Aging, Technology and Health

Aging, Technology and Health

Richard Pak

Clemson University, Clemson, SC, United States

Anne Collins McLaughlin

North Carolina State University, Raleigh, NC, United States

ACADEMIC PRESS

An imprint of Elsevier

Academic Press is an imprint of Elsevier
125 London Wall, London EC2Y 5AS, United Kingdom
525 B Street, Suite 1800, San Diego, CA 92101-4495, United States
50 Hampshire Street, 5th Floor, Cambridge, MA 02139, United States
The Boulevard, Langford Lane, Kidlington, Oxford OX5 1GB, United Kingdom

Notices
Knowledge and best practice in this field are constantly changing. As new research and experience broaden our understanding, changes in research methods, professional practices, or medical treatment may become necessary.

Practitioners and researchers must always rely on their own experience and knowledge in evaluating and using any information, methods, compounds, or experiments described herein. In using such information or methods they should be mindful of their own safety and the safety of others, including parties for whom they have a professional responsibility.

To the fullest extent of the law, neither the Publisher nor the authors, contributors, or editors, assume any liability for any injury and/or damage to persons or property as a matter of products liability, negligence or otherwise, or from any use or operation of any methods, products, instructions, or ideas contained in the material herein.

British Library Cataloguing-in-Publication Data
A catalogue record for this book is available from the British Library

Library of Congress Cataloging-in-Publication Data
A catalog record for this book is available from the Library of Congress

ISBN: 978-0-12-811272-4

For Information on all Academic Press publications
visit our website at https://www.elsevier.com/books-and-journals

Working together
to grow libraries in
developing countries

www.elsevier.com • www.bookaid.org

Publisher: Nikki Levy
Acquisition Editor: Emily Ekle
Editorial Project Manager: Barbara Makinster
Production Project Manager: Kiruthika Govindaraju
Cover Designer: Limbert Matthew

Typeset by MPS Limited, Chennai, India

Contents

List of contributors

Renato F. L. Azevedo University of Illinois at Urbana-Champaign, Champaign, IL, United States

Chandramallika Basak Center for Vital Longevity, University of Texas at Dallas, Richardson, TX, United States

Dina Battisto Clemson University, Clemson, SC, United States

Jenay M. Beer University of South Carolina, Columbia, SC, United States

Ronald W. Berkowsky University of Miami School of Medicine, Miami, FL, United States

Michael T. Bixter Arizona State University, Tempe, AZ, United States

Kenneth A. Blocker University of Illinois at Urbana-Champaign, Champaign, IL, United States

Philipp Brauner RWTH Aachen University, Aachen, Germany

Kelly Caine Clemson University, Clemson, SC, United States

HeeSun Choi North Carolina State University, Raleigh, NC, United States

Maribeth Gandy Coleman Georgia Institute of Technology, Atlanta, GA, United States

Kay Connelly Indiana University, Bloomington, IN, United States

Sara J. Czaja University of Miami School of Medicine, Miami, FL, United States

Cheryl J. Dye Clemson University, Clemson, SC, United States

Jing Feng North Carolina State University, Raleigh, NC, United States

Sanjiv Jain Carle Foundation Hospital, Urbana, IL, United States

Yifang Li Clemson University, Clemson, SC, United States

Laura A. Matalenas North Carolina State University, Raleigh, NC, United States

Anne Collins McLaughlin North Carolina State University, Raleigh, NC, United States

Daniel G. Morrow University of Illinois at Urbana-Champaign, Champaign, IL, United States

Otis L. Owens University of South Carolina, Columbia, SC, United States

Vignesh R. Paramathayalan Advanced Digital Sciences Center, Illinois at Singapore PTE Ltd, Singapore, Singapore

Shuo Qin Center for Vital Longevity, University of Texas at Dallas, Richardson, TX, United States

Rama Ratnam University of Illinois at Urbana-Champaign, IL, United States; Advanced Digital Sciences Center, Illinois at Singapore PTE Ltd, Singapore, Singapore

Wendy A. Rogers University of Illinois at Urbana-Champaign, Champaign, IL, United States

Subina Saini Clemson University, Clemson, SC, United States

Robert Sall North Carolina State University, Raleigh, NC, United States

Jacob J. Sosnoff University of Illinois at Urbana-Champaign, IL, United States

Ruopeng Sun University of Illinois at Urbana-Champaign, IL, United States

Ellen Vincent Clemson University, Clemson, SC, United States

Wiktoria Wilkowska RWTH Aachen University, Aachen, Germany

Martina Ziefle RWTH Aachen University, Aachen, Germany

Preface

Technology has been used by people of all ages to help manage their health, from the first branch crafted into a toothbrush to a home glucose monitor for people with diabetes. People over 65 now have many technologies to track everything from activity to diet to medication. Most of these include a social dimension for sharing health information, progress, and goals with loved ones or healthcare providers. However, as is often true with a boom in new technology, these health technologies do not always take into account the ease of use for older adults. For example, smartphones are often the gateway and controller to many health technologies. But the smartphone form factor may not be the optimal choice, merely the most convenient. Such usability issues become even more apparent when the user has age-related challenges in vision, hearing, cognition, and movement control.

How can we ensure that technology facilitates health at older ages? How can we ensure that technologies are easy to use? Given the sensitive and personal nature of health, how can information be kept private while communicating what is private (and what is not) to users? What are best practices for design in safety-critical tasks, such as driving? What are the best ways for technology to bring people together? What advice do we give regarding emerging technologies before they hit the market? These are the core questions addressed in this volume: technology adoption, basic human factors, cognitive aging, training, mobile technology, aging and usability, privacy, and trust of automation.

This book covers the challenges and solutions involved in designing health technologies for the older user. The chapter authors apply a problem-centered approach to understanding how different knowledge and methods of human factors apply to older adults' use of technology for health. Each chapter discusses the human factors design challenges associated with older adults' use of a specific type of health technology, often with principles, guidelines, or recommendations for translating this knowledge into application.

Each chapter represents a unique problem that is studied by a different set of researchers with unique perspectives. Through these chapters and topics, the reader will gain a better understanding of how current and future technology can assist older adults and enhance their health and well-being. The key takeaways from these chapters include an understanding of the process of problem identification, development of evidence-based solutions, and, finally, methods of evaluation.

The chapters in this book are organized into present-day application and future research directions. In the first chapters, authors discuss how existing human factors methodologies, ideas, and concepts can be immediately applied to enhance the health and wellbeing of older adults in domains such as transportation, the built environment, and online health information. Each of the chapters propose unique solutions using various methods. The second part of the book retains a focus on older adult well-being, but looks into the future. Authors review cutting-edge technologies, such as social robots, ubiquitous and pervasive computing, privacy in an increasingly shared world, and design of virtual cognitive training and augmented reality for health promotion.

Design for aging is crucial yet lacking, and nowhere is that more apparent than in products for health. Our chapter authors are deeply invested in not only enhancing our scientific knowledge base, but also the practical problems of solving these present and future concerns to make growing older easier through well-designed technology. With the general goals of improved quality of life, extending independence, and addressing specific diseases, this book aims to inspire other researchers to continue the difficult and fine balance of conducting scientifically rigorous work that enhances the well-being of adults in what should be a vibrant stage of life.

Rethinking technology development for older adults: A responsible research and innovation duty

1

Wiktoria Wilkowska, Philipp Brauner and Martina Ziefle
RWTH Aachen University, Aachen, Germany

Starting point: Challenges for aging societies

Motivation

One of the largest and most powerful trends of our time is the global demographic shift resulting from changes in the population structures of many nations (Bloom, Canning, & Fink, 2010). Thereby, globally the population aged 60 years and over is growing at the fastest pace (United Nations, 2009). Rapid population aging and the development of the main drivers of the demographic change (i.e., increased life expectancy, birthrate decline, and migration) trigger complex social, political, and socioeconomic consequences, with which many nations already find themselves confronted.

Such consequences have become noticeable in Germany and are in line with many other Western societies: Public sector, which is especially affected by the demographic development, refers in particular to the statutory social insurance schemes, where, there is a strong link between service provision and age (Arnds & Bonin, 2002). Thus, financing of social insurance systems is strained and policymakers face difficult decisions about changes to the benefit structures and taxes to support the so-called graying society. In addition, it is uncertain how economies will fare due to the demographic transition and how policies will affect the global flows of labor and capital in the economic development (Arnds & Bonin, 2002; Little & Triest, 2001; Wilkowska, 2015).

The globally increasing number of people aged 60 years and over as well as the extended life expectancy result in the increased likelihood of chronic diseases which, according to WHO, mostly manifest in the later stages of life (WHO, 2003). Consequently, less people are contributing to health and welfare systems that more and more people depend on. This fact is connected to a substantial increase of costs in the area of healthcare and nursing services (Little & Triest, 2001). In addition to the financial bottlenecks due to the increasing treatment and nursing requirements, some issues from the medical supply chain arise. In the last decades, several weaknesses in the German healthcare system have become

Aging, Technology and Health. DOI: http://dx.doi.org/10.1016/B978-0-12-811272-4.00001-4

apparent (Leonhardt, 2006; Wilkowska, 2015). A combination of lower fertility rates and higher longevity of the society results in a number of those needing nursing care which is significantly higher than the number of persons who can offer the health support. This applies to physicians as well as nursing staff (Korzilius, 2008; Terschüren, Mensing, & Mekel, 2012).

These facts and the resulting challenges in various public spheres require effective, innovative, and efficient solutions. To obviate, as far as possible, the onset of chronic illnesses in the graying society, long-term prevention measures, constant health monitoring, and early diagnostics gain importance. These actions to be taken are the first step to generally achieve better health and, at the same time, to reduce health-related costs. For instance, targeted prevention programs regarding fitness and/or diet regulation can be realized during younger ages of individuals. For those who already suffer from a chronic condition (CC)—and this topic is specifically addressed in the below presented studies—a powerful disease management should be established (i.e., a sensible, as much as possible unobtrusive monitoring of relevant vital parameters and a continuous dialog with the supervising medical staff). Moreover, an efficient system should be created to include supply structures as well as inpatient and outpatient, curative, rehabilitative, and nursing services.

One possible solution to achieve such ambitious goals lies in the use of technology or, more specifically, of advancements in ubiquitous computing in combination with sophisticated, intelligent sensor networks (Holzinger, Röcker, & Ziefle, 2015; Nehmer, Becker, Karshmer, & Lamm, 2006; Yan, Huo, Xu, & Gidlund, 2010). Modern technologies which are integrated in home environments have a huge potential to assist elderly and individuals with CCs in their daily life: They can support their independency, sovereignty, and autonomy, uphold their social network, and maintain the comfort of living in familiar surroundings, rather than relocate in a nursing home or a long-term rehabilitation clinic (Wilkowska, 2015). Technologies that support health, well-being, a balanced and satisfactory lifestyle, be it sports programs, serious exercise games, appropriate dietary programs and/or a vital parameter monitoring system individually adapted to the inhabitant's needs, are feasible and can be realized even with existing devices.

In the areas of health prevention, cure, and rehabilitation, electronic health (eHealth) and electronic homecare (eHomecare) provide a meaningful framework for both the users and the healthcare that is useful to be focused from the user-centered perspective. Taking as an example diseases with the highest prevalence in today's society, cardiovascular diseases—e.g., acute cardiac infarction, cardiac insufficiency, disturbed blood flow through cardiac muscle—are the leading cause of death in Germany, causing a total of about 40% of all deaths (Destatis, 2014). According to experts, people who have suffered from a cardiovascular disease are, firstly, urged to regularly monitor their vital signs, such as blood pressure, heart rate, body weight, temperature, and coagulation. Secondly, these persons must, under certain circumstances, strictly adhere to their prescribed medication intake, follow special dietary requirements, and absolve trainings to maintain physical health (Klack et al., 2011; Lee, 2010). Here, eHealth technology embedded in their home environment could assist with many of these obligations commonplace for heart patients or vulnerable persons, e.g., the storage and transmission of the health data (Eloy, Plácido, & Duarte, 2007). The two empirical studies presented later in this chapter leverage such assistive home environment that supports its inhabitant(s) to meet their health requirements.

To reach a successful adoption of health-supporting technologies, however, high acceptance, high perceived meaningfulness of its use, and, therefore, high intention to use are needed. According to the Extended Unified Theory of Acceptance and Use of Technology Model (UTAUT 2; Venkatesh, Thong, & Xu, 2012), the use behavior is directly linked to the behavioral intention to use a technology system which, in turn, is modeled by different influencing factors, such as, among other things, expected performance of the system, hedonic motivation to use it, and social influence, which can be reached by using it. In addition, the intention to use technology is moderated by user factors, like age and gender which considerably impact on the willingness to use such technologies (Wilkowska, Gaul, & Ziefle, 2010; Wilkowska, Himmel, & Ziefle, 2015; Ziefle & Schaar, 2011). Using UTAUT 2 as a theoretical framework, the two presented research studies dedicate special attention to the user factors and identify perceived benefits and barriers that relate to the acceptance of two distinct healthcare applications.

A consequent consideration of the users' perceptions on technology innovations and their acceptance to use novel technologies—especially in the area of health-supporting ambient technologies—is particularly important for older users as the main target group of homecare environments. It has been shown that seniors desire to keep a livelong independency in their own "four walls" as this allows for a higher life quality in a conversant environment (e.g., Wilkowska & Ziefle, 2011) and preservation of their intimacy, self-reliance, and autonomy, as opposed to living in an old peoples' homes (Dewsbury & Edge, 2001; Mynatt, Melenhorst, Fisk, & Rogers, 2004). In this regard, the idea of technology-enhanced homes fits perfectly with older adults' attitudes. However, on the other hand, older adults were found to face greater difficulties in general in dealing with technology. A high usability of devices in line with smart interfaces are vital prerequisites of universal access (Pak & McLaughlin, 2010; Pak, Price, & Thatcher, 2009), seniors' perception of the usefulness of such a technology, and, eventually, making use of the technology (Pak & McLaughlin, 2010; Wilkowska & Ziefle, 2009). In addition, older adults' experience with technology is grounded on completely different forms, appearances, and types of technologies which do not match the seamlessly integrated smart home technology (Arning & Ziefle, 2007a; Gaul & Ziefle, 2009). The ambient technology which is possibly not even visible for them (as it is integrated into the surrounding) could elicit unfamiliar and even embarrassing feelings. In the traditional view, the home environment is highly intimate and perceived as being safe and comfortable. For older adults and their mental model of technology this seems to be not easily combinable with smart care technology as an integral part of their living space. In this context, privacy concerns and supposed loss of intimacy as well as the feeling of being continuously monitored is a serious barrier (Wilkowska et al., 2015; Ziefle, Himmel, & Wilkowska, 2011). Nobody likes a vision of technology that stigmatizes them as old, ill, and dependent, particularly since there is still a quite negative image of elderly prevailing in public perceptions of societies as well as in working and family environments (Iweins, Desmette, Yzerbyt, & Stinglhamber, 2013; John, 2013; Ziefle & Schaar, 2014). Thus, from a social point of view, the integration of technology into the sanctuary of the "own four walls" is a delicate issue and needs to be developed with sensitivity (Stronge, Rogers, & Fisk, 2007; Wilkowska et al., 2015; Ziefle & Schaar, 2014; Ziefle et al., 2011). Understanding older adults' concerns, their requirements, social values, and hopes in the context of a technology that really supports them is inevitable (Ziefle & Schaar, 2014). Thus, a successful adoption of smart-home technologies is inextricably linked with an understanding of the users, but also their unhesitant willingness to use and integrate technical devices in their personal spaces.

The research objectives and chapter structure

The main aim of this chapter is to show our idea of a smart home: An environment that contains useable medical applications merged into one ubiquitous system that can simplify its users' life in different areas. The main research goal was to examine intention to future use of different health-supporting applications after interaction with them in an experimental setting. We describe two studies, referring to the evaluation of two exemplary applications: Firstly, to the health aspect based on measurements of vital parameters necessary in case of a cardiovascular disease (see "Study I: Health assistance at home" section), and secondly, to the aspect of a person's physical mobility in the context of serious games (see "Study II: Serious exercise games in AAL" section).

Both applications were created using the design process by Gould and Lewis (Gould & Lewis, 1985) that builds on three principles: (1) Early focus on the users and their tasks; (2) An iterative design process; and (3) empirical measurement of the product use. For a better understanding, we introduce Maria who is an (imaginary) prototypic inhabitant of the smart home. Maria is one of several archetypal personas, a common method in user-centered design (Cooper, 1999), that guided the development of the Ambient Assisted Living (AAL) Lab between participatory user studies. As a potential persona (LeRouge, Ma, Sneha, & Tolle, 2013) in terms of a prototypic older adult as target user of smart home technology, Maria is 74 years old, lives alone, and, as a result of a cardiac infarction she suffered a few years previously, she must keep track of some vital parameters daily (i.e., blood pressure, weight) and consult her doctor within certain time intervals. Additionally, she has some mild, age-related physical impairments, but she is generally in relative good health and interested in maintaining her independence within her "own four walls."

The two studies reported subsequently in this chapter will show meaningful health applications for persons in similar situations and with comparable ailments as Maria. In the first one, a health-assistive application that is embedded into the living environment and allows to monitor relevant vital parameters is evaluated. The intention to use the health-supporting ambient technology after an interaction with the system is the main research subject. The second study reports on serious games for physical exercise in the technology-augmented habitat. Here, apart from the rendered performance and factors influencing the willingness to play the game, factors affecting the intention to use the ambient technology in the entertaining context will be presented.

Future Care Lab© and its applications as experimental environment

The studies to be described in the following were conducted in the Future Care Lab© at RWTH Aachen University. This environment resembles a living room of comfortable size (25 m²) and enables the integration of different existing and prototypic medical technologies. Following the user-centered design approach (Gould & Lewis, 1985), this environment is used to include the users' perspective into the design and development of upcoming medical technologies, since their feedback is very valuable for the desired user acceptance and can be integrated into later stages of the design process. In the next iterative cycle then, a further evaluation and optimization of the ambient system begins (participatory design approach).

The idea was to make use of currently available technologies and integrate them into an overall consistent usage concept. Thus, the Future Care Lab© was meant to be a medical and living environment at the same time: i.e., the room should, on the one hand, provide the necessary medical equipment and assistance features without compromising comfort, and, on the other hand, preserve the intimacy and personal privacy of a living room (Klack et al., 2011). For the communication interface, which is the key requirement for remote diagnostics and communication between patient and physician, the room was equipped with high-definition cameras and a wall-sized interactive display as presented in Fig. 1.1. The multi-touch, sensitive display-wall serves as a screen and an input device for various applications (Heidrich, 2015; Kasugai, Ziefle, Röcker, & Russell, 2010), ranging from monitoring of relevant health parameters, medication, nutrition, and exercise management

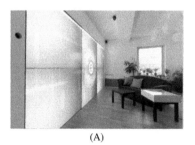
(A)

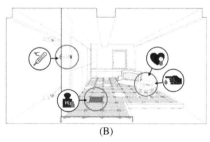
(B)

Figure 1.1 Future Care Lab© with its interactive wall display, serving as the visual communication tool and a diagnostic interface in the patient−doctor communication: (A) unobtrusive interior of the living lab environment, (B) schematic visualization of the health-monitoring system (side table: blood pressure and coagulation; wall: body temperature; floor: weight).

to daily multimedia entertainment (e.g., serious games (Brauner, Holzinger, & Ziefle, 2015), movies), virtual environments (e.g., myGreenSpace, meetingMeEating (Röcker & Kasugai, 2011)), or meetings with physicians, family, and friends (Beul et al., 2010). Focusing on the health aspect (the main objective of the Study I described later) this feature allows the inhabitant to measure vital signs and easy access their data as well as their medication histories without using different devices and without having to manually recording the results for a (video) consultation with their physician.

The term Ambient Assisted Living (AAL) describes the basic idea behind the development of the living lab: A space to foster the emergence of systematic innovations for the autonomous living of elderly and individuals with chronic illnesses which, on the one side, increases the quality of their lives, and, on the other side, reduces the expenditures of the possibly necessary nursing care. Such smart homes that include innovative smart health concepts, reaching from electronic health monitoring to serious gaming as will be described in the second study, are meant to be individually suited to the resident(s), adaptive to the (changing) needs (e.g., disease progress), and sensitive with regard to the living conditions (Klack et al., 2011).

Study I: Health assistance at home

The first study was intended to examine if potential users, after a real interaction with the health-supporting application, would use such assistive systems at home in the future. For this purpose, an experimental study with middle-aged and older individuals was performed in the Future Care Lab©. The target group were persons with chronic heart conditions, who have to monitor some of their health parameters on a daily basis. Their opinions were compared to those of individuals without any ailments.

Getting back to the example of Maria, the main question was whether she intends to use the application in the future, which is meant to simplify measuring and recording her vital parameters, ease the storage of her health data, and facilitate communication with the responsible physician in case of deterioration of the relevant values. In the following, the experimental design and procedure of the first study are described.

Materials and methods

Research method

As the aim was to get an impression of the real use of the assistive system, this study was designed to examine how persons with chronic heart conditions can effectively monitor their relevant vital signs by means of unobtrusively integrated specific medical devices in a domestic environment. For this purpose, the participants were asked to perform two exemplary measurements, common for heart patients: The first was taking their blood pressure (via a standard sphygmo-manometer, comprising an inflatable cuff to restrict blood flow and a manometer to measure the pressure), the second was a weight measurement (via a digital scale integrated in the floor). Both are, according to experts, reliable parameters for (negative) changes in cardiovascular processes of the human body. Participants were requested to use the health-app of the system (Fig. 1.2A, top left) which initiates the particular measurement and, afterwards, to appropriately save the data in the system. The app also provides the possibility to compare the current result with previous results (imaginary but strongly related to the real one) in a measurement overview (Fig. 1.2B, bottom right).

Between the trials and after interaction with the health application of the system, the individuals were asked to assess if they would use such technology at home, provided that the circumstances are acceptable—i.e., transparent financing, technical maintenance, telemedical servicing. In a semistructured interview as well as using the method of a quantitative questionnaire, participants answered questions such as: "Can you imagine using an eHealth system like this in your home in the future?" and "Do you think you would like to frequently use such technology system in the future?" The questions based on the original items for behavioral intention in UTAUT 2 (Venkatesh et al., 2012) were adjusted to the purposes of the present study. The statements in the questionnaire had to be rated on a five-point Likert scale ranging from "strongly disagree" ($=1$) to "strongly agree" ($=5$). In addition, opinions about the system's usability, assessed via the System Usability Scale (Brooke, 1996), and general perceptions pertaining to the reliability of the system, data security, and personal privacy were collected (for details see Wilkowska, 2015).

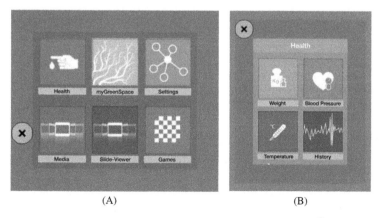

(A)   (B)

Figure 1.2 Control panel on the large wall screen in the Future Care Lab©: (A) front panel for different applications; (B) the health-app tailored to Marias needs of monitoring vital parameters relevant for the cardiovascular system.

Experimental procedure

Experimental testing was carried out within a period of about two weeks. The sessions were held individually and in German, the native language of all participants. Before the experiment started, each participant was asked about special needs as well as objections or restrictions with respect to the planned study. The experimental trials took on average 20–30 minutes.

In the first step, the participants were introduced to the concepts of AAL and telemedicine to provide an idea of the broad possibilities connected to eHealth technology in a domestic environment. Monitoring of vital parameters in a comfortable way at home and the reminder function to do so, an efficient digital transmission of the sensitive health data, facilitated patient–physician communication and exchange with other patients or support groups on the Internet. To evaluate the interaction with the technology, participants had to perform two tasks—taking their blood pressure and body weight using the health-app on the system. Each action was previously demonstrated by the experimenter. After each measurement, the participants were requested to interact with the app by taking a look at the weekly or monthly overview of particular results. Fictitious values for the previous weeks and months were generated automatically, using an algorithm based on the real measurement. During the interaction, the participants were informed that the storage and transmission of their personal health data would take place via secure, specialized medical services which would facilitate the communication with medical staff. There was also no time limit for the user's interaction with the health-app. After each measurement and the subsequent interaction, participants assessed the functionality and usability of the system. They also filled in a questionnaire to evaluate their willingness of using the technology in future (as described in "Research method").

In the final part of the experimental session, interviews gave participants the opportunity to comment on their perceived advantages and disadvantages in comparison to current solutions in the healthcare sector. This gave the researchers an idea of the general attitude toward the future use of such complex and sophisticated technologies in the domestic setting.

Participants of the Study I

To get volunteers to participate in this experimental study, posters were placed in local hospitals in cardiology departments and public places for about three weeks. Attending the experiment was voluntary and was neither compensated with payments or other incentives, nor were any direct or indirect health benefits promised or suggested to the test group.

A total of 25 German adults between the ages of 35 and 86 years ($M = 61.1$, $SD = 12.4$) participated in the study, 56% of them female. More than half of the participants (52%) reported to suffer from some kind of chronic heart disease (e.g., tachycardia, myocardial infarction, coronary heart disease), and as many to regularly visit a physician to check their actual health status. In the group with chronic conditions (CCs), all persons used medical assistive devices to monitor relevant vital signs (e.g., blood pressure, heart rate, weight, body temperature); the majority (70%) reported to write down the results of the measurements by pen and paper. In the group with healthy participants (H), only one person reported to use medical devices on a regular basis and to visit a physician periodically for checkups.

The participants presented different educational levels: 52% reported a university degree (including business administration, domestic science and nutrition, psychology, mechanical engineering, teaching profession, biology, etc.), 20% completed a vocational training, and 28% indicated secondary school qualifications. When asked about their current or last profession before their retirement, various occupational fields were named, e.g., psychologists, doctor's assistants, engineers, administrative assistants, teachers, business economists, translators, etc. In this way, the presented study reflects a broad spectrum of users.

Research variables

To examine the intention for a future use of the eHealth technology by different users, the following research variables were involved in the statistical analyses.

Independent variables: The first independent variable was the age of the tested persons. Here, middle-aged (age range: 35−59 years; $M = 51.4$, $SD = 6.6$; $n = 13$) and people in the older adulthood (age range: 60−86 years; $M = 71.6$, $SD = 7.7$; $n = 12$) were compared. In addition, the participants' self-reported health status (chronic heart condition ($n = 13$) versus healthy/without heart condition ($n = 12$)) distinguished between the participants. Also, gender-specific perceptions (males ($n = 11$) vs females ($n = 14$)) were contemplated in the analyses.

Dependent variables: The main focus lies on the intention to use (ItU) the complex but, at the same time, versatile technology which is integrated into the residential area. Methodologically, this topic is considered from both the qualitative and quantitative point of view. In the quantitative analysis, the two assessments about the intention to use eHealth in the future, evaluated after each measurement event, were merged to form a single variable (ItU: min. = 2, max. = 10). The other dependent variables are the fun ("I had fun using the system") and the perceived meaningfulness of the use ("I consider the monitoring of my vital parameters (e.g., blood pressure and weight) with the help of integrated technology at home reasonable"). The latter two had to be rated on a five-point scale as described earlier.

Results of Study I

The results of the first study mainly focused on the users' intention to use complex assistance technologies in a smart home environment, here exemplified by the health context as to allude to the strain of increasing numbers of older people and persons who need medical monitoring. In the following, it is firstly analyzed how the intention to use such eHealth technology correlates to the enjoyment of its use and its perceived meaningfulness, as well as how all the research variables are connected. Secondly, it is examined whether there are fundamental differences between users who either promote or negate the intention to use the system. Thirdly, a qualitative analysis will provide a complementary picture of the opinions about intended future use.

For the analyses of the results, different statistical techniques were chosen, depending on the properties of the data, number of the variables and groups, and in accordance with the achievement of the statistical assumptions. When possible, parametric methods were preferred. The cut-off for the significance level in all statistical analyses lies by 5% ($P = .05$), the effect size is calculated with eta squared (η^2), the values of which can range from 0 to 1 and indicate the strength of effect sizes (Cohen, 1988).

Relationships between research variables

To gain a general impression of the associations between the research variables, Pearson product−moment correlation coefficients (parametric analysis between continuous variables) and Spearman's rho correlation coefficients (nonparametric alternative) were generated, depending on the respective data structure. Table 1.1 summarizes the strengths of the particular relationships.

From the correlation analysis' results, it is evident that age is strongly associated with the intention to use the ambient technology ($r = 0.53$, $P < .01$) and with the meaningfulness of its use ($r = 0.40$, $P < .05$), which means that both get higher with increasing age. The above coefficients affirm the fact that with increasing age the occurrence of the chronic heart diseases grows ($r = 0.48$, $P \leq .01$), and there is a substantial positive association with the intention to use the eHealth technology ($r = 0.43$, $P < .05$): Persons with chronic heart condition showed higher willingness to utilize it than the healthy participants. In contrast, for gender there is no evidence of links to the focused aspects (n.s.).

From Table 1.1, also high positive relationships between the focused dependent variables become evident. The intention to use the technology is positively related to the perceived meaningfulness of use ($r = 0.42$, $P \leq .05$) and fun ($r = 0.49$, $P \leq .05$); the latter two, in turn, are strongly associated with each other ($r = 0.63$, $P \leq .001$).

Table 1.1 Bivariate correlation coefficients between the research variables (gender: male = 1, female = 2; health status: healthy = 1, chronic heart condition = 2) ($N = 25$)

	Age	Gender	Hs	ItU	F	M
Age	1	–	0.48*	0.53**	0.13	0.40*
Gender		1	–	−0.07	0.15	0.09
Health status (Hs)			1	0.43*	−0.15	0.22
Intention to Use (ItU)				1	0.49*	0.42*
Fun (F)					1	0.63***
Meaningfulness (M)						1

***$P < .001$; **$P < .01$; *$P < .05$.

These substantial relationships among the target variables give reason to take a closer look at the effects of different users on the future usage behavior in the health context.

User differences

In the next step, the effects of the independent variables on the intention to use, fun, and perceived meaningfulness with respect to the use of ambient health-supporting technology are examined. To compare the research groups according to the properties of the data, independent-samples t-tests were used.

Since, in the context of eHealth technology, the *physical health* of the inhabitants can be decisive for an opinion of its use, the first analysis refers to a comparison between persons with chronic heart conditions and healthy individuals. The t-test revealed significant differences with respect to the intention to use eHealth in the future between these research groups [$t(23) = 2.3$, $P = .033$, $\eta^2 = 0.17$]. Those who suffered from illness wanted, almost without exception, to use the technology in the future ($M = 9.7$ out of 10 points, $SD = 0.6$). In the healthy group, the opinions in this regard were positive too, but much less pronounced ($M = 7.7$, $SD = 3$). The mean differences are depicted in Fig. 1.3. Apparently, all participants had a positive attitude towards the technology innovation as the average values were high. However, people with chronic diseases see more benefits in the use of technical assistance (at least in the context of the health-app) in comparison to persons without permanent ailments. Moreover, the health status had no significant effect on the perceived fun with the technology [$t(23) = 1.1$, *n.s.*] and the perceived meaningfulness of its use [$t(23) = 1.2$, *n.s.*].

In addition to the health aspect, it is also of interest whether the *age* factor influenced the opinions about willingness for future use of a medical assistance system in the home environment. The analysis revealed that the examined age groups significantly differed in regard to the intention to use [$t(23) = -2.5$, $P = .025$, $\eta^2 = 0.22$] and the perceived meaningfulness of the use [$t(23) = -2.9$, $P = .012$,

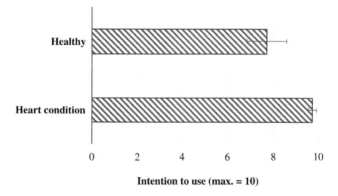

Intention to use (max. = 10)

Figure 1.3 Main effect of the health status on the intention to use eHealth technology at home [$t(23) = 2.3$, $P < .05$].

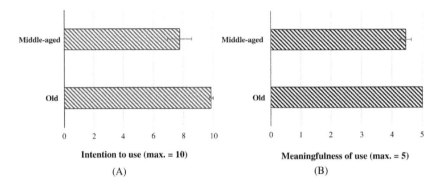

Figure 1.4 Main effect of age: (A) on the intention to use eHealth technology at home [$t(23) = -2.5$, $P < .05$]; (B) on perceived meaningfulness of use [$t(23) = -2.9$, $P < .05$].

$\eta^2 = 0.26$]. Here, older participants showed averagely higher, almost the maximum possible intention to use eHealth ($M = 9.8$ out of 10 points, $SD = 0.4$) and considered the monitoring of their vital parameters by means of the medical assistive system invariably more meaningful ($M = 5$ of 5 possible points, $SD = 0$) than the middle-aged individuals (ItU: $M = 7.8$, $SD = 2.9$; meaningfulness: $M = 4.4$, $SD = 0.7$). The effect of age is visualized in Fig. 1.4. With respect to the evaluations of fun after the interaction with the system, both age groups showed high mean values (middle-aged group: $M = 4.6$, $SD = 0.8$; old age group: $M = 4.8$, $SD = 0.4$); the differences were not significant [$t(23) = -0.9$, n.s.].

In the final step, it was examined whether the *gender* factor influenced opinions in a relevant way. The independent-samples *t*-test analysis revealed no statistical significance for gender differences [ItU: $t(23) = -1$, n.s.; fun: $t(23) = 0.6$, n.s.; meaningfulness of use: $t(23) = 0.7$, n.s.]: Men and women reached similarly high mean values in all the mentioned aspects. These results testify that, unlike previous technology generations, gender no longer splits the users with respect to the latest technological achievements. On the contrary, women and men are equally willing to use, have comparable fun with, and consider the technical medical assistance at home meaningful to the same extent.

Intention to use eHealth: Qualitative analysis

To complement the research analysis, in this section a brief report of the qualitative results will be offered. The benefits of qualitative methods, like interviews, are not only a far more personal form of research, but working directly with the respondent eases the expression of opinions and impressions, and it also allows for follow-up questions or redirection if someone strays from the topic.

As was described in "Experimental procedure" section, after the interaction with the ambient assistive system in the Future Care Lab© and the subsequent completion of the questionnaire, participants were involved in a short, semistructured interview. Therein, they had to respond, among other things, to the question whether they could imagine (or not) using a technical system like the one used in the test experiment in their homes in the future.

According to the final statements, more than three quarters of the participants ($n = 19$; which makes 76%) showed a positive attitude towards the (future) use of the system after their interaction with the prototypic eHealth environment. In the following, some exemplary statements are listed:

> I think it is totally fine! Luckily, until now I hadn't had to deal with bigger health issues, but I think that has a future and I can imagine to use it not only in the health context.
>
> *(male, 53 years, no chronic conditions)*

> I think, when the technology is fully developed and it works properly, the results of the measurements would be absolutely reliable. If I had that, I would also regularly measure my blood pressure, like I also should. In this form, it is too large for my apartment, but I think it's great and I would definitely use it in the future.
>
> *(female, 56 years, hypertension)*

> That's really interesting and also fun! I could certainly use it.
>
> *(female, 73 years, no chronic condition)*

Another 20% of the interviewed persons ($n = 5$) displayed a positive attitude, but they also showed a certain skepticism, or declared some reservations for the future use. Below some examples are listed:

> You certainly can learn how to use that thing, but most people are reluctant to deal with it; my wife, for example. I think it is very good, however, space limits and the financing could be reasons not to use it.
>
> *(male, 74 years, cardiac insufficiency)*

> I think it's great that you can operate it with the whole hand (instead of only one finger). But I would like to see additional functions: electronic calendar, reminder, etc. You could also retrofit the floor.
>
> *(male, 71 years, myocardial infarction, stroke)*

One person rejected the use of the ambient system in the future:

> Human contact gets lost, the sensory organs come off badly, life would be very mechanized. That's not for me! I'm less concerned about my health monitoring than about the [social] isolation.
>
> *(female, 58, arrhythmia, tachycardia)*

Summary of the results for the Study I

According to the presented results, the greatest enthusiasm for the use of health-related technology in terms of ambient assistance systems in a domestic environment emerges from elderly and chronically ill people. Their intention to use such ambient technology is significantly higher than in healthy and individuals in their midlife, even though the vast majority of participants acknowledged it as a meaningful and enriching supplement. The participants showed great enthusiasm with the technology, reaching mean values between $M = 4.6$ and $M = 4.8$ out of maximum five points. In addition, the absence of significant effects for gender indicates that women and men comparably evaluate the technology with respect to the focused aspects.

Accordingly, we can assume that Maria is pleased with the surrounding technology in her home and she enjoys taking her vital signs regularly. She definitely wants to use this innovation in the future.

Study II: Serious exercise games in AAL

After the measurement of her vital parameters, Maria is interested in playing a game. The technology-augmented habitat provides different types of games. Maria can choose to play conventional computer games, or she might use one of the several serious games for healthcare offered by the AAL environment. One serious game couples the motivational incentives of games with explicit and thought-out purposes outside the actual game (Zyda, 2005). For example, the game Cook It Right (Wittland, Brauner, & Ziefle, 2015) uses a cooking scenario to address the improvement of cognitive functioning, i.e., remembering and planning abilities. Maria decides to launch the exercising game Fruit Garden this time.

Physical inactivity is linked to diabetes, hypertension, coronary, and cerebrovascular diseases. It is also connected with a lower life expectancy (Knight, 2012). In contrast, exercising has benefits for health, such as lower risk and lower intensity of cardiovascular diseases (Perez-Terzic, 2012), higher physical and cognitive abilities (Ahlskog, Geda, Graff-Radford, & Petersen, 2011), as well as positive influences on mood and depression (Thayer, Newman, & McClain, 1994). Sportive physical activities reduce the probability of silent brain infarcts (Willey et al., 2011). Therefore, performing regular exercises—in or outside a game environment—is beneficial for the overall health status.

The Fruit Garden game involves full-body movement exercises, captured with nearly invisible motion-capturing cameras, and aims at picking fruit in a garden environment presented on the large wall of the technology-augmented habitat (Brauner et al., 2015; see Fig. 1.5). Previous research (De Schutter & Van Den Abeele, 2008) has identified this as a suitable game core. In several levels with increasing difficulty, distinct movement gestures address different body and muscle areas and the training should retain, or improve, the overall stamina of its players. The game offers different single and multiplayer modes, and players can decide to compete against their own high scores or against friends, relatives, or others over a network. Today, Maria chooses to play the single player mode, as she wants to break her personal record for the levels with more difficult movements.

Figure 1.5 An elderly player interacting with a prototype of the fruit picking game.

Materials and methods

To investigate how people interact with an exercise game in a technology-augmented environment, and to understand under which conditions it is likely to be used, a formal user study was conducted. This section presents the evaluated prototype of the above mentioned exercise game, followed by the description of the independent, explanatory, and dependent variables. Finally, the sample of the experimental study is described.

The evaluated game prototype

In the exercise game, the player's task is to pick different fruits (e.g., apples, pears) in a comic-like garden environment presented on the large wall of the AAL lab. The body movements are captured through hidden Kinect sensors, which capture a high resolution color image, a depth image, as well as a skeleton model with 3D coordinates of 20 joints in high temporal and spatial resolution. The picture of the player is directly integrated into the game environment by compiling the different images from the Kinect sensor (see Fig. 1.6): The RGB-image of the player is separated from the background by using the depth image, then the background-separated image is integrated into the game's scenery.

For each type of fruit, a specific full body movement gesture is required. The gestures were developed with medical professionals and each gesture captures a specific, medically sound, exercise. For example, for picking an apple on the right side of the screen, the left hand must be used. This trains hand-eye-coordination and the shoulder and back muscles. During the first levels of the game, the different gestures are sequentially introduced and repeatedly trained.

Research variables

Before and after the serious game intervention, a questionnaire assesses the independent (explicitly used for creating the sample), explanatory (measured but not

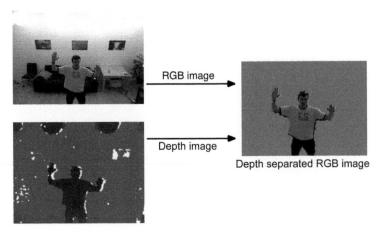

Figure 1.6 Schematic illustration of the separation of the player's background using the depth image.

used for creating the sample), and dependent variables (capturing the evaluation of the game) of the user study.

Independent variables: Besides age and gender as independent variables, the questionnaire collected data regarding the participants' self-efficacy in interacting with technology (SET, e.g., "I have fun solving technical problems"), their gaming frequency across multiple game types (GF, e.g., "I frequently play board games"), and their need for achievement (NAch, e.g., "I am attracted to difficult problems") as additional explanatory variables.

Self-efficacy in interacting with technology relates to Banduras Self-efficacy Theory (Bandura, 1982) and describes an individual's perceived ability to successfully interact with a technical device and to attain certain goals with these devices. Previous research has identified tremendous gender (e.g., Brauner, Leonhardt, Ziefle, & Schroeder, 2010; Busch, 1995; Wilkowska et al., 2010) and age effects (e.g., Arning & Ziefle, 2007b; Wilkowska & Ziefle, 2009) in performance and acceptance of technological systems. Self-efficacy in interacting with the technology was measured and analyzed by the scale of Beier (1999).

Gaming frequency was determined as an index across nine playful activities ranging from playing cards or ball games (not computer mediated), to computer or console games.

The participant's need for achievement was measured on a scale by Schuler and Prochaska (2001). An individual's need for achievement relates to the choice of tasks and the performance attained within the tasks. Therefore, players with higher need for achievement will attain a higher performance in the game than players with a lower need for achievement.

Dependent variables: In addition to the aforementioned personality factors, the participants' current subjective pain levels for several body parts (e.g., head, shoulder, back, legs) and the perceived current level of exertion—collected on the scale by Borg (1982) that strongly correlates with the actual heart rate—were queried. To investigate the effect of the game on perceived pain and exertion, both measures were captured directly before and after the game intervention (repeated measure).

The evaluation of the game was measured using the items of the Technology Acceptance Model (TAM (Davis, 1989; Davis, Bagozzi, & Warshaw, 1989)) and the Extended Unified Theory of Acceptance and Use of Technology (UTAUT 2 (Venkatesh et al., 2012)). Following Davis' TAM model, there is a strong relationship between the intention to use a system and the later actual system use. Therefore, the intention to use (ItU)—similar to the first study—is captured as the target variable to predict the actual use of the system (e.g., "I intend to continue using this game in the future"). A detailed description of the other constructs of UTAUT 2 for this exercise game is given in (Brauner et al., 2015).

In addition to the participants' assessments of the game, the attained performance was captured via log files and then combined with the data from the questionnaires. All items, apart from age and gender, were rated on a six-point Likert scales ranging from "I fully disagree" (=0) to "I fully agree" (=5). The acquired data is analyzed using bivariate correlations (Spearman's rho (ρ) coefficient is reported), univariate analysis of variance (ANOVA) and repeated measures, as the data meets the assumptions of parametric calculations. Effect sizes are reported as η^2, corresponding to the first study. Multiple linear regressions were calculated using the step-wise method and models with high variance inflation factors were excluded (VIF $\gg$ 1). The level of significance is set to $P = .05$.

Participants

In total, $N = 64$ participants ($n = 32$ males and $n = 32$ females) ranging from 17 to 85 years of age participated in the user study voluntarily and without any financial compensation. The participants were gathered through public posters in the city and personal social networks. The reported current or last occupations were in the social (20%), health (8%), business (9%), technical (41%), or other sectors (22%).

As above, the sample was split into a younger ($M = 26$, $SD = 4.6$, age ≤ 35 years) and an older group ($M = 61.6$, $SD = 10.4$, age > 35 years) to differentiate between age-dependent evaluations, using factorial methods. By the design of the sample, age groups and gender were not correlated [$\chi^2(2,64) = 0.563$, n.s.].

About one quarter of the participants (26%) reported a chronic illness, mainly asthma, hypertension, and diabetes; the prevalence of chronic illness grew with the increasing age ($\rho = 0.41$, $P \leq .001$).

Elderly subjects indicated a lower technical self-efficacy ($\rho = -0.37$, $P < .01$). Also, gender affected technical self-efficacy and women reported significantly lower scores than men ($\rho = -0.33$, $P < .01$). Gender [$F(1,60) = 4.3$, $P = .043$] as well as age [$F(1, 60) = 24.6$, $P < .001$] are significantly related to technical self-efficacy. Though, there is no significant interaction between age and gender [$F(2, 59) = 0.1$, n.s.].

The subjective gaming frequency decreased with the increasing age ($\rho = -0.49$, $P < .001$), but gender did not affect the reported gaming frequency ($\rho = -0.16$, n.s.).

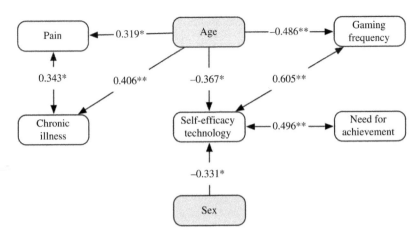

Figure 1.7 Interrelationships between the investigated user factors (**$P < .01$; *$P < .05$).

Although the gaming frequency scale captures the frequency of use of the technology-mediated and nontechnology mediated playful activities, there is a strong positive relationship between gaming frequency and self-efficacy in interacting with technology ($\rho = 0.60$, $P < .001$). Fig. 1.7 depicts the dependencies between the investigated user factors.

Results of Study II

In the results section of the second study, firstly, the overall effect of the game on the perceived pain levels and the perceived exertion is presented. Secondly, the factors that contribute to performance in the game are identified. Finally, the participants' intention to use the game in the future and factors contributing to that are analyzed.

Effects of the game

Exertion: To understand the effect of the game on the perceived exertion, a repeated measures ANOVA with the factors age and gender as independent variables, time as within-subject variable, and perceived exertion as dependent variable was calculated. The analysis reveals that the perceived exertion doubles from $M = 0.8$ ($SD = 1.2$) to $M = 1.7$ ($SD = 1.3$) of 5 points and that this increase is statistically significant [$F(1,60) = 13.3$, $P = .001$, $\eta^2 = 0.182$]. Gender does not affect the change in exertion [$F(1,60) = 0.5$, *n.s.*], but there is a significant effect of age [$F(1,60) = 7.7$, $P = .007$, $\eta^2 = 0.113$]. Specifically, the exertion of the younger participants increases from $M = 0.7$ ($SD = 0.8$) to $M = 2.2$ ($SD = 1$) of 5 points, whereas there is only a negligibly increase from $M = 1.0$ ($SD = 1.5$) to $M = 1.2$ ($SD = 1.1$) of 5 points for the elderly.

 Pain: An investigation of the changes of the perceived pain levels further reveals a significant overall effect of the game [$F(1,60) = 20.2$, $P < .001$, $\eta^2 = 0.25$]. On average across all participants, the perceived pain level decreased over the course of the exercise game. Although the absolute decrease from $M = 0.5$ ($SD = 0.6$) to $M = 0.2$ ($SD = 0.3$) of 5 points seems rather small, the relative change of -62% is astonishing. Again, age [$F(1,60) = 6.4$, $P = .015$, $\eta^2 = 0.09$] but not gender [$F(1,60) = 0.4$, $n.s.$] affected the decrease in pain perception and the decrease is stronger for older (-68%) than for younger participants (-33%). The other investigated factors, such as a chronic illness, did not or to a much smaller extent influence the change in perceived pain.

Performance

Only one 85-year-old female participant had difficulties to use the game due to movability constraints. The other 63 participants picked 9−30 fruits in each level of the game, with an average of $M = 19.6$ ($SD = 5.2$) fruits per level ($Md = 20$). All investigated user diversity factors were found to influence the attained performance in the game as shown in Fig. 1.8.

As the description of the sample has shown, all considered factors of user diversity are closely interrelated. To untangle this net of dependencies and to identify the true drivers for performance, a multiple linear regression analysis is calculated. Thereby, the user factors were considered the independent variables and the average performance across the three levels was included as the dependent variable.

The analysis revealed a linear model for performance based on age, need for achievement, and gender that explains over 63% of the variance in performance ($r^2 = 0.63$). The model's parameters are given in Table 1.2.

Intention to use

Now, the important question is whether and under which premises the game is likely to be used by the future residents of technology-augmented habitats. This section provides two perspectives on this question: Firstly, the variables that govern the intention to use the game are identified. Secondly, the evaluation of the game's assessment with regard to the identified influencing factors is presented.

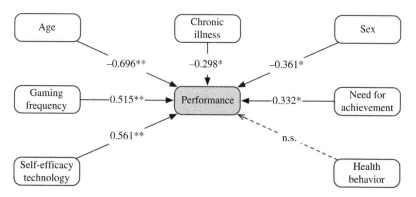

Figure 1.8 User factors contributing to performance (**$P < 0.01$; *$P < .05$).

Table 1.2 Linear regression model for performance
$(VIF_{max} = 1.39)$

Factor	B	SE B	β	T
(const)	26.5	2.03		13.04
Age	−0.17	0.02	−0.66	−8.26
Need for achievement	1.24	0.36	0.27	3.43
Gender	−2.64	0.79	−0.27	−3.34

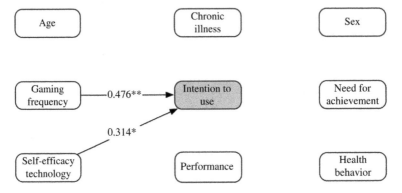

Figure 1.9 User factors contributing to intention to use ($**P < .01$; $*P < .05$).

A correlation analysis shows that the intention to use the game is solely governed by the participant's prior gaming frequency ($\rho = 0.47$, $P < .001$) and their self-efficacy in interacting with technology ($\rho = 0.31$, $P < .05$). None of the other investigated facets of user diversity, like age, gender, chronic illness, or the need for achievement, has a significant influence on the intention to use the game. A considerable finding was that the performance attained in the game is not meaningfully related to the projected later use ($\rho = 0.17$, n.s.). Hence, some people might express a desire to play, or not to play, the game again regardless of whether they were rather slow or rather fast in the game. Fig. 1.9 illustrates the two variables influencing the projected use of the game.

A multiple linear regression revealed that the effect of self-efficacy in interacting with technology on the intention to use fades if controlled for gaming frequency. Hence, gaming frequency is the single most significantly influencing factor on the intention to use serious games for healthcare in technology-augmented home environments.

Considering the absolute values of the intention to use the game, overall, the intention is rather high ($M = 3.9$, $SD = 1.2$ out of 5 points) and above the midpoint of the scale (2.5 points). The participants attested that the had game a high entertainment value ($M = 4.6$, $SD = 0.6$ out of 5 points) and wanted to play it again (replay value: $M = 4.3$, $SD = 0.9$). Yet, the desire to use this game in their home was much lower, but still above the center of the scale ($M = 3$, $SD = 1.6$ out of 5 points).

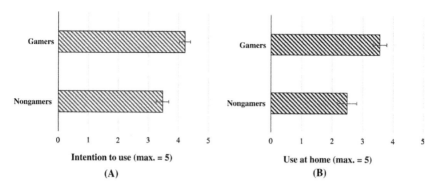

Figure 1.10 Evaluation of the serious exercise game by gamers and nongamers: (A) on the intention to use serious games; (B) on the use at home.

As gaming frequency was identified as the main factor for the intention to use this game in the future, it was further examined whether absolute evaluations differ. The overall intention to use it in future was significantly higher for gamers ($M = 4.2$, $SD = 1$) than for nongamers ($M = 3.5$, $SD = 1.2$) [$F(1,62) = 7$, $P = .010$, $\eta^2 = 0.102$]. However, both gamers and nongamers attested that the game had a similarly high entertainment value [$M = 4.6$, $SD = 0.6$; $F(1,62) = 0.3$, $n.s.$]. Also, the desire to play the game again did not differ significantly between gamer types [$F(1,62) = 3.4$, $n.s.$]. Fig. 1.10 illustrates the relevant findings.

According to the analyses, the participants were less inclined to use the game in their homes ($M = 3$, $SD = 1.6/5$ points) and both gamer groups differed significantly [$F(1,62) = 7.3$, $P = .009$, $\eta^2 = 0.106$]. Gamers expressed a higher desire to play the game at home ($M = 3.6$, $SD = 1.3$) than nongamers ($M = 2.5$, $SD = 1.8$). Surprisingly, the standard deviations on this question were considerably higher in comparison to previous questions which hints at different evaluations among the participants.

Discussion and limitations

In the following, a résumé of the results of both studies will be presented, interpreted, and discussed in terms of smart health. The subsequent section deals with limitations and future research. In this paper, we introduced two different health-related applications for which the broad acceptance and the intention to use these tools in the (smart) home environment were under study, using a strictly user-centered and participatory design methodology. As the above presented studies showed, both chronically ill persons as well as healthy (aged) individuals successfully interacted with the electronic health system integrated into a prototypical living room. In addition, a simulated gaming environment meant to motivate the (older) inhabitants to keep active by physical exercise, was found to increase the intention to use such ambient technologies in the future.

The current results show that, unlike previous trends in the use of technology innovations (where scientific studies have demonstrably revealed that young, mostly male individuals show significantly higher technical interest, knowledge, and skills), the greatest enthusiasm and willingness to use technology in the context of health-related assistance systems in domestic environments emerges from elderly and chronically ill people, regardless of gender. This finding originated especially from individuals with chronic heart diseases who did not only interact with the ambient system smoothly and in an intuitive way, but also showed a high motivation to use the technology in the future. Their opinions were possibly influenced by the fact that the technology is meant to be directly accessible in their living room and individually tailored to their personal needs, allowing the individual to cope easier with their particular disease. Their intention to use such ambient technology is higher than in healthy and middle-aged persons. Also, according to the high average assessments of the perceived meaningfulness and fun, an overwhelming majority of the participants acknowledged the eHealth system was a useful, enriching, and sensible facility.

In addition, as the findings clearly demonstrated, it was advantageous to integrate serious games in the ambient technology systems. Although, it has also been shown that not every person in old age displays the same enthusiasm for gaming, technical aptitude, and self-efficacy, suggesting a great diversity of individual factors. This diversity among the users has to be considered whenever developing innovative healthcare solutions. Thus, engineers need to be adequately trained to understand and consider the users' diversity in this regard. Moreover, from the presented studies, it can be learned that basically all investigated user factors affected the attained performance in the game, however, age and the need for achievement were identified as the strongest predictors for the performance. This finding is in line with prior research (Fisk & Rogers, 1997; Fisk, Rogers, Charness, Czaja, & Sharit, 2009). From the users' evaluation, it was evident that the inclination towards gaming and gaming frequency are the strongest predictors for the intention to use the exercise game in the future. This finding seems obvious at first sight, but it is more deceptive under further scrutiny. On the one hand, exercise games are an excellent way to increase the fitness and overall health of the residents of technology-augmented home environments. They increase individual mobility and independence, and contribute to the idea of successful aging. On the other hand, according to the presented results these exercise games are much more likely to be used only by gamers. The nongamers are therefore at risk to be excluded from this motivating, entertaining, and preventive form of health-supporting intervention. Hence, future research should address alternative forms of technology-mediated exercising, for instance, by linking the creation of music or images with cognitive or physical exercises. Corresponding to the users' diversity, the different inhabitants of technology-augmented habitats have varying interests. Therefore, a multifaceted set of exercising applications with different connecting points (e.g., games, music, paintings) should be offered. Finally, the game affected the individual's perceived exertion levels, which indicates that the players were actually involved in the game and aimed at achieving a decent score. And, even more importantly, playing the game had a strong positive effect on the perceived levels of pain. The younger participants started at a low level of pain, permitting only little space for a further decrease. In contrast, the older test participants reported a significant amount of initial pain that decreased over the course of the game. This result should not suggest that exercise games can substitute any medical therapies. Instead, they might be a valuable addition. The theory of pain mechanisms (Melzack & Wall, 1965) is further backed by the present data. As a consequence, the medical therapy of a resident of a health-supporting home environment may include a game-based exercise component. As outlined at the beginning of "Study II: Serious exercise games in AAL" section, this form of entertaining distraction from the actual therapy leads then to a lower perceived pain, as well as increased fitness, mood, and overall well-being.

However, there are also some limitations that need to be considered for future research. The presented studies consider how smart health technology is perceived, and how it is intended to be used by the residents of technology-enhanced habitats. Obviously, this view into the future is tainted with uncertainty. On the one hand, the development of technology may follow different and currently unimagined paths. On the other hand, future elderly persons may have different perceptions of technology in general, and computer games in particular. It is evident that technology expertise is formed by individual upbringing and by the technology types that dominate each generation. It follows that technology experience might differ between the generations (Prensky, 2001; Sackmann & Winkler, 2013) and that there is a need to examine in how far different generations might get familiar with using such complex systems, adopting them as a natural part of their lives.

Another interesting line of research is to concentrate on gender effects. One reason for this is that women still have a higher average life expectancy and live longer than their husbands or partners. Thus, in the next decades, we can expect a superior number of women as senior users (Barford, Dorling, Davey Smith, & Shaw, 2006; Durndell & Haag, 2002). Besides, although slightly in contrast with the results presented in Study I (health-related context), there is a strong empirical evidence that women show a lower interest in technology and a higher level of anxiety when handling novel technologies. This goes hand-in-hand with a lower self-efficacy with digital devices, which makes women much more careful and reluctant to interact with technology (Durndell & Haag, 2002). From this point of view, the general use of smart ambient technologies might be a serious hurdle for this user group. However, regarding the use of social media, women show a higher emotional involvement and social engagement in digital communication in comparison to men (Sun, Wang, Shen, & Zhang, 2015). There is also a high social motivation to be friends with, and stay in contact with, family members or peers (Barker, 2009; Thelwall, Wilkinson, & Uppal, 2010; Woolham & Frisby, 2002). Thus, a high involvement in the use of social media could be a powerful motivational anchor or trigger point to attract women to use health-supporting applications at home.

In conclusion, the presented findings provide evidence for a basically motivated attitude towards, and a high intention to use, such technology solutions at home, especially of elderly and chronically diseased persons. According to the resulting high scores for fun and perceived meaningfulness, the combination of the entertaining games and the serious background gives reason to conclude that Maria, who is autonomously checking her relevant health parameters, might be able to enjoy her independence, as characterized by self-determination and dignity in life for longer, and also to improve her social network through the game-based interactions with her grandchildren.

Responsible research and innovation in technology development for older adults

A final thought of this chapter regards the claim for responsible research and the consideration of ethical, legal, and social implications of technology development. In times in which technology developments, fostered by the huge and tremendously fast evolving innovations through modern information and communication technologies, enter private spheres and come into close contact with individual, private, and intimate activities, it is a mandatory claim that any technology development should be carefully developed and balanced within societal, cultural and individual values and norms. Within the European Union, the term "responsible research and innovation (RRI)" was formed under the prospective EU Framework Programme for Research and Innovation "Horizon 2020" (Stahl, 2013; Stahl, Eden, & Jirotka, 2013; von Schomberg, 2013). The concept was recently introduced as across countries there is—beyond the market itself, which might dictate which product is successful in the end—no normative instance which might define best practices or might assess and evaluate consequences, responsibilities and impacts of technology for the countries, the society, and the users (von Schomberg, 2013). Stahl (2013) points out that RRI is a social concept "that is meant to mediate the consequences of technical and other innovations on our individual and social lives" (p. 202). In Germany, a similar movement can be observed. With the ELSI (ethical, legal, social implications) and the ELSA (ethical, legal and social aspects) the German Ministry for Education and Research fosters the consequent consideration of these aspects in all research projects in which technology development, education and social aspects for different stakeholder groups are under study. As the RRI concept and the ELSA/ELSI approach are currently quite normative, the individual's rights and ethics when using technology should be the base for the ELSI perspective (Nelles et al., 2017; Owen, Macnaghten, & Stilgoe, 2012; Sutcliffe, 2011).

To come back to the issue of responsible research and technology development for older adults, we argue that any of these developments should comply with the claim for a socially responsible technology design. Beyond the normative aspect and the impact of RRI and ELSA concepts for policy, however, we strongly vote for including older adults in a bottom up process and asking for participation exactly those persons, for which these technologies are designed. It is important to keep in mind that smart homes and embedded health-supporting technologies have an enormous potential to bring forward and facilitate some crucial mechanisms regarding consequences of demographic change. And this is not only because the so-called eHealth technologies promise to deliver significant improvements in the access and quality, and to increase the efficiency of care as well as the productivity of the health sector (Holzinger, Dorner, Födinger, Calero Valdez, & Ziefle, 2010; Kleinberger, Becker, Ras, Holzinger, & Müller, 2007). It is much more a long-term success of smart health-technologies, depending on the sensitivity with which the users and their specific requirements, needs, values, as well as their culturally and individually formed wishes are considered during the development and implementation process.

To conclude, the responsibility in the research can be outlined on the basis of three major cornerstones of the age-appropriate technology developments: First is the *holistic and interdisciplinary technology development.* In contrast to the standard technology development currently practiced, in which mostly medical or technical facets are the center of attention, there is an urgent need to develop integrative models for the design of user-centered healthcare systems. The new concepts of health-monitoring systems within ambient living environments should be suited to support users individually (i.e., according to the users' profiles and specific needs), adaptively (i.e., in accordance with the age-related changes and/or depending on the course of disease), and sensitively (i.e., corresponding to the living conditions under all circumstances) (Blanchard-Fields, Hertzog, Stein, & Pak, 2001; Klack et al., 2011). A second important point is the *novel understanding of age and aging.* The technical development in the context of health-supporting ambient systems should be based on a sensitive concept of human needs and specifically tailored to the requirements of the most frequent user group: Seniors. This could mean that the devices and technical systems then unveil their reverse side: Smart health systems being not only compensatory for the negative effects of aging (e.g., general frailty, cognitive or physical deficiencies), but rather the complete opposite. The support of the positive aspects of aging like life-experience, domain knowledge, skills and expertise, wisdom, and fun in the old age should be deeply anchored as benchmarks in a sustainable technology development (Blanchard-Fields et al., 2001; Sackmann & Winkler, 2013). As such, technology development then has the responsibility to empower elderly people as an active part of the society (Ziefle & Schaar, 2014). Eventually, the third cornerstone refers to *integrating the users in the whole design process.* The most important modification to traditional technology development approaches in the field of medical engineering is to include the users actively during the whole process of the technology innovation (participative design). A coherent, user-centered design of health-supporting devices integrated in home environments will result in ambient technology which is not only functional in an engineering way of thinking, but it also addresses the users' fundamental needs in terms of unobtrusiveness (nonstigmatizing design), ease of use, perceived usefulness, and overall usability (Wilkowska, 2015). Especially in case of AAL and smart health systems, this is a vital precondition. For the majority of us, the home is the most intimate and conversant place, and technology that is integrated into this sensitive piece of one's identity must unconditionally adapt to the lifestyle and requirements of its inhabitant(s). Therefore, it is obvious—and should appropriately be acknowledged in both the research and in the industry—that involvement of the users as well as careful considering of their perspectives, wishes, and requirements into the technical development process prospect a reasonable chance of successful adoption and in the long run is able to bear the burden of a graying society.

Acknowledgments

This work has been funded by Excellence Initiative of Germany's Federal Ministry of Education and Research and the German Research Foundation.

References

Ahlskog, J. E., Geda, Y. E., Graff-Radford, N. R., & Petersen, R. C. (2011). Physical exercise as a preventive or disease-modifying treatment of dementia and brain aging. *Mayo Clinic Proceedings*, *86*(9), 876−884.

Arnds, P., & Bonin, H. (2002). *Arbeitsmarkteffekte und finanzpolitische Folgen der demographischen Alterung in Deutschland [Labor market effects and financial policy consequences of demographic aging in Germany]*. Institute for the Study of Labor (IZA).

Arning, K., & Ziefle, M. (2007a). Barriers of information access in small screen device applications: The relevance of user characteristics for a transgenerational design. In C. Stephanidis, & M. Pieper (Eds.), *User interfaces for all: Universal access in ambient intelligence environments* (pp. 117−136). Berlin, Heidelberg: Springer, LNCS 4397.

Arning, K., & Ziefle, M. (2007b). Understanding age differences in PDA acceptance and performance. *Computers in Human Behavior*, *23*(6), 2904−2927.

Bandura, A. (1982). Self-efficacy mechanism in human agency. *American Psychologist*, *37* (2), 122−147.

Barford, A., Dorling, D., Davey Smith, G., & Shaw, M. (2006). Life expectancy: Women now on top everywhere. *BMJ*, *332*, 800.

Barker, V. (2009). Older adolescents' motivations for social network site use: The influence of gender, group identity, and collective self-esteem. *CyberPsychology & Behavior*, *12* (2), 209−213.

Beier, G. (1999). Kontrollüberzeugungen im Umgang mit Technik [Control convictions in dealing with technology]. *Report Psychologie*, *9*, 684−693.

Beul, S., Klack, L., Kasugai, K., Möllering, C., Röcker, C., Wilkowska, W., & Ziefle, M. (2010). Between innovation and daily practice in the development of AAL systems: Learning from the experience with today's systems. In *Proceedings of the 3rd international ICST conference on electronic healthcare for the 21st century*. Casablanca, 2010.

Blanchard-Fields, F., Hertzog, C., Stein, R., & Pak, R. (2001). Beyond a stereotyped view of older adults' traditional family values. *Psychology and Aging*, *16*(3), 483−496.

Bloom, D. E., Canning, D., & Fink, G. (2010). The greying of the global population and its macroeconomic consequences. *Twenty-First Century Society*, *5*(3), 233−242.

Borg, G. A. V. (1982). Psychophysical bases of perceived exertion. *Medicine and Science in Sports and Exercise*, *14*(5), 377−381.

Brauner, P., Holzinger, A., & Ziefle, M. (2015). Ubiquitous computing at its best: Serious exercise games for older adults in ambient assisted living environments − A technology acceptance perspective. *EAI Endorsed Transactions on Serious Games*, *15*(4), 1−12.

Brauner, P., Leonhardt, T., Ziefle, M., & Schroeder, U. (2010). The effect of tangible arti-facts, gender and subjective technical competence on teaching programming to seventh graders. Proceedings of the 4th International Conference on Informatics in Secondary Schools. In J. Hromkovic, R. Královiè, & J. Vahrenhold (Eds.), *Lecture Notes in Computer Science 5941* (pp. 61–71). Berlin Heidelberg: Springer.

Brooke, J. (1996). SUS-A quick and dirty usability scale. *Usability Evaluation in Industry, 189,* 4–7.

Busch, T. (1995). Gender differences in self-efficacy and attitudes toward computers. *Journal of Educational Computing Research, 12,* 147–158.

Cohen, J. (1988). *Statistical power analysis for the behavioral sciences.* Hillsdale, NJ: Erlbaum.

Cooper, A. (1999). *The inmates are running the asylum.* Indianapolis, IN: Sams.

Davis, F. D. (1989). Perceived usefulness, perceived ease of use, and user acceptance of information technology. *MIS Quarterly, 13*(3), 319–340.

Davis, F. D., Bagozzi, R. P., & Warshaw, P. R. (1989). User acceptance of computer technol-ogy: a comparison of two theoretical models. *Management Science, 35*(8), 982–1003.

De Schutter, B., & Van Den Abeele, V. (2008). Meaningful Play in Elderly Life. In *Proceedings of the 58th annual conference of the international communication associa-tion.* Montreal: Canada.

Destatis. (2014). *Most frequent causes of dead.* Available online <https://www.destatis.de/EN/FactsFigures/SocietyState/Health/CausesDeath/CausesDeath.html>. Accessed 09.12.16.

Dewsbury, G., & Edge, M. (2001). Designing the home to meet the needs of tomorrow... today: smart technology, health and well-being. *Open House International, 26*(2), 33–42.

Durndell, A., & Haag, Z. (2002). Computer self-efficacy, computer anxiety, attitudes towards the Internet and reported experience with the Internet, by gender, in an East European sample. *Computers in Human Behavior, 18*(5), 521–535.

Eloy, S., Plácido, I., & Duarte, J. P. (2007). Housing and information society: Integration of ICT in the existing housing stock. In Braganca, et al. (Eds.), *SB 2007, Sustainable con-struction, materials, practices.* Portugal: IOS Press.

Fisk, A. D., & Rogers, W. A. (1997). *Handbook of human factors and the older adult.* San Diego, CA: Academic Press.

Fisk, A. D., Rogers, W. A., Charness, N., Czaja, S. J., & Sharit, J. (2009). *Designing for older adults: Principles and creative human factors approaches.* Boca Raton, FL: CRC Press.

Gaul, S., & Ziefle, M. (2009). Smart home technologies: Insights into generation-specific acceptance motives. *Symposium of the Austrian HCI and usability engineering group* (pp. 312–332). Berlin Heidelberg: Springer.

Gould, J. D., & Lewis, C. (1985). Designing for usability: Key principles and what designers think. *Communications of the ACM, 28*(3), 300–311.

Heidrich, F. (2015). *Inhabitable Bits. Adaptive User Interfaces for Smart Environments.* Aachen: Apprimus.

Holzinger, A., Dorner, S., Födinger, M., Calero Valdez, A., & Ziefle, M. (2010). *Chances of increasing youth health awareness through mobile wellness applications. Symposium of the Austrian HCI and usability engineering group* (pp. 71–81). Berlin Heidelberg: Springer.

Holzinger, A., Röcker, C., & Ziefle, M. (2015). From smart health to smart hospitals. In A. Holzinger, C. Röcker, & M. Ziefle (Eds.), *Smart health* (pp. 1–20). Switzerland: Springer International Publishing.

Iweins, C., Desmette, D., Yzerbyt, V., & Stinglhamber, F. (2013). Ageism at work: The impact of intergenerational contact and organizational multi-age perspective. *European Journal of Work and Organizational Psychology*, *22*(3), 331−346.

John, B. (2013). Patterns of ageism in different age groups. *Journal of European Psychology Students*, *4*(1), 16−36.

Kasugai, K., Ziefle, M., Röcker, C., & Russell, P. (2010). Creating spatio-temporal contiguities between real and virtual rooms in an assistive living environment. In J. Bonner, M. Smyth, S. O'Neill, & O. Mival (Eds.), *Proceedings of Create 10 innovative interactions* (pp. 62−67). Loughborough: Elms Court.

Klack, L., Schmitz-Rode, T., Wilkowska, W., Kasugai, K., Heidrich, F., & Ziefle, M. (2011). Integrated home monitoring and compliance optimization for patients with mechanical circulatory support devices (MCSDs). *Annals of Biomedical Engineering*, *39*(12), 2911−2921.

Kleinberger, T., Becker, M., Ras, E., Holzinger, A., & Müller, P. (2007). Ambient intelligence in assisted living: Enable elderly people to handle future interfaces. *International conference on universal access in human-computer interaction* (pp. 103−112). Berlin Heidelberg: Springer.

Knight, J. A. (2012). Physical inactivity: Associated diseases and disorders. *Annals of Clinical & Laboratory Science*, *42*(3), 320−337.

Korzilius, H. (2008). Hausärztemangel in Deutschland: die große Landflucht [Shortage of GPs in Germany: the rural exodus]. *Deutsches Aerzteblatt*, *105*, 373−374.

Lee, M. L. (2010). Embedded assessment of wellness with smart home sensors. *Proceedings of the 12th ACM international conference adjunct papers on Ubiquitous computing-Adjunct* (pp. 473−476). ACM.

Leonhardt, S. (2006). Personal healthcare devices. In S. Mekherjee, et al. (Eds.), *AmIware Hardware Technology Drivers of Ambient Intelligence* (pp. 349−370). Dordrecht: Springer Netherlands.

LeRouge, C., Ma, J., Sneha, S., & Tolle, K. (2013). User profiles and personas in the design and development of consumer health technologies. *International Journal of Medical Informatics*, *82*(11), e251−e268.

Little, J.S., & Triest, R.K. (2001). Seismic shifts: the economic impact of demographic change. An overview. In *Conference Series-Federal Reserve Bank of Boston* (Vol. 46, pp. 1−30). Federal Reserve Bank of Boston; 1998.

Melzack, R., & Wall, P. D. (1965). Pain mechanisms: A new theory. *Survey of Anesthesiology*, *11*(2), 89−90.

Mynatt, E. D., Melenhorst, A.-S., Fisk, A. D., & Rogers, W. A. (2004). Aware technologies for aging in place: Understanding user needs and attitudes. *Pervasive Computing*, *3*(2), 36−41.

Nehmer, J., Becker, M., Karshmer, A., & Lamm, R. (2006). Living assistance systems: An ambient intelligence approach. *Proceedings of the 28th international conference on software engineering* (pp. 43−50). Shanghai: ACM.

Nelles, J., Kohns, S., Spies, J., Bröhl, C., Brandl, C., Mertens, A., & Schlick, C. M. (2017). *Best-practice approach for a solution-oriented technology assessment: Ethical, legal, and social issues in the context of human-robot collaboration. Advances in ergonomic design of systems, products and processes* (pp. 1−14). Berlin Heidelberg: Springer.

Owen, R., Macnaghten, P., & Stilgoe, J. (2012). Responsible research and innovation: From science in society to science for society, with society. *Science and Public Policy*, *39*(6), 751−760.

Pak, R., & McLaughlin, A. (2010). *Designing displays for older adults*. Hoboken, NJ: CRC Press.

Pak, R., Price, M., & Thatcher, J. (2009). Age-sensitive design of online health information: Comparative usability study. *Journal of Medical Internet Research*, *11*(4), e45.

Perez-Terzic, C. M. (2012). Exercise in cardiovascular diseases. *Exercise and Sports for Health Promotion, Disease, and Disability*, *4*(11), 867–873.

Prensky, M. (2001). Digital natives, digital immigrants Part 1. *On the Horizon*, *9*, 1–6.

Röcker, C., & Kasugai, K. (2011). *Interactive architecture in domestic spaces. International joint conference on ambient intelligence* (pp. 12–18). Berlin Heidelberg: Springer.

Sackmann, R., & Winkler, O. (2013). Technology generations revisited: The internet generation. *Gerontechnology*, *11*(4), 493–503.

Schuler, H., & Prochaska, M. (2001). *LMI: Leistungsmotivationsinventar [Need for achievement inventory]*. Test hand manual. Göttingen: Hogrefe.

Stahl, B. C. (2013). Responsible research and innovation: The role of privacy in an emerging framework. *Science and Public Policy*, *40*(6), 708–716.

Stahl, B. C., Eden, G., & Jirotka, M. (2013). Responsible research and innovation in information and communication technology: Identifying and engaging with the ethical implications of ICTs. *Responsible Innovation*, 199–218.

Stronge, A. J., Rogers, W. A., & Fisk, A. D. (2007). Human factors considerations in implementing telemedicine systems to accommodate older adults. *Journal of Telemedicine and Telecare*, *13*, 1–3.

Sun, Y., Wang, N., Shen, X. L., & Zhang, J. X. (2015). Location information disclosure in location-based social network services: Privacy calculus, benefit structure, and gender differences. *Computers in Human Behavior*, *52*, 278–292.

Sutcliffe, H. (2011). *A report on Responsible Research and Innovation*. MATTER and the European Commission.

Terschüren, C., Mensing, M., & Mekel, O. C. (2012). Is telemonitoring an option against shortage of physicians in rural regions? Attitude towards telemedical devices in the North Rhine-Westphalian health survey, Germany. *BMC Health Services Research*, *12*(1), 1–9.

Thayer, R. E., Newman, J. R., & McClain, T. M. (1994). Self-regulation of mood: Strategies for changing a bad mood, raising energy, and reducing tension. *Journal of Personality and Social Psychology*, *67*(5), 910–925.

Thelwall, M., Wilkinson, D., & Uppal, S. (2010). Data mining emotion in social network communication: Gender differences in MySpace. *Journal of the American Society for Information Science and Technology*, *61*(1), 190–199.

United Nations. (2009). *World Population Prospects*. The 2008 Revision. CD-ROM Edition – Extended Dataset United Nations.

Venkatesh, V., Thong, J., & Xu, X. (2012). Consumer acceptance and use of information technology: Extending the unified theory of acceptance and use of technology. *MIS Quarterly*, *36*(1), 157–178.

Von Schomberg, R. (2013). A vision of responsible research and innovation. In R. Owen, M. Heintz, & J. Bessant (Eds.), *Responsible innovation*. London: John Wiley.

WHO, J., & FAO Expert Consultation (2003). Diet, nutrition and the prevention of chronic diseases. *World Health Organ Tech Rep Ser*, *916*, i–viii.

Wilkowska, W. (2015). *Acceptance of eHealth technology in home environments: Advanced studies on user diversity in ambient assisted living*. Aachen: Apprimus.

Wilkowska, W., Gaul, S., & Ziefle, M. (2010). A small but significant difference – The role of gender on the acceptance of medical assistive technologies. In G. Leitner, M. Hitz, & A. Holzinger (Eds.), *HCI in work & learning, life & leisure*, LNCS 6389 (pp. 82–100). Berlin, Heidelberg: Springer.

Wilkowska, W., Himmel, S., & Ziefle, M. (2015). Perceptions of personal privacy in smart home technologies: Do user assessments vary depending on the research method? *International conference on human aspects of information security, privacy, and trust* (pp. 592−603). New York: Springer International Publishing.

Wilkowska, W., & Ziefle, M. (2009). Which factors form older adults' acceptance of mobile information and communication technologies? In A. Holzinger, & K. Miesenberger (Eds.), *Human−computer interaction for eInclusion, LNCS 5889* (pp. 81−101). Berlin, Heidelberg: Springer.

Wilkowska, W., & Ziefle, M. (2011). *User diversity as a challenge for the integration of medical technology into future smart home environments. Human-centered design of E-Health technologies: Concepts, methods and applications* (pp. 95−126). Hershey, PA: Medical Information Science Reference.

Willey, J. Z., Moon, Y. P., Paik, M. C., Yoshita, M., DeCarli, C., Sacco, R. L., … Wright, C. B. (2011). Lower prevalence of silent brain infarcts in the physically active: The Northern Manhattan Study. *Neurology, 76*(24), 2112−2118.

Wittland, J., Brauner, P., & Ziefle, M. (2015). *Serious games for cognitive training in ambient assisted living environments−A technology acceptance perspective. Human-Computer Interaction* (pp. 453−471). New York: Springer International Publishing.

Woolham, J., & Frisby, B. (2002). Social Care Online Search Social Care Online… Building a local infrastructure that supports the use of assistive technology in the care of people with dementia. *Research Policy and Planning, 20*(1), 11−24.

Yan, H. R., Huo, H. W., Xu, Y. Z., & Gidlund, M. (2010). Wireless sensor network based e-health system−implementation and experimental results. *IEEE Transactions on Consumer Electronics, 56*(4), 2288−2295.

Ziefle, M., Himmel, S., & Wilkowska, W. (2011). When your living space knows what you do: Acceptance of medical home monitoring by different technologies. In A. Holzinger, & K.-M. Simonic (Eds.), *Human-computer interaction: Information quality in eHealth, LNCS 7058* (pp. 607−624). Berlin, Heidelberg: Springer.

Ziefle, M., & Schaar, A. K. (2011). Gender differences in acceptance and attitudes towards an invasive medical stent. *Electronic Journal of Health Informatics, 6*(2), e13, 1−18.

Ziefle, M., & Schaar, A. K. (2014). Technology acceptance by patients: Empowerment and stigma. In J. van Hoof, G. Demiris, & E. Wouters (Eds.), *Handbook of smart homes, health care and well-being* (pp. 1−10). New York: Springer International Publishing.

Zyda, M. (2005). From visual simulation to virtual reality to games. *Computer, 38*(9), 25−32.

Challenges associated with online health information seeking among older adults

2

Ronald W. Berkowsky and Sara J. Czaja
University of Miami School of Medicine, Miami, FL, United States

In 2008, Czaja, Sharit, and Nair conducted a study wherein 112 adults aged 50+ were tasked with using the Medicare.gov website to answer a series of questions regarding eligibility for home healthcare services, selecting home health agencies, making enrollment decisions associated with Medicare Part D, selecting a drug plan, and assessing associated costs. The participants, who had prior computer experience, were also tasked with rating the usability of the Medicare.gov website by assessing how difficult it was to navigate the website, and how frustrating it was to search for information on the site. The results, published in *JAMA*, were shocking: 68.8% of participants were unable to correctly identify eligibility criteria for home healthcare services, 80.4% were unable to choose the correct home health agency, and 83.9% were unable to compute the costs associated with selecting a drug plan. Participants performed best in making an enrollment decision, but even in this case only 57.1% were able to make the correct decision based on the task parameters. In addition, over half of participants found it difficult to navigate the Medicare.gov website, frustrating to use, and difficult to find the information needed. As shown by this study, seeking online health information is not always an easy endeavor, especially for older adults.

Information and communication technologies or ICTs (i.e., Internet-connected devices and applications used for the dissemination of information or for communication purposes) have developed and evolved at a pronounced and rapid pace over the past few decades, and ICTs have also become more widely available to consumers. Along with availability of, and access to, ICTs, there has also been an increase in e-health (i.e., digital information and communication processes related to health, wellness, and healthcare) wherein more consumers are using technology devices and applications to assume a more pronounced role in managing their health and in making healthcare decisions (Czaja, Sharit, Nair, & Lee, 2009). While there now exist numerous devices and applications which fall under the purview of e-health, such as wearable technologies to track vital signs or mobile phone apps to manage health lifestyles, one of the most common types of e-health is that of online health information seeking. The Pew Research Center reports that in 2013, 59% of US adults indicated that they went online to look up health information over the past year and that 35% of US adults indicated they went online to search for information on specific illnesses or symptoms in an attempt to self-diagnose a condition,

Aging, Technology and Health. DOI: http://dx.doi.org/10.1016/B978-0-12-811272-4.00002-6

or to diagnose the condition of someone close to them (Fox & Duggan, 2013). Over half of US smartphone users have indicated using their devices to look up health information (Fox & Duggan, 2012).

Yet, while ICTs provide consumers with unprecedented access to health information on a variety of topics, there exist a number of barriers and challenges associated with finding the relevant information needed, interpreting it, and successfully using it (e.g., Czaja, Sharit, Hernandez, Nair, & Loewenstein, 2010; Czaja et al., 2008; Sharit, Hernandez, Czaja, & Pirolli, 2008). This chapter specifically discusses the challenges older adults face when attempting to search for health information online. Specifically, we discuss the unique characteristics and risk factors relevant to older adults, which may increase the probability of unsuccessful information searches, or contribute to a decreased ability among older adults in being able to successfully utilize the information found. These challenges include those associated with physical health limitations, cognitive limitations, issues with literacy (including health literacy, numeracy, and digital literacy), and negative attitudes toward technology. By identifying where and why older adults struggle when searching for health information online, designers may more aptly take into account the limitations of this population when designing health-based websites and/or smartphone apps. In addition, by identifying the challenges older adults face in online health information seeking, technology training interventionists may better tailor their training protocols to the specific needs (e.g., physical limitations, cognitive issues, etc.) of this vulnerable group.

Older adults and ICT use

The percentage of older adults who report using the Internet has been steadily increasing over the past two decades and at a pace higher than younger age groups. As reported by the Pew Research Center, approximately 14% of older adults aged 65+ reported going online in 2000. By 2016, that number had increased to 64%, a noticeable and significant change. However, despite the increase in usage, the percentage of older adults reportedly going online is still much lower compared to younger age groups: in 2016, 99% of those aged 18−29 went online, while 96% of those aged 30−49 and 87% of those aged 50−64 went online. Similar trends are found when examining broadband use, as older adults are much less likely to report being broadband users (51% in 2016) compared to younger age groups (77% 18−29, 81% 30−49, 75% 50−64). Lack of Internet use and broadband access is especially pronounced among those in the older cohorts (e.g., age 75+).

Older adults may greatly benefit from ICT use, as these devices and applications give unprecedented access to information on a variety of topics (including health, entertainment, financial considerations, education, etc.) as well as a new communication avenue to connect or reconnect with social ties and foster new ties. Older adults who report using the Internet have been shown to experience less loneliness (e.g., Cotten, Anderson, & McCullough, 2013; Czaja et al., 2017), increased life satisfaction and psychological well-being (Heo, Chun, Lee, Lee, & Kim, 2015), and fewer depressive symptoms (e.g., Cotten, Ford, Ford, & Hale, 2014). Yet despite the potential benefits of ICT use, older adults are less likely to be online compared to younger age groups.

The disparities associated with Internet use are commonly referred to as the digital divide and manifest in two broad "levels": The first-level digital divide (which primarily includes issues of access), and the second-level digital divide (which primarily includes issues of knowledge and skill). With the increase in availability of various types of ICTs as well as the costs of these ICTs and of Internet connectivity dropping, many researchers have turned to the second-level digital divide as a means of explaining why older adults are less likely to be online. Indeed, compared to younger groups older adults tend to have less experience and fewer skills associated with ICT use (Hargittai, 2002), and they may also lack the confidence to learn to use ICTs or lack the social/technical support to promote learning (Cotten, Yost, Berkowsky, Winstead, & Anderson, 2016). An older adult may have a desktop computer sitting in their home, or they may have access to one at a public library, or in the activity room of a continuing care retirement community (CCRC), but simply having the technology available does not dictate that they will be able to use the technology to their benefit. ICTs are complex machines for those who have never used them or have little experience with them. In addition, because these technologies are constantly upgrading and updating, it can be difficult for older learners and users to "keep up," as they may constantly have to learn new online skills. Despite lower skill levels and perceived difficulties in mastering new technologies, many older adults cite learning to use ICTs as a worthwhile endeavor (Boulton-Lewis, Buys, & Lovie-Kitchin, 2006).

With regards to e-health, Pew reports that looking for health information ranks as the third-most popular activity to do online among older adults aged 65+, behind only email use and searching for general information (Zickuhr, 2010). While the Internet is not typically perceived as the most referenced or most trustworthy sources of health information among older adults, among those who are online the Internet is ranked high as a preferred source of health information (behind only healthcare providers and pharmacists), and it is common for older Internet users to supplement the information they receive from other sources with information found on the Internet (Medlock et al., 2015; Renahy, Parizot, & Chauvin, 2008). In this way, ICTs provide older adults a vital tool in learning more information about health, wellness, and healthcare, and allow them to take a more active role in managing their health; in some instances, a preliminary search for health information online assists older Internet users with making a decision as to whether or not to seek medical assistance or to search for health information online to prepare for an appointment with a physician, although it is more common for older adults to seek health information after an appointment rather than before (Medlock et al., 2015).

Information search strategies

With online health searching being a particularly popular activity among Internet-using older adults, researchers have focused on how older adults go about searching for information as well as how successful they are in finding and using health information. While individual strategies for online information seeking can be more detailed (Thatcher, 2008), in general the literature on the subject identifies two primary and broad strategies employed by web users (Marchionini, 1997): analytic strategies (wherein users extract keywords from a given problem scenario and use these terms to search for information through the use of a search engine) and browsing strategies (wherein users explore websites or categories within a specific website by following links and tabs that may yield appropriate information). The strategies defined by Marchionini (1997) are comparable to the bottom-up and top-down strategies defined by Navarro-Prieto, Scaife, and Rogers (1999) wherein *bottom-up* is comparable to an analytic search strategy and *top-down* is comparable to a browsing search strategy. Navarro-Prieto et al. (1999) and Hölscher and Strube (2000) also reference a *mixed* search strategy wherein a user employs both a bottom-up and top-down strategy in one of two manners: Either by conducting separate bottom-up and top-down searches simultaneously in different web browsers or windows, or by alternating between the two strategies during a single search.

Most research shows that those with more Internet experience tend to employ a bottom-up strategy when searching for information online, including health information (Aula & Nordhausen, 2006; Navarro-Prieto et al., 1999; Sharit, Taha, Berkowsky, Profita, & Czaja, 2015). Drabenstott (2001) elaborates on the bottom-up strategy by proposing 6 keyword formulation and utilization profiles:

1. *Shot in the dark*—the user enters one keyword into a search bar.
2. *Bingo*—the user enters a series of keywords into a search bar.
3. *Kitchen sink*—the user enters numerous keywords into a search bar, throwing everything in "but the kitchen sink."
4. *Big bite*—the user enters additional keywords to the original search term to narrow down the results of the search query.
5. *Citation pearl growing*—the user recycles previously successful keywords in a new search.
6. *Help from your friends*—the user utilizes subject directories to aid in the search.

In addition to Internet experience, cognitive ability also tends to be a significant predictor of using a bottom-up strategy for searching (Aula & Nordhausen, 2006; Navarro-Prieto et al., 1999; Sharit et al., 2015).

Interestingly, while there tends to be significant differences between younger adults and older adults with regards to search strategies employed, the time it takes to conduct a search, and the "amount" (i.e., the number of individual searches done to answer a query or the number of websites accessed to find the necessary information), when it comes to health information studies suggest that younger and older adults tend to score similarly with regards to search accuracy; i.e., all else equal, an older ICT user may perform just as well on a simple health search task compared to a younger user (Sharit, Taha, Berkowsky, & Czaja, 2016; Sharit et al., 2015) but perhaps not as well on more complex tasks that involve integrating information across several websites. Older adults may be more likely to use a top-down strategy, exhibit longer search times, and exhibit lower "amounts" of search, but may still be able to score relatively similarly to younger groups. The key phrase here is *all else equal*—assuming similar scores on Internet experience, cognitive abilities, etc., both younger and older adults can perform successful health searches online. However, there are a number of barriers and challenges unique to older populations that tip the scale in a way that can prevent successful health searches, including physical barriers, cognitive limitations, literacy levels, and attitudes toward technology.

Physical barriers

Many US older adults aged 65+ have a physical health issue (i.e., disability, handicap, or chronic disease) which impacts on participation in everyday activities and completing everyday tasks. For example, among Medicare beneficiaries in the United States, which comprises older adults who receive coverage for various medical services by the government, 69% have two or more chronic health conditions, 37% have four or more, and 14% have six or more chronic conditions such as diabetes, high blood pressure, and ischemic heart disease (Centers for Medicare and Medicaid Services, 2012). Compared to those who report not having any physical limitations, older adults with physical disabilities are much less likely to go online—49% of those with physical limitations report going online versus 66% with no physical limitations (Smith, 2014). It is an unfortunate conundrum, as those who experience physical health issues may be the most in need of health information but are also less likely to be able to get online to *retrieve* the information they need, as their physical health issues may prevent them from doing so. With regards to ability to use an ICT and navigate the Internet for health information, problems with visual impairment and problems with motor skills can be especially detrimental for older adults.

Visual impairment

As an individual ages, vision deteriorates, and changes in visual ability can significantly affect an older adult's ability to learn how to use an ICT to search for health information as well as use said ICT to conduct a successful search (Becker, 2004; Charness, 2001; Hanson, 2010). Common visual changes that occur as an individual ages include (but are not limited to): a decline in visual acuity (i.e., the ability to resolve detail and see objects clearly), a reduced ability to focus on an object, a decline in contrast sensitivity (i.e., the ability to distinguish an object from a background based on color and brightness), declines in color perception and differentiation, decreased light sensitivity, and increased sensitivity to glare (Becker, 2004;

Czaja & Sharit, 2013). According to Charness (2001), these changes in vision as an individual ages can affect the user's ability to conduct an online search and navigate a website; changes in vision can affect legibility of content, reading speed, comprehension of content, ability to navigate a website and navigate between websites, and the amount of visual content that poses as a distraction.

If the font size of a health- or healthcare-related website it small, or if the font style is particularly difficult to read, older adults with visual impairments may not be able to locate or read the information provided on the site. If there is not enough contrast between colors on the website, older adults with visual impairments may not be able to differentiate between the text and background, or between different sections of the site. Even something as innocuous as a mouse cursor can pose an issue for an individual with vision issues—if an older adult is using a laptop or desktop computer to navigate the Internet and the mouse cursor is too small to see clearly, the user may not be able to click on the necessary tabs and links or may not be able to navigate the cursor to a search bar. Besides being able to see what is on a computer or smartphone screen and to differentiate between various different on-screen cues, visual impairment can also cause discomfort that manifests in other physical ways. An example described by Hanson (2010) is that of an older adult who requires bifocal lenses—an older adult who uses such lenses may be required to reposition their neck and shoulders in a way that is uncomfortable for long stretches of time, thus demotivating the individual from putting a lot of physical strain and effort into conducting an online health search.

Motor skills

In addition to decreased visual ability, older adults experience declines in motor skills and mobility as they age. There may be declines in coordination, loss of motor control, reduced ability to make continuous movements for long periods of time, and slower response times, to name but a few potential impairments. These changes in motor skills can greatly reduce an individual's ability to get to a stationary ICT or to successfully use the hardware associated with the ICT to search for health information.

Mouse control can be especially difficult for older adults, not just for those with limited ICT experience but also for those with limited dexterity, pain due to arthritis, or those with chronic diseases that can cause tremors in the hands (Cotton et al., 2016; Czaja & Sharit, 2013). In fact, Czaja and Sharit (2013, p. 19) state, "…we have found that mastering the use of a mouse can be more challenging for older people than learning to use a software program." Many online activities require the use of a mouse to give a command to a laptop or desktop computer through moving and positioning the cursor, clicking or double-clicking, and clicking-and-dragging, all activities that can be nearly impossible for an older adult with decreased hand control.

While ICT training (and, specifically, mouse training) may be an appropriate avenue to overcome decreased hand control, it may not be enough for those with chronic issues. It may behoove the older user to switch to a more accommodating mouse (such as a larger mouse with a trackball, which remains stationary while the user moves the cursor with the trackball) or to switch to using an ICT with a touchscreen interface. Such ICTs, like tablet computers, are gaining in popularity among older adults as they do not require the motor skills needed for mouse control and the devices are small enough so that the user can carry them wherever they please (Tsai, Shillair, & Cotten, 2017; Tsai, Shillair, Cotten, Winstead, & Yost, 2015). For older adults with mobility issues, a tablet can be with them at all times to search for health information, rather than the user having to travel to a stationary laptop or desktop computer when attempting to answer a health query.

Cognitive ability

Using an ICT and searching for information online can be a cognitively demanding endeavor, as information searches require locating, filtering, and consolidating a large amount of information potentially across multiple different online sources (Bhavnani, 2005). Searching for health information online, in particular, can be quite demanding—whether looking up information on a specific illness or looking up information on a care provider, medical information can be difficult to interpret and understand for laypeople, and coupling the confusing language of medicine with the taxing nature of online searches can be cognitively draining for ICT users. Previous research has shown that cognitive abilities such as memory and speed of processing are essential to successful performance of technology-based tasks (Charness, Kelley, Bosman, & Mottram, 2001; Czaja, Sharit, Ownby, Roth, & Nair, 2001; Sharit, Czaja, Nair, & Lee, 2003) and that cognitive abilities are a significant predictor of online health information seeking performance (Czaja et al., 2010; Sharit et al., 2008, 2015).

Cognitive abilities tend to decline with age, particularly fluid abilities. Broadly speaking, fluid abilities include those related to the active processing of new or current information (e.g., working memory, wherein an individual simultaneously stores and processes new information); by contrast, abilities that are more knowledge-based are referred to as crystalized abilities. In general, fluid abilities decline as people age, whereas crystalized abilities remain relatively stable until late life. Fluid abilities tend to be more associated with learning processes—i.e., when an individual is provided with new information to interpret, they rely on fluid abilities in order to do so. Having said that, both fluid and crystalized abilities have been shown to be important in the learning and mastery of ICTs (Czaja et al., 2006). Holt and Morrell (2002) contend that lessening the number of steps needed to conduct a successful online search would decrease the cognitive demands of the search, specifically those on working memory. With regards to health-related searches, Holt and Morrell (2002) also contend that presenting the material in an easily digestible format (e.g., written in plain language) lessens the cognitive effort of the older user; in this instance, the older adult would be less likely to be overwhelmed by the complexities of the information while simultaneously over-whelmed by the complexity of the technology.

While cognitive limitations may prevent older adults from successfully using ICTs or from being able to conduct accurate online health searches, there is evidence to suggest that some cognitive limitations can be overcome. As an example, when presented with an information search task older adults with lower cognitive abilities tend to utilize a top-down strategy or browsing strategy to find the relevant information (Chin, Fu, & Kannampallil, 2009; Sharit et al., 2015), and utilization of a top-down strategy did not necessarily predict task failure (Sharit et al., 2015). It is thus possible for older adults experiencing cognitive declines to make adjustments to enable successful searches of online health information.

Literacy

As previously mentioned, a significant barrier which may prevent older adults from successfully searching for health information may be ICT knowledge and skills. As digital divide researchers will contend, those with limited ICT knowledge and skills will be less likely to use the technologies to their full capacity. Knowledge and skills associated with being able to use ICTs is often referred to as *digital literacy*. Yet as described below, digital literacy is not the only "type" of literacy associated with searching for health information on the Internet.

Health literacy

Health literacy, as defined by the Institute of Medicine of the National Academies, is "the degree to which individuals can obtain, process, and understand the basic health information and services they need to make appropriate health decisions" (Institute of Medicine, 2004). Expanding on this, Jensen, King, Davis, and Guntzviller (2010, p. 807) argue:

> ...health literacy is an individual's ability to find and use health information. As such, health literacy could include basic skills (e.g., reading, writing, mathematics, speaking), cognitions (e.g., self efficacy, health motivation), and environmental factors (e.g., access). Put another way, what constitutes health literacy may be situationally dependent. It is whatever an individual needs to successfully navigate their health care environment.

In 2003, the National Assessment of Adult Literacy (NAAL) for the first time included a health literacy component and found that only 12% of US adults had proficient health literacy levels, with 53% having intermediate levels, 22% having basic levels, and 14% having below basic levels. The results for older adults aged 65+ were even more troubling; only 3% had proficient health literacy levels, while 38% had intermediate levels, 30% had basic levels, and 29% had below basic levels (Kutner, Greenburg, Jin, & Paulsen, 2006). Previous research has shown that low health literacy is significantly associated with less knowledge about personal health issues, higher hospitalization rates, higher costs of care, and worse health status (Berkman, Sheridan, Donahue, Halpern, & Crotty, 2011). Low health literacy may also prevent effective communication between patients and healthcare providers, as providers may present information in a manner the patient does not understand, or the patient does not have the knowledge to ask their provider the necessary questions.

Regardless of health literacy levels, the primary source of health information tends to be healthcare providers (Gutierrez, Kindratt, Pagels, Foster, & Gimpel, 2014). However, health literacy tends to be one of the more consistent predictors of successful online health searches (Gutierrez et al., 2014), including among older populations. In a study comparing younger and older adults on online task performance and answering health-related questions using the Internet, researchers found that increased health literacy was associated with increased search success and increased success in answering questions wherein prior health knowledge was required (e.g., flu vaccine recommendations), regardless of the age of the participant (Agree, King, Castro, Wiley, & Borzekowski, 2015). In addition, in the aforementioned work by Jensen et al. (2010), it was found that health literacy (in addition to numeracy, outlined in the next section) mediated the relationship between age and online health information seeking—i.e., those with higher health literacy were more likely to use the Internet to search for health information.

Numeracy

Another consideration health information providers need to take into account is that of numeracy ability of older consumers. Numeracy (specifically health numeracy) is defined as "...the degree to which individuals have the capacity to access, process, interpret, communicate, and act on numerical, quantitative, graphical, biostatistical, and probabilistic health information needed to make effective health decisions" (Golbeck, Ahlers-Schmidt, Paschal, & Dismuke, 2005, p. 375). Because health information provided online can be given in a variety of formats including charts, tables, and graphs, an individual's numeracy ability may have a significant impact on their ability to interpret online health information even when they successfully find the information they were looking for. Low numeracy levels may also prevent an individual from being able to make mathematical computations with quantitative data from a website without assistance (e.g., calculating and interpreting BMI scores). A study by Taha, Sharit, and Czaja (2014) investigated the association between numeracy ability and an older adult's ability to complete health management tasks on an online patient portal. What the investigators found was that numeracy ability has a significant impact on patient portal task performance even when accounting for health literacy; i.e., even older adults who scored high on health literacy showed problems in being able successfully read and interpret health data when presented in a more quantitative format (such as a table or graph). Moreover, 39.2% of those in the study found the tables in the patient portal to be confusing, indicating that "...tables displaying numeric information in the portal need to be formatted to provide information in a way that is more readily under-stood by those with low numeracy" (Taha et al., 2014, p. 432).

Taha and colleagues suggest that to account for an older adult's decreased numeracy skills, patient portals (and online health information sources in general) should highlight values that are significant or abnormal (e.g., lab results that are out of the proper range for a patient) or include supplemental audio or video files to more fully explain the values and significance of numeric information. Other recent studies have found similar results. As an example, Sharit et al. (2014) found that when assessing the usability of online personal health records by veterans, signifi-cant predictors of task performance included age, health literacy, objective numer-acy, and graph literacy. The authors suggest that when designing an e-health interface, potential improvements may include offering "analogies" to assist the user in interpreting numeric information and to provide aids in audio and/or visual formats that can be easily accessed but are also not obtrusive. In another study examining use of personal health records by veterans, Ruiz et al. (2016) found that lower graph literacy was associated with a decreased likelihood of using an online personal health record.

Digital literacy

Whereas health literacy refers to the skills and knowledge associated with proces-sing and understanding health information, digital literacy (broadly speaking) refers to the skills and knowledge associated with successful use of ICTs, including lap-tops and desktop computers, smartphones, and tablet computers. Common sense dictates that in order for an individual to be able to find health information online, they would first need a basic understanding of digital devices and applications they would be using to conduct the search. Digital literacy encompasses both hardware and software skills/knowledge; as an example, an older adult intending to look up a location of a healthcare provider in the community using a smartphone would need to know (1) how to activate the smartphone, (2) what maneuvers (i.e., tapping the screen) are required to operate the smartphone, (3) how to access the Internet from the home screen (through the use of an app or by opening a browser), (4) how to navigate to a search engine, (5) how to use a search bar, and (6) how to choose a search result, to name but a few of the skills needed. In this case, not only does the older user need to know how to use the Internet, they also have to know how to operate a smartphone in general. For most tech-savvy individuals, these processes may seem straightforward and simple; however, for an individual with little-to-no ICT experience, they can be quite challenging.

Lacking ICT knowledge is often a deterrent to use ICTs such as smartphones (e.g., Neves, Amaro, & Fonseca, 2013). Even so, just being online and having pass-ing knowledge of ICTs may not be enough to promote health and well-being; as an example, Leung (2010) found that Internet-connectedness does not alone predict quality of life (i.e., being online did not significantly predict increased well-being), but digital literacy *was* significantly associated with quality of life. This implies that those with more technical knowledge may be better equipped to use the digital tools at their disposal to fulfill online tasks. With regards to health information searches, those with decreased digital literacy tend to be less successful in completing health-based tasks like looking up information on specific illnesses, information on treatment options, information on prescriptions, etc. (Feufel & Stahl, 2012; Sharit et al., 2015).

It is no wonder that, in much of the literature examining health information seeking among older adults, the concept of literacy is found to be a significant and powerful predictor of success. Searching for health information requires multiple competencies: a basic understanding of health and healthcare, some numeric proficiency, and digital know-how.

Attitudes toward technology

A significant barrier to successful ICT adoption and use particularly among older adults is that of attitudes toward technology (e.g., Vroman, Arthanat, & Lysack, 2015). Many older adults perceive themselves as unable to learn to successfully use ICTs or lack the confidence in their ability to learn and master the technology, which in turn can inhibit learning (Boulton-Lewis, Buys, Lovie-Kitchin, Barnett, & David, 2007; Gatto & Tak, 2008). As argued by Berkowsky, Cotten, Yost, and Winstead (2013), "In order to undertake the often tedious process of learning to use technology, older adults must be persuaded that the outcome is worth the effort involved." Indeed, when comparing younger and older technology users, attitudes toward technology is often overlooked; while most would believe the largest difference between these groups would be in digital literacy, research has shown that differences in confidence and overall attitudes can be just as drastic, if not more so (Mitzner et al., 2010).

Research has shown that tailored technology training interventions can successfully improve older adults' attitudes toward technology and decrease perceived limitations to ICT use. In a study examining ICT use in CCRCs, older adults took part in an 8-week technology training course designed specifically to address the physical and cognitive learning needs of older adults in this setting. The specially-designed training included the development of a tailored training manual, use of specialized equipment (large trackball mice, large keyboards), and both formal class instruction as well as optional one-on-one instruction. The results of the study found that when comparing pre-intervention survey responses to post-intervention survey responses, CCRC residents reported more positive attitudes toward using a computer and the Internet (such as feeling less intimidated by computers); in addition, CCRC residents reported experiencing fewer perceived limitations to using ICTs—as an example, fewer participants reported that computers and the Internet were too complicated and hard to use (Berkowsky et al., 2013; Cotten et al., 2016). Other studies support the notion of tailored training promoting more positive attitudes toward technology (Laganà, 2008; Laganà, Oliver, Ainsworth, & Edwards, 2011);

research shows that the benefit of technology training can go well beyond that of increased digital literacy and skill.

Yet while having more negative attitudes toward technology may be a significant barrier for general ICT use and getting online in the first place (Vroman et al., 2015), online search performance itself may be less affected by attitudes among older adults. Previous research has shown that, when examining older adults' health information seeking task performance, there tends to be no significant difference between the best and worst performers on attitude measures (Czaja et al., 2010). Also, in the aforementioned CCRC study, while significant changes were found in the study population on measures of attitudes toward technology and perceived limitations to using ICTs by the end of the technology interventions, no significant change was found with regards to the amount of health information searches that were conducted (Cotten et al., 2016, p. 92). Such studies imply that while negative attitudes toward technology may prevent older adults from using the Internet to conduct health information searches, it does not pose a significant barrier to conducting a successful search among those who are already online; in such cases, technology experience and/or digital literacy may be more of an important factor (Czaja et al., 2010).

Related to attitudes toward technology, attitudes toward e-health websites may also play a role in health information seeking. Consumers are more likely to utilize a health-oriented website for health information if they deem the website trustworthy. Numerous factors may go into a consumer's decision on whether or not to trust a website—they may evaluate the content of the website, the design and layout of the website, and the source of the information, among other things, before deeming the website trustworthy and the information reliable (e.g., Sillence, Briggs, Harris, & Fishwick, 2007).

Addressing the challenges older adults face

There is the potential for older adults to greatly benefit from being online (Cotten et al., 2016), particularly from being able to use ICTs to search for health information and successfully integrate it into their healthcare plan (Sharit et al., 2016). While the number of older adults who are utilizing ICTs to search for and use online health information is increasing, there are significant barriers to successful use and conducting successful searches. As previously outlined, these barriers manifest in many forms, including physical limitations (vision, motor skills), cognitive issues and/or impairment, decreased literacy (health literacy, numeracy, digital literacy), and more negative attitudes toward technology (which has less of an effect on search performance, but may still significantly prevent older adults from being able to conduct an online health search). We conclude this chapter with recommendations for technology designers and technology training interventionists looking to decrease the digital divide (or more specifically, the e-health divide) to keep in mind when creating technologies or classes specifically catered toward older consumers.

Designing interfaces that are friendly to older users

Becker (2004) investigated the usability of 125 online health resource websites using guidelines for older adult-friendly web design recommended by the National Institute on Aging and found that a majority of resources did not score high on usability. Many of the challenges older adults face in seeking health information can be tackled in the technology design phase. Some suggestions based on previous literature and our own experiences in the field of technology and aging are outlined here, and can be applied to both immobile ICTs (e.g., desktop and laptop computers) or mobile devices (e.g., smartphones):

- *Accommodating visual impairment*—Use large font sizes, use font styles that are easy-to-read (Becker, 2004; suggests sans serif styles such as Arial), use highly contrasted colors between the foreground and background, avoid use of patterned images and backgrounds that may cause eye strain, create a search bar that is large and easy to locate on a screen, and avoid overloading the webpage with visual content that may be viewed as "clutter" (and thus distracting) by the user. In addition, provide audio content for users to listen to (i.e., a video which summarizes the content on the page). Those that focus on hardware design can also develop screens that reduce glare and allow the user to easily change the brightness of the screen.
- *Accommodating declines in motor skills*—Consider designing website navigation to minimize more advanced mouse skills (i.e., make all clickable tabs and links large enough for those who experience difficulty steadying the cursor, or avoid including buttons that require the user to double-click). This includes minimizing the use of a mouse to scroll, as scrolling requires a precise mouse click on page-up and page-down arrows that can be hard to locate and hard to click on for those with unsteady hands. In addition, designing the health website for use with a touchscreen interface allows older adults who cannot successfully use a mouse to still have options with regards to accessing health information.
- *Accommodating diminished cognitive ability*—Organize material in a standard and consistent format and avoid creating visual content that can be viewed as "clutter" (and confuse the user). Health information should be written in plain language, such as at a fifth grade reading level, that is easy to understand and interpret, and when possible use an active rather than passive voice when presenting content (as research shows that an active voice reduces cognitive demands such as working memory; see Park, 1992).
- *Presenting content for all literacy levels*—Presenting the content in easily digestible formats can more easily accommodate those with low literacy. Presenting health information in lay terms (and at a fifth grade reading level) with appropriate illustrations and photos can assist those with low health literacy; as suggested by Sharit et al. (2014), "analogies" may also assist those with low health literacy. Keeping sentence structure simple can also help, and presenting content in multiple languages can assist those for whom English is not their primary language. Minimizing the use of complicated charts or graphs, or including additional audio/video content to help explain these charts and graphs, can assist those with low numeracy skills. Minimizing the quantitative expectations of the user also avoids confusion (e.g., rather than provide a user with a formula to calculate BMI by hand,

include a calculator right into the webpage for users to input numbers and have the site conduct the calculation for them). To accommodate those with low digital literacy, include a site map and a help feature to make navigation easier and make sure a search bar is easily visible and easy to use, in addition to some of the already-mentioned recommendations that minimize complicated mouse procedures (e.g., scrolling).

- *Promoting trust between the user and the health source*—The National Institutes of Health (2011) along with many other organizations have come out with help-sheets for consumers to use when evaluating health information online; it would behoove designers to use these help-sheets as a starting point to know what information to include on a health resource site to promote trust between the site and the user. This includes incorporating detailed information on who runs the website and who funds it (e.g., government organization or a pharmaceutical company), who provides the content of the site (e.g., a physician vs. a layperson) and who reviews it, is there an easily findable privacy statement and/or terms of service statement, and how the site interacts with users (e.g., is there a physical or email address to contact the content's writer). Transparency is key when promoting trust.

The benefit of technology training

As mentioned earlier in this chapter, Cotten et al. (2016) conducted a technology intervention study and found that older adults who took part in the classes reported more positive attitudes toward technology, fewer limitations to using ICTs, and decreased feelings of loneliness. Technology training interventions can provide older adults who lack the confidence or appropriate physical/cognitive resources to learn to use ICTs more effectively. As previously outlined, the digital divide (and, thus, the e-health divide) does not simply encompass issues of access, but also issues of literacy and skill. Technology training can help overcome these issues. Some suggestions for those looking to create their own technology training courses include:

- *Cater to the needs of the older learner*—When conducting a class, know what the physical and cognitive limitations of your group are. If there are participants with vision or hearing issues, seat them close to the front of the class and use a microphone. Speak loudly and slowly to allow those with cognitive issues to be able to more easily process new information. On the topic of cognitive ability: as previously demonstrated, those with lower cognitive ability may have difficulty with online searches using a bottom-up search approach; as such, be open to teaching numerous different search procedures to cater to the needs of the specific students.
- *Have the appropriate equipment*—Those with issues with motor skills may require a mouse that is different from a typical mouse (e.g., a mouse with a large trackball). Those with vision issues may need keyboards with larger keys and computers with large screens and high resolutions.
- *Present class content in numerous formats*—Have both formal class sessions as well as one-on-one sessions for those who need more personal assistance and more individualized instruction. Create a custom training manual that contains the lesson plans (and minimize extraneous material; too much seldom-used material may confuse those with low cognitive ability). Include step-by-step instructions in the manual as well as screenshots.

These suggestions are merely a sample of the considerations technology designers and trainers may take into consideration when promoting health information seeking among older adults. By taking a more active and applied approach, researchers can help decrease the digital divide and enable more older adults to take a more active role in their health management.

References

Agree, E. M., King, A. C., Castro, C. M., Wiley, A., & Borzekowski, D. L. (2015). "It's got to be on this page": Age and cognitive style in a study of online health information seeking. *Journal of Medical Internet Research*, *17*(3), e79.

Aula, A., & Nordhausen, K. (2006). Modeling successful performance in Web searching. *Journal of the American Society for Information Science and Technology*, *57*(12), 1678–1693.

Becker, S. A. (2004). A study of web usability for older adults seeking online health resources. *ACM Transactions on Computer-Human Interaction (TOCHI)*, *11*(4), 387–406.

Berkman, N. D., Sheridan, S. L., Donahue, K. E., Halpern, D. J., & Crotty, K. (2011). Low health literacy and health outcomes: An updated systematic review. *Annals of Internal Medicine*, *155*(2), 97–107.

Berkowsky, R. W., Cotten, S. R., Yost, E. A., & Winstead, V. P. (2013). Attitudes towards and limitations to ICT use in assisted and independent living communities: Findings from a specially-designed technological intervention. *Educational Gerontology*, *39*(11), 797–811.

Bhavnani, S. K. (2005). The retrieval of highly scattered facts and architectural images: Strategies for search and design. *Automation in Construction*, *14*(6), 724–735.

Boulton-Lewis, G. M., Buys, L., & Lovie-Kitchin, J. (2006). Learning and active aging. *Educational Gerontology*, *32*(4), 271–282.

Boulton-Lewis, G. M., Buys, L., Lovie-Kitchin, J., Barnett, K., & David, L. N. (2007). Ageing, learning, and computer technology in Australia. *Educational Gerontology*, *33*(3), 253–270.

Centers for Medicare and Medicaid Services, Chronic conditions among Medicare beneficiaries, chartbook: 2012 edition, Baltimore, MD, CMS. 2012.

Charness, N. (2001). *Aging and communication: Human factors issues. Communication, technology, and aging: Opportunities and challenges for the future* (pp. 3–29). New York: Springer Publishing Company.

Charness, N., Kelley, C. L., Bosman, E. A., & Mottram, M. (2001). Word-processing training and retraining: Effects of adult age, experience, and interface. *Psychology and Aging, 16* (1), 110–127.

Chin, J., Fu, W.T., & Kannampallil, T. (2009). Adaptive information search: Age-dependent interactions between cognitive profiles and strategies. In *Proceedings of the SIGCHI conference on human factors in computing systems* (pp. 1683–1692).

Cotten, S. R., Anderson, W. A., & McCullough, B. M. (2013). Impact of internet use on loneliness and contact with others among older adults: Cross-sectional analysis. *Journal of Medical Internet Research*, *15*(2), e39.

Cotten, S. R., Ford, G., Ford, S., & Hale, T. M. (2014). Internet use and depression among retired older adults in the United States: A longitudinal analysis. *The Journals of Gerontology Series B: Psychological Sciences and Social Sciences*, 69(5), 763−771.

Cotten, S. R., Yost, E. A., Berkowsky, R. W., Winstead, V., & Anderson, W. A. (2016). *Designing technology training for older adults in continuing care retirement communities*. Boca Raton, FL: CRC Press.

Czaja, S. J., Charness, N., Fisk, A. D., Hertzog, C., Nair, S. N., Rogers, W. A., & Sharit, J. (2006). Factors predicting the use of technology: Findings from the Center for Research and Education on Aging and Technology Enhancement (CREATE). *Psychology and Aging*, 21(2), 333.

Czaja, S. J., & Sharit, J. (2013). *Designing training and instructional programs for older adults*. Boca Raton, FL: CRC Press.

Czaja, S. J., Sharit, J., Hernandez, M. A., Nair, S. N., & Loewenstein, D. (2010). Variability among older adults in Internet health information-seeking performance. *Gerontechnology*, 9(1), 46−55.

Czaja, S. J., Sharit, J., & Nair, S. N. (2008). Usability of the Medicare health web site. *JAMA*, 300(7), 790−792.

Czaja, S. J., Sharit, J., Nair, S. N., & Lee, C. C. (2009). Older adults and Internet health information seeking. *Proceedings of the Human Factors and Ergonomics Society Annual Meeting*, 53(2), 126−130.

Czaja, S. J., Sharit, J., Ownby, R., Roth, D. L., & Nair, S. (2001). Examining age differences in performance of a complex information search and retrieval task. *Psychology and Aging*, 16(4), 564−579.

Czaja, S. J., Boot, W. R., Charness, N., Rogers, W. A., & Sharit, J. (2017). Improving social support for older adults through technology: Findings from the PRISM randomized controlled trial. *The Gerontologist*. Available from http://dx.doi.org/10.1093/geront/gnw249.

Drabenstott, K. M. (2001). Web search strategy development. *Online*, 25(4), 18−27.

Feufel, M. A., & Stahl, S. F. (2012). What do web-use skill differences imply for online health information searches? *Journal of Medical Internet Research*, 14(3), e87.

Fox, S., & Duggan, M. (2012). *Mobile health 2012*. Pew Research Center. Retrieved from <http://www.pewinternet.org/~/media//Files/Reports/2012/PIP_MobileHealth2012_FINAL.pdf>.

Fox, S., & Duggan, M. (2013). *Health online 2013*. Pew Research Center. Retrieved from <http://www.pewinternet.org/~/media//Files/Reports/PIP_HealthOnline.pdf>.

Gatto, S. L., & Tak, S. H. (2008). Computer, Internet, and e-mail use among older adults: Benefits and barriers. *Educational Gerontology*, 34(9), 800−811.

Golbeck, A. L., Ahlers-Schmidt, C. R., Paschal, A. M., & Dismuke, S. E. (2005). A definition and operational framework for health numeracy. *American Journal of Preventive Medicine*, 29(4), 375−376.

Gutierrez, N., Kindratt, T. B., Pagels, P., Foster, B., & Gimpel, N. E. (2014). Health literacy, health information seeking behaviors and internet use among patients attending a private and public clinic in the same geographic area. *Journal of Community Health*, 39(1), 83−89.

Hanson, V. L. (2010). Influencing technology adoption by older adults. *Interacting with Computers*, 22(6), 502−509.

Hargittai, E. (2002). Second-level digital divide: Differences in people's online skills. *First Monday*, 7(4). Retrieved from <http://firstmonday.org/issues/issue7_4/hargittai/index.html>.

Heo, J., Chun, S., Lee, S., Lee, K. H., & Kim, J. (2015). Internet use and well-being in older adults. *Cyberpsychology, Behavior, and Social Networking, 18*(5), 268–272.

Hölscher, C., & Strube, G. (2000). Web search behavior of Internet experts and newbies. *Computer Networks, 33*(1), 337–346.

Holt, B. J., & Morrell, R. W. (2002). *Guidelines for web site design for older adults: The ultimate influence of cognitive factors. Older Adults, Health Information, and the World Wide Web* (pp. 109–129). Hillsdale, NJ: L. Erlbaum Associates Inc.

Institute of Medicine. 2004. *Health literacy: A prescription to end confusion.* Report Brief. Retrieved from <http://www.nationalacademies.org/hmd/~/media/Files/Report%20Files/2004/Health-Literacy-A-Prescription-to-End-Confusion/healthliteracyfinal.pdf>.

Jensen, J. D., King, A. J., Davis, L. A., & Guntzviller, L. M. (2010). Utilization of internet technology by low-income adults: The role of health literacy, health numeracy, and computer assistance. *Journal of Aging and Health, 22*(6), 804–826.

Kutner, M., Greenburg, E., Jin, Y., & Paulsen, C. (2006). *The health literacy of America's adults: Results from the 2003 National Assessment of Adult Literacy.* NCES 2006-483. National Center for Education Statistics.

Laganà, L. (2008). Enhancing the attitudes and self-efficacy of older adults toward computers and the internet: Results of a pilot study. *Educational Gerontology, 34*(9), 831–843.

Laganà, L., Oliver, T., Ainsworth, A., & Edwards, M. (2011). Enhancing computer self-efficacy and attitudes in multi-ethnic older adults: A randomised controlled study. *Ageing and Society, 31*(6), 911–933.

Leung, L. (2010). Effects of Internet connectedness and information literacy on quality of life. *Social Indicators Research, 98*(2), 273–290.

Marchionini, G. (1997). *Information seeking in electronic environments.* New York: Cambridge University Press.

Medlock, S., Eslami, S., Askari, M., Arts, D. L., Sent, D., de Rooij, S. E., & Abu-Hanna, A. (2015). Health information–seeking behavior of seniors who use the internet: a survey. *Journal of Medical Internet Research, 17*(1), e10.

Mitzner, T. L., Boron, J. B., Fausset, C. B., Adams, A. E., Charness, N., Czaja, S. J., ... Sharit, J. (2010). Older adults talk technology: Technology usage and attitudes. *Computers in Human Behavior, 26*(6), 1710–1721.

National Institutes of Health. (2011). *How to evaluate health information on the Internet: Questions and Answers.* Department of Health and Human Services. Retrieved from <https://ods.od.nih.gov/Health_Information/How_To_Evaluate_Health_Information_on_the_Internet_Questions_and_Answers.aspx>.

Navarro-Prieto, R., Scaife, M., & Rogers, Y. (1999). Cognitive strategies in web searching. In *Proceedings of the 5th Conference on Human Factors & the Web* (pp. 43–56).

Neves, B. B., Amaro, F., & Fonseca, J. R. (2013). Coming of (old) age in the digital age: ICT usage and non-usage among older adults. *Sociological Research Online, 18*(2), 6.

Park, D. C. (1992). Applied cognitive aging research. *The handbook of aging and cognition* (pp. 449–493). Hillsdale, NJ: Psychology Press.

Renahy, E., Parizot, I., & Chauvin, P. (2008). Health information seeking on the Internet: a double divide? Results from a representative survey in the Paris metropolitan area, France, 2005–2006. *BMC Public Health, 8*(1), 69.

Ruiz, J. G., Andrade, A. D., Hogue, C., Karanam, C., Akkineni, S., Cevallos, D., ... Sharit, J. (2016). The association of graph literacy with use of and skills using an online personal health record in outpatient veterans. *Journal of Health Communication, 21*(Suppl. 2), 83–90.

Sharit, J., Czaja, S. J., Nair, S., & Lee, C. C. (2003). Effects of age, speech rate, and environmental support in using telephone voice menu systems. *Human Factors: The Journal of the Human Factors and Ergonomics Society, 45*(2), 234−251.

Sharit, J., Hernandez, M. A., Czaja, S. J., & Pirolli, P. (2008). Investigating the roles of knowledge and cognitive abilities in older adult information seeking on the web. *ACM Transactions on Computer-Human Interaction (TOCHI), 15*(1), 3.

Sharit, J., Lisigurski, M., Andrade, A. D., Karanam, C., Nazi, K. M., Lewis, J. R., & Ruiz, J. G. (2014). The roles of health literacy, numeracy, and graph literacy on the usability of the VA's personal health record by veterans. *Journal of Usability Studies, 9*(4), 173−193.

Sharit, J., Taha, J., Berkowsky, R. W., & Czaja, S. J. (2016). Seeking and resolving complex online health information: Age differences in the role of cognitive abilities. *Proceedings of the human factors and ergonomics society annual meeting, 60*(1), 1−5.

Sharit, J., Taha, J., Berkowsky, R. W., Profita, H., & Czaja, S. J. (2015). Online information search performance and search strategies in a health problem-solving scenario. *Journal of Cognitive Engineering and Decision Making, 9*(3), 211−228.

Sillence, E., Briggs, P., Harris, P. R., & Fishwick, L. (2007). How do patients evaluate and make use of online health information? *Social Science & Medicine, 64*(9), 1853−1862.

Smith, A. (2014). *Older adults and technology use.* Pew Research Center. Retrieved from <http://www.pewinternet.org/files/2014/04/PIP_Seniors-and-Tech-Use_040314.pdf>.

Taha, J., Sharit, J., & Czaja, S. J. (2014). The impact of numeracy ability and technology skills on older adults' performance of health management tasks using a patient portal. *Journal of Applied Gerontology, 33*(4), 416−436.

Thatcher, A. (2008). Web search strategies: The influence of Web experience and task type. *Information Processing & Management, 44*(3), 1308−1329.

Tsai, H. Y. S., Shillair, R., & Cotten, S. R. (2017). Social support and "playing around": An examination of how older adults acquire digital literacy with tablet computers. *Journal of Applied Gerontology, 36*(1), 29−55.

Tsai, H. Y. S., Shillair, R., Cotten, S. R., Winstead, V., & Yost, E. (2015). Getting grandma online: Are tablets the answer for increasing digital inclusion for Older Adults in the US? *Educational Gerontology, 41*(10), 695−709.

Vroman, K. G., Arthanat, S., & Lysack, C. (2015). "Who over 65 is online?" Older adults' dispositions toward information communication technology. *Computers in Human Behavior, 43*, 156−166.

Zickuhr, K. (2010). *Generations 2010.* Pew Research Center. Retrieved from <http://www.pewinternet.org/ ~ /media//Files/Reports/2010/PIP_Generations_and_Tech10.pdf>.

Improving older adults' comprehension and use of patient portal-based health information

Renato F. L. Azevedo and Daniel G. Morrow
University of Illinois at Urbana-Champaign, Champaign, IL, United States

Introduction

Within the next 40 years the number of older adults (over 65 years of age) in the world is expected to exceed the number of younger adults for the first time in history (Goldstein, 2010; UN, 2010; 2011). In the United States, older adults are the fastest growing segment of the population and the most frequent consumers of health information. Not surprisingly, the occurrence of chronic illnesses increases with age, with 69% of older adults having two or more chronic illnesses (Bayliss, Steiner, Fernald, Crane, & Main, 2003; Hoffman, Rice, & Sung, 1996). Successful management of chronic illness is a complex endeavor that requires patient engagement and participation by their families and friends. Daily self-management has multiple components, such as interacting with health care providers and electronic health record (EHR) systems, following medication instructions, adherence to treatment recommendations, and engaging in activities that promote physical and psychosocial health (e.g., exercises, changes in diet), just to mention a few examples. These activities in turn depend on several factors including the patient's physical condition, financial constraints, system resources, logistics to obtain care (e.g., patient-centered care), patient's needs for social and emotional support, adequate health literacy and numeracy skills, and cognitive abilities more broadly. To sum up, older adults constitute the most vulnerable demographic group, because, while they are more likely to need to self-manage chronic illness, they are more disproportionally affected by inadequate health literacy and lower numeracy skills essential to self-care (Finucane et al., 2002; Galesic & Garcia-Retamero, 2010; Speros, 2009).

In this chapter we focus on health literacy in relation to self-management of chronic illness. Health literacy is often defined as the degree to which individuals have the capacity to obtain, process, and understand basic health services and information needed to make appropriate health decisions (Ratzan & Parker, 2000). These activities depend on the cognitive and social skills that determine the ability to maintain, and promote, good health (Speros, 2009; World Health Organization, 2009).

Approximately only 20% of American adults have adequate health literacy to successfully understand health information and navigate the demands of the health

Aging, Technology and Health. DOI: http://dx.doi.org/10.1016/B978-0-12-811272-4.00003-8

care system (Brach et al., 2014; Kutner, Greenberg, Jin, & Paulsen, 2006). According to the 2003 National Assessment of Adult Literacy, which surveyed 19,000 adults and was the first-ever US national assessment of health literacy, only 3% of older adults who were surveyed were considered proficient, having lower health literacy scores compared with all other age groups surveyed (Kutner et al., 2006).

Health tasks that involve numeric information may pose particular challenges for older adults—numeric-based concepts are prominent in health-related communication and self-care (Schapira, Mozal, Shofer, Gonzalez, & Apter, 2017). The tasks needed to navigate health care systems (e.g., navigating patient portals) often require the ability to make sense of numbers—"mathematical literacy" or numeracy (Nielsen-Bohlman, Panzer, & Kindig, 2004; Peters, 2012; Rothman, Montori, Cherrington, & Pignone, 2008). Patients with lower numeracy are more likely to struggle with such tasks. For example, they may misunderstand test results, undermine health decisions, behaviors, and outcomes (Apter et al., 2008; Gardner, McMillar, Raynor, Woolf, & Knapp, 2011; Schapira et al., 2017), which are problems that especially affects older adults (Delazer, Kremmler, & Benke, 2013).

Traditionally, providers help patients understand medical information, reducing the mismatch between patient's health literacy and numeracy skills and the demands of the health system (Black et al., 2015; Brach et al., 2014). During face-to-face interactions, they discuss the meaning of the numbers and help patients plan actions and treatment to address the risks indicated by their test results and diagnosis. While there is general agreement that face-to-face communication between patients and providers is central to effective patient education, there is also recognition of diminishing time for that to happen, so that critical information is less likely to be consistently conveyed. In addition, information that is presented may not be remembered (Kessels, 2003) or correctly understood by patients (Street et al., 2009).

Health information technology and the Internet have tremendous potential to transform health care, particularly through EHR portal-based systems, which allow patients to access health information and services when needed and desired (Black et al., 2015; Sharit et al., 2014; Sharit et al., 2016; Taha, Czaja, Sharit, & Morrow, 2013). EHR systems have the potential to support collaboration between patients and providers, despite diminished opportunities for face-to-face communication. These systems have expanded the delivery of health information to patients because of federal requirements for "meaningful use" of EHRs (IOM, 2012), with some evidence that they improve patient outcomes (Ammenwerth, Schnell-Inderst, & Hoerbst, 2012). However, these systems' full potential for supporting patient-centered care has still to be realized (Stead & Lin, 2009; IOM, 2012) for at least two inter-related reasons. Firstly, EHR portals and other forms of health technology are underutilized by patients. Secondly, this underutilization increasingly reflects limited "cognitive access" rather than technology access because poorly designed systems increase demands on patients' cognitive ability, posing a barrier to self-care (Gardner et al., 2011; Griffin et al., 2016; Schapira et al., 2017). For example, EHR systems often function more as information repositories than as tools to engage patients in self-care. Simply having access to health information is insufficient to guarantee that patients will be able to use that information to improve their health care (Zikmund-Fisher et al., 2017). As a consequence, those patients with greater abilities are more likely to be able to use these systems, while the less capable, who are most in need of self-care support, are less likely to use them ("the rich get richer and the poor get poorer," a.k.a. the "Matthew effect," Merton, 1968). This is especially the case for patients with limited numeracy-based skills because of the prevalence of numeric information on patient portals. Research suggests that even when controlling for decline in cognitive ability, EHR use among older adults is predicted by limited numeracy (Delazer et al., 2013; Sharit et al., 2014, 2016; Taha et al., 2013).

In this chapter we describe the importance of theory, principles from the cognitive science of teaching and learning, and research methods in designing technology for older adults in the domain of health care. To exemplify this central argument, we adopt our framework to design and use EHR portals (Fig. 3.1), which encompasses theories from cognitive and behavioral science as well as human factors/engineering approaches (Morrow et al., 2017).

We next elaborate that argument and specific components of the framework. "The role of education, knowledge and health literacy in EHR portal use" section expands on the role of patient's education, knowledge and health literacy in EHR portal use. "The role of numeracy skills in EHR portal use" section focuses on the role of numeracy skills, as a special case of literacy (mathematical literacy) and its relation with health decision-making and EHR portal use (e.g., *fuzzy-trace theory* (FTT)). "Affective responses, gist comprehension and decision making" section describes the interaction between affective processing, gist comprehension, and decision making (e.g., behavior change theories). "Enhancing EHR portal message formats to support older adult's self-care" section details how our framework guides design of EHR portal-based information that reduces the demands of comprehension and decision-making on health literacy and numeracy skills, and cognitive

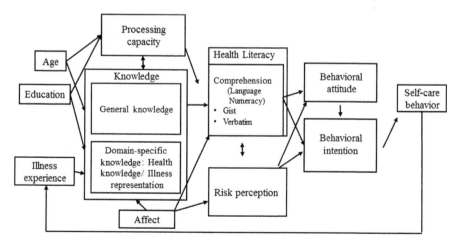

Figure 3.1 Framework guiding the design and evaluation of EHR portal-based information (Morrow et al., 2017).

abilities more broadly, so that EHR systems can better support patient-centered care. Finally, "Conclusion" section presents final considerations.

The role of education, knowledge and health literacy in EHR portal use

Literacy is defined as the basic ability to read and write a given language, while functional literacy is the ability to use reading, writing, and computational skills at a given proficiency that is compatible with the needs of daily life situations (e.g., self-managing illness; self-managing personal finances), in order to function in society (Andrus & Roth, 2002; Baker, Williams, Parker, Gazmararian, & Nurss, 1999; Parker, Baker, Williams, & Nurss, 1995; Ratzan & Parker, 2000).

Inadequate health literacy skills are a significant barrier to self-care (see Andrus & Roth, 2002). Patients are constantly expected to read and understand textual and/or numerical information often written at levels that exceed their general education and reading level (Doak & Doak, 1980; Davis, Crouch, Wills, Miller, & Abdehou, 1990; Davis et al., 1994; Jackson et al., 1991; Williams et al., 1995). The process-knowledge model of health literacy (Chin et al., 2011; Morrow & Chin, 2015) draws on theories of text comprehension to identify the mechanisms and processes involved in patients' comprehension of health information. These include word recognition and the integration of concepts associated with words into propositions. Furthermore, comprehension processes depend on cognitive resources (e.g., speed of processing, working memory (WM) capacity, and executive function), (e.g., Kintsch, 1988, 1994). In addition, comprehension of health information depends on patients' goals and illness experience, as information (e.g., clinical scores) may be integrated with knowledge (see the lower left part of Fig. 3.1) in order to create a mental model of the self-care plan or task described by the text (Morrow & Chin, 2015).

Lifespan theories of cognitive development postulate that the acquisition of knowledge, which includes domain-specific knowledge (e.g., health knowledge), varies tremendously across the lifespan (Baltes, 1987; Cattell, 1963; Horn & Cattell, 1967; Salthouse, 2003). As seen in the left part of Fig. 3.1, aging influences health literacy and comprehension of health-information, because of age-related changes in the cognitive and affective resources needed for comprehension (Finucane et al., 2002). Processing capacity tends to decline with age (e.g., attention control, response inhibition, working memory/problem solving, self-awareness) (Barrington & Yoder-Wise, 2006; Salthouse, 2003; Salthouse & Babcock, 1991; Speros, 2009). On the other hand, knowledge (of language and domain-specific: health-related concepts) tends to grow with age-related increases in experience (Cattell, 1963; Beier & Ackerman, 2005; Horn & Cattell, 1967; Salthouse & Babcock, 1991; Salthouse, 2003).

Hence, comprehension processes depend on several types of cognitive abilities or resources, as well as age and education (see Fig. 3.1). In addition, age-related abilities (limits and gains) interact to influence health literacy (Chin et al., 2011) and comprehension of health information (Chin et al., 2015), such that high levels of general knowledge can offset processing capacity limits on comprehension. Regardless of processing capacity, those individuals with higher levels of knowledge can recall more self-care information. However, older adults with low health literacy may not have high levels of knowledge to offset age-related declines in processing capacity. For example, Cheng et al. (2005) report that adults generally know little about their current or target cholesterol scores, and even patients with previous history of cardiovascular diseases were no better at comprehending their cholesterol targets than those without cardiac problems, which suggests that while health literacy is important it does not solely account for all aspects of comprehension. Specifically, health decisions that are heavily based on numeric information, as in the case of cholesterol test results, pose additional challenges for comprehension (Peters et al., 2009; Peters, Västfjäll, Slovic, et al., 2006).

The role of numeracy skills in EHR portal use

Numeracy, the "ability to understand and use numbers in daily life" (Rothman et al., 2008), complements the concept of literacy, and is sometimes also called "mathematical literacy". At its core, numeracy refers to one's ability to represent, store, and accurately process mathematical operations (Peters, 2012) and, as a component of health literacy, it is particularly important for utilizing EHR systems because so much portal-based information is numeric.

Goldbeck, Ahlers-Schmidt, Paschal, and Dismuke (2005) suggest that numeracy consists of four main skills: Basic (e.g., identifying numbers), computational (e.g., simple manipulation of numbers), analytical (e.g., inferences, estimations and proportions), and statistical (e.g., probability, risk evaluation). Analogous to the concept of "functional literacy" is the concept of "functional numeracy" which involves the ability to appropriately apply math skills to perform particular tasks and figuring out which math skills are needed in a given context. It has been commonplace to accept that both literacy and numeracy skills are essential to everyday life given the variety of numerical information that we process daily (Castel, 2007; Peters, 2012). As mentioned by Peters (2012), numerical information must frequently be considered when making decisions, but numbers can be difficult to evaluate because they are abstract symbols, and context changes their evaluative meaning (e.g., 9°F, $9 billion, 9% chance of a tsunami).

In the health-domain, Federal "meaningful use" EHR guidelines require health organizations to provide patients results from lipid panel, blood glucose, MRI, and other complex tests through portals (IOM, 2012). This use arises from the Medicare and Medicaid EHRs Incentive Programs, designed to improve patient care (Black et al., 2015; Schapira et al., 2017). Although these requirements mandate providing patients with this information, there is no corresponding guidance about effective formats for communicating the information to older adults. In health care, patients with lower numeracy are more likely to misunderstand test results, undermining health decisions, behaviors, and outcomes (Apter et al., 2008; Black et al., 2015).

As shown in the Health Literacy/Comprehension box in Fig. 3.1, as with all complex skills, individual differences in numeracy will reflect the interaction of many cognitive and affective mechanisms that vary by context and situation. Health numeracy declines with age, in part as a result of cognitive declines in executive functions and calculation abilities (Delazer et al., 2013). However, evidence also suggests that individual differences in numeracy are often independent of fluid ability (Peters, 2012). Hence, not surprisingly, limited numeracy is an important predictor of portal use among older adults, even when controlling for cognitive ability (Delazer et al., 2013; Sharit et al., 2014, 2016; Taha et al., 2013). For example, the comprehension of lipid panel results requires understanding each component results with different scales. For example, a higher "low density lipoproteins" (LDLs) score means more risk, but a higher "high density lipoproteins" (HDLs) score means less risk. It also requires integrating the components information into a global interpretation (high HDL protects against higher LDL). It requires identifying numbers and comparing them with each respective scale (basic and computational skills), as well as making inferences and calculating proportions to obtain an overall evaluation of risk—analytical and statistical (Goldbeck et al., 2005). This may help explain why adults generally know little about their current or target cholesterol levels (Black et al., 2015; Cheng et al., 2005; Nash et al., 2003).

FTT provides a framework to understand the relation between numeracy and health decision-making, explaining differences in numerical processing in terms of cognitive representations and memory. According to FTT (Reyna, 2004; Reyna & Lloyd, 2006; Reyna, Nelson, Han, & Dieckmann, 2009) cognition is said to involve simultaneous encoding of verbatim information ("literal numbers and facts," e.g., 7:00 a.m.) and gist information ("fuzzy meaning or interpretations," e.g., "time to wake up") into two separable and distinct forms of memory. The verbatim memory trace has been described as an accurate (nonelaborated) representation of experienced events. It corresponds to the surface-level of comprehension and information source. The gist memory trace is defined as "an abstract representation of semantic content that does not incorporate details of surface form" (Reyna & Kiernan, 1994, p. 180). Gist reasoning combines details with previous knowledge to generate meaning and it is personally salient (Chapman & Mudar, 2013). For example, when evaluating two options with different prices, individuals can be shown to encode both verbatim information (e.g., "option one costs $25 dollars and option two costs $0") as well as gist information (e.g., "the cost is something versus nothing" or "the first option is more expensive than the second option").

Slovic and Peters (2006) suggest that individuals may process the gist of information more than its verbatim meaning, but highly numerate individuals may derive richer gist from numbers, including their affective meaning. In that sense, when individuals are able to link new information to familiar and past experiences, they can extract number magnitudes more readily, use early controlled processes to generate qualitative, and evaluative gist representations or desire greater accuracy with numbers.

Overall, unless the task requires specific verbatim information retrieval, older adults should demonstrate superior understanding of numerical health information by integrating domain-related knowledge and affective responses, using heuristics at the level of gist representation, which should mitigate the demands on health literacy and numeracy skills, and cognitive abilities more broadly, as illustrated on Fig. 3.1. More specifically, the affective avenue and the associations to familiar and previous experiences can be used to leverage EHR designs and gist comprehension (Morrow & Chin, 2015; Morrow et al., 2017; see also Garcia-Retamero & Cokely, 2011).

Affective responses, gist comprehension and decision making

As motivated by our framework (see: lower central part of Fig. 3.1), aging is also accompanied by increasing focus on affect and emotion, which influences comprehension, risk perception and decision making about health information. Peters, Västfjäll, Gärling, & Slovic (2006) highlights the importance of affect in decision-making and numeracy. First, according to the "affect-as-information" hypothesis, affect can act as information itself. People consult their feelings at the moment of making decisions or judgments, by asking "How do I feel about this?" (Clore et al., 2001; Loewenstein, Weber, Hsee, & Welch, 2001; Schwarz & Clore, 2003; Slovic, Finucane, Peters, & MacGregor, 2002). The feelings themselves are often based on prior experiences and thoughts (Damasio, 1994) or the result of an ephemeral emotional state (e.g., mood, Bower, Monteiro, & Gilligan, 1978; Hess, Popham, Emery, & Elliott, 2012). Emotional processing and emotional regulation increasingly develop across the lifespan (Blanchard-Fields, 2007; Carstensen, 2006; Carstensen, Pasupathi, Mayr, & Nesselroade, 2000; Scheibe & Carstensen, 2010). For example, according to socioemotional theory, older adults are better at regulating their emotions and favor positive over negative stimuli in cognitive processing—positivity effect, Carstensen, 2006; Carstensen, Isaacowitz, & Charles, 1999; Charles & Carstensen, 2010; Reed & Carstensen, 2012. Other theories conceptualize changes in affective response as compensatory strategies to adapt to age declining effects and diminishing cognitive capacities associated with age (Labouvie-Vief, 2003).

Secondly, affective processing is a key component of gist comprehension, which facilitates appropriate judgment and decision-making (Loewenstein & Lerner, 2003; Loewenstein et al., 2001; Reyna & Brainerd, 2008). Complex thoughts and information are translated into simpler affective evaluations, allowing decision makers to compare and integrate good and bad feelings rather than attempt to make sense out of a multitude of conflicting logical reasons. In that sense, affective information can be more easily and effectively integrated into judgments than nonaffective information (Peters, Västfjäll, Gärling, et al., 2006; Loewenstein & Lerner, 2003; Loewenstein et al., 2001).

Furthermore, affective processing plays a crucial role in health decisions based on numeric information (Peters et al., 2009; Peters, Västfjäll, Gärling, et al., 2006). Affect appears to serve as a common currency in comprehension, allowing us to compare the values of very different decision options or information without imposing heavy demands on processing capacity (Peters, Västfjäll, Gärling, et al., 2006). For instance, older adults can also capitalize on domain-knowledge and expertise to improve verbatim memory for numeric information. Castel (2005) found that older adults were particularly better at remembering the price of grocery items that were at market value (e.g., milk $3.29), relative to younger adults, assumed to be less experienced with the current prices. However, that age-related verbatim memory-advantage was nonexistent when items were priced unrealistically (e.g., bread $12.49). Thus, Castel (2005) shows that expertise helped older adults remember numerical information when prices were somewhat consistent with their prior knowledge.

Moreover, emotions have also been linked to health-related risk perception, or "judgments about the likelihood of a given outcome" (Ferrer, Klein, Lerner, Reyna, & Keltner, 2014). For example, it is believed that risk perceptions may be systematically influenced by fear, anger, and happiness (Ferrer et al., 2014; Rogers, 1975). Because illness threats so often underlie decisions about an individual's health care, the interaction between risk perception and affective response plays a prominent role in making these types of health care decisions. In that sense, affective processing should influence decisions based on avoiding losses to acquiring equivalent gains (e.g., framing effects, Tversky & Kahneman, 1974). Peters, Västfjäll, Slovic, et al. (2006) provided an experimental example to support this hypothesis. They asked participants to rate the work quality of undergraduates described in positive frames (e.g., Emily got 74% correct) or negative frames (e.g., Emily got 26% incorrect). As predicted by the authors, highly numerate decision makers showed significantly smaller framing effects than did the novices or less numerate, who rated work quality substantially higher in a positive than negative frame. One explanation for this effect using the framework of FTT is that, highly numerate decision makers (experts) were able to reevaluate the same question (Emily got 74% correct or 26% incorrect) in terms of gist representation (Peters, Västfjäll, Slovic, et al., 2006) mitigating the effects of framing. On the other hand, Garcia-Retamero and Cokely (2011) demonstrated that by adding visual aids to health information brochures, younger adults became equally and highly effective in understanding and promoting health behaviors, both in gain- and loss-framed messages. In that sense, the authors were able to show desirable means of risk communication and effects on health care attitudes and behavioral intentions by enhancing messages with well-designed formats that promote gist comprehension and affective reactions. Considering that less numerate decision makers are more vulnerable to the effects of framing, the benefits of enhanced messages (e.g., graphics and multimedia) should be even greater for comprehension comparatively with standard text-based formats.

It is known that there is a long pathway between comprehension and actual changes in behavior. Theories of behavior change (Ajzen & Fishbein, 1977; Ajzen & Madden, 1986; Meyer, Leventhal, & Gutmann, 1985; Schwarzer, Luszczynska, Ziegelmann, Scholz, & Lippke, 2008) indicate that risk-perception shapes attitudes toward actions intended to mitigate the perceived risks. Then, these behavioral attitudes predict intention to perform the corresponding behaviors, which predict performance of the behaviors (for a review, see: Webb & Sheeran, 2006). In addition, changes in health behaviors are also influenced by other factors as well, such as beliefs about whether the perceived actions are linked to the illness (Brewer et al., 2007) and the patient's readiness to change (e.g., transtheoretical model, Prochaska & DiClemente, 2005). For instance, patients may comprehend that their cholesterol results indicate high risk for cardiovascular illness, but they do not believe that exercising or changing their diet will reduce risk. In that sense, affect serves as a motivator of information processing and behavior (Peters, Västfjäll, Gärling, et al., 2006). Affect is linked to behavioral tendencies of approach or avoidance (Chen & Bargh, 1999), and incidental mood states also have been shown to motivate behavior as people tend to act to maintain or attain positive mood states (Bower et al., 1978; Isen, 2000).

Affect-processing also appears to play a role to allocate attention and on encoding of new information. The extent or type of affective feelings (e.g., weak vs strong affect or anger versus fear) focuses the decision maker on new information (Nabi, 2003; Peters, Västfjäll, Gärling, et al., 2006). Furthermore, affect can be experienced as feedback (Clore & Huntsinger, 2007; Clore et al., 2001). In many situations, people engage in relational processing, or in other words, they relate new information to what is already known or believed. Overall, positive affect tends to reinforce this tendency, leading to gist (relational, cognitive, interpretive, category-level, and global) processing, whereas negative affect tends to inhibit this tendency, leading to verbatim (referential, perceptual, item-level and local) processing (Clore & Storbeck, 2006; Clore et al., 2001). That effect seems to be more prominent and amplified with low-knowledge readers.

Enhancing EHR portal message formats to support older adult's self-care

We now describe an interdisciplinary research project that leverages expertise in computer science, medicine, human factors, and educational psychology to improve portal-based information needed for self-care (for details see Morrow et al., 2017). Guided by the framework in Fig. 3.1, we developed portal message formats predicted to improve gist comprehension by reducing demands on abilities that decline with age (numeracy, literacy and cognitive abilities) and leverage age-related assets (knowledge and affective processing).

Text-based formats

Clinicians at our partner health organization have expressed concern that their patients can become confused about test results presented in text-based formats currently delivered through their EHR portal without prior discussion with their provider. According to their experience, patients need to call for assistance to understand their results. In their view, the portal may sometimes increase, rather than reduce, clinical workload and impacts on the quality of care delivered to

"Your XXX screening test(s) is (are) negative.

Test performed: YYY Test, ZZZ test, and WWW test.

If you have any questions, please call the office nurse at (XXX) XXX-XXXX"

Figure 3.2 Example of text-only message.

Component	Your value	Standard range	Units
Total cholesterol	184	<200−	mg/dL
Triglycerides	42	<150−	mg/dL
HDL cholesterol	47	40−60	mg/dL
LDL cholesterol	130	<100−	mg/dL

"Your test results require discussion to assess your future plan of care.
A follow up appointment is recommended to discuss your results."

Figure 3.3 Standard message format (Morrow et al., 2017).

patients. Several clinical test results provided on portals are composed mostly of text information (e.g., Figs. 3.2 and 3.3).

While simplicity is often beneficial (the principle of parsimony, a.k.a. Occam's Razor), often these formats do not provide the affordances and cognitive resources that patients need in order to deal with complex operations. Firstly, text formats are inadequate because they are hard to understand in many cases. Research has documented innumerous ways in which providers and patients struggle to grasp basic concepts that are prerequisite for accurate judgement and communication of risks (Gigerenzer et al., 2007; Peters, Västfjäll, Slovic, et al., 2006; Schwartz et al., 1997). Secondly, text formats for test results are inadequate because they are not informative enough to support guide-appropriate self-care management (e.g., Fig. 3.2).

Patients often desire to compare their results with previous numerical scores or with average numbers of other patients under similar conditions. In order to do that, typically a numerical reference point (e.g., range), or some basic descriptive statistics (e.g., percentage scores or average scores) are needed.

Typically, messages in EHR portals contain numerical information in table formats (Zikmund-Fisher et al., 2017). For example, clinical test results are presented as a table of numbers accompanied by minimal information about the scale of each score (e.g., Fig. 3.3). Sometimes, this table is followed by a textual summary statement about the overall level of risk associated with the test results, or some other verbal commentary.

Enhanced-formats

There is evidence that actively generating and elaborating on explanations of complex materials promotes understanding. Memory demands are attenuated when information is presented in formats that encourage abstraction, integration, elaboration, in terms of gist representations (Douglas & Caldwell, 2011; Galesic & Garcia-Retamero, 2010; Garcia-Retamero & Cokely, 2011, 2013; Garcia-Retamero & Galesic, 2009; Wolfe et al., 2015).

Comparatively with the previous format, one learning principle utilized is to reduce the unnecessarily extraneous cognitive load (Sweller, 1988) to compare different columns on a table, representing the information in a more consolidated way into each respective cell (Spool et al., 1997). That should reduce some demands on working memory. It is known that users can remember relatively few items of information for a relatively short period of time (Baddeley, 1992; Cowan, 2001; Miller, 1956). An explanation of a number should be given spatially near the numeric information on the display, as an application of the contiguity learning principle (Mayer, 2001; Wickens, Hollands, Banbury, & Parasuraman, 2013). In addition, if users must make comparisons, it is best to have the items being compared side-by-side so that the design reduces the demands on working memory (Leavitt & Shneiderman, 2006; Wickens et al., 2013).

Verbally enhanced formats

Both previous formats (Figs. 3.2 and 3.3) challenge patients with limited numeracy and literacy skills, making it difficult to understand the gist of the test results (Black et al., 2015; Gardner et al., 2011; Schapira et al., 2017; Zikmund-Fisher et al., 2017). Verbally enhanced formats add verbal support for comprehension, especially at the gist level. The same information as in the numeric and text-based format (EHR typical standard) is presented, but annotated with verbal labels to indicate the degree of risk for diseases and health complications. Words that label the level of risk associated with results provide more information about the range of scores for a test and how they map into evaluative qualitative categories that support meaningful processing (Peters et al., 2009) and gist-level understanding of implications for risk (Reyna, Lloyd, & Whalen, 2001). The verbally enhanced format should impose fewer demands on numeracy and processing capacity (e.g., working memory) and take advantage of age-related increases in linguistic knowledge and affective processing. More specifically, the textual and numerical information is enhanced with verbal cues related to the risk level associated with numbers (Fig. 3.4). In that way, older adults can develop affectively as well as cognitively meaningful gist representations that support health decisions (Peters et al., 2009). The column of units has been integrated to the corresponding headers. In addition, the column headings and components indicate to users how each score should be labeled or identified, focusing on the significance of the score in the overall ranges presented.

Furthermore, adding the complete information about the regions of risk associated with the scale for each score, and the labels for evaluative categories (low, borderline, high risk levels) can provide context for interpreting the specific numbers in relation to the appropriate risk category. These labels are evaluative, helping patients interpret the numbers in terms of affectively meaningful gist representations (Peters et al., 2009; Reyna et al., 2001).

Component	Your value (mg/dL)	Range of scores (mg/dL)
Total cholesterol	184 **Desirable**	< 200 (Desirable) 200–240 (Borderline) >240 (High)
Triglycerides	42 **Optimal**	< 100 (Optimal) 101–149 (Normal) 150–199 (Borderline) 200–499 (High) >500 (Very High)
HDL cholesterol	47 **Borderline**	< 40 (Low/Bad) 41–59 (Borderline) >60 (High/Good)
LDL cholesterol	130 **Borderline**	< 100 (Optimal) 101–129 (Near optimal) 130–159 (Borderline) 160–189 (High) >190 (Very High)

"Your risk for heart disease is borderline. I recommend a follow up appointment to discuss your future plan of care."

Figure 3.4 Verbally enhanced message format (Morrow et al., 2017).

Because patients are often confused about the different meaning of total cholesterol, triglycerides, LDL, and HDL numbers and how to integrate these numbers into an overall interpretation of risk (Goldman et al., 2006), a brief verbally enhanced summary statement about the overall level of risk associated with the results may be helpful. The summary statement helps patients understand the overall risk for heart disease associated with the set of test scores.

In that account, the verbally enhanced format can provide patients with meaningful strategies for retaining the most relevant information of each clinical component score. A caveat to that format that requires further investigation is that formats that rely on "viewing the text" without much efforts to generate their own information might enhance learning acquisition, but at the expense of long term retention. However, EHR portals have the benefit to allow older adults to access the information as needed, without the need to store most of the information in memory, it is important to consider that a reasonable level of effort should happen, so patients can learn and retain the necessary gist information that produces actions towards self-care.

Graphical representations

As mentioned by Okan, Garcia-Retamero, Cokely, and Maldonado (2011) the popular saying "a picture is worth a thousand words" reflects widespread beliefs that graphical displays and images can promote superior communication and facilitate comprehension of complicated information. Indeed, many studies shown that better comprehension can result from learning with text and picture (Eitel, Scheiter, &

Schuler, 2013; Eitel, Scheiter, Schuler, Nystrom, & Holmqvist, 2013; Fletcher & Tobias, 2005; Glenberg & Langston, 1992; Hegarty, 1992; Oliva & Torralba, 2006; Vekiri, 2002; Winn, 1991).

On the other hand, research has shown that individual differences are substantial in the ways people vary in their abilities to understand graphically presented information (for more on graph literacy, see Okan et al., 2011; Galesic & Garcia-Retamero, 2011; Garcia-Retamero & Cokely, 2017). Furthermore, the research on graphical representations becomes a complex endeavor as a myriad of different types of graphics exist. Typically, graphs vary simultaneously in distinct aspects, presenting challenges for controlling experimental conditions.

By representing lab reports, such as cholesterol test results, in a graphical as well as verbal context for categorical or ordinal gist comprehension, older adults can become participants on their health, making sense of their numbers. Research has shown that graphics and other visual aids can increase appropriate risk-avoidance behaviors, promote healthy behaviors, reduce errors induced by narratives (Cox, Sturm, & Zimet, 2010; Fagerlin, Wang, & Ubel, 2005; Galesic & Garcia-Retamero, 2011; Schirillo & Stone, 2005), and can improve comprehension of risks associated with different medical treatments, screenings, and lifestyles (Zikmund-Fisher, Fagerlin, & Ubel, 2008).

The use of icons (pictures, diagrams, and other graphic formats) to convey health information (e.g., risk levels of clinical test results) may be more effective than text for supporting gist-level understanding and affective responses, especially benefiting older adults with limited numeracy abilities, for several reasons. Firstly, icons are often more explicit than text, therefore reducing demands on working memory (Glenberg & Langston, 1992; Morrow et al., 1998). Secondly, pictures are often more easily remembered than words (picture superiority effect) for both younger and older adults (Park, Puglisi & Smith, 1986).

Thirdly, icon-based displays can be useful for integrating information, and reducing demands on comprehension. Morrow et al. (1998) found that older and younger adults better recalled medication dose and time information when presented using icons rather than by text in medication instructions. This finding suggests that icons, if well designed, can improve older and younger adults' comprehension by reducing the need to draw inferences.

Fourthly, the use of icon arrays and grids to represent the number in a population affected by some event (e.g., disease) can be used to illustrate relative magnitude, proportions and base rates, and therefore support risk perception, especially for older adults with lower numeracy abilities (Brust-Renck, Royer, & Reyna, 2013; Reyna & Brainerd, 1995; Reyna & Brainerd, 2008). According to FTT, people can easily and automatically estimate relative magnitudes perceptually, reducing the demands on numeracy and cognitive abilities. People in general have trouble estimating proportions and base rates (e.g., base rate neglect) (Tversky & Kahneman, 1974) and the inclusion of icons allows for visual representation of risk information that patients can understand quickly, making the denominator salient (Brust-Renck et al., 2013). This design enables quick comparisons, and patients can appreciate the gist of the graphic without becoming overwhelmed in the details of the numbers and ranges. When designing EHR interfaces, the icons should not be displayed at random (Leavitt & Shneiderman, 2006; Wickens et al., 2013), but rather in systematic ways and with distinguishable aspects, otherwise readers would have a harder time to "obtain the gist."

Furthermore, some icons can be more effective for conveying affect. If older adults rely on affective responses to encode the gist of their clinical test results, the use of face icons can encourage corresponding emotions associated with each level of risk. For example, Fig. 3.5 capitalizes on the iconic representation of smile faces, typically adopted in hospitals (e.g., pain scales, Wong-Baker Faces Pain Rating Scale, Wong, Hockenberry-Eaton, Wilson, Winkelstein, & Schwartz, 2001) to represent the different levels of risk of a cholesterol component (e.g., Triglycerides).

Contemporary decision research places a heavy and multifaceted focus on the role of affect in decision-making (Loewenstein & Lerner, 2003; Loewenstein et al., 2001; Peters, Västfjäll, Slovic, et al., 2006). This phenomenon may pose a compensatory opportunity for older adults, as a large body of literature has shown that older adults rely on emotional reactions (Labouvie-Vief, 2003; for a review see: Scheibe & Carstensen, 2010). Lastly, from a motivational perspective, someone may not want to read a block of text, but be more willing to interpret a face icon (Hancock, Bowles, Rogers & Fisk, 2006).

For example, Fig. 3.6 exemplifies gradual "enhancements" of graphical representations. Overall, these visual displays facilitate inferences about conceptual relations that are made on the basis of spatial relations and precedence of global features in visual perception—e.g., icons and color coding (Eitel, Scheiter, & Schuler, 2013; Navon, 1977; Wickens et al., 2013). All four variations, similarly to the verbally enhanced format, integrate the test score with the verbal label for each risk category represented by the numbers. In addition, these graphic formats provide information about the number's scale in an integrated format that should facilitate inferences. In that sense, comparatively, with Fig. 3.4 (verbally enhanced format), Fig. 3.6A should ease the demands on positioning each cholesterol test score in relation to their respective ranges, and correspondent risk associated to each category on the basis of spatial relations. While Fig. 3.6B incorporates the benefits of using face icons, the graph on Fig. 3.6C represents the test results adding colors (using common green-yellow-red coding for level of hazard/risk), but without the icons, and Fig. 3.6D the enhancement adopts both visual aids. By representing each risk region on the scale with color-codes and face icons, we expect to reinforce and promote gist-based understanding for each level of risk relying less on numeracy skills, as these cues convey additional evaluation/affective response meaning (Leckart, 2010; Oliva & Schyns, 2000).

Figure 3.5 Example of risk levels with integrated icons.

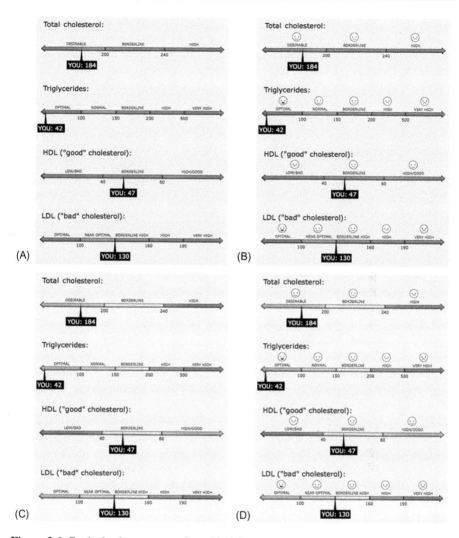

Figure 3.6 Gradual enhancements of graphical formats.
Source: Condition (D) from Morrow, D. G., Hasegawa-Johnson, M., Huang, T., Schuh, W., Azevedo, R. F. L., Gu, K., ... Garcia-Retamero, R. (2017). A multidisciplinary approach to designing and evaluating Electronic Medical Record portal messages that support patient self-care. Journal of Biological Informatics, 69, 63−74.

Leckart (2010) consulted expert physicians and experts in communicating data to patients and proposed a lab report makeover. Standard blood tests, cholesterol tests, and prostate tests were simplified in graphical representations, which translated the most relevant numbers augmented with qualitative gist interpretations in color-coded designs, as in Fig. 3.6D. For instance, many patients tend to confuse LDL and HDL scores, and are forced to come up with mnemonic strategies to recall which score refers to the "bad" or "good" cholesterol components, such as "L for lousy" and "H for happy" cholesterol. However, by incorporating color, it should be more salient that the HDL scale has an opposite polarity from the other scales—a case in which lower values indicate higher risk rather than low risk (Douglas & Caldwell, 2011; Leckart, 2010; Morrow et al., 2017). For example, considering the most enhanced graphical representation (Fig. 3.6D), the test scores are embedded within the corresponding scale for each of the four component scores, with color coding and facial expression icons reinforcing the verbal labels of risk regions, which are ordered into a scale.

One challenge on designing graphics comes from the learning principle of coherence (Kalyuga, Chandler, & Sweller, 1999; Mayer, 2001). Patients need to get a coherent form of delivery of medical information (e.g., test results) that represents a well-connected form of representation of the main ideas needed to promote self-care. In that way, the graphical representation design faces a trade-off to remove distracting and irrelevant details—e.g., seductive distractions. Some graphical information might seem artistically appealing and motivational, but are detrimental to performance. It is important to consider that sometimes the formats that are most likely to be preferred by patients are not the most effective for enhancing performance. While graphics tend to be seductive and attractive, challenges in comprehension includes the previous aspects of literacy and numeracy, as well as graphical literacy (Galesic & Garcia-Retamero, 2011). Conversely, formats that sometimes yield lower levels of satisfaction can be the ones that bolster comprehension or objective measures of performance. Moreover, and not surprisingly, differences in numeracy skills (Wright et al., 2009), age (Garcia-Retamero, Galesic, & Gigerenzer, 2010), and familiarity with the content (Roth & Bowen, 2003; Shah & Hoeffner, 2002) also affect patient's reactions to different graphic representation formats.

As in previous formats, a summary statement is recommended to facilitate gist comprehension of the whole message (Fig. 3.7, right image), and in this case is also a graphic scale with color-coded lower, borderline and higher risk regions, with the appropriate region marked to indicate the overall risk level associated with the test results.

Zikmund-Fisher et al. (2017) compared three different gradual enhanced graphic formats (simple line graph, a solid block line graph and a gradient line graph) against a standard table of numbers, finding that even by using a simple line, it was possible to decrease the sense of urgency about values at the normal standard range.

Audio-enhanced formats

Cognitive theories offer important contributions to EHR design (e.g., *cognitive theory of multimedia learning*, Mayer, 2001; *integrative model of text and picture comprehension*, Schnotz & Bannert, 2003). One advantage of audio-enhanced formats is that information is encoded and remembered better when it is delivered in multiple channels for representing and manipulating knowledge (auditory-verbal and visual-pictorial) and sensory modalities (auditory and visual) (Baddeley, 1992; Moreno & Valdez, 2005; Mayer, 2001; Schnotz & Bannert, 2003; Wickens et al.,

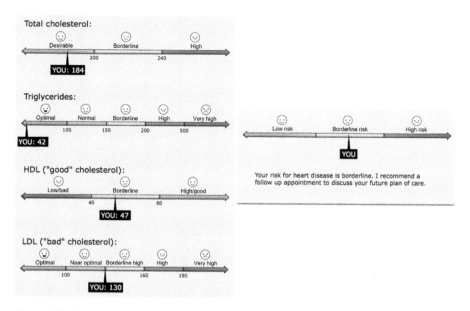

Figure 3.7 Graphically enhanced message format (Morrow et al., 2017).

2013). Older adults should benefit from richer and varied forms of representation, as it allows different memory retrieval routes (Ainsworth, 1999; Pachman & Ke, 2012; Paivio, 1986).

One could argue whether message formats should accompany speech (Fig. 3.8), or if patients should receive only speech. It is important to consider that multimedia messages could be potentially less effective than other enhanced formats because the demands of integrating information from the audio or video and the graphic display, as it may overload older adults' visual attention (Kalyuga et al., 1999; Mayer & Moreno, 2003) or when listeners are distracted by noise (Banbury, Macken, Tremblay, & Jones, 2001). As motivated by our framework (Fig. 3.1), age-related differences in processing capacity and knowledge influence comprehension.

Print has an advantage over speech, as the latter is transient and imposes a greater load on working memory. Nevertheless, speech could also support patients with low numeracy and literacy by providing commentary about the meaning of the numbers with cues (e.g., prosody and intonation conveying risk severity and sense of urgency) to guide gist comprehension. Key-terms can be emphasized as illustrated by the "bolded speech" on Fig. 3.8.

The use of multimedia often mitigates information overload when we are learning new information, in part because designers can capitalize on the tendency of learners to switch attention to contextually pertinent material (e.g., auditory split/divided-attention and cognitive capacities) (Mayer, 2001; Mayer & Moreno, 2003; Wickens et al., 2013). Some researchers have demonstrated that when the text and the audio are identical and presented simultaneously learning is less effective than text alone or audio alone (Clark & Mayer, 2011; Moreno & Valdez, 2005).

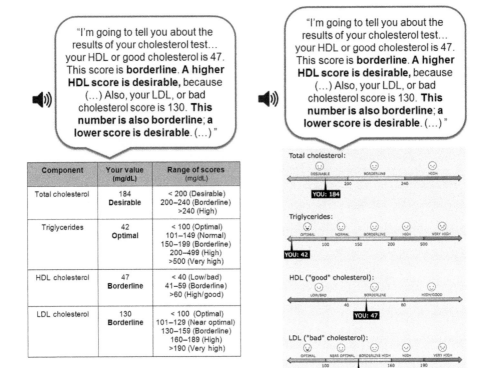

Figure 3.8 Two examples of audio-enhanced message formats.

The central argument is that presenting the same text and audio together overloads the learner channels, and if the information is identical, one modality is redundant. In addition, audio is spoken typically at about half the speed of average reading. The mismatch between the two processing speeds has been, in some cases, demonstrated to be detrimental to learning. For example, Kalyuga et al. (1999) showed that a group presented with audio alone performed better on an assessment than a group that learnt from text and audio together.

On the other hand, some researchers found benefits of providing redundant information to older adults, consistently with the environment support hypothesis of cognitive aging (Craik, 1986; Dingus et al., 1997; Morrow & Rogers, 2008) by enhancing task-relevant information, increasing processing opportunity and externalizing the task. For instance, in a study on driving navigation, older adults benefited more from receiving information comprised by a map, text and audio narration, compared with map and text-only (Dingus et al., 1997). This evidence suggests that audio has potential benefits to reduce task demands and support use of cognitive resources, particularly when used without much screen text. A possibility to further exploration will be to reduce the demands on older adults' visual attention, substituting the graphical representation by elaborated gist-based verbal information—e.g., verbally enhanced format, Fig. 3.8 left.

Video-enhanced formats

Patient portal messages may be most effective if the numeric information is accompanied by a video of a provider adding commentary about the meaning of the numbers. In this way, benefits of face-to-face communication can be incorporated into portal messages. This "video-enhanced format" has the following advantages. First, the physician provides high-level commentary about the results, using nonverbal cues (e.g., tone of voice and facial expressions), and verbal cues, as in ideal face-to-face communication, to signal information relevance and guide affective interpretation. Fig. 3.9 indicates an example of a provider delivering cholesterol test results presented by a graphical format. Second, to help patients integrate verbal commentary with the relevant information in the graphic display, the corresponding part of the graphic loomed as each test score was discussed by the physician, providing a dynamic attentional cue to help participants integrate information from the video and the graphic display.

The multimedia video format may be most effective because the verbal and non-verbal cues reinforce each other (Pachman & Ke, 2012; Van Gerven, Paas, Van

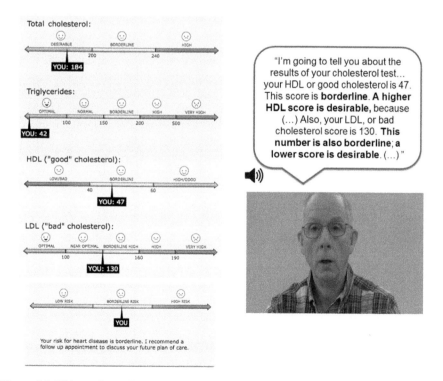

Figure 3.9 Video-enhanced message format (Morrow et al., 2017).

Merriënboer, Hendriks, & Schmidt, 2003). For example, prosodic (e.g., intonation) and facial cues (viewing speaker lips) support older adults' speech comprehension (Brault et al., 2010), and redundantly presenting numeric information visually and aurally improves older adults' problem solving performance (Pachman & Ke, 2012). Visual cues that guide attention (e.g., highlighting key graphical features) may improve comprehension of visual or spoken information in older adults (Ouwehand et al., 2012). Challenges to older adults' comprehension and performance that are associated with numeracy and literacy skills may also be reduced, by decreasing the need for numeracy-based skills and encouraging the use of affect to understand risk. Some evidence suggests that even when presented alone, the video format yields superior performance than the standard text-numeric format (Azevedo et al., 2015).

Nevertheless, in practical terms, challenges to implementing these videos in actual patient EHR portals emerge as different videos would be required for each patient and set of test results, which would impose an unreasonable burden on providers. Alternatively, a computer-based conversational agent (CA), or "virtual provider" could be used to deliver health information in EHR portals, being generative and emulating the same benefits of face-to-face communication. By being generative, CAs have the capability of tailoring different messages and a wide range of health information to diverse patients.

Computer-generated formats

CAs may be well suited for explaining complex concepts to patients with limited health literacy and numeracy by using exemplary communication techniques in health care without the time constraints and delivery inconsistencies previously addressed (Bertrand, Babu, Polgreen, & Segre, 2010; Bickmore, Pfeifer, & Paasche-Orlow, 2009; Bickmore et al., 2010; Wolfe et al., 2015). Furthermore, CAs are not designed to replace human interaction, but to complement face-to-face communication potentially reducing the amount of time physicians need to spend instructing individual patients. CAs can be implemented in home devices or phone applications to serve as reminders or to repeat essential information—e.g., patient discharge information, Bickmore et al., 2009. In fact, CAs have been shown to be at least as effective as human professionals in explaining medical information to patient, and particularly effective for patients with low health literacy (Bickmore et al., 2009, 2010).

CAs in EHR portals may especially help patients with low numeracy and literacy because, as in face-to-face communication, they can provide commentary with non-verbal cues (e.g., prosody, facial expressions) and verbal cues (e.g., risk category labels) to guide gist comprehension. CAs can emulate facial expressions, gestures, and other relational cues to improve learning, support a variety of patient goals, and help diverse patients follow self-care recommendations, as compared to text-based or lower fidelity interfaces (Bertrand et al., 2010; Bickmore et al., 2010; Schroeder, Adesope, & Gilbert, 2013; Wolfe et al., 2015).

Like the videos, the CA messages (Fig. 3.10) contain spoken commentary, using direct and active language (Morrow & Conner-Garcia, 2013) with appropriate evaluative/affective cues (both verbal and nonverbal) that should help patients create gist representations of risk (Reyna et al., 2009), and provide context to help patients extract more meaning from the numbers (Peters et al., 2009). In this project the commentaries provided by the CA are organized around information relevance and key-concepts for gist interpretation (e.g., risk category of numbers) can be emphasized by "tagging" the scripts for relevance, and inputting into the speech synthesizer of the CA system (Morrow et al., 2017).

Equally important, the CA conveys risk information nonverbally as well as verbally through facial expressions that express emotions consistent with the risk level. For example, for high LDL scores, the CA can express concern (e.g., frowning). Evidence suggests that both the video-enhanced format and the CA-enhanced format are equally able to effectively communicate facts about cholesterol test results, and inspire patients' satisfaction (Azevedo et al., 2017). As illustrated on Fig. 3.10, the CA is accompanied by the graphical representation of the test results. Previous study demonstrates greater user recall with audiovisual information that was combined with conversational style speech and animations (Meppelink, van Weert, Haven, & Smit, 2015).

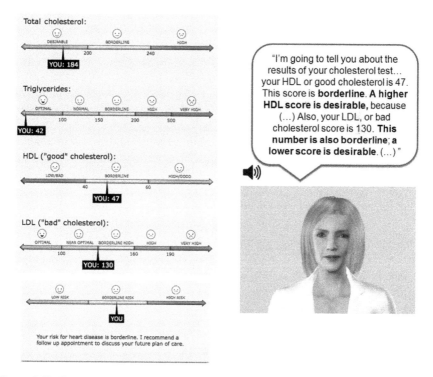

Figure 3.10 Conversational agent (CA) enhanced message format: realistic female CA. Generated using *Reallusion's CrazyTalk 8 Pro* Software.

An alternative to the use of CAs (or videos) that depict providers, would be the use CAs that depict and represent other patients. It has been known for decades that stories and other forms of narrative are easier to comprehend and remember than typical expository texts (Bower & Clark, 1969). In that sense, one application for CAs and videos (e.g., Bickmore & Ring, 2010) is to use stories with concrete situations, emotions, characters, and actions that bear similarity with the intentions needed to self-care and everyday experiences. Videos and CAs could be used to convey affective reactions and to convey specific points—e.g., encourage changes in exercises and/or diets, quit smoking, or promoting readiness to change: trans-theoretical model (Prochaska & DiClemente, 2005). The understanding of an abstract concept improves with examples and cases, in addition to be potentially more persuasive, memorable and easy to comprehend. A hypothesis to test is to verify a potential disassociation, in which videos are more effective to convey affective responsive through the use of "war stories" that are built on empathy and social responses, whereas the use of providers as videos or CAs, would bolster comprehension.

Conclusion

Our project is intended to improve use of portal information by older adults with diverse numeracy and literacy abilities, so that portals can better support patient-centered care. The project has three phases (for more details see, Morrow et al., 2017).

Firstly, develop portal message formats for clinical test results and evaluate them in a simulated patient portal environment. In order to achieve that first phrase, we propose scenario-based experimental studies to evaluate whether enhanced formats improve patient comprehension of health care information compared to the standard text-based portal format. The study scenarios describe cholesterol or diabetes test results, and were developed in collaboration with two physicians from our partner health care organization (Morrow et al., 2017). Secondly, develop a tool for clinicians to annotate test results for their patients, facilitating collaborative use of portals by providers and patients. Thirdly, evaluate use of the tool and analyze patient responses to the clinician-constructed messages in an actual portal system.

These methods include experimental and individual difference techniques to evaluate messages and investigate whether enhanced formats especially benefit adults with lower numeracy and literacy abilities comparatively with standard text-based formats, using both quantitative measures of message memory (e.g., FTT) and intention to perform behaviors in response to the messages (e.g., behavior change theories), and more qualitative measures.

We predict that differences in performance associated with lower numeracy and health literacy skills may be especially reduced by the exemplified enhanced formats, which encourage the use of affective-based resources in order to understand risk concepts and decrease the need for numeracy-based skills. In order to illustrate the importance of theory, principles of cognitive sciences for teaching and learning, and research methods in designing technology for older adults, we describe a project that is focused on helping patients understand and use health information, such as test results, which are presented through an EHR system patient portal (Morrow et al., 2017). Each message format illustrated here proposes strategies that could to be used to improve comprehension, particularly reducing numeracy demands, compared with current baselines of information that heavily rely on text and numerical information, by leveraging gist comprehension and affective-response. In addition, formal studies will focus on the impact of video-enhanced format and then compare CA-enhanced to video-enhanced formats (see also: Azevedo et al., 2017).

Further directions include different graphical formats. While the graphs represented in Fig. 3.6 are snapshots of one single test result, for multiple test results over time, line graphs with risk regions indicated are more effective (Shah & Hoeffner, 2002), as they allow to emphasize key change in values/trends over time (Fagerlin & Peters, 2011). When only one result is made available at the time, line graphs can be used in many applications that enable patients to see their scores relatively to a range of values (Zikmund-Fisher et al., 2017). Additional reference points could be implemented to the graphic to make direct comparisons with previous scores more easily available.

Moreover, we intend to improve the CAs to include features of interactivity. For example, one possibility is to implement "teach back" techniques and adaptive learning strategies. Another direction, is to provide the option of choosing from a set of CAs that vary in gender, age, and race, which may improve patients' satisfaction and patients' self-identification (Wolfe et al., 2015). There is also debate about the appropriate level of realism for CAs (animated vs photorealistic) that produces trust and "social stance" that primes learning.

However, increasing realism, as exemplified on Fig. 3.11, until the CA appears almost, but not quite human may have drawbacks and produce negative responses (e.g., "uncanny valley" effect, Mori, 2012). That would suggest that less realistic versions of the CA will be more effective when compared to a human recording, a hypothesis that needs further investigation.

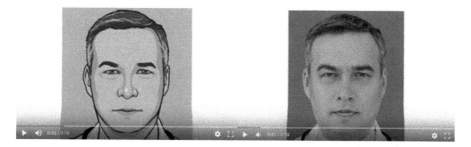

Figure 3.11 2D conversational agent enhanced message format: animated versus photorealistic.

References

Ainsworth, S. (1999). The functions of multiple representations. *Computers & Education, 33*, 131−152.

Ajzen, I., & Fishbein, M. (1977). Attitude-behavior relations: A theoretical analysis and review of empirical research. *Psychological bulletin, 84*, 888−918.

Ajzen, I., & Madden, T. J. (1986). Prediction of goal-directed behavior: Attitudes, intentions and perceived behavioral control. *Journal of Personality and Social Psychology, 22*, 453−474.

Ammenwerth, E., Schnell-Inderst, P., & Hoerbst, A. (2012). The impact of electronic patient portals on patient care: A systematic review of controlled trials. *Journal of Medical Internet Research, 14*, e162.

Andrus, M. R., & Roth, M. T. (2002). Health literacy: A review. *Pharmacotherapy, 22*, 282−302.

Apter, A. J., Paasche-Orlow, M. K., Remillard, J. T., Bennett, I. M., Ben-Joseph, E. P., Batista, R. M., ... Rudd, R. E. (2008). Numeracy and communication with patients: They are counting on us. *Journal of General Internal Medicine, 23*, 2117−2124.

Azevedo, R. F. L., Gu, K., Zhang, Y., Sadauskas, V., Sakakini, T., Morrow, D., . . . Schuh, W. (2017). Using computer agents to explain clinical test results. In *Proceedings of the American Medical Informatics Association (AMIA) annual symposium*; 2017 November 4−8; Washington, DC.

Azevedo, R. F. L., Morrow, D. G., Hasegawa-Johnson, M., Gu, K., Soberal, D., Huang, T., Garcia-Retamero, R. (2015). Improving patient comprehension of numeric health information. In Proceedings of the *human factors and ergonomics society annual meeting* (Vol. 59 (10) pp. 488−492).

Baddeley, A. (1992). Working memory. *Science, 255*, 556−559.

Baker, D. W., Williams, M. V., Parker, R. M., Gazmararian, J. A., & Nurss, J. (1999). Development of a brief test to measure functional health literacy. *Patient Education and Counseling, 38*, 33−42.

Baltes, P. B. (1987). Theoretical propositions of life-span developmental psychology: On the dynamics between growth and decline. *Developmental Psychology, 23*, 611−626.

Banbury, S., Macken, W. J., Tremblay, S., & Jones, D. M. (2001). Auditory distraction and short-term memory: Phenomena and practical implications. *Human Factors, 45*, 12−29.

Barrington, L., & Yoder-Wise, P. S. (2006). Executive control function: A clinically practical assessment. *Journal of Gerontological Nursing, 32*, 28−34.

Bayliss, E., Steiner, J. F., Fernald, D. H., Crane, L. A., & Main, D. S. (2003). Descriptions of barriers to self-care by persons with comorbid chronic diseases. *Annals of Family Medicine, 1*, 15−21.

Beier, M. E., & Ackerman, P. L. (2005). Age, ability, and the role of prior knowledge on the acquisition of new domain knowledge: Promising results in a real-world learning environment. *Psychology and Aging, 20*(2), 341−355.

Bertrand, J., Babu, S. V., Polgreen, P., & Segre, A. (2010). Virtual agents based simulation for training healthcare workers in hand hygiene procedures. In *Proceedings of the 10th international conference on intelligent virtual agents (IVA 2010)* (pp. 125−131). Springer Verlag Berlin/Heidelberg, 6395.

Bickmore, T., Pfeifer, L., & Paasche-Orlow, M. (2009). Using computer agents to explain medication information documents to patients with low health literacy. *Patient Education Counseling, 75*, 315−320.

Bickmore, T., Pfeifer, L. M., Byron, D., Forsythe, S., Henault, L. E., Jack, B. W., ... Passche-Orlow, M. K. (2010). Usability of conversational agents by patients with inadequate health literacy: Evidence from two clinical trials. *Journal of Health Communication, 15*, 197−210.

Bickmore, T. W., & Ring, L. (2010). Making it personal: End-user authoring of health narratives delivered by virtual agents. In *Proceedings of the 10th international conference on intelligent virtual agents (IVA 2010)* (pp. 399−405). Springer Verlag Berlin/Heidelberg, 6395.

Black, H., Gonzalez, R., Priolo, C., Schapira, M. M., Sonnad, S. S., Hanson, C. W., 3rd, ... Apter, A. J. (2015). True "meaningful use": Technology meets both patient and provider needs. *The American Journal of Managed Care, 21*, e329−337.

Blanchard-Fields, F. (2007). Everyday problem solving and emotion: An adult developmental perspective. *Current Directions in Psychological Science, 16*, 26−31.

Bower, G. H., & Clark, M. C. (1969). Narrative stories as mediators for serial learning. *Psychonomic Science, 14*(4), 181−182.

Bower, G. H., Monteiro, K. P., & Gilligan, S. G. (1978). Emotional mood as a context of learning and recall. *Journal of Verbal Learning and Verbal Behavior, 17*, 573−585.

Brach, C., Dreyer, B. P., & Schillinger, D. (2014). Physicians' roles in creating health literate organizations: A call to action. *Journal of General Internal Medicine, 29*(2), 273−275.

Brault, L. M., Gilbert, J. L., Lansing, C. R., McCarley, J. S., & Kramer, A. F. (2010). Bimodal stimulus presentation and expanded auditory bandwidth improve older adults' speech perception. *Human Factors, 52*, 479−491.

Brewer, N. T., Chapman, G. B., Gibbons, F. X., Gerrard, M., McCaul, K. D., & Weinstein, N. D. (2007). Meta-analysis of the relationship between risk perception and health behavior: The example of vaccination. *Health Psychology, 26*, 136−145.

Brust-Renck, P. G., Royer, C. E., & Reyna, V. F. (2013). Communicating numerical risk: Human factors that aid understanding in health care. *Reviews of Human Factors and Ergonomics, 8*, 235−276.

Carstensen, L. L. (2006). The influence of a sense of time on human development. *Science, 312*, 1913−1915.

Carstensen, L. L., Isaacowitz, D. M., & Charles, S. T. (1999). Taking time seriously: A theory of socioemotional selectivity. *American Psychologist, 54*, 165.

Carstensen, L. L., Pasupathi, M., Mayr, U., & Nesselroade, J. R. (2000). Emotional experience in everyday life across the adult life span. *Journal of Personality and Social Psychology, 79*, 644−655.

Castel, A. D. (2005). Memory for grocery prices in younger and older adults: The role of schematic support. *Psychology and Aging, 20*, 718−721.

Castel, A. D. (2007). Aging and memory for numerical information: The role of specificity and expertise in associative memory. *Journal of Gerontology: Psychological Sciences, 62*, 194−196.

Cattell, R. B. (1963). Theory of fluid and crystallized intelligence: A critical experiment. *Journal of Educational Psychology, 54*, 1−22.

Chapman, S. B., & Mudar, R. A. (2013). Discourse gist: A window into the brain's complex cognitive capacity. *Discourse Studies, 15*, 519−533.

Charles, S. T., & Carstensen, L. L. (2010). Social and emotional aging. *Annual Review of Psychology, 61*, 383−409.

Chen, M., & Bargh, J. A. (1999). Consequences of automatic evaluation: Immediate behavioral predispositions to approach or avoid the stimulus. *Personality & Social Psychology Bulletin, 25*, 215−224.

Cheng, S., Lichtman, J. H., Amatruda, J. M., Smith, G. L., Mattera, J. A., Roumanis, S. A., & Krumholtz, H. M. (2005). Knowledge of cholesterol levels and targets in patients with coronary artery disease. *Preventive Cardiology*, *8*, 11–17.

Chin, J., Morrow, D. G., Stine-Morrow, E. A. L., Conner-Garcia, T., Graumlich, J. F., & Murray, M. D. (2011). The process-knowledge model of health literacy: Evidence from a componential analysis of two commonly used measures. *Journal of Health Communication*, *16*, 222–241.

Chin, J., Payne, B., Gao, X., Conner-Garcia, T., Graumlich, J. F., Murray, M. D., ... Stine-Morrow, E. A. L. (2015). Memory and comprehension for health information among older adults: Distinguishing the effects of domain-general and domain-specific knowledge. *Memory*, *23*, 577–589.

Clark, R. C., & Mayer, R. E. (2011). *E-Learning and the science of instruction: Proven guidelines for consumers and designers of multimedia learning*. San Francisco, CA: Pfeiffer.

Clore, G. L., & Huntsinger, J. R. (2007). How emotions inform judgment and regulate thought. *Trends in Cognitive Sciences*, *11*, 393–399.

Clore, G. L., & Storbeck, J. (2006). Affect as information about liking, efficacy, and importance. In J. Forgas (Ed.), *Affect in social thinking and behavior*. New York: Psychology Press.

Clore, G. L., Wyer, R. S., Dienes, B., Gasper, K., Gohm, C., & Isbell, L. (2001). Affective feelings as feedback: Some cognitive consequences. In L. L. Martin, & G. L. Clore (Eds.), *Theories of mood and cognition: A user's guidebook* (pp. 27–62). Mahwah, NJ: Erlbaum.

Cowan, N. (2001). The magical number 4 in short-term memory: A reconsideration of mental storage capacity. *Behavioral and Brain Sciences*, *24*(1), 87–114, discussion 114–85.

Cox, D. S., Cox, A. D., Sturm, L., & Zimet, G. (2010). Behavioral interventions to increase HPV vaccination acceptability among mothers of young girls. *Health Psychology*, *29*, 29–39.

Craik, F. I. M. (1986). A functional account of age differences in memory. In F. Klix, & H. Hagendorf (Eds.), *Human memory and cognitive capabilities: Mechanisms and performances* (pp. 409–422). Amsterdam: Elsevier Science Publishers.

Damasio, A. R. (1994). *Descartes' error: Emotion, reason, and the human brain*. New York: Avon.

Davis, T., Crouch, M., Wills, G., Miller, S., & Abdehou, D. (1990). The gap between patient reading comprehension and the readability of patient education materials. *Journal of Family Practice*, *31*, 533–538.

Davis, T., Mayeaux, E., Fredrickson, D., Bocchini, J., Jackson, R., & Murphy, R. (1994). Reading ability of parents compared with reading level of pediatric patient education materials. *Pediatrics*, *93*, 460–468.

Delazer, M., Kremmler, G., & Benke, T. (2013). Health numeracy and cognitive decline in advanced age. *Neuropsychology, Development, and Cognition*, *20*, 639–659.

Dingus, T. A., Hulse, M. C., Mollenhauser, M. A., Fleischman, R. N., Mcgehee, D. V., & Manakkal, N. (1997). Effects of age, system experience, and navigation techniques on driving with an advanced traveller information system. *Human Factors*, *39*, 177–199.

Doak, L., & Doak, C. (1980). Patient comprehension profiles: Recent findings and strategies. *Patient Counselling and Health Education*, *2*, 101–106.

Douglas, S. E., & Caldwell, B. S. (2011). Design and validation of an Individual Health Report (IHR). *International Journal of Industrial Ergonomics*, *41*, 352–359.

Eitel, A., Scheiter, K., & Schuler, A. (2013). How inspecting a picture affects processing of text in multimedia learning. *Applied Cognitive Psychology*, *27*, 451–461.

Eitel, A., Scheiter, K., Schuler, A., Nystrom, M., & Holmqvist, K. (2013). How a picture facilitates the process of learning from text: Evidence for scaffolding. *Learning and Instruction*, *28*, 48−63.

Fagerlin, A., & Peters, E. (2011). Quantitative information. In B. Fischhoff, N. Brewer, & J. Downs (Eds.), *Evidence-based communication of risk and benefits: A user's guide.* (pp. 53−64). Silver Spring, MD: Food and Drug Administration.

Fagerlin, A., Wang, C., & Ubel, P. A. (2005). Reducing the influence of anecdotal reasoning on people's health care decisions: Is a picture worth a thousand statistics? *Medical Decision Making*, *25*, 398−405.

Ferrer, R., Klein, W., Lerner, J. S., Reyna, V. F., & Keltner, D. (2014). Emotions and health decision-making: Extending the appraisal tendency framework to improve health and healthcare. In C. Roberto, & I. Kawachi (Eds.), *Behavioral economics and public health.* Cambridge, MA: Harvard University Press.

Finucane, M. L., Slovic, P., Hibbard, J. H., Peters, E., Mertz, C., & MacGregor, D. G. (2002). Aging and decision-making competence: An analysis of comprehension and consistency skills in older versus younger adults considering health-plan options. *Journal of Behavioral Decision Making*, *15*, 141−164.

Fletcher, J. D., & Tobias, S. (2005). The multimedia principle. In R. E. Mayer (Ed.), *The Cambridge handbook of multimedia learning* (pp. 117−133). Cambridge, MA: Cambridge University Press.

Galesic, M., & Garcia-Retamero, R. (2010). Statistical numeracy for health: A cross-cultural comparison with probabilistic national samples. *Archives of Internal Medicine*, *170*(5), 462−468.

Galesic, M., & Garcia-Retamero, R. (2011). Graph literacy: A cross-cultural comparison. *Medical Decision Making*, *31*(3), 444−457.

Garcia-Retamero, R., & Cokely, E. T. (2011). Effective communication of risks to young adults: Using message framing and visual aids to increase condom use and STD screening. *Journal of Experimental Psychology-Applied*, *17*(3), 270.

Garcia-Retamero, R., & Cokely, E. T. (2013). Communicating health risks with visual aids. *Current Directions in Psychological Science*, *22*(5), 392−399.

Garcia-Retamero, R., & Cokely, E. T. (2017). Designing visual aids that promote risk literacy: A systematic review of health research and evidence-based design heuristics. *Human Factors: The Journal of the Human Factors and Ergonomics Society*, *59*(4), 582−627.

Garcia-Retamero, R., & Galesic, M. (2009). Communicating treatment risk reduction to people with low numeracy skills: A cross-cultural comparison. *American Journal of Public Health*, *99*, 2196−2202.

Garcia-Retamero, R., Galesic, M., & Gigerenzer, G. (2010). Do icon arrays help reduce denominator neglect? *Medical Decision Making*, *30*(6), 672−684.

Gardner, P. H., McMillar, B., Raynor, D. K., Woolf, E., & Knapp, P. (2011). The effects of numeracy on the comprehension of information about medicines in users of a patient information website. *Patient Education and Counseling*, *83*, 398−403.

Gigerenzer, G., Gaissmaier, W., Kurz-Milke, E., Schwartz, L., & Woloshin, S. (2007). Helping doctors and patients make sense of health statistics. *Psychological Science in the Public Interest*, *8*(2), 53−96.

Glenberg, A. M., & Langston, W. E. (1992). Comprehension of illustrated text: Pictures help to build mental models. *Journal of Memory and Language*, *31*, 129−151.

Goldbeck, A. L., Ahlers-Schmidt, C. R., Paschal, A. M., & Dismuke, S. E. D. (2005). A definition and operational framework for health numeracy. *American Journal of Preventive Medicine*, *29*, 375−376.

Goldman, R. E., Parker, D. R., Eaton, C. B., Borkan, J. M., Gramling, R., Cover, R. T., & Ahern, D. K. (2006). Patients' perceptions of cholesterol, cardiovascular disease risk, and risk communication strategies. *The Annals of Family Medicine*, *4*(3), 205−212.

Goldstein, D. R. (2010). Aging, imbalanced inflammation and viral infection. *Virulence*, *1* (4), 295−298.

Griffin, A., Skinner, A., Thornhill, J., & Weinberger, M. (2016). Patient portals. *Applied Clinical Informatics*, *7*(2), 489−501. (2016).

Hancock, H. E., Bowles, C. T., Rogers, W. A., & Fisk, A. D. (2006). Comprehension and retention of warning information. In M. S. Wogalter (Ed.), *Handbook of warnings* (pp. 267−277). Mahwah, NJ: Erlbaum.

Hegarty, M. (1992). Mental animation: Inferring motion from static displays of mechanical systems. *Journal of Experimental Psychology: Learning, Memory, and Cognition*, *18*, 1084−1102.

Hess, T. M., Popham, L. E., Emery, L., & Elliott, T. (2012). Mood, motivation, and misinformation: Aging and affective state influences on memory. *Neuropsychology, Development and Cognition*, *19*, 13−34.

Hoffman, C., Rice, D., & Sung, H. Y. (1996). Persons with chronic conditions. Their prevalence and costs. *Journal of the American Medical Association*, *276*, 1473−1479.

Horn, J. L., & Cattell, R. B. (1967). Age differences in fluid and crystallized intelligence. *Acta Psychologica*, *26*, 107−129.

Institute of Medicine (IOM). (2012). *Health IT and patient safety: Building safer systems for better care*. Washington, DC: The National Academies Press.

Isen, A. M. (2000). Positive affect and decision making. In M. Lewis, & J. Haviland-Jones (Eds.), *Handbook of emotions* (2nd ed., pp. 417−435). New York: Guilford.

Jackson, R., Davis, T., Bairnsfather, L., George, R., Crouch, M., & Gault, H. (1991). Patient reading ability: An overlooked problem in health care. *The Southern Medical Journal*, *84*, 1172−1175.

Kalyuga, S., Chandler, P., & Sweller, J. (1999). Managing split-attention and redundancy in multimedia learning. *Applied Cognitive Psychology*, *13*, 351−371.

Kessels, R. P. (2003). Patients' memory for medical information. *Journal of the Royal Society of Medicine*, *96*, 219−222.

Kintsch, W. (1988). The role of knowledge in discourse comprehension construction-integration model. *Psychological Review*, *95*, 163−182.

Kintsch, W. (1994). Text comprehension, memory, and learning. *American Psychologist*, *49*, 294−303.

Kutner, M., Greenberg, E., Jin, Y., & Paulsen, C. (2006). The health literacy of America's adults: Results from the 2003 National Assessment of Adult Literacy (NCES 2006−483). *U.S. Department of Education*. Washington, DC: National Center for Education Statistics.

Labouvie-Vief, G. (2003). Dynamic integration: Affect, cognition, and the self in adulthood. *Current Directions in Psychological Science*, *12*, 201−206.

Leavitt, M. O., & Shneiderman, B. (2006). *Research-based web design & usability guidelines*. Washington, DC: U.S. General Services Administration.

Leckart, S. (2010). The blood test gets a makeover [Internet]. *Wired*. <http://www.wired.com/magazine/2010/11/ff_bloodwork/> Accessed 21.04.17.

Loewenstein, G. F., & Lerner, J. S. (2003). The role of affect in decision making. In R. Davidson, K. Scherer, & H. Goldsmith (Eds.), *Handbook of affective science* (pp. 619−642). New York: Oxford University Press.

Loewenstein, G. F., Weber, E. U., Hsee, C. K., & Welch, N. (2001). Risk as feelings. *Psychological Bulletin, 127,* 267−286.

Mayer, R. E. (2001). *Multimedia learning.* New York: Cambridge University Press.

Mayer, R. E., & Moreno, R. (2003). Nine ways to reduce cognitive load in multimedia learning. *Educational Psychologist, 38,* 43−52.

Meppelink, C. S., van Weert, J. C., Haven, C. J., & Smit, E. G. (2015). The effectiveness of health animations in audiences with different health literacy levels: An experimental study. *Journal of Medical Internet Research, 17,* e11.

Merton, R. K. (1968). The Matthew effect in science. *Science., 159*(3810), 56−63.

Meyer, D., Leventhal, H., & Gutmann, M. (1985). Common-sense models of illness: The example of hypertension. *Health Psychology, 4,* 115−135.

Miller, G. A. (1956). The magical number seven, plus or minus two: Some limits on our capacity for processing information. *Psychological Review., 63*(2), 81−97.

Moreno, R., & Valdez, A. (2005). Cognitive load and learning effects of having students organize pictures and words in multimedia environments: The role of student interactivity and feedback. *Educational Technology Research and Development., 53,* 35−45.

Mori, M. (2012). *The uncanny valley* (K. F. MacDorman, N. Kageki, Trans.). IEEE Robotics and Automation (Vol. 19, pp. 98−100).

Morrow, D. G., & Chin, J. (2015). Health literacy and health decision making among older adults. In T. Hess, J. Strough, & C. Lockenhoff (Eds.), *Aging and decision-making: Empirical and applied perspectives* (pp. 261−282). London: Elsevier.

Morrow, D. G., & Conner-Garcia, T. (2013). Improving comprehension of medication information: Implications for nurse-patient communication. *Journal of Gerontological Nursing, 39,* 22−29.

Morrow, D. G., Hasegawa-Johnson, M., Huang, T., Schuh, W., Azevedo, R. F. L., Gu, K., ... Garcia-Retamero, R. (2017). A multidisciplinary approach to designing and evaluating Electronic Medical Record portal messages that support patient self-care. *Journal of Biological Informatics, 69,* 63−74.

Morrow, D. G., Hier, C. M., Menard, W. E., & Leirer, V. O. (1998). Icons improve older and younger adults' comprehension of medication information. *Journal of Gerontology: Psychological Sciences, 53B*(4), P240−P254.

Morrow, D. G., & Rogers, W. A. (2008). Environmental support: An integrative framework. *Human Factors, 50,* 589−613.

Nabi, R. L. (2003). Exploring the framing effects of emotion: Do discrete emotions differentially influence information accessibility, information seeking, and policy preference? *Communication Research, 30,* 224−247.

Nash, I. S., Mosca, L., Blumenthal, R. S., Davidson, M. H., Smith, S. C., Jr, & Pasternak, R. C. (2003). Contemporary awareness and understanding of cholesterol as a risk factor: Results of an American Heart Association national survey. *Archives of Internal Medicine, 163*(13), 1597.

Navon, D. (1977). Forest before trees: The precedence of global features in visual perception. *Cognitive Psychology., 9*(3), 353−383.

Nielsen-Bohlman, L., Panzer, A. M., & Kindig, D. A. (2004). *Health literacy: A prescription to end confusion.* Washington, DC: The National Academies Press.

Okan, Y., Garcia-Retamero, R., Cokely, E., & Maldonado, A. (2011). Individual differences in graph literacy: Overcoming denominator neglect in risk comprehension. *Behavioral Decision Making, 25,* 390−401.

Oliva, A., & Schyns, A. (2000). Diagnostic colors mediate scene recognition. *Cognitive Psychology, 41,* 176−210.

Oliva, A., & Torralba, A. (2006). Building the gist of a scene: The role of global image features in recognition. *Progress in Brain Research, 155,* 23–26.

Ouwehand, K., van Gog, T., & Paas, F. (2012). The use of gesturing to facilitate older adults' learning from computer-based dynamic visualizations. In R. Hill, R. Zheng, & M. Gardner (Eds.), *Engaging older adults with modern technology: Internet use and information access needs* (pp. 33–58). Hershey, PA: IGI Publishing.

Pachman, M., & Ke, F. (2012). Environmental support hypothesis in designing multimedia training for older adults: Is less always more? *Computers & Education, 58,* 100–110.

Paivio, A. (1986). *Mental representations: A dual coding approach.* New York: Oxford University Press.

Park, D. C., Puglisi, J. T., & Smith, A. D. (1986). Memory for pictures: Does an age-related decline exist? *Psychology and Aging, 1*(1), 11–17.

Parker, R. M., Baker, D. W., Williams, M. V., & Nurss, J. R. (1995). The test of functional health literacy in adults: A new instrument for measuring patient's literacy skills. *Journal of General Internal Medicine, 10,* 537–541.

Peters, E. (2012). Beyond comprehension: The role of numeracy in judgments and decisions. *Current Directions in Psychological Science, 21,* 31–35.

Peters, E., Dieckmann, N. F., Västfjäll, D., Mertz, C. K., Slovic, P., & Hibbard, J. (2009). Bringing meaning to numbers: The impact of evaluative categories on decisions. *Journal of Experimental Psychology: Applied, 15,* 213–227.

Peters, E., Västfjäll, D., Gärling, T., & Slovic, P. (2006). Affect and decision making: A "hot" topic. *Journal of Behavioral Decision Making, 19*(2), 79–85.

Peters, E., Västfjäll, D., Slovic, P., Mertz, C. K., Mazzoco, K., & Dickert, S. (2006). Numeracy and decision making. *Psychological Science, 17,* 408–414.

Prochaska, J. O., & DiClemente, C. C. (2005). The transtheoretical approach. In J. C. Norcross, & M. R. Goldfried (Eds.), *Handbook of psychotherapy integration* (pp. 147–171). New York: Oxford University Press.

Ratzan, S. C., & Parker, R. M. (2000). *Introduction. In National Library of Medicine Current Bibliographies in Medicine: Health Literacy.* Bethesda, MD: National Institutes of Health, U.S. Department of Health and Human Services.

Reed, A. E., & Carstensen, L. L. (2012). The theory behind the age-related positivity effect. *Frontiers in Psychology, 3,* 1–9.

Reyna, V. F. (2004). How people make decisions that involve risk: A dual-processes approach. *Current Directions in Psychological Science, 13,* 60–66.

Reyna, V. F., & Brainerd, C. J. (1995). Fuzzy-trace theory: An interim synthesis. *Learning and Individual Differences, 7,* 1–75.

Reyna, V. F., & Brainerd, C. J. (2008). Numeracy, ratio bias, and denominator neglect in judgments of risk and probability. *Learning and Individual Differences, 18,* 89–107.

Reyna, V. F., & Kiernan, B. (1994). Development of gist versus verbatim memory in sentence recognition: Effects of lexical familiarity, semantic content, encoding instructions, and retention interval. *Developmental Psychology, 30,* 178–191.

Reyna, V. F., & Lloyd, F. (2006). Physician decision making and cardiac risk: Effects of knowledge, risk perception, risk tolerance, and fuzzy processing. *Journal of Experimental Psychology: Applied, 12,* 179–195.

Reyna, V. F., Lloyd, F., & Whalen, P. (2001). Genetic testing and medical decision making. *Archives of Internal Medicine, 161,* 2406–2408.

Reyna, V. F., Nelson, W. L., Han, P. K., & Dieckmann, N. F. (2009). How numeracy influences risk comprehension and medical decision making. *Psychological Bulletin, 135,* 943–973.

Rogers, R. W. (1975). A protection motivation theory of fear appeals and attitude change. *Journal of Psychology: Interdisciplinary and Applied, 91,* 93–114.

Roth, W. M., & Bowen, G. M. (2003). When are graphs worth ten thousand words? An expert-expert study. *Cognition and Instruction, 21*(4), 429–473.

Rothman, R. L., Montori, V. M., Cherrington, A., & Pignone, M. P. (2008). Perspective: The role of numeracy in health care. *Journal of Health Communication: International Perspectives, 13*, 583–595.

Salthouse, T. A. (2003). Interrelations of aging, knowledge and cognitive performance. In U. M. Staudinger, & U. Lindenberger (Eds.), *Understanding human development. Dialogues with lifespan psychology* (pp. 267–287). Norwell, MA: Kluwer Academic.

Salthouse, T. A., & Babcock, R. L. (1991). Decomposing adult age differences in working memory. *Developmental Psychology, 27*, 763–776.

Schapira, M. M., Mozal, C., Shofer, F. S., Gonzalez, R., & Apter, A. J. (2017). Alignment of patient health numeracy with asthma care instructions in the patient portal. *Health Literacy Research and Practice, 1*, e1–10.

Scheibe, S., & Carstensen, L. L. (2010). Emotional aging: Recent findings and future trends. *The Journals of Gerontology, 65B*, 135–144.

Schirillo, J. A., & Stone, E. R. (2005). The greater ability of graphical versus numerical displays to increase risk avoidance involves a common mechanism. *Risk Analysis, 25*, 555–566.

Schnotz, W., & Bannert, M. (2003). Construction and interference in learning from multiple representation. *Learning and Instruction, 13*, 141–156.

Schroeder, N. L., Adesope, O. O., & Gilbert, R. B. (2013). How effective are pedagogical agents for learning? A meta-analytic review. *Journal of Educational Computing Research, 49*, 1–39.

Schwarz, N., & Clore, G. L. (2003). Mood as information: 20 years later. *Psychological Inquiry, 14*, 294–301.

Schwarzer, R., Luszczynska, A., Ziegelmann, J. P., Scholz, U., & Lippke, S. (2008). Social-cognitive predictors of physical exercise adherence: Three longitudinal studies in rehabilitation. *Health Psychology*.

Schwartz, L. M., Woloshin, S., Black, W. C., & Welch, H. G. (1997). The role of numeracy in understanding the benefit of screening mammography. *Annals of Internal Medicine, 127*(11), 966–972.

Shah, P., & Hoeffner, J. (2002). Review of graph comprehension research: Implications for instruction. *Educational Psychology Review, 14*, 47–69.

Sharit, J., Idrees, T., Andrade, A. D., Anam, R., Karanam, C., Valencia, W., ... Ruiz, J. G. (2016). Use of an online personal health record's track health function to promote positive lifestyle behaviors in Veterans with prediabetes. *Journal of Health Psychology*, 1–10.

Sharit, J., Lisigurski, M., Andrade, A. D., Karanam, C., Nazi, K. M., Lewis, J. R., & Ruiz, J. G. (2014). The roles of health literacy, numeracy, and graph literacy on the usability of the VA's personal health record by veterans. *Journal of Usability Studies, 9*, 173–193.

Slovic, P., Finucane, M. L., Peters, E., & MacGregor, D. G. (2002). The affect heuristic. In T. Gilovich, D. Griffin, & D. Kahneman (Eds.), *Heuristics and biases: The psychology of intuitive judgment* (pp. 397–420). New York: Cambridge University Press.

Slovic, P., & Peters, E. (2006). Risk perception and affect. *Current Directions in Psychological Science, 15*, 322–325.

Speros, C. (2009). More than words: Promoting health literacy in older adults. *The Online Journal of Issues in Nursing, 14*(3), Manuscript 5.

Spool, J. M., Scanlon, T., Schroeder, W., Snyder, C., & DeAngelo, T. (1997). *Web site usability: A designer's guide, user interface engineering*. North Andover MA: Morgan Kaufmann.

Stead, W. W., & Lin, H. S. (Eds.), (2009). *Computational technology for effective health care: Immediate steps and strategic directions*. Washington, DC: National Academies Press.

Street, R. L., Jr, Makoul, G., Arora, N. K., & Epstein, R. M. (2009). How does communication heal? Pathways linking clinician-patient communication to health outcomes. *Patient Education and Counseling*, *74*(3), 295−301.

Sweller, J. (1988). Cognitive load during problem solving: Effects on learning. *Cognitive Science*, *12*, 257−285.

Taha, J., Czaja, S., Sharit, J., & Morrow, D. (2013). Factors affecting the usage of a personal health record (PHR) to manage health. *Psychology and Aging*, *28*(4), 1124−1139.

Tversky, A., & Kahneman, D. (1974). Judgment under uncertainty: Heuristics and biases. *Science*, *185*, 1124−1131.

United Nations, Department of Economic and Social Affairs, Population Division (2011). *World population prospects: The 2010 revision, Volume I: Comprehensive tables*. ST/ESA/SER.A/313.

United Nations Population Division. (2010). World Population Ageing 195-2050 Executive summary. www.un.org/esa/population/pulibcations/worldageing19502050/pdf/62executivesummary_english.pdf.

Van Gerven, P. W. M., Paas, F., Van Merriënboer, J. J. G., Hendriks, M., & Schmidt, H. G. (2003). The efficiency of multimedia learning into old age. *British Journal of Educational Psychology*, *73*, 489−505.

Vekiri, I. (2002). What is the value of graphical displays in learning? *Educational Psychology Review*, *14*, 261−312.

Webb, T. L., & Sheeran, P. (2006). Does changing behavioral intentions engender behavior change? A meta-analysis of the experimental evidence. *Psychological Bulletin*, *132*, 249−268.

Wickens, C. D., Hollands, J. G., Banbury, S., & Parasuraman, R. (2013). *Engineering psychology and human performance* (4th ed.). Boston, MA: Pearson.

Williams, M. V., Parker, R. M., Baker, D. W., Parikh, N. S., Pitkin, K., Coates, W. C., & Nurss, J. R. (1995). Inadequate functional health literacy among patients at two public hospitals. *Journal of the American Medical Association*, *274*, 1677−1682.

Winn, W. (1991). Learning from maps and diagrams. *Educational Psychology Review*, *3*, 211−247.

Wolfe, C. R., Reyna, V. F., Widmer, C. L., Cedillos, E. M., Fisher, C. R., Brust-Renck, P. G., & Weil, A. M. (2015). Efficacy of a web-based intelligent tutoring system for communicating genetic risk of breast cancer: A fuzzy-trace theory approach. *Medical Decision Making*, *35*, 46−59.

Wong, D. L., Hockenberry-Eaton, M., Wilson, D., Winkelstein, M. L., & Schwartz, P. (2001). *Wong's essentials of pediatric nursing* (6th ed., p. 1301)St. Louis, MI: Mosby Inc.

World Health Organization (2009). *Health literacy and health behavior*. Available <www.who.int/healthpromotion/conferences/7gchp/track2/en/> Accessed 22.04.17.

Wright, K. (2009). The assessment and development of drug calculation skills in nurse education—a critical debate. *Nurse Education Today*, *29*(5), 467−572.

Wright, A. J., Whitwell, S. C. L., Takeichi, C., Hankins, M., & Marteau, T. M. (2009). The impact of numeracy on reactions to different graphic risk presentation formats: An experimental analogue study. *British Journal of Health Psychology*, *14*, 107−125.

Zikmund-Fisher, B. J., Fagerlin, A., & Ubel, P. A. (2008). Improving understanding of adjuvant therapy options by using simpler risk graphics. *Cancer*, *113*, 3382−3390.

Zikmund-Fisher, B. J., Scherer, A. M., Witteman, H. O., Solomon, J. B., Exe, N. L., Tarini, B. A., & Fagerlin, A. (2017). Graphics help patients distinguish between urgent and non-urgent deviations in laboratory test results. *Journal of the American Medical Informatics Association*, *24*, 520−528.

Bringing older drivers up to speed with technology: Cognitive changes, training, and advances in transportation technology

4

Robert Sall, HeeSun Choi and Jing Feng
North Carolina State University, Raleigh, NC, United States

Introduction

Improving the driving performance and safety of older drivers has become an important issue in 21st century human factors, likely due to the expected rapid growth of their presence on the road in the near future (Lyman, Ferguson, Braver, & Williams, 2002; Retchin & Anapolle, 1993), their increased risk of crash involvement (Evans, 2000), and the disproportionately high risk of experiencing fatal injuries from a crash (Li, Braver, & Chen, 2003). As a result, many researchers have devoted themselves to understanding the ways that late-life cognitive changes may affect driving performance, and have started to develop training interventions that are intended to improve age-related declines that hinder older drivers' abilities. While the study of aging drivers has historically been of interest to scientists, the rapid expansion of dynamic transportation-related technologies gives rise to new pressures and opportunities for older drivers, as well as novel areas of work for human factors researchers.

In this chapter, readers should first expect to find relevant literature on age-related changes in attention, memory, spatial cognition, perception, and executive function, as well as information regarding ways that those changes might affect interactions with newer transportation technologies. In addition, this chapter will discuss countermeasures that can be used to combat decrements in aging drivers' performance, including driver assessments, cognitive and driver training, along with compensatory strategies taken by aging drivers. Finally, the chapter will include research on the newer advances in technology that have shaped, and will continue to shape, the way older adults maintain mobility, both with and without vehicles. Given the extensive coverage of these topics in scientific literature, this chapter should be treated as an introduction to the nature of aging drivers' interactions with transportation and transportation technologies. The authors of this chapter encourage interested parties to continue investigating the comprehensive details involved in this topic, and hope that this section might serve as a foundation for that study.

Aging, Technology and Health. DOI: http://dx.doi.org/10.1016/B978-0-12-811272-4.00004-X

Age-related changes in sensory, perceptual, and cognitive functions

Sensory processing

Many age-related declines in a driver's ability to correctly identify a piece of information may result from cognitive errors, such as a decline in spatial deployment of the attentional "spotlight" (discussed later in this chapter). However, late-life degradation of sensory organs may also greatly influence an older driver's ability to locate relevant stimuli on the road. Before delving into the specific sensory changes that plague aging drivers, it will be important to delineate and differentiate the sensory and cognitive systems, as well as the two competing components of attention fueled by those two respective systems. When navigating an unfamiliar city with directions studied before the journey begins, the driver deploys a *top-down* attentional guidance to search for street signs and landmarks in their route. That is, the driver's attention will be strategically ushered by previous knowledge, expertise, and their goals. Conversely, a driver whose attention is abruptly captured by a fire truck's siren will have experienced a *bottom-up*, or stimulus driven, capture of attention. Both the bottom-up and top-down systems have evolved to assist humans with the scrupulous guidance of attention that is required by our species. The interaction of these two systems reveals much of what is known about humanity's ability to detect events (Egeth & Yantis, 1997).

Visual impairments

In terms of age-related differences in these two attentional systems, many of the changes in bottom-up attentional guidance are thought to be related to the degeneration of the visual sensory system (Sandell & Peters, 2001; Schneider & Pichora-Fuller, 2000; Spear, 1993). In other words, a deficit in the system that receives physical stimulation (e.g., light wave), and converts the stimulus into a neural signal (via transduction) to be carried through the rest of the nervous system. While lapses in a driver's attention may result from cognitive shortcomings without perceptual deficits (Owsley, Ball, & Keeton, 1995), sensory changes later in life have been known to increase the risk of crash involvement (Owsley & McGwin, 1999), though empirical support for the latter may fall short of evidence for the former. For example, while some studies have demonstrated a modest association between basic visual acuity and the risk for automobile collisions (Ball, Owsley, Sloane, Roenker, & Bruni, 1993; Hofstetter, 1976; Liessma, 1975), others have failed to unveil significant relationships between the two (Cross et al., 2009; Keeffe, Jin, Weih, McCarty, & Taylor, 2002; Owsley & McGwin, 1999). Additionally, many clinical conditions of the eye that are commonly observed in the elderly, such as cataracts, glaucoma, macular degeneration, and diabetic retinopathy, have often failed to be significant predictors of car crashes in older adults, though other geriatric neurological conditions (e.g., multiple sclerosis, Parkinson's, and stroke) are known to be strong predictors of certain types of motor vehicle crashes

(Cross et al., 2009; Margolis et al., 2002; McGwin, Sims, Pulley, & Roseman, 2000; Sims, McGwin, Allman, Ball, & Owsley, 2000). Thus, an appropriate screening measure for visual function in older drivers should combine both low-level sensory characteristics of driving with the higher order cognitive process described elsewhere in this chapter.

Hearing loss

While the primary sensory modality demanded during driving is vision, hearing is also a necessary attribute to avoiding automobile crashes (e.g., hearing the car horn of a neighboring traveler on the road, localizing the source of an emergency vehicle siren that cannot be seen). Much like vision, hearing loss is an inevitable impairment for many older adults (Li-Korotky, 2012) and is prevalent in nearly two thirds of the population (Lin, Thorpe, Gordon-Salant, & Ferrucci, 2011), though its impact on driving performance tends to be studied less often than vision. Nonetheless, reports of an association between hearing loss and motor vehicle crashes have been made (Edwards et al., 2016; Ivers, Mitchell, & Cumming, 1999). However, others have found this to be true only when hearing impairments are seen alongside a decline in visual function, rather than hearing impairments being the sole predictor of crash risks (Green, McGwin, & Owsley, 2013). Support for this interaction is also reinforced by theoretical accounts for the interplay between hearing and vision loss, and overall cognitive functions (e.g., Wahl & Heyl, 2003).

Unfortunately, degradation of the sensory system is an inescapable component of aging. Future research in the field of assisted or automated driving may want to consider the aforementioned declines for components of vehicle technologies to come, like cues for the transition of control in conditionally automated vehicles (Level 3, SAE International, 2014, p. 2, Table 1). Older operators of these vehicles who are unable to detect auditory or visual cues may face catastrophe as they are unknowingly given back manual control over the car. Such changes in sensory processing are likely to be areas of great interest for transportation research, for more than just optimizing the transfer of control in conditionally automated vehicles. Rather, these considerations should be of interest for those who aim to convey any signal to drivers in the next generations of vehicle technology.

Attention

A particularly important facet of understanding age-related changes can be seen in the literature examining declines in attention. One of the earliest, and most well-known, definitions of attention posits that "everyone knows what attention is. It is the taking possession by the mind, in clear and vivid form, of one out of what seem several simultaneously possible objects or trains of thought. Focalization, or concentration, of consciousness is of its essence. It implies withdrawal from some things in order to deal effectively with others..." (James, 1890, p. 404). Though much work from pioneering psychologists, like William James, lacked the empirical support seen in contemporary theories of cognition, James's definition still encompasses many elements regarded as factual by today's researchers. While his definition describes many unique components of human attention, this section will limit its review to those components that are most relevant to driving, and interacting with technology in automobiles.

Some of the most studied aspect of attention in the context of driving are the spatial limitations of attention demonstrated by tasks like the Useful Field of View (UFOV) Test (Ball, 1997; Ball & Owsley, 1993; Ball & Rebok, 1994; Owsley, 1994), the Attentional Visual Field (Feng et al., 2016), and similar laboratory measures (Hassan et al., 2008; Sekuler, Bennett, & Mamelak, 2000; West et al., 2010). Rather than just measuring a driver's perceptual or sensory sensitivity, tasks like these require a distribution of attention to discriminate targets among distractors across an extended field of view. The tasks assess an ability to spatially allocate attention and avoid distractions. Spatial abilities of attention are particularly important for predicting incidents involving oncoming traffic from the periphery (De Raedt & Ponjaert-Kristoffersen, 2001), including some of the most dangerous types of collision for older adults that occur at intersections (Hakamies-Blomqvist, 1993; Owsley, Ball, Sloane, Roenker, & Bruni, 1991).

Given the strong concurrent validity with a number of basic cognitive and perceptual abilities, as well as other measures of driving performance (for a review, see Clay et al., 2005), measures of spatial selective attention hold a great deal of value for assessing older adult's fitness to drive at the regulatory level. In addition, measures of spatial attention offer the potential for researchers to continue to understand the neurocognitive deficits that may accompany a decline in driving performance later in life. For example, Owsley and colleagues (1995) demonstrated that many older adults who possessed good perceptual sensitivity were still unable to adequately detect, localize, and identify a target in their visual field. These findings have paved the way for the understanding of a weakened attentional "spotlight" in older drivers that contributes to failures in their ability to detect relevant visual information while driving across the visual field, particularly when that information occurs in their visual periphery. Thus, rather than merely a decline in the physical components of visual perception, the visuospatial deficits seen in failures related to the tests of spatial attention among older drivers are more likely to come from the simultaneous reduction in cognitive and perceptual abilities (Atchley & Hoffman, 2004; Hartley & McKenzie, 1991; Madden & Gottlob, 1997). Nonetheless, physiological changes to the nervous system that contribute to drivers attentional limitations may also have importance in predicting reductions in cognitive performance (Kramer, Fabiani, & Colcombe, 2006; Li et al., 2015; Madden, Whiting, & Huettel, 2005).

Particular aspects of declines in spatial attention may have greater impacts on specific driving performance. For example, with advancing age, declines in the ability to select a target among distractors do not occur equally in the upper and lower visual fields. It has been demonstrated that while younger adults show an advantage of attentional selection in the upper visual field (Feng & Spence, 2014), such advantages are largely diminished among older adults (Feng et al., 2016). In other words, older adults experience a disproportionate decline in their ability to select a target among distractors when those targets appear in the upper, rather than lower visual field. These differential age-related changes in the upper and lower visual fields may have implications for driving hazard detection with older drivers, such that hazards occurring at a great eccentricity in the upper visual field may be particularly difficult for older drivers. Changes in selective and spatial attention may also be hindering for older driver's ability to use certain in-vehicle displays. Particularly with center console display screens, and dashboard systems that are designed to show more information than previous generations of those devices. As car manufacturers add more screens to the insides of cars, and the range of functionality for those screens increase, older drivers may experience more difficulty with the technological interactions they have behind the wheel.

Another important area of attention research, is that pertaining to divided attention, even though it has received less interest than the spatial attention for its specific application to aging drivers. There has been mixed evidence for distracted driving performance reductions that are different for older adults. While some have shown that distractions may yield larger decrements in driving performance than younger drivers (Alm & Nilsson, 1995; Lam, 2002), there has also been evidence that both older and younger drivers suffer equally from mobile phone-induced distraction while driving (Strayer & Drews, 2004), indicating that both older and younger drivers will incur a greater risk for crashes when they engage in distracted driving. However, older drivers have been known to be less likely to voluntarily engage in distracting behaviors while driving, like using a cell phone (Lamble, Rajalin, & Summala, 2002). When engaging in distracted driving, older drivers are also known to employ compensatory strategies, like reducing speeds (Young, Regan, & Hammer, 2007).

An important consideration for future researchers is how these trends will change in 30 or so years, when the cohort of older drivers is composed of those who currently make up the population of younger drivers. It is possible that when millennials reach seniority, they will take with them their affinity for regular technology use. In addition to possible increases in rates of distracted driving for older adults of the future, having been raised in the current, technology-rich, environment may contribute to greater confidence in their ability to operate a vehicle under distraction. Therefore, those compensatory strategies used by the current generation of older drivers may change greatly, if present at all. It will be of increasing importance to understand the role of divided attention in future generations of aging drivers. Not only will researcher need to understand how cohort effects might influence the performance of distracted driving in older adults, but it may be necessary to revise what is known about distracted driving as changes are made to the nature of in-vehicle technologies that facilitate both involuntary and voluntary distractions (e.g., heads-up displays, touchscreen radio displays).

Just as the construct of attention can be parsed into many distinct components, some have found it useful to distinguish between different types of divided attention to better understand the attentional limitations of older adults (Zanto & Gazzaley, 2014). The first, referred to here as intramodal divisions of attention, describes the ability to attend to multiple items presented in the same modality (e.g., all visual stimuli). Some have refuted the idea of robust age-related difference in intramodal divisions of attention from studies where older adults perform similarly to younger adults in their ability to detect or compare multiple targets in static visual fields (Hahn & Kramer, 1995; Somberg & Salthouse, 1982). However, differences do begin to become apparent when the complexity of the tasks increase (McDowd & Craik, 1988), and when the tasks transition from still scenes to moving stimuli (Trick, Perl, & Sethi, 2005; Tsang & Shaner, 1998). Differences also become particularly noticeable with tasks that require older adults to sustain intramodal divisions of attention for longer periods of time, or when the velocity of moving stimuli increases (Sekuler, McLaughlin, & Yotsumoto, 2008). This difficulty in tracking dynamic objects in visually complex scenes is paramount when considering older adults having to manage the cognitive demands placed on them by driving while surrounded by new technologies. Augmented reality heads-up displays, e.g., are thought to have unintended effects in their dividing driver's attention, even when the two sets of stimuli share space (Sun, Wu, & Spence, 2015). However, it has not yet been tested whether or not this cost is disproportionately present for older drivers.

Age-related differences in divided attention have also been demonstrated with multimodal divisions—i.e., those in which the attended stimuli are of different modalities, typically auditory and visual. For example, Hawkins, Kramer, and Capaldi (1992) demonstrated that differences in multimodal divisions can be ameliorated with aerobic exercise while intramodal attention performance did not seem to have any improvements after this intervention (Zanto & Gazzaley, 2014). However, understanding the unique age-related changes to multimodal attention may be particularly advantageous for design considerations to vehicle alert systems, particularly when it comes to multisensory cueing of attention. Though a fair amount is known about the benefits of multisensory cues in facilitating the attention of drivers (Ho, Reed, & Spence, 2007; Spence & Ho, 2008), there has not been much research devoted to understanding how multisensory attention changes with age. In one study however, Mahoney and colleagues (2012) demonstrated superiority for visual-somatosensory cues' ability to orient attention (i.e., direct attention to one spatial location) for both older and younger drivers, while audio-visual cues provided a unique benefit for older adults.

While many conceptions of divided attention while driving primarily involve voluntary distractions from inside of the vehicle (e.g., cell phone usage), roughly 25% of collisions due to distracted driving are the result of distractions occurring *outside* of the vehicle (Trezise et al., 2006). There also exists evidence of involuntary distractions from sources outside of the vehicle, like the red light running camera flashes (Sall, Wright, & Boot, 2014). This phenomenon has also been demonstrated with older drivers, who appear to have particular difficulty disengaging attention from these types of targets (Wright, Vitale, Boot, & Charness, 2015). What this means, is that when an older driver's attention is involuntarily captured by the flash from a camera at an intersection or the siren of a police car, they are likely to take longer to regain control of their attention and reorient their eyes to the road. However, contrary to some theoretical studies of attentional capture that suggest the existence of larger age-related differences in attentional capture with irrelevant and salient stimuli (Kramer, Hahn, Irwin, & Theeuwes, 2000; Munoz, Broughton, Goldring, & Armstrong, 1998), Wright et al. (2015) reported no age-related differences in the initial capture of attention. The results of this study make clear two things for the future of transportation technology. First, while theoretical paradigms are invaluable aids to the understanding of the cognitive limitations faced by drivers, it is paramount that they are replicated using real-world simulations. Second, special considerations may need to be made for gadgetry that is intended to convey messages to older drivers with abrupt flashes of salient images, as they are likely to reorient their attention back to the road at a much slower rate than younger drivers. In other words, the future transportation and safety research will benefit from ecological studies of aging driver's attentional limitations in the face of such systems.

Memory

In cognitive aging research, memory is one of the constructs for which there has been considerable work done (e.g., for a review, see McDaniel, Einstein, & Jacoby, 2008). The fears of late life lapse in memory, experiencing dementia, and developing Alzheimer's disease have made this work particularly important for human longevity. While age-related deteriorations in memory can play a minor role in one's driving performance, they appear to do so in less direct forms than those same deteriorations of attention or the visual and auditory sensory systems. However, empirical findings on the direct relationship between driving and memory declines in aging populations are much sparser than those for other cognitive domains, like attention. Nonetheless, this section will review some of the memory-related factors that have been shown to contribute to changes in driving for older adults.

Overall, changes in memory do seem to have some predictive value for determining driving fitness, with greater declines in memory being associated with higher crash risks (Anstey, Wood, Lord, & Walker, 2005). However, this relationship tends to be modest (Hu, Trumble, Foley, Eberhard, & Wallace, 1998; McKnight & McKnight, 1999; Stutts, Stewart, & Martell, 1998), with some failing to find any link at all (Ball et al., 2006). Unsurprisingly though, stronger associations between memory and driving performance are reported in samples who experience dementia (Odenheimer et al., 1994; Szlyk, Myers, Zhang, Wetzel, & Shapiro, 2002) as well as mild progression of Alzheimer's Disease (Frittelli et al., 2009). However, it is likely that the "multidimensional" nature of memory, as it relates to other cognitive domains (Glisky, 2007) means that older adults whose driving skill has been hindered with greater memory loss (i.e., dementia) may also have more compromised attentional abilities.

When it comes to reflecting on one's own cognitive function, the concept of memory is likely the single most tangible. It is not surprising then that, contrary to just driving performance, memory loss appears to be a key factor in older adult's complete cessation of driving (Ackerman, Edwards, Ross, Ball, & Lunsman, 2008; Anstey, Windsor, Luszcz, & Andrews, 2006; Edwards et al., 2008). Overall though, the connection between memory loss and driving is still one that will require considerable research in the future, particularly as neuroimaging becomes more accessible to a larger number of researchers. Many constructs of memory that may factor heavily into older adults' risk of a vehicle crash, like procedural memory, do not have clear methods of testing (Glisky, 2007), though researchers have some insights as to the neuroanatomical structures dealing with these types of memory.

Executive function

Arguably, the most prominent changes in the late-life cognitive process which may impact driving performance are those related to attention and visual perception (e.g., Mathias & Lucas, 2009). However, it is likely that a truly comprehensive understanding of aging drivers' crash risks may also involve an understanding of several other areas of cognition that have been known to decline with age (Anstey et al., 2006; Glisky, 2007; Lundberg, Hakamies-Blomqvist, Almkvist, & Johansson, 1998). For example, a laboratory study conducted by Freund and colleagues (2008) showed scores on a basic measure of executive function to be the strongest predictor of unintended accelerations during simulated driving. Other examinations of executive function have also demonstrated it to be a good predictor of crash risk, though the studies failed to consider other measures of attention (e.g., spatial or divided attention) as possible covariates in their analyses (Adrian, Postal, Moessinger, Rascle, & Charles, 2011; Daigneault, Joly, & Frigon, 2002; Stutts et al., 1998). The need to parse executive functioning from other areas of cognition, as a significant predictor of driving performance and safety, becomes particularly salient when considering arguments for uniquely distinct dimensions of executive functioning (Salthouse, 2003, 2005). Therefore, it is difficult to determine whether or not the more robust reductions in driving performance are a result of selective attention, executive functioning, or the combination.

Future research on older adults' executive function should seek to determine the unique ability of this domain to predict driving performance by including an analysis of covariate cognitive constructs like attention, memory, and speed of processing. In addition, researchers will need to consider the unique demands that newer in-vehicle technologies present to older drivers, especially with the growth of this driver populations. As discussed previously, failure in drivers' executive control is known to result in procedural errors, like unintended accelerations. How will an older driver's ability to employ their executive function be hindered by the influx of new technology? Will incorporating extra elements like conditionally automated driving, where drivers will need to go from a "cold" state of exhibiting little awareness, to high alert as the computer brings accelerating, braking, and steering duties back to the driver, result in greater executive function-related driving mistakes? Or, will advances like automatic high-beam control reduce the cognitive demand for older drivers allowing their executive process to manage fewer elements of the vehicle? The answers to these questions will be a critical component to the future of driver safety in the golden years.

Physical and psychomotor functioning

In addition to the myriad of cognitive, sensory, and perceptual functions required for optimal driving performance, a number of physical disabilities have been implicated as barriers for aging drivers (Foley, Wallace, & Eberhard, 1995; McGwin et al., 2000). While many of the complications that drivers with those disabilities face can be overcome with vehicle modifications (Jones, McCann, & Lassere, 1991), many older adults forgo those modifications (Hawley & Dunne, 2003). Rheumatological conditions, like arthritis, represent one of the largest contributors to late-life physical disability in the United States and Canada (Badley, 2005; Helmick et al., 2008) and have been known to have critical impacts on older adults' ability to perform tasks like steering and maintaining foot pedal functions while driving (Hawley & Dunne, 2003; Jones et al., 1991; Vrkljan et al., 2010). While understanding and ameliorating the debilitating motor deficits which occur from specific medical conditions is essential for successful driving of older adults, compensating for more general reductions in psychomotor skills will be of equal importance.

In a study examining older adults with a balanced distribution of medical conditions (rather than just arthritis or dementia), Ferreira and colleagues (2013) found measures of reaction time to be the strongest predictors of driving performance. Although basic changes in motor speed for older adults who are free of stroke or dementia are known behavioral manifestations of changes in brain matter density (Au et al., 2006; Guo et al., 2001; Rosano, Aizenstein, Studenski, & Newman, 2007), specific causes of those cortical changes are unknown. While the solution of this mystery will certainly be unveiled in future research, current theories have posited cardiovascular health as a predictor of loss of cerebral white-matter and blunted cognitive functions, including psychomotor speed (Breteler et al., 1994; Gorelick et al., 2011; Grodstein, 2007). In line with this hypothesis, researchers have demonstrated physical fitness interventions as successfully being able to improve skills contributing to driving performance (Marmeleira, Godinho, & Fernandes, 2009; Marottoli et al., 2007).

Countermeasures for increased crash risks among older drivers

Given the significant impacts of age-related declines in cognitive and physical functions on older drivers' increased crash risks, it is essential to develop effective countermeasures for older drivers to maintain driving performance and safety. A variety of countermeasure approaches and methods can be used to mitigate the impacts of increased crash risks of at-risk older drivers. For instance, a report from National Highway Traffic Safety Administration (NHTSA; Staplin, Lococo, Martell, & Stutts, 2012), developed a comprehensive taxonomy of critical functional deficits of older drivers and associated crash risks, and evaluated a wide set of existing countermeasures that have the potential to reduce the severity of the identified functional deficits as well as reduce critical driving errors among older drivers. The reviewed countermeasures included surgical and nonsurgical visual sensory system enhancements, physical and motor training, driver education, driver aids and assistance systems, and cognitive training (Staplin et al., 2012). Each countermeasure method can be used as an intervention for a targeted functional deficit and may have varying effectiveness (see Figure 4 in Staplin et al., 2012 for the countermeasure-by-deficit association and effectiveness ratings). Technological advances have expanded countermeasure solutions and enhanced the effectiveness of existing approaches. This section addresses different countermeasure approaches that have the potential to accommodate elevation in functional deteriorations and crash risks among the older driver population.

Driver assessment

A widely used countermeasure approach is the use of screening or assessment tools to identify older drivers at risks. Measuring a driver's competence and crash risk has been commonly used for professional evaluations, such as a medical review process concerning driver licensing, but also for self-assessments by individual drivers. There are a variety of types of measures for fitness-to-drive including questionnaires and scales, paper-and-pencil or computerized cognitive assessments, and multifaceted assessment batteries. While traditional assessment tools had primarily depended on paper-and-pencil or self-reported survey methods, modern technologies including personal computers have extended availability of alternative assessment methods and allowed individual drivers to self-assess their driving competence using various tools.

Self-reported assessment tools or checklists have been most widely used to measure driving behavior and safety (Choi, Grühn, & Feng, 2015; Reason, Manstead, Stradling, Baxter & Campbell, 1990; Reimer et al., 2005). For instance, American Automobile Association (AAA) provided a self-rating tool that includes safety information suggestions for safe driving, *Drivers 65 Plus: Check Your Performance* (AAA Foundation for Traffic Safety, 2013a). Researchers have also proposed a number of questionnaires and scales that aim to assess general or specific aspects of driving behaviors and risks. The Manchester Driver Behavior Questionnaire assesses the frequency of involvement in driving errors, lapses, and violations (Reason et al., 1990; Reimer et al., 2005). The Susceptibility to Driver Distraction Questionnaire is used to assess a driver's tendency to engage in distracting behaviors, both voluntarily and involuntarily (Chen, Donmez, Hoekstra-Atwood, & Marulanda, 2016; Feng, Marulanda, & Donmez, 2014). The Adelaide Driving Self-Efficacy Scale measures how confident a driver is in various driving situations, such as driving at night or turning left across the oncoming traffic (George, Clark, & Crotty, 2007). The Attentional Failures during Driving Questionnaire was developed to assess older drivers' increased crash risks that are due particularly to age-related declines in attentional abilities (Choi et al., 2015).

Cognitive assessment and functional competence measurements can also be used to assess fitness to drive and identify older drivers who are at substantial risks. Measurements for visual impairments or cognitive deficits have been found to predict drivers' safety, such as the previously mentioned UFOV (Ball, Beard, Roenker, Miller, & Griggs, 1988) and the Mini-Mental State Exam (Crizzle, Classen, Bedard, Lanford, & Winter, 2012) (see Vrkljan, McGrath, & Letts, 2011 for a review of the widely used fitness-to-drive assessment tools). While these general cognitive assessments were found to be effective to identify older drivers' increased crash risks, they measured general functional efficiency without taking any driving context into account. There have been attempts at combining the rigorous procedures of traditional cognitive tasks with driving environments to assess drivers' performance more precisely within the driving context. For instance, the DriverScan (Hoffman, Yang, Bovaird, & Embretson, 2006), which was designed as a change detection task with real-world driving scenes, assesses a driver's ability to identify the change between driving scenes. Older drivers' performance on the DriverScan task was found to be a better indicator of their simulated driving performance than a comparable attentional task using abstract stimuli (Hoffman, McDowd, Atchley, & Dubinsky, 2005). Similarly, the Driver Aware Task (DAT; Feng et al., 2015) combines the procedures of computerized visual detection tasks and the stimuli of simulated driving environments to assess a driver's ability in hazard perception. The DAT has been examined, and the findings showed that older drivers' performance levels on the DAT were aligned with simulated driving performance, which demonstrates the validity and effectiveness of the DAT as a potential assessment tool for cognitive fitness to drive among older drivers (Feng et al., 2015).

Multifaceted assessment batteries often combine sets of surveys and questionnaires, vision- and motor-tests, cognitive assessments, and simulated and/or on-road driving tests to better assess one's fitness to drive. For instance, a clinical tool, which includes a list of tests of vision, motor, and cognitive functions, was proposed by the American Medical Association, with support from the NHTSA (McCarthy & Mann, 2006). This Assessment of Driving-Related Skills (ADReS) was designed to be used by physicians for identifying potentially unsafe older drivers. Many states also provide a multifaceted assessment battery for their medical advisory board or physicians and residents. Maryland provides a 30-minute Functional Capacity Test screening that can be taken at their motor vehicle admiration locations. The test consists of a series of tests that measure basic visual perception, memory, cognitive, and physical abilities, including the UFOV and rapid-pace walk test (Maryland Department of Transportation Motor Vehicle Administration, n.d.).

Although some assessment tools have shown to be useful in predicting older drivers' abilities and crash risks, many of the currently available screening procedures or mandatory licensing policies have limited effectiveness. For instance, data analysis comparing the driver licensing policies and crash involvement among older drivers across 46 US states showed that, while mandatory in-person renewal and vision test procedures were associated with significant crash reductions, requiring a knowledge test or an on-road driving test did not lead to additional crash reductions (Tefft, 2014). A number of studies investigating the effectiveness of different licensing procedures and policies used for older drivers also found that many of the policies and procedures in use were ineffective tools to identify older drivers at high risks (Dobbs, 2008). Studies have also demonstrated limitations of the ADReS regarding its sensitivity and specificity as a screening tool (McCarthy & Mann, 2006; Ott et al., 2013). These findings emphasize that further efforts are needed for developing and implementing an accurate and effective driver assessment tool. Rapid advances in technology may further advance availability and effectiveness of existing and new driver assessment and screening tools. The primary benefit of driver assessment and screening tools is being easy to implement and cost-effective. However, this resolution has the disadvantage that it primarily aims to screen out older drivers whose fitness-to-drive have declined to an unsafe level, without considering the potential to improve driving competence among these drivers.

Driver training and cognitive intervention

While the driver assessment and screening approach can be useful for identifying at-risk older drivers, more preventative resolutions might be found in providing cognitive or driving training programs to older drivers so that they can keep mobility without compromising road safety (Gamache, Hudon, Teasdale, & Simoneau, 2010). Accumulated evidence of cognitive plasticity has suggested that many aspects of the age-related declines in cognitive function can be delayed, slowed, or reversed (Anguera et al., 2013; Bavelier, Levi, Li, Dan, & Hensch, 2010; Bavelier, Green, Pouget, & Schrater, 2012). Studies investigating training effects on driving performance have demonstrated that training targeted for specific aspects of cognitive functions improved driving performance (Ball et al., 2002; Ball, Edwards, & Ross, 2007; Ball, Edwards, Ross & McGwin, 2010; Cassavaugh & Kramer, 2009; Roenker, Cissell, Ball, Wadley, & Edwards, 2003). For instance, Ball et al. (2010) showed that crash involvement was significantly reduced among older drivers after a training for reasoning and speed of processing, lasting up to 10 sessions. There are also effective driver training programs that aim more directly at improving driving skills. Increased availability of advanced technologies has been a predominant factor in improvements of driving skill training for older adults. For instance, driving simulation technology and virtual reality have enabled the development of simulator-based driver training programs which can be more efficient and cost-effective compared to traditional on-road training. There has been an increasing use of a simulators for driver training programs and observations have shown effectiveness of this method in improving driving performance (Casutt, Theill, Martin, Keller, & Jäncke, 2014; Roenker et al., 2003; Romoser & Fisher, 2009). Drivers who received simulator-based training were found to improve certain aspects of driving performance such as turning into the correct lane and proper signal use (Roenker et al., 2003), and it was also suggested that the simulator-based training can be transferred to on-road driving performance (Casutt et al., 2014). When comparing the simulator and cognitive training, the simulator training is possibly more powerful for improving older drivers' safety on the road, likely due to its higher ecological validity, greater attractiveness, and being more motivating (Casutt et al., 2014).

Identifying factors contributing to the effectiveness of driver training is essential to developing an effective intervention program. Tailoring the intervention to fit individual drivers' specific needs was found to be an effective way to improve training effects. The personalized learning approach has proven to be far superior to the one-size-fits-all method in general educational settings (for a review, see Mulwa, Lawless, Sharp, Arnedillo-Sanchez, & Wade, 2010). There may be greater challenges to adopting the tailored method in the cognitive intervention or driver training for older drivers compared to a general training, but programs designed to meet an individual's needs may produce greater outcomes. For instance, research showed that older drivers improved visual scanning behaviors in simulated driving when they received personalized feedback on their scanning behaviors. On the other hand, driving performance was not improved after nontailored training in the form of a lecture about how to scan intersections (Romoser & Fisher, 2009). In addition, driver intervention using a training task that is more dynamic and complex may produce greater outcomes. While training using a static perceptual task has provided some promising training outcomes, studies have suggested that training in virtual environments, such as video games, have a greater potential to improve training effects (Basak, Boot, Voss, & Kramer, 2008; Bavelier et al., 2012; Feng, Spence, & Pratt, 2007; Spence & Feng, 2010). The training effects were greater when a training required multiple tasks performed simultaneously (Anguera et al., 2013) and when there were changing emphases and priorities among the tasks (Boot et al., 2010; Gopher, Kramer, Wiegmann, & Kirlik, 2007), which provides significant implications on the design of driver intervention and training programs. Simulated driving is one of the key technologies that will enhance effectiveness of driver intervention and training. The capability to manipulate driving tasks and variable scenarios one can build using simulated driving enables tailored training that targets a driver's specific needs and performance levels in a dynamic and complex environment.

Compensatory driving strategies and educational program

Age-related functional declines are often observed as early as the 1950s and 1960s depending on the type of functions. Elevation in crash risks, however, tends to begin appearing much later in life (Ryan, Legge, & Rosman, 1998). One possible reason that many older drivers continue to drive without an incident, despite significant cognitive and physical declines, is the strategic use of compensatory behaviors to accommodate their increased risks. Studies have shown that older drivers often self-regulate driving behaviors according to their functional impairments (Molnar & Eby, 2008; Moták, Gabude, Bougeant, & Huet, 2014; Staplin et al., 2012). Common compensatory driving behaviors adopted by older drivers include traveling fewer miles (Langford, Koppel, McCarthy, & Srinivasan, 2008), driving more slowly

(Kaber, Zhang, Jin, Mosaly, & Garner, 2012; Trick, Toxopeus, & Wilson, 2010), keeping a longer headway distance (Andrews & Westerman, 2012; Trick et al., 2010), and avoiding challenging driving situations such as making a left turn or driving in heavy traffic (Andrews & Westerman, 2012; Horberry, Anderson, Regan, Triggs, & Brown, 2006). In addition, there have been extensive advances to and increases in availability of safety control measures using technologies. Using advanced driver assistance systems (ADASs), that have proven benefits in improving driver safety, can also be an effective compensatory strategy for older drivers with decreasing driving competence due to functional declines. These devices include adaptive cruise control, blind spot monitoring, forward collision warning, lane departure warning, automatic parking, and collision avoidance systems.

Some studies have observed large individual differences in self-regulatory driving practices and there are various factors influencing the use of compensatory driving strategies among older drivers (Devlin & McGillivray, 2014; Molnar et al., 2014). Furthermore, contrary to the general expectation, a study found that more self-reported compensatory driving behaviors were not associated with reduced crash risks among older drivers (Choi, 2016). These findings suggest that many older drivers who are at risk may not have accurate knowledge of effective compensatory driving behaviors, which might have resulted in failing to adopt necessary compensatory driving practices or using ineffective strategies. Studies suggested that compensatory driving behaviors are more likely to be predicted by self-confidence in driving or self-perceived functional abilities, but less likely to be associated with one's actual functional impairments or driving performance (Choi, 2016; Devlin & McGillivray, 2014; Molnar et al., 2014). This may explain why some older drivers at higher risks do not regulate their driving or fail to adopt compensatory driving behaviors at an appropriate level. Thus, providing accurate information about age-related functional declines and the risks associated with those declines, as well as effective compensatory driving behaviors a driver can use, is a key to promote compensatory driving practices among older drivers. The NHTSA, together with the USAA Educational Foundation and AARP, developed a booklet which outlines the potential impacts of various functional declines with aging, and the associated compensatory driving strategies that can be taken to cope with each type of decline, so that older drivers remain safe drivers (*Driving safely while aging gracefully*, n.d.). This booklet provides a list of compensatory driving behaviors for drivers who are experiencing declines in attention and reaction time that might contribute to things like planning a route in advance, keeping a safe distance with a car ahead, avoiding making left turns at intersections where no green arrow signal is present to provide protected turns, and scanning far down the road constantly. In order to help effective driving practices, it provides specific compensatory actions that a driver can take. For example, to keep a safe distance behind another vehicle, a driver can find a marker located ahead (e.g., a tree, sign or lamp post). When the leading vehicle passes this marker, the driver can count to themselves, "1001, 1002, 1003, 1004," so that the driver leaves enough space to reach 1004 before they reach the same place of the leading vehicle when the count began.

A variety of educational programs has already been made available to older drivers. Seattle has demonstrated targeted education efforts toward older adults through partnerships with AARP and local media to run public service announcements and speak in person with older drivers (Curtin & Schwartz, 2016). A fair amount of research has also indicated that driver educational programs designed to change self-perceptions and to promote self-regulatory driving have been effectively able to increase compensatory driving practices and reduce crash risks among older drivers (Curtin & Schwartz, 2016; Kua, Korner-Bitensky, Desrosiers, Man-Son-Hing, & Marshall, 2007; Owsley, Stalvey, & Phillips, 2003). Findings showed that, although some interventions improved awareness of a driver's own limitations of driving exposure and avoidance of challenging driving situations (Owsley et al., 2003), they often failed to directly reduce crashes (Kua et al., 2007; Nasvadi & Vavrik, 2007), which may suggest limited effectiveness of the currently available programs. Furthermore, while various safety-related ADASs are available and have great potential, use of those technologies as compensatory strategies may be limited among older drivers. Older driver education aiming to improve acceptance and familiarity with the technologies may facilitate strategic driving behaviors using technological solutions.

Advanced vehicle technologies

Another potential solution to improve older adults' driving safety is to use advanced vehicle technology. These technologies providing automated functions may assist older drivers in tasks that become increasingly difficult due to the cognitive and physical declines that are known to occur with age, or could reduce the severity of crash by taking over vehicle control when necessary. For example, a crash mitigation system could detect a hazard (e.g., another vehicle or a cyclist) on the collision course of the vehicle and present a warning to the driver. If no manual braking is subsequently applied, automatic braking will be engaged to prevent a crash. In other situations, when a driver applies vigorous braking to try to stop the vehicle as quickly as possible, the system would apply extra braking force to facilitate vehicle speed reduction. Crash mitigation systems have been found to be effective in avoiding crashes or mitigate the consequence of an unavoidable crash (Fecher et al., 2008). Given the fragility and cognitive changes associated with advanced age, older drivers could benefit greatly from this type of technology. Research has shown that older drivers in general hold very positive attitudes toward such technology and prefer earlier warnings (e.g., more than 3 seconds of time-to-collision; Wilschut, Kroon, Goede, Cremers, & Hoedemaeker, 2014). Blind spot warning is another technology that has the potential to significantly benefit older drivers. As drivers age, flexibility in head and trunk rotation declines (Chen, Xu, Lin, & Radwin, 2015; Malfetti, 1985). As a result of limited neck mobility, older drivers experience difficulties to observe blind spots (Janke, 1994), thus make far less checks of blind spots than younger drivers (Lavallière et al., 2011), which led to increased crash risks in older age (Marottoli et al., 1998). Blind spot warning technology provides notifications to a driver when a car in the adjacent lane enters in the driver's blind spot. Furthermore, with blind spot assistance, the system may even automatically take an action to avoid collisions with hazards in the blind spot. Despite concerns of system reliability in conditions such as poor weather and potential distraction from the warning signals on driving, drivers including those in the older age responded positively to the effectiveness of blind spot warning systems (Braitman, McCartt, Zuby, & Singer, 2010; Cicchino & McCartt, 2014). A comprehensive review of older drivers' attitude, use and benefits of various advanced in-vehicle technologies is presented in Eby et al. (2016). In addition to the development and evaluation of these technology, another important step is to bring these safety features to the awareness of older drivers that facilitates drivers' decisions when buying new vehicles. Efforts have been made, such as the recent update to *Smart Features for Older Drivers* (AAA Foundation for Traffic Safety, 2013b), *MyCarDoesWhat.org* (National Safety Council, 2015) and the *CarTech VR360* app (National Safety Council, 2017).

Vehicles with high-level automation (and even full automation) have been proposed as another method to potentially improve the mobility of older adults (Zmud, Ecola, Phleps, & Feige, 2013). This technology may be particularly useful for providing a stress-free mode of transportation to older adults with certain driving restriction, those who have ceased driving altogether, or older adults with limited access to public transit services. While the modern high-level vehicle automation has lots of promises, human factors research aimed at understanding driver behavior when interacting with highly automated vehicles is still in its infancy. This is especially true for research aimed at older drivers' interaction with highly automated vehicles. It is not clear how cognitively demanding it is to use this vehicle technology under dynamic driving situations (e.g., to monitor whether automation is working properly). Research is also needed to investigate how to help older drivers develop an accurate understanding of the capabilities and limitations of such high-level automation. As older drivers, on average, may be less experienced with advanced vehicle technology, more training and support would be necessary to enable older drivers to adopt and correctly use these technologies.

Older drivers, on average, differ from younger drivers in a set of characteristics that are important to consider when designing highly automated vehicles that are intended to serve the needs of older drivers. As mentioned earlier, older drivers experience declines in cognitive functions such as attention, executive function and proceeding speed (for a review, see Glisky, 2007). It is likely that these differences in cognitive processing will become apparent with future generations of vehicle technologies, like instances where an older driver would be required to takeover the vehicle control after a period of automated driving (i.e., when the vehicle was controlling its operation without the intervention of a driver). During takeovers from automated states to periods of manual control, older drivers may require warnings that are of higher intensity, more salient, and are provided earlier on, than warnings needed by younger drivers. If unexpected takeovers could happen, an important consideration is if this transition would be too cognitively challenging for older drivers who experience significant cognitive declines. As mentioned earlier, older drivers are also less likely to take risks and more likely adopt compensatory driving behaviors (for a review, see Staplin et al., 2012) such as driving slower (Kaber et al., 2012; Trick et al., 2010), braking more frequently (Case, Hulbert, & Beers, 1970), and keeping a longer headway distance from the vehicle ahead (Andrews & Westerman, 2012; Trick et al., 2010). These age-related differences in driving behavior imply disparate vehicle dynamics for drivers of different age groups, like the differential demands for vehicle automations designed for drivers of different ages. For instance, to make the riding experience comfortable for older adults, a highly automated vehicle may need to keep a greater headway distance. In addition, older adults are generally less experienced with newer technology and often lack access to necessary technical support to help them when encountering difficulties with technology (Heart & Kalderon, 2011; Peek et al., 2015). Therefore, more extensive training and assistance would be necessary to support older adults' successful interaction with highly automated vehicle technology.

The human factors domain recognizes the importance of understanding the issues around aging and advanced vehicle technologies, and there is a growing interest and effort in conducting research on this topic. In a study comparing younger and older drivers' performance during the takeover of vehicle control during simulated driving with conditional automation in different levels of traffic (i.e., no traffic, medium, or high traffic), researchers found older drivers were more likely to take on compensatory driving behaviors, like maintaining a longer headway distance and applying the brakes more frequently (Körber, Gold, Lechner, & Bengler, 2016). These compensatory driving behaviors allowed older drivers to achieve a comparable level of takeover performance as younger drivers. Similarly, in another study, both younger and older drivers were instructed to engage in a secondary task such as watching a movie, reading a story, or overseeing vehicle operation (Miller et al., 2016). The researchers compared younger and older drivers' takeover performance under these secondary task conditions in simulated driving with high-level automation. No age difference was found in takeover performance, while older drivers in general drove more slowly than younger drivers. In a recent study from our research group, we observed engagement in nondriving-related activities during simulated automated driving in both younger and older drivers when they could freely choose the time and form of engagement (Clark & Feng, 2016). We found that both age groups engaged in various activities with distinct preferences for the type of activity. Younger drivers were mostly interested in interacting with their electronic personal device during the autonomous phase, while older drivers tended to converse with another individual. When a request to takeover was presented, older drivers responded (e.g., hands back to the wheel, or foot back to a pedal) as quickly as younger drivers to regain control of the vehicle. Findings from these studies suggest that older drivers are capable of interacting with autonomous vehicles, although the vehicle dynamics may vary between the two age groups. Such age differences have significant implications for vehicle automation interface design.

Given the novelty of vehicle technology with high-level automation and its yet-to-develop market, a few studies examined drivers' concern, trust, and willingness to adopt the technology. In a survey study that examined public opinions about highly automated vehicles in the United States, United Kingdom, and Australia

(Schoettle & Sivak, 2014), older drivers reported greater concerns than younger drivers over the technology. In a more recent survey study in the United States, older drivers were less comfortable with high-level vehicle automation and were particularly skeptical about fully automated vehicles (Abraham et al., 2017). In this study, older drivers also expressed less willingness to pay for autonomous vehicles than younger drivers. These age differences in the trust and willingness to adopt the technology are important to consider when designing advanced vehicle technology to benefit older drivers.

Alternative mobility services and accessible transportation in age-friendly communities

In addition to automated vehicle technology, a wide variety of modern technological advances may provide alternative solutions for safe and efficient means of transportation for older drivers (Rosenbloom, 2009). Individual ownership of a vehicle may lead to environmental and financial demands. In recent years, new technologies have emerged that seek to reduce individual ownership. These systems are intended to help maintain independence and well-being for older adults, reduce transportation costs, eliminate the need for and cost of parking, as well as improve road safety.

Shared mobility service

Shared mobility services, or on-demand vehicles, are one of the important innovations that have greatly changed mobility solutions in the past decade. The ride/car sharing services (e.g., Uber, Lyft, Zipcar, etc.) are based on the concept of sharing by connecting people who are in need of a ride with available drivers or vehicles. Key technologies that enable the process of real-time matching between a shared mobility service and a need, based on the geographical location, include smartphone and mobile apps, social networks, and GPS navigation (Bajpai, 2016). Shared mobility services provide a convenient and cost-effective mode of transportation. Instead of owning and driving a car, people who live in an urban area can ride a shared car to reduce or even eliminate stress from traffic congestion, and costs of parking and fuel.

Beyond the primary benefits for individual riders, there are potential mobility benefits as well as safety implications associated with this innovative solution. In particular, they provide alternative transportation for older and disabled populations that have limited access to affordable transportation. Disabled or older people may still be able to maintain mobility and independence after losing their capability to drive safely. Shared mobility services also have safety benefits for general road users, given the potential reduction in vehicles and traffic on the road. The availability of ride-sharing services may decrease the number of cars on the road and reduce travel mileage (Bajpai, 2016), which could lead to improving flows of traffic and minimize delays. The overall reduction of road use would potentially result in the more efficient transportation system and better road safety. In addition, given the more accessible and convenient ride-sharing services compared to traditional public transportation (e.g., an older adult does not need to walk to a bus stop in the winter with snow and ice on ground), drivers who perceived themselves as being at higher crash risks may favor shared mobility services given its ease.

Age-friendly communities

Over the past decade, there has been growing interest in the development of age-friendly communities. The World Health Organization (WHO) launched the Global Age-Friendly Cities project, which aims to help cities around the world make their communities more accessible and responsive to the needs of older adults with varying levels of ability (Lui, Everingham, Warburton, Cuthill, & Bartlett, 2009; World Health Organization, 2007). This project emphasizes that an age-friendly community should be designed to support older adults having an active and healthy life with the appropriate physical and social environments. As an affiliate of the WHO Age-Friendly Cities program, the AARP initiated the network of age-friendly communities in the United States (Warth, 2016). Similar efforts have been made around the world including the United Kingdom (e.g., lifetime neighborhood) and Canada (e.g., Calgary Elder Friendly Communities (EFC) program) (Lui et al., 2009).

Age-friendly communities are different from retirement villages, nursing homes, or assisted living facilities. The aim of the age-friendly communities is to provide older people places that actively involve, value, and support both active and frail older adults, with infrastructure and services that effectively accommodate their changing needs (Alley, Liebig, Pynoos, Banerjee, & Choi, 2007). Different models and approaches proposed key features of an age-friendly community, which include policies, services, and products to meet the needs of the older population in the community (Alley et al., 2007; Steels, 2015; Lui et al., 2009). Among the critical physical infrastructure and social environment, providing a better mobility solution has been heavily recognized as a key basis for the development of a supportive community for older people (Alley et al., 2007; Steels, 2015; Lui et al., 2009). For example, the WHO Age-Friendly Cities program identifies a list of aspects of urban settings and services in eight major domains that can contribute to the participation, health, independence, and security of older persons (World Health Organization, 2007). The list indicates accessible public and private transportation as a key to ensuring participation and independence. This Age-Friendly Cities guide indicates that a number of aspects of the transportation system, including affordability, reliability and frequency, travel destinations, safety and comfort, age-friendly vehicles, and road design and condition, needs to be carefully designed to improve mobility and maximize the independence of older residents. The guide also suggests that age-friendly communities should help driving competence by providing and promoting refresher driving courses.

Much of the aspiration for developing age-friendly transportation in senior community settings has revolved around two major aspects: improving accessible public and community transportation and designing a road for the needs of older drivers (see Brewer, Murillo, & Pate, 2014 for the suggested roadway designs for the aging population). As addressed in the previous section, creating alternative transportation networks can be an effective approach to improving mobility in the age-friendly communities. In a recent study, Shaheen, Cano, and Carnel (2013) investigated the potentials of car sharing services in an active older adult community setting. The study aimed to evaluate the feasibility of an Electric Vehicle car-sharing program and examine if this program might change travel behaviors and improve the mobility of older adults. In the study, surveys and interviews were conducted to understand general travel behaviors and preferences for a shared car use system among the residents in a senior community in the San Francisco area. A majority of the respondents reported that they typically plan their driving trips in advance, which suggests on-demand vehicle services might be an appropriate form of transportation in the older population. While a significant number of respondents did not believe they would give up their own vehicles, even if they were to join such a program, 38% reported that they would or might sell their household vehicles (Shaheen et al., 2013). Also, more than half of the survey respondents said they would or might use public transit and carpool more if a car sharing service were available and assisted those forms of transportation (Shaheen et al., 2013). The findings suggest opportunities for using shared mobility service as an alternative transportation option among older adults in a community setting. Although more evidence is yet to be collected, the promising findings in this study warrant further research to investigate how a variety of technological advances and innovative solutions can improve mobility and safety in the older population.

Summary

While some of the areas discussed in this chapter have been covered in great detail by the scientific community, there remains a great deal of work to be done in order to maximize older adults' safe and effective methods of transportation. The progression of neuroimaging technology is likely to become a prominent asset for researchers interested in the well-being of older adults. In addition to the more theoretical investigations on aging and driving, applied and translational explorations on this topic are also likely to experience significant revelations as previous generations of transportation technology become antiquated, and are replaced by novel gadgets. Even though such machinery is currently being developed with the best intentions, special considerations are necessary to accommodate for older adults' known differences in cognitive processing, and driving strategies that might leave them unable to benefit from, or even be harmed by, these technologies. Fortunately, though, much of future engineering has already been oriented toward addressing these concerns, like human factors research on how older drivers use advanced vehicle technologies, the shared mobility services, and age-friendly communities. With the expectation for broader availability to research tools, and unknown challenges faced by the next generation of transportation technologies, the scientific study of aging drivers is likely to be one with tremendous importance in the future.

References

AAA Foundation for Traffic Safety. (2013a). *Drivers 65 plus: Check your performance.* Washington, DC. Retrieved from <https://www.aaafoundation.org/sites/default/files/driver65.pdf>.

AAA Foundation for Traffic Safety. (2013b). *Smart features for older drivers.* Heathrow, FL. Retrieved from <http://seniordriving.aaa.com/wp-content/uploads/2015/11/Smart-Features-for-Older-Drivers-Brochure-lores.pdf>.

Abraham, H., Lee, C., Brady, S., Fitzgerald, C., Mehler, B., Reimer, B., & Couglin, J.F. (2017). Autonomous vehicles, trust, and driving alternatives: A survey of consumer preferences. In *Proceedings of the transportation research board 96th annual meeting,* Washington, D.C., USA.

Ackerman, M. L., Edwards, J. D., Ross, L. A., Ball, K. K., & Lunsman, M. (2008). Examination of cognitive and instrumental functional performance as indicators for driving cessation risk across 3 years. *The Gerontologist, 48*(6), 802−810.

Adrian, J., Postal, V., Moessinger, M., Rascle, N., & Charles, A. (2011). Personality traits and executive functions related to on-road driving performance among older drivers. *Accident Analysis & Prevention, 43*(5), 1652−1659.

Alley, D., Liebig, P., Pynoos, J., Banerjee, T., & Choi, I. H. (2007). Creating elder-friendly communities: Preparations for an aging society. *Journal of Gerontological Social Work, 49*(1−2), 1−18.

Alm, H., & Nilsson, L. (1995). The effects of a mobile telephone task on driver behavior in a car following situation. *Accident Analysis & Prevention, 27*(5), 707−715.

Andrews, E. C., & Westerman, S. J. (2012). Age differences in simulated driving performance: Compensatory processes. *Accident Analysis & Prevention, 45,* 660−668.

Anguera, J. A., Boccanfuso, J., Rintoul, J. L., Al-Hashimi, O., Faraji, F., Janowich, J., ... Gazzaley, A. (2013). Video game training enhances cognitive control in older adults. *Nature, 501*(7465), 97−101.

Anstey, K. J., Windsor, T. D., Luszcz, M. A., & Andrews, G. R. (2006). Predicting driving cessation over 5 years in older adults: Psychological well-being and cognitive competence are stronger predictors than physical health. *Journal of the American Geriatrics Society, 54*(1), 121−126.

Anstey, K. J., Wood, J., Lord, S., & Walker, J. G. (2005). Cognitive, sensory and physical factors enabling driving safety in older adults. *Clinical Psychology Review, 25*(1), 45−65.

Atchley, P., & Hoffman, L. (2004). Aging and visual masking: Sensory and attentional factors. *Psychology and Aging, 19,* 57−67.

Au, R., Massaro, J. M., Wolf, P. A., Young, M. E., Beiser, A., Seshadri, S., ... DeCarli, C. (2006). Association of white matter hyperintensity volume with decreased cognitive functioning: The Framingham Heart Study. *Archives of Neurology, 63*(2), 246−250.

Badley, E. M. (2005). Arthritis in Canada: What do we know and what should we know? *The Journal of Rheumatology, 72,* 39−41.

Bajpai, J. N. (2016). Emerging vehicle technologies & the search for urban mobility solutions. *Urban, Planning and Transport Research, 4*(1), 83−100.

Ball, K. K. (1997). Attentional problems and older drivers. *Alzheimer Disease and Associated Disorders, 11,* 42−47.

Ball, K. K., Beard, B. L., Roenker, D. L., Miller, R. L., & Griggs, D. S. (1988). Age and visual search: Expanding the useful field of view. *Journal of the Optical Society of America A, 5*(12), 2210−2219.

Ball, K. K., Berch, D. B., Helmers, K. F., Jobe, J. B., Leveck, M. D., Marsiske, M., ... Willis, S. L. (2002). Effects of cognitive training interventions with older adults. *Journal of American Medical Association, 288*(18), 2271−2281.

Ball, K. K., Edwards, J. D., & Ross, L. A. (2007). The impact of speed of processing training on cognitive and everyday functions. *The Journals of Gerontology Series B: Psychological Sciences and Social Sciences, 62*(Special Issue 1), 19−31.

Ball, K. K., Edwards, J. D., Ross, L. A., & McGwin, G. (2010). Cognitive training decreases motor vehicle collision involvement of older drivers. *Journal of the American Geriatrics Society, 58*(11), 2107−2113.

Ball, K. K., & Owsley, C. (1993). The useful field of view test: A new technique for evaluating age-related declines in visual function. *Journal of the American Optomological Association, 63*, 71−79.

Ball, K. K., Owsley, C., Sloane, M. E., Roenker, D. L., & Bruni, J. R. (1993). Visual attention problems as a predictor of vehicle crashes in older drivers. *Investigative Ophthalmology & Visual Science, 34*(11), 3110−3123.

Ball, K. K., & Rebok, G. (1994). Evaluating the driving ability of older adults. *Journal of Applied Gerontology, 13*, 20−38.

Ball, K. K., Roenker, D. L., Wadley, V. G., Edwards, J. D., Roth, D. L., McGwin, G., ... Dube, T. (2006). Can high-risk older drivers be identified through performance-based measures in a department of motor vehicles setting? *Journal of the American Geriatrics Society, 54*(1), 77−84.

Basak, C., Boot, W. R., Voss, M. W., & Kramer, A. F. (2008). Can training in a real-time strategy video game attenuate cognitive decline in older adults? *Psychology and Aging, 23*(4), 765−777.

Bavelier, D., Green, C. S., Pouget, A., & Schrater, P. (2012). Brain plasticity through the life span: Learning to learn and action video games. *Annual Review of Neuroscience, 35*, 391−416.

Bavelier, D., Levi, D. M., Li, R. W., Dan, Y., & Hensch, T. K. (2010). Removing brakes on adult brain plasticity: From molecular to behavioral interventions. *Journal of Neuroscience, 30*(45), 14964−14971.

Boot, W. R., Basak, C., Erickson, K. I., Neider, M., Simons, D. J., Fabiani, M., ... Low, K. A. (2010). Transfer of skill engendered by complex task training under conditions of variable priority. *Acta Psychologica, 135*(3), 349−357.

Braitman, K. A., McCartt, A. T., Zuby, D. S., & Singer, J. (2010). Volvo and Infiniti drivers; experience with select crash avoidance technologies. *Traffic Injury Prevention, 11*, 270−278.

Breteler, M. M., van Amerongen, N. M., van Swieten, J. C., Claus, J. J., Grobbee, D. E., Van Gijn, J., ... Van Harskamp, F. (1994). Cognitive correlates of ventricular enlargement and cerebral white matter lesions on magnetic resonance imaging. The Rotterdam Study. *Stroke, 25*(6), 1109−1115.

Brewer, M., Murillo, D., & Pate, A. (2014). *Handbook for designing roadways for the aging population, (No. FHWA-SA-14-015).*

Case, H. W., Hulbert, S., & Beers, J. (1970). Driving ability as affected by age. *Final Report No. 70-18*. Los Angeles, CA: Institute of Transportation and Traffic Engineering, University of California.

Cassavaugh, N. D., & Kramer, A. F. (2009). Transfer of computer-based training to simulated driving in older adults. *Applied Ergonomics, 40*(5), 943−952.

Casutt, G., Theill, N., Martin, M., Keller, M., & Jäncke, L. (2014). The drive-wise project: Driving simulator training increases real driving performance in healthy older drivers. *Frontiers in Aging Neuroscience, 6*, 85.

Chen, H. Y. W., Donmez, B., Hoekstra-Atwood, L., & Marulanda, S. (2016). Self-reported engagement in driver distraction: An application of the theory of planned behaviour. *Transportation Research Part F: Psychology and Behaviour, 38*, 151–163.

Chen, K. B., Xu, X., Lin, J.-H., & Radwin, R. G. (2015). Evaluation of older driver head functional range of motion using portable immersive virtual reality. *Experimental Gerontology, 70*, 150–156.

Choi, H. (2016). Older drivers' attentional functions and crash risks in various hazardous situations: Relationship, taxonomy, and compensatory behaviors *(Unpublished doctoral dissertation)*. Raleigh, NC: North Carolina State University.

Choi, H., Grühn, D., & Feng, J. (2015). Self-reported attentional failures during driving relates to on-road crashes and simulated driving performance of older drivers. In *Proceedings of the transportation research board 94th annual meeting* (No. 15-5079), Washington, DC.

Cicchino, J. B., & McCartt, A. T. (2014). *Experiences of dodge and jeep owners with collision avoidance and related technologies.* Arlington, TX: Insurance Institute for Highway Safety.

Clark, H., & Feng, J. (2016). Age differences in the takeover of vehicle control and engagement in non-driving-related activities in simulated semi-autonomous driving. *Accident, Analysis & Prevention.* Available from http://dx.doi.org/10.1016/j.aap.2016.08.027.

Clay, O. J., Wadley, V. G., Edwards, J. D., Roth, D. L., Roenker, D. L., & Ball, K. K. (2005). Cumulative meta-analysis of the relationship between useful field of view and driving performance in older adults: Current and future implications. *Optometry & Vision Science, 82*(8), 724–731.

Crizzle, A. M., Classen, S., Bédard, M., Lanford, D., & Winter, S. (2012). MMSE as a predictor of on-road driving performance in community dwelling older drivers. *Accident Analysis & Prevention, 49*, 287–292.

Cross, J. M., McGwin, G., Rubin, G. S., Ball, K. K., West, S. K., Roenker, D. L., & Owsley, C. (2009). Visual and medical risk factors for motor vehicle collision involvement among older drivers. *British Journal of Ophthalmology, 93*(3), 400–404.

Curtin, J., & Schwartz, A. (2016). Vision zero IN Seattle WA, USA: Part 1. Institute of Transportation Engineers. *ITE Journal, 86*(6), 18–21.

Daigneault, G., Joly, P., & Frigon, J. Y. (2002). Executive functions in the evaluation of accident risk of older drivers. *Journal of Clinical and Experimental Neuropsychology, 24*(2), 221–238.

De Raedt, R., & Ponjaert-Kristoffersen, I. (2001). Predicting at-fault car accidents of older drivers. *Accident Analysis & Prevention, 33*(6), 809–819.

Devlin, A., & McGillivray, J. A. (2014). Self-regulation of older drivers with cognitive impairment: A systematic review. *Australasian Journal on Ageing, 33*(2), 74–80.

Dobbs, B. M. (2008). Aging baby boomers — A blessing or challenge for driver licensing authorities. *Traffic Injury Prevention, 9*(4), 379–386.

Eby, D. W., Molnar, L. J., Zhang, L., St. Louis, R. M., Zanier, N., Kostyniuk, L. P., & Stanciu, S. (2016). Use, perceptions, and benefits of automotive technologies among aging drivers. *Injury Epidemiology, 3*(28), 1–20.

Edwards, J. D., Lister, J. J., Lin, F. R., Andel, R., Brown, L., & Wood, J. M. (2016). Association of hearing impairment and subsequent driving mobility in older adults. *The Gerontologist, gnw009.* https://doi.org/10.1093/geront/gnw009.

Edwards, J. D., Ross, L. A., Ackerman, M. L., Small, B. J., Ball, K. K., Bradley, S., & Dodson, J. E. (2008). Longitudinal predictors of driving cessation among older adults from the ACTIVE clinical trial. *The Journals of Gerontology Series B: Psychological Sciences and Social Sciences, 63*(1), 6–12.

Egeth, H. E., & Yantis, S. (1997). Visual attention: Control, representation, and time course. *Annual Review of Psychology, 48*(1), 269–297.

Evans, L. (2000). Risks older drivers face themselves and threats they pose to other road users. *International Journal of Epidemiology, 29*(2), 315–322.

Fecher, N., Fuchs, K., Hoffmann, J., Abendroth, B., Bruder, R., & Winner, H. (September 2008). Analysis of the driver behavior in autonomous emergency hazard braking situations. In *FISITA world automotive congress*, September (pp. 14–19).

Feng, J., Craik, F.I.M., Levine, B., Moreno, S., Naglie, G., & Choi, H. (2015). Drive aware: Measuring attention in the context of driving. In *The proceedings of the 94th transportation research board annual meeting* (No. 15-4960), Washington, DC.

Feng, J., Craik, F. I. M., Levine, B., Moreno, S., Naglie, G., & Choi, H. (2016). Differential age-related changes in attention across an extended visual field. *European Journal of Ageing*. Available from http://dx.doi.org/10.1007/s10433-016-0399-7.

Feng, J., Marulanda, S., & Donmez, B. (2014). Susceptibility to Driver Distraction Questionnaire: Development and relation to relevant self-reported measures. *Transportation Research Record: Journal of the Transportation Research Board, 2434*, 26–34.

Feng, J., & Spence, I. (2014). Upper visual field advantage in localizing a target among distractors. *i-Perception, 5*(2), 97–100.

Feng, J., Spence, I., & Pratt, J. (2007). Playing an action video game reduces gender differences in spatial cognition. *Psychological Science, 18*(10), 850–855.

Ferreira, I. S., Simões, M. R., & Marôco, J. (2013). Cognitive and psychomotor tests as predictors of on-road driving ability in older primary care patients. *Transportation Research Part F: Traffic Psychology and Behaviour, 21*, 146–158.

Foley, D. J., Wallace, R. B., & Eberhard, J. (1995). Risk factors for motor vehicle crashes among older drivers in a rural community. *Journal of the American Geriatrics Society, 43*(7), 776–781.

Freund, B., Colgrove, L. A., Petrakos, D., & McLeod, R. (2008). In my car the brake is on the right: Pedal errors among older drivers. *Accident Analysis & Prevention, 40*(1), 403–409.

Frittelli, C., Borghetti, D., Iudice, G., Bonanni, E., Maestri, M., Tognoni, G., … Iudice, A. (2009). Effects of Alzheimer's disease and mild cognitive impairment on driving ability: A controlled clinical study by simulated driving test. *International Journal of Geriatric Psychiatry, 24*(3), 232–238.

Gamache, P.-L., Hudon, C., Teasdale, N., & Simoneau, M. (2010). Alternative avenues in the assessment of driving capacities in older drivers and implications for training. *Current Directions in Psychological Science, 19*(6), 370–374.

George, S., Clark, M., & Crotty, M. (2007). Development of the Adelaide driving self-efficacy scale. *Clinical Rehabilitation, 21*(1), 56–61.

Glisky, E. L. (2007). Changes in cognitive function in human aging. In D. R. Riddle (Ed.), *Brain aging: Models, methods and mechanisms*. Boca Raton, FL: CRC Press, Taylor & Francis Group.

Gopher, D., Kramer, A., Wiegmann, D., & Kirlik, A. (2007). Emphasis change as a training protocol for high-demand tasks. In A. F. Kramer, D. A. Wiegmann, & A. Kirlik (Eds.), *Attention: From theory to practice* (pp. 209–224). New York: Oxford University Press.

Gorelick, P. B., Scuteri, A., Black, S. E., DeCarli, C., Greenberg, S. M., Iadecola, C., … Petersen, R. C. (2011). Vascular contributions to cognitive impairment and dementia a statement for healthcare professionals from the American Heart Association/American Stroke Association. *Stroke, 42*(9), 2672–2713.

Green, K. A., McGwin, G., & Owsley, C. (2013). Associations between visual, hearing, and dual sensory impairments and history of motor vehicle collision involvement of older drivers. *Journal of the American Geriatrics Society*, *61*(2), 252−257.

Grodstein, F. (2007). Cardiovascular risk factors and cognitive function. *Alzheimer's & Dementia*, *3*(2), S16−S22.

Guo, X., Steen, B., Matousek, M., Andreasson, L. A., Larsson, L., Palsson, S., ... Skoog, I. (2001). A population-based study on brain atrophy and motor performance in elderly women. *The Journals of Gerontology, Series A: Biological Sciences and Medical Sciences*, *56*(10), M633−M637.

Hahn, S., & Kramer, A. F. (1995). Attentional flexibility and aging: You don't need to be 20 years of age to split the beam. *Psychology and Aging*, *10*(4), 597−609.

Hakamies-Blomqvist, L. E. (1993). Fatal accidents of older drivers. *Accident Analysis & Prevention*, *25*(1), 19−27.

Hartley, A. A., & McKenzie, C. R. (1991). Attentional and perceptual contributions to the identification of extrafoveal stimuli: Adult age comparisons. *Journal of Gerontology*, *46*, 202−206.

Hassan, S. E., Turano, K. A., Muñoz, B., Munro, C., Roche, K. B., & West, S. K. (2008). Cognitive and vision loss affects the topography of the attentional visual field. *Investigative Ophthalmology & Visual Science*, *49*, 4672−4678.

Hawkins, H. L., Kramer, A. F., & Capaldi, D. (1992). Aging, exercise, and attention. *Psychology and Aging*, *7*(4), 643−653.

Hawley, L. M., & Dunne, C. A. (2003). Driving with rheumatoid arthritis, no problem! Or is it? *Rheumatology*, *42*, 21−22.

Heart, T., & Kalderon, E. (2011). Older adults: Are they ready to adopt health-related ICT? *International Journal of Medical Informatics*, *82*, e209−e231. Available from http://dx.doi.org/10.1016/j.ijmedinf.2011.03.002.

Helmick, C. G., Felson, D. T., Lawrence, R. C., Gabriel, S., Hirsch, R., Kwoh, C. K., ... Pillemer, S. R. (2008). Estimates of the prevalence of arthritis and other rheumatic conditions in the United States: Part I. *Arthritis & Rheumatism*, *58*(1), 15−25.

Ho, C., Reed, N., & Spence, C. (2007). Multisensory in-car warning signals for collision avoidance. *Human Factors*, *49*(6), 1107−1114.

Hoffman, L., McDowd, J. M., Atchley, P., & Dubinsky, R. (2005). The role of visual attention in predicting driving impairment in older adults. *Psychology and Aging*, *20*(4), 610−622.

Hoffman, L., Yang, X., Bovaird, J. A., & Embretson, S. E. (2006). Measuring attentional ability in older adults development and psychometric evaluation of driver scan. *Educational and Psychological Measurement*, *66*(6), 984−1000.

Hofstetter, H. W. (1976). Visual acuity and highway accidents. *Journal of the American Optometric Association*, *47*(7), 887−893.

Horberry, T., Anderson, J., Regan, M. A., Triggs, T. J., & Brown, J. (2006). Driver distraction: The effects of concurrent in-vehicle tasks, road environment complexity and age on driving performance. *Accident Analysis & Prevention*, *38*(1), 185−191.

Hu, P. S., Trumble, D. A., Foley, D. J., Eberhard, J. W., & Wallace, R. B. (1998). Crash risks of older drivers: A panel data analysis. *Accident Analysis & Prevention*, *30*(5), 569−581.

Ivers, R. Q., Mitchell, P., & Cumming, R. G. (1999). Sensory impairment and driving: The Blue Mountains Eye Study. *American Journal of Public Health*, *89*(1), 85−87.

James, W. (1890). *The principles of psychology*. New York: Henry Holt & Company.

Janke, M.K. (1994). *Age-related disabilities that may impair driving and their assessment: Literature review*. Report No. RSS-94-156. Sacramento, CA: California Department of Motor Vehicles.

Jones, J. G., McCann, J., & Lassere, M. N. (1991). Driving and arthritis. *Rheumatology, 30*(5), 361–364.

Kaber, D., Zhang, Y., Jin, S., Mosaly, P., & Garner, M. (2012). Effects of hazard exposure and roadway complexity on young and older driver situation awareness and performance. *Transportation Research Part F: Traffic Psychology and Behaviour, 15*, 600–611.

Keeffe, J. E., Jin, C. F., Weih, L. M., McCarty, C. A., & Taylor, H. R. (2002). Vision impairment and older drivers: Who's driving? *British Journal of Ophthalmology, 86* (10), 1118–1121.

Körber, M., Gold, C., Lechner, D., & Bengler, K. (2016). The influence of age on the take-over of vehicle control in highly automated driving. *Transportation Research Part F: Traffic Psychology and Behaviour, 39*, 19–32.

Kramer, A. F., Fabiani, M., & Colcombe, S. J. (2006). Contributions of cognitive neuroscience to the understanding of behavior and aging. In J. E. Birren, K. W. Schaie, R. P. Abeles, M. Gatz, & T. A. Salthouse (Eds.), *Handbook of the psychology of aging* (6th ed.). Amsterdam: Elsevier Inc.

Kramer, A. F., Hahn, S., Irwin, D. E., & Theeuwes, J. (2000). Age differences in the control of looking behavior: Do you know where your eyes have been? *Psychological Science, 11*, 210–217.

Kua, A., Korner-Bitensky, N., Desrosiers, J., Man-Son-Hing, M., & Marshall, S. (2007). Older driver retraining: A systematic review of evidence of effectiveness. *Journal of Safety Research, 38*(1), 81–90.

Lam, L. T. (2002). Distractions and the risk of car crash injury: The effect of drivers' age. *Journal of Safety Research, 33*(3), 411–419.

Lamble, D., Rajalin, S., & Summala, H. (2002). Mobile phone use while driving: Public opinions on restrictions. *Transportation, 29*(3), 223–236.

Langford, J., Koppel, S., McCarthy, D., & Srinivasan, S. (2008). In defence of the 'low-mileage bias'. *Accident Analysis & Prevention, 40*(6), 1996–1999.

Lavallière, M., Reimer, B., Mehler, B., D'Ambrosio, L., Wang, Y., Teasdale, N., & Coughlin, J.F. (2011). The effect of age and gender on visual search during lane changing. In *Proceedings of the 6th international driving symposium on human factors in driver assessment, training, and vehicle design* (pp. 621–628).

Li, G., Braver, E. R., & Chen, L. H. (2003). Fragility versus excessive crash involvement as determinants of high death rates per vehicle-mile of travel among older drivers. *Accident Analysis & Prevention, 35*(2), 227–235.

Li, H. J., Hou, X. H., Liu, H. H., Yue, C. L., Lu, G. M., & Zuo, X. N. (2015). Putting age-related task activation into large-scale brain networks: A meta-analysis of 114 fMRI studies on healthy aging. *Neuroscience & Biobehavioral Reviews, 57*, 156–174.

Liessma, M. (1975). *The influence of a driver's vision in relation to his driving. Proceedings of the first international congress on vision and road safety* (pp. 31–34). Stockholm: LA Prevention Routiere Internationale.

Li-Korotky, H. S. (2012). Age-related hearing loss: Quality of care for quality of life. *The Gerontologist, 52*(2), 265–271.

Lin, F. R., Thorpe, R., Gordon-Salant, S., & Ferrucci, L. (2011). Hearing loss prevalence and risk factors among older adults in the United States. *The Journals of Gerontology Series A: Biological Sciences and Medical Sciences, 66*(5), 582–590.

Lui, C. W., Everingham, J. A., Warburton, J., Cuthill, M., & Bartlett, H. (2009). What makes a community age-friendly: A review of international literature. *Australasian Journal on Ageing*, *28*(3), 116−121.

Lundberg, C., Hakamies-Blomqvist, L., Almkvist, O., & Johansson, K. (1998). Impairments of some cognitive functions are common in crash-involved older drivers. *Accident Analysis & Prevention*, *30*(3), 371−377.

Lyman, S., Ferguson, S. A., Braver, E. R., & Williams, A. F. (2002). Older driver involvements in police reported crashes and fatal crashes: Trends and projections. *Injury Prevention*, *8*(2), 116−120.

Madden, D. J., & Gottlob, L. R. (1997). Adult age differences in strategic and dynamic components of focusing visual attention. *Aging, Neuropsychology, and Cognition*, *4*, 185−210.

Madden, D. J., Whiting, W. L., & Huettel, S. A. (2005). Age-related changes in neural activity during visual perception and attention. In R. Cabeza, L. Nyberg, & D. Park (Eds.), *Cognitive neuroscience of aging: Linking cognitive and cerebral aging* (pp. 157−185). New York: Oxford University Press.

Mahoney, J. R., Verghese, J., Dumas, K., Wang, C., & Holtzer, R. (2012). The effect of multisensory cues on attention in aging. *Brain Research*, *1472*, 63−73.

Malfetti, J. W. (1985). *Needs and problems of older drivers: Survey results and recommendations*. Falls Church, VA: AAA Foundation for Traffic Safety.

Margolis, K. L., Kerani, R. P., McGovern, P., Songer, T., Cauley, J. A., & Ensrud, K. E. (2002). Risk factors for motor vehicle crashes in older women. *The Journals of Gerontology Series A: Biological Sciences and Medical Sciences*, *57*(3), 186−191.

Marmeleira, J. F., Godinho, M. B., & Fernandes, O. M. (2009). The effects of an exercise program on several abilities associated with driving performance in older adults. *Accident Analysis & Prevention*, *41*(1), 90−97.

Marottoli, R. A., Allore, H., Araujo, K. L., Iannone, L. P., Acampora, D., Gottschalk, M., ... Peduzzi, P. (2007). A randomized trial of a physical conditioning program to enhance the driving performance of older persons. *Journal of General Internal Medicine*, *22*(5), 590−597.

Marottoli, R. A., Richardson, E. D., Stowe, M. H., Miller, E. G., Brass, L. M., Cooney, L. M., Jr., & Tinetti, M. E. (1998). Development of a test battery to identify older drivers at risk for self-reported adverse driving events. *American Geriatrics Society Journal*, *46*, 562−568.

Maryland Department of Transportation Motor Vehicle Administration. (n.d.). *What is a functional capacity test (FCT) screening?* Retrieved from <http://www.mva.maryland. gov/safety/older/fct-screening.htm>.

Mathias, J. L., & Lucas, L. K. (2009). Cognitive predictors of unsafe driving in older drivers: A meta-analysis. *International Psychogeriatrics*, *21*(04), 637−653.

McCarthy, D. P., & Mann, W. C. (2006). Sensitivity and specificity of the American Medical Association's Assessment of Driving-Related Skills (ADReS). *Topics in Geriatric Rehabilitation*, *22*, 139−152.

McDaniel, M. A., Einstein, G. O., & Jacoby, L. L. (2008). In F. I. M. Craik, & T. A. Salthouse (Eds.), *The handbook of aging and cognition* (3rd ed., pp. 251−310). New York: Psychology Press.

McDowd, J. M., & Craik, F. I. (1988). Effects of aging and task difficulty on divided attention performance. *Journal of Experimental Psychology: Human Perception and Performance*, *14*(2), 267.

McGwin, G., Sims, R. V., Pulley, L., & Roseman, J. M. (2000). Relations among chronic medical conditions, medications, and automobile crashes in the elderly: A population-based case-control study. *American Journal of Epidemiology, 152*(5), 424–431.

McKnight, A. J., & McKnight, A. S. (1999). Multivariate analysis of age-related driver ability and performance deficits. *Accident Analysis & Prevention, 31*(5), 445–454.

Miller, D., Johns, M., Ive, H. P., Gowda, N., Sirkin, D., Sibi, S., … Ju, W. (2016). Exploring transitional automation with new and old drivers. *SAE Technical Paper 2016-01-1442.* Available from http://dx.doi.org/10.4271/2016-01-1442.

Molnar, L. J., Charlton, J. L., Eby, D. W., Langford, J., Koppel, S., Kolenic, G. E., & Marshall, S. (2014). Factors affecting self-regulatory driving practices among older adults. *Traffic Injury Prevention, 15*(3), 262–272.

Molnar, L. J., & Eby, D. W. (2008). The relationship between self-regulation and driving-related abilities in older drivers: An exploratory study. *Traffic Injury Prevention, 9*(4), 314–319.

Moták, L., Gabaude, C., Bougeant, J. C., & Huet, N. (2014). Comparison of driving avoidance and self-regulatory patterns in younger and older drivers. *Transportation Research Part F: Traffic Psychology and Behaviour, 26*(Part A), 18–27.

Mulwa, C., Lawless, S., Sharp, M., Arnedillo-Sanchez, I., & Wade, V. (2010). *Adaptive educational hypermedia systems in technology enhanced learning: A literature review. Proceedings of the 2010 ACM conference on information technology education* (pp. 73–84). ACM.

Munoz, D. P., Broughton, J. R., Goldring, J. E., & Armstrong, I. T. (1998). Age-related performance of human subjects on saccadic eye movement tasks. *Experimental Brain Research, 121*, 391–400.

Nasvadi, G. E., & Vavrik, J. (2007). Crash risk of older drivers after attending a mature driver education program. *Accident Analysis & Prevention, 39*(6), 1073–1079.

National Highway Traffic Safety Administration. (n.d.). *Driving safely while aging gracefully.* Retrieved from <http://www.nhtsa.dot.gov/people/injury/olddrive/driving%20safely%20aging%20web/>.

National Safety Council. (2015). *MyCarDoesWhat.org.* Retrieved from <https://mycardoeswhat.org>.

National Safety Council. (2017). *CarTech VR360 (smartphone app).* Retrieved from <https://appadvice.com/app/cartech-vr360/1200913564>.

Odenheimer, G. L., Beaudet, M., Jette, A. M., Albert, M. S., Grande, L., & Minaker, K. L. (1994). Performance-based driving evaluation of the elderly driver: Safety, reliability, and validity. *Journal of Gerontology, 49*(4), 153–159.

Ott, B. R., Davis, J. D., Papandonatos, G. D., Hewitt, S., Festa, E. K., Heindel, W. C., … Carr, D. B. (2013). Assessment of driving-related skills prediction of unsafe driving in older adults in the office setting. *Journal of the American Geriatrics Society, 61*(7), 1164–1169.

Owsley, C. (1994). Vision and driving in the elderly. *Optometry and Vision Sciences, 71*, 727–735.

Owsley, C., Ball, K., & Keeton, D. M. (1995). Relationship between visual sensitivity and target localization in older adults. *Vision Research, 35*, 579–587.

Owsley, C., Ball, K., Sloane, M. E., Roenker, D. L., & Bruni, J. R. (1991). Visual/cognitive correlates of vehicle accidents in older drivers. *Psychology and Aging, 6*(3), 403–415.

Owsley, C., & McGwin, G. (1999). Vision impairment and driving. *Survey of Ophthalmology, 43*(6), 535–550.

Owsley, C., Stalvey, B. T., & Phillips, J. M. (2003). The efficacy of an educational intervention in promoting self-regulation among high-risk older drivers. *Accident Analysis & Prevention, 35*(3), 393–400.

Peek, S. T., Luijkx, K. G., Rijnaard, M. D., Nieboer, M. E., van der Voort, C. S., Aarts, S., ... Wouters, E. J. (2015). Older adults' reasons for using technology while aging in place. *Gerontology, 62*(2), 226–237.

Reason, J., Manstead, A., Stradling, S., Baxter, J., & Campbell, K. (1990). Errors and violations on the roads: A real distinction? *Ergonomics, 33*(10–11), 1315–1332.

Reimer, B., D'Ambrosio, L. a, Gilbert, J., Coughlin, J. F., Biederman, J., Surman, C., ... Aleardi, M. (2005). Behavior differences in drivers with attention deficit hyperactivity disorder: The driving behavior questionnaire. *Accident Analysis and Prevention, 37*(6), 996–1004.

Retchin, S. M., & Anapolle, J. (1993). An overview of the older driver. *Clinics in Geriatric Medicine, 9*(2), 279–296.

Roenker, D. L., Cissell, G. M., Ball, K. K., Wadley, V. G., & Edwards, J. D. (2003). Speed-of-processing and driving simulator training result in improved driving performance. *Human Factors, 45*(2), 218–233.

Romoser, M. R., & Fisher, D. L. (2009). The effect of active versus passive training strategies on improving older drivers' scanning in intersections. *Human Factors, 51*(5), 652–668.

Rosano, C., Aizenstein, H. J., Studenski, S., & Newman, A. B. (2007). A regions-of-interest volumetric analysis of mobility limitations in community-dwelling older adults. *The Journals of Gerontology, Series A: Biological Sciences and Medical Sciences, 62*(9), 1048–1055.

Rosenbloom, S. (2009). Meeting transportation needs in an aging-friendly community. *Generations, 33*(2), 33–43.

Ryan, G. A., Legge, M., & Rosman, D. (1998). Age related changes in drivers' crash risk and crash type. *Accident Analysis & Prevention, 30*(3), 379–387.

SAE International. (2014). Taxonomy and definitions for terms related to on-road motor vehicle automated driving systems. J3016-201401.

Sall, R. J., Wright, T. J., & Boot, W. R. (2014). Driven to distraction? The effect of simulated red light running camera flashes on attention and oculomotor control. *Visual Cognition, 22*, 57–73. Available from http://dx.doi.org/10.1080/13506285.2013.873509.

Salthouse, T. A. (2005). Relations between cognitive abilities and measures of executive functioning. *Neuropsychology, 19*(4), 532–545.

Salthouse, T. A., & Ferrer-Caja, E. (2003). What needs to be explained to account for age-related effects on multiple cognitive variables? *Psychology and Aging, 18*(1), 91–110.

Sandell, J. H., & Peters, A. (2001). Effects of age on nerve fibers in the rhesus monkey optic nerve. *Journal of Comparative Neurology, 429*, 541–553.

Schneider, B. A., & Pichora-Fuller, M. K. (2000). Implications of perceptual deterioration for cognitive aging research. In F. I. M. Craik, & T. A. Salthouse (Eds.), *Handbook of aging and cognition* (2nd ed., pp. 155–219). Mahwah, NJ: Erlbaum.

Schoettle, B., & Sivak, M. (2014). *A survey of public opinion about autonomous and self-driving vehicles in the U.S., the U. K., and Australia.* The University of Michigan Transportation Research Institute. Report No. UMTRI-2014-21.

Sekuler, A. B., Bennett, P., & Mamelak, M. (2000). Effects of aging on the useful field of view. *Experimental Aging Research, 26*, 103–120.

Sekuler, R., McLaughlin, C., & Yotsumoto, Y. (2008). Age-related changes in attentional tracking of multiple moving objects. *Perception, 37*, 867–876.

Shaheen, S.A., Cano, L.A., & Camel, M.L. (2013). Electric vehicle carsharing in a senior adult community in San Francisco Bay area. In: *Transportation research board 92nd annual meeting* (No. 13-4491), Washington, DC.

Sims, R. V., McGwin, G., Jr, Allman, R. M., Ball, K., & Owsley, C. (2000). Exploratory study of incident vehicle crashes among older drivers. *Journals of Gerontology, Series A: Biological Sciences and Medical Sciences, 55*(1), 22−27.

Somberg, B. L., & Salthouse, T. A. (1982). Divided attention abilities in young and old adults. *Journal of Experimental Psychology: Human Perception and Performance, 8*(5), 651−653.

Spear, P. D. (1993). Neural bases of visual deficits during aging. *Vision Research, 33*(18), 2589−2609.

Spence, C., & Ho, C. (2008). Multisensory warning signals for event perception and safe driving. *Theoretical Issues in Ergonomics Science, 9*(6), 523−554.

Spence, I., & Feng, J. (2010). Video games and spatial cognition. *Review of General Psychology, 14*(2), 92−104.

Staplin, L., Lococo, K. H., Martell, C., & Stutts, J. (2012). *Taxonomy of older driver behaviors and crash risk*. Washington, DC: U.S. Department of Transportation, DOT HS 811 468A.

Steels, S. (2015). Key characteristics of age-friendly cities and communities: A review. *Cities, 47*, 45−52.

Strayer, D. L., & Drew, F. A. (2004). Profiles in driver distraction: Effects of cell phone conversations on younger and older drivers. *Human Factors, 46*(4), 640−649.

Stutts, J. C., Stewart, J. R., & Martell, C. (1998). Cognitive test performance and crash risk in an older driver population. *Accident Analysis & Prevention, 30*(3), 337−346.

Sun, Y., Wu, S., & Spence, I. (2015). The commingled division of visual attention. *PLoS One, 10*(6), e0130611. Available from http://dx.doi.org/10.1371/journal.pone.0130611.

Szlyk, J. P., Myers, L., Zhang, Y. X., Wetzel, L., & Shapiro, R. (2002). Development and assessment of a neuropsychological battery to aid in predicting driving performance. *Journal of Rehabilitation Research and Development, 39*(4), 483−496.

Tefft, B. C. (2014). Driver license renewal policies and fatal crash involvement rates of older drivers, United States, 1986−2011. *Injury Epidemiology, 1*(25), 1−11.

Trezise, I., Stoney, E. G., Bishop, B., Eren, J., Harkness, A., Langdon, C., & Mulder, T. (2006). Report of the road safety committee on the inquiry into driver distraction *(Rep. No. 209)*. Melbourne, VIC: Road Safety Committee, Parliament.

Trick, L. M., Perl, T., & Sethi, N. (2005). Age-related differences in multiple-object tracking. *Journals of Gerontology, Series B: Psychological Sciences and Social Sciences, 60*, 102−105.

Trick, L. M., Toxopeus, R., & Wilson, D. (2010). The effects of visibility conditions, traffic density, and navigational challenge on speed compensation and driving performance in older adults. *Accident Analysis and Prevention, 42*(6), 1661−1671.

Tsang, P. S., & Shaner, T. L. (1998). Age, attention, expertise, and time-sharing performance. *Psychology and Aging, 13*(2), 323−347.

Vrkljan, B. H., Cranney, A., Worswick, J., O'Donnell, S., Li, L. C., Gélinas, I., ... Marshall, S. (2010). Supporting safe driving with arthritis: Developing a driving toolkit for clinical practice and consumer use. *American Journal of Occupational Therapy, 64*(2), 259−267.

Vrkljan, B. H., McGrath, C. E., & Letts, L. J. (2011). Assessment tools for evaluating fitness to drive: A critical appraisal of evidence. *Canadian Journal of Occupational Therapy, 78*(2), 80−96.

Wahl, H. W., & Heyl, V. (2003). Connections between vision, hearing, and cognitive function in old age. *Generations*, *27*(1), 39−45.

Warth, L. (2016). The WHO global network of age-friendly cities and communities: Origins, developments and challenges. In T. Moulaert, & S. Garon (Eds.), *Age-friendly cities and communities in international comparison: Political lessons, scientific avenues, and democratic issues* (pp. 37−46). New York: Springer International Publishing.

West, S. K., Hahn, D. V., Baldwin, K. C., Duncan, D. D., Munoz, B. E., Turano, K. A., … Bandeen-Roche, K. (2010). Older drivers and failure to stop at red lights. *Journal of Gerontology: Biological Sciences & Medical Sciences*, *65A*, 179−183.

Wilschut, E.S., Kroon, E.C.M., de Goede, M., Cremers, A., & Hoedemaeker, M. (2014). The older adult road user: Recommendations for driver assistance. In *International interdisciplinary conference "Ageing and Safe Mobility" held at the Federal Highway Research Institute (BASt) in Bergisch Gladbach* (pp. 1−10).

World Health Organization. (2007). *Global age-friendly cities: A guide*. Retrieved from <http://www.who.int/ageing/age_friendly_cities_guide/en/>.

Wright, T. J., Vitale, T., Boot, W. R., & Charness, N. (2015). The impact of red light running camera flashes on younger and older drivers' attention and oculomotor control. *Psychology and Aging*, *30*(4), 755−767.

Young, K., Regan, M., & Hammer, M. (2007). Driver distraction: A review of the literature. In I. J. Faulks, M. Regan, M. Stevenson, J. Brown, A. Porter, & J. D. Irwin (Eds.), *Distracted driving* (pp. 379−405). Sydney, NSW: Australasian College of Road Safety.

Zanto, T. P., & Gazzaley, A. (2014). Attention and ageing. In A. C. Nobre, & S. Kastner (Eds.), *The oxford handbook of attention* (pp. 927−971). New York: Oxford University Press.

Zmud, J., Ecola, L., Phleps, P., & Feige, I. (2013). *The future of mobility: Scenarios for the United States in 2030*. Santa Monica, CA: RAND Corporation.

Technological supports to increase nature contact for older adults

Dina Battisto, Ellen Vincent and Cheryl J. Dye
Clemson University, Clemson, SC, United States

Introduction

Maintaining an older adult's health is crucial to achieving a high quality of life. However, as older adults age, many face issues that compromise their health. Consequently, ongoing efforts focus on seeking ways to promote individual health particularly with advancing age. One strategy that has consistently been effective on health promotion for people of all ages is connections to natural elements such as trees, grass, water, and living animals. Nature has shown to have therapeutic benefits dating back to ancient times with mounting evidence proving it is a positive stimulus that promotes health. However, as health declines due to advancing age, it is not always practical or safe to venture outdoors to immerse oneself in the natural environment. Therefore, the premise of this chapter is that the use of technology to evoke a positive health effect (a technological support) is effective for connecting older adults to natural environments. The focus of many of these emerging technological supports is to help maintain health and a high quality of life. This emerging field is showing promise by simulating natural landscapes such as nature scenes of landscapes into the built environment for therapeutic purposes. Technological supports are useful when immersion in, and access to, nature is not possible due to reasons such as safety concerns and physical limitations. Technological supports that connect older adults to nature are vehicles to promote healthy lifestyles and quality of life in various ways. Firstly, technological supports encourage physical functioning and physical activity as well as aiding pain management and stress reduction. Secondly, technological supports boost cognitive functioning through exposure to multisensory stimulation and lifelong learning and entertainment opportunities. Finally, technological supports facilitate social connectedness with family and friends, which enhances cognitive and physical activity, emotional health, and enjoyment. In summary, the potential for connecting people to natural environments using various technological innovations is possible while the simulations are becoming more realistic. However, the verdict is still out as to whether virtual landscapes provide the same therapeutic benefits as actually immersing oneself in a natural environment.

This chapter is organized into three main sections. The first section argues that promoting health is essential for the growing number of older adults to maintain a high quality of life. Next, the second section makes the case that natural environments are therapeutic, and simulating landscapes using technological supports has

Aging, Technology and Health. DOI: http://dx.doi.org/10.1016/B978-0-12-811272-4.00005-1

the potential to promote the health of older adults. Finally, in the last section, examples of technological supports connecting older adults to nature are discussed. More specifically, innovations in simulations, virtual environments (VEs) and interactive screens are being studied and integrated into built environments showing positive benefits for health promotion.

Promoting health is essential for older adults to maintain a high quality of life

In the first section, the context of the chapter is discussed, particularly the implications of the growth of the aging population. Older adults face many challenges with maintaining health and healthy lifestyles, both of which are prerequisites to achieving a higher quality of life.

Growth of the aging population and challenges to maintaining health

The United States, similar to many other parts of the world, is experiencing an increase in the older population due to population growth, an increase in life expectancy and a decline in mortality rates. According to the US Department of Health and Human Services, in 2015 one in seven Americans was over 65 years of age representing about 14.9% of the population and this percentage is expected to increase at a staggering rate. The US Census Bureau predicts that the 65 + population will grow to represent almost 22% of the overall population by 2040 as shown in Fig. 5.1 (Administration on Aging, Administration for Community Living, US Department of Health, & Human Services, 2016). This growth pattern is presenting challenges since older adults desire to have a high quality of life up until the end of life. Despite this desire, older adults often face many challenges in maintaining a high quality of life influenced by the interrelated factors contributing to the health of an older adult.

Health is a multidimensional concept influenced by many intrinsic and extrinsic factors. According to the World Health Organization's original and unchanged definition of health since 1948, health is a "complete state of physical, mental and social well-being and not merely the absence of disease or infirmity" (World Health Organization, 2017). As such, there are multiple dimensions contributing to the ever-changing state of one's health. Fig. 5.2 shows that health has various levels and operates as a dynamic continuum ranging from optimum health to approaching death. The status of one's health influences one's needs, capabilities, and resources, which often compromise choices such as whether or not a person can remain at home independently.

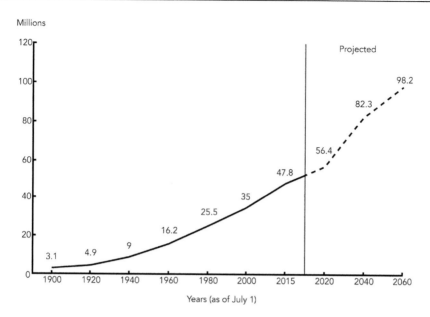

Millions

Figure 5.1 Number of persons 65+: 1900–2060 (numbers in millions).
From Administration on Aging, Administration for Community Living, U.S. Department of
Health and Human Services. (2016). *Profile of older Americans.* Retrieved from Administration
for Community Living <https://aoa.acl.gov/aging_statistics/profile/index.aspx>.

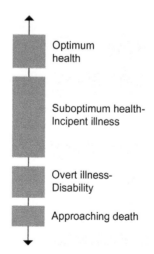

Figure 5.2 Levels of health.
From Fanshel, S., & Bush, J. W. (1970). A health-status index and its application to health-
services outcomes. *Operations Research, 18*(6), 1021–1066. doi:10.1287/opre.18.6.1021.

Over 87% of older adults want to continue to live independently in their homes and communities as they age, yet the preference to live at home is often not possible due to the gradual decline in an older adult's health as they age (Farber, Shinkle, Lynott, Fox-Grage, & Harrell, 2011). It is estimated that, at least 90% of the growing population of those 65+ will have one or more chronic conditions, while at the same time, the population of professional and informal caregivers is declining (The Schmieding Center for Senior Health and Education, The International Longevity Center-USA, n.d.). To achieve the desire to live independently and retain quality of life, older adults must maintain their physical, mental, and social health as they age. Therefore, the question explored in this chapter is: Can technologies be used to promote health among older adults? One area that is showing promise is using technology to gain access to nature, because humans have innate tendencies to seek connections with nature and various life forms (Wilson, 1984).

Quality of life indicators for older adults

Health is a significant indicator of quality of life for older adults. The WHO defines quality of life as "individuals' perception of their position in life in the context of the culture and value systems in which they live and in relation to their goals, expectations, standards, and concerns" (The WHOQOL Group, 1995). As stated previously, goals, expectations, standards, and concerns for older adults include independent living as they age which is enhanced by physical and mental health, emotional well-being, and social functioning (Baernholdt, Hinton, Yan, Rose, & Mattos, 2012). Quality of life is frequently measured using the Quality of Life Index which is a generic satisfaction with life tool that accounts for individual's reactions to four life domains: Health and functioning, socioeconomic, psychological/spiritual, and family (Levasseur, Desrosiers, & Tribble, 2008).

Health as a concept has evolved over time into a multidimensional concept that encompasses various interrelated dimensions as shown in Fig. 5.3. Scientists generally recognize five factors or determinants of health. The first determinant is genes and biological factors such as sex and age. The second determinant is health behaviors such as physical activity, eating habits, smoking, and alcohol use. Third, one's social environment or social characteristics such as income, gender, and family composition, which influence an individual's health. The fourth factor that influences one's health is the total ecology or physical environment that an individual inhabits, such as where a person lives and works, community characteristics and natural resources. Finally, access to medical care and quality healthcare services influence an individual's health. While it has been debatable on the exact factors and percentages that influence one's health, there has been some consistency in these five determinants of health (Schroeder, 2017; Tarlov, 1999).

Initiatives focused on advocating for the role of healthy communities and healthy cities have long argued that the built and natural environment a person occupies

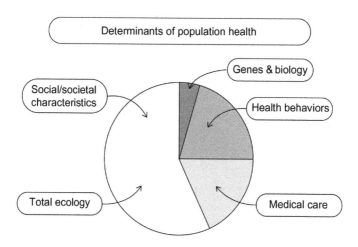

Figure 5.3 Determinants of health.
From Tarlov, A. R. (1999). Public policy framework for improving population health. *Annals of the New York Academy of Sciences, 896,* 281–293. doi:10.1111/j.1749-6632.1999. tb08123.x.

influences his or her health. Proponents of this mindset believe that, "Health encompasses not just the absence of disease, but the full range of quality of life issues, including lifestyle and behavioral choices, genetic endowment, and the socioeconomic, cultural and physical environment. Health is a byproduct of a wide array of choices and factors—not simply the result of medical intervention" (Norris & Pittman, 2000).

This expanded view of health builds upon several research studies. For example, Lawton, Windley, and Byerts (1982) and Lawton (1983a, 1983b). Dr. Powell Lawton, a highly respected researcher who was a strong advocate for the needs of the elderly, found several components linked to the quality of life. He concluded six components of quality of life as follows: (1) Psychological well-being including mental health status, cognitive judgements of life satisfaction, positive–negative emotions, and positive outlook; (2) external, objective, and physical environment such as housing and neighborhood resources; (3) adequate financial circumstances; (4) health and functioning; (5) social relationships; and (6) leisure activities. He also found that independent living was especially important. In another study, Bowling, Banister, Sutton, Evans, and Windsor (2002) found that independent predictors of self-rated global quality of life included: Social comparisons and expectations, personality and psychological characteristics (optimism–pessimism), health and functional status, and person and neighborhood social capital. Additionally, Barton and Grant (2006) expanded on the determinants of health and well-being to include the neighborhood/community, built, and natural environment (see Fig. 5.4). As more research unfolds, there is increasing evidence showing that environmental conditions (built and natural environments) are contributing factors to health and quality of life.

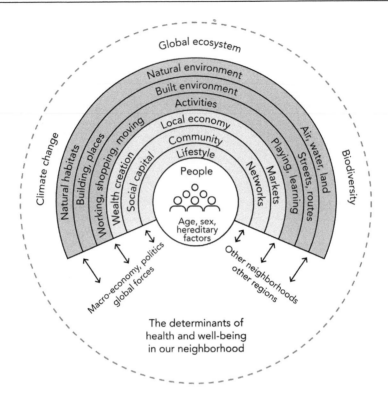

Figure 5.4 Determinants of health and well-being in our neighborhoods.
Adapted from Barton, H., & Grant, M. (2006). A health map for the local human habitat. *The Journal for the Royal Society for the Promotion of Health*, *126*(6), 252–253. doi:10.1177/1466424006070466.

Thus, the dimensions of health have expanded over time as well as the interconnectedness and relationships across all of the dimensions as noted in numerous studies. For example, the 2005–2006 National Health and Nutrition Examination Survey (NHANES) survey data (*n* = 911) collected from Americans 60 years and older revealed that physical functioning, specifically activities of daily living (ADLs), was associated with physical and mental health, emotional well-being, and social functioning (Baernholdt et al., 2012). Likewise, the study showed that physical activity was related to social functioning, and that healthcare utilization was linked to emotional well-being. In another study, Levasseur et al. (2008) found that older adults' quality of life decreased according to activity limitations. However, they agree with other researchers that adaptation to activity limitations has more influence on quality of life than activity limitations by themselves.

Still other studies show the role of social connections in maintaining a quality of life. In a secondary data analysis of the English Longitudinal Study of Ageing, which included 4848 adults over age 50 years living in England, findings revealed that becoming depressed and developing difficulties with ADLs contributed to decreases in quality of life. Conversely, the study showed that improvements in family relationships, the neighborhood, and perceived financial position all counteracted the decline in quality of life. Therefore, the authors concluded that the maintenance of good quality of life in older adults is necessary to avoid depression, maintain physical functioning, and enjoy good family relationships, financial stability, and high-quality neighborhoods (Webb, Blane, McMunn, & Netuveli, 2011).

Promoting healthy lifestyles and health-promoting behaviors are essential requirements for older adults to have a high quality of life, yet many factors have moderating effects on each other. In regards to lifestyle, The Baltimore Longitudinal Study of Aging (BLSA), which began in 1958, has revealed that exercise, healthy eating and social activities are cornerstones to healthy aging (National Institute on Aging, National Institutes of Health, US Department of Health & Human Services, 2010). People who exercise regularly live longer and have better quality of life because of enhanced physical and cognitive functioning, reduced risk of falls, and reduced risk for diseases such as cardiovascular disease and osteoporosis. Exercise is also an effective treatment for several chronic conditions such as arthritis, high blood pressure, or diabetes. In addition to exercise and healthy eating, people who volunteer and are sociable, generous, and goal-oriented, report higher levels of happiness and lower levels of depressions than others. Involvement in hobbies, social, and leisure activities enhance longevity and reduce risk for dementia. Due to this and other evidence, there has been increasing emphasis in seeking ways older adults can increase physical activity, the promotion of healthy lifestyles and social connectedness with families and friends.

Technology supports for quality of life

Technology is a promising vehicle for promoting health and quality of life. In fact, technology has been applied to various applications to enhance an older adult's ability to enjoy a high quality of life by facilitating a healthy lifestyle, social connections, and access to needed services. Technology has equipped healthcare professionals and informal caregivers to more effectively meet the needs of their patients and care recipients. According to the 2014 report update of "The New Era of Connected Aging: A Framework for Understanding Technologies that Support Older Adults in Aging" emerging technologies are enabling both older adults and their caregivers to meet medical, health, social, and functional needs (Center for Technology & Aging (CTA), Center for Information Technology Research in the Interest of Society (CITRIS), Public Health Institute (PHI), 2014). For example, older adults are monitoring their physiological and mental health status with body-worn sensors and activity monitors that offer automated coaching.

Using technological simulations, physical and cognitive health has been improved through games and training such as Lumosity.com, PositScience.com and Wii Fit. Technology has also been used to improve medication adherence with medication reminder alerts using interactive voice response, text messaging, or e-mail. Medication dispensers have been used to provide the correct dosage of medication at the right time. GPS navigation devices have been used to help caregivers of those with early dementia keep track of their location. Likewise, "Smart home" technologies are increasingly being used to monitor ADLs and generate alerts if activities appear abnormal or a fall is detected. Moreover, technology is being used to help healthcare providers through remote patient monitoring (RPM), care transitions, medication optimization, and mHealth tools (Center for Technology & Aging, 2014).

Perhaps one of the greatest benefits of technology is the ability to stay connected to family, friends, and communities. Loneliness has been shown to be a predictor of functional decline and death (Perissinotto, Cenzer, & Covinsky, 2012). Social communication technologies such as Skype, social networking through sites such as Facebook.com and Aarp.org/onlinecommunity, and increasing volunteer opportunities through SeniorCorps.org are being used to enhance social connectedness and reduce loneliness. While all of these various technologies are developing at breakneck speed, an untapped resource is the use of technologies to simulate the feeling of being outside in nature.

Natural environments are therapeutic

The second section of this chapter posits that natural environments have been linked to a wide array of health indicators and quality of life issues. The question explored in this section is whether technology can be an effective substitute to connect older adults to nature when actual immersion in nature is not possible. There is an increasing number of studies suggesting that various technologies are being used to simulate natural environments and nature. While it is still an emerging area of study, examples suggest that technologies simulating nature scenes and landscapes are positively influencing health and quality of life.

Health benefits of nature

While many factors influence health and quality of life, one aspect that is often overlooked is the role of natural environments and nature in promoting health. Nature's therapeutic benefits for people have a rich and ancient tradition. Ancient Greeks conducted pilgrimages to the Temples of Asclepius to experience healing dreams. The temples were often located in sheltered landscapes surrounded by hills and trees, with streams, pools of water, or mineral springs (Gesler, 2003). Roman baths were associated with health, well-being, and healing and often located at hot springs (Cunliffe, 1971). Likewise, medieval monastery gardens were frequently installed near hospital wards and recuperating patients were encouraged to stroll through the aromatic medicinal plants and shrubs (van den Berg, 2005). More recently, the restorative effects of nature have been studied scientifically which was

Figure 5.5 Modern day spas, Grove Park Inn Spa, Asheville, NC (left) and Mohonk Mountain House, New Paltz, NY (right).
Photos by Ellen Vincent.

captured in a landmark study published in *Science* in 1984. Dr. Roger Ulrich conducted a comparative analysis of 23 matched surgical patients where half of the patients were assigned to a view overlooking a nature scene out the patient room window and the other half assigned to view overlooking a brick building wall. Results found that patients overlooking the natural setting had shorter postoperative hospital stays, fewer complaints, and took fewer pain medications (Ulrich, 1984). The tradition of blending natural and built environments to foster healing and well-being continues today. Modern day spas, such as the renowned Grove Park Inn in Asheville, NC and Mohonk Mountain House in New Paltz, NY sport extensive views of stone, wood, gardens, and water as shown in Fig. 5.5. Elements of wood, stone, and "old" are used in these spas associated with restorative health benefits according to the survey research (Kaplan & Kaplan, 1989).

An increasing number of studies are showing that older adults' health and quality of life is being improved in various ways through contact with nature. For example, nature contact facilitates greater physical activity, lower perceived stress, and better recovery from surgery (Largo-Wight, 2011; Ulrich, Simons, Losito, & Zelson, 1991). There are multiple ways older adults can access nature. For example, interaction with plants, animals and landscape views can be achieved through outdoor contact, indoor contact or indirectly. It has also been shown that outdoor nature contact offers the most benefit perhaps because of the multisensory stimulation occurring from seeing, hearing, and smelling natural elements (Largo-Wight, 2011). Green and "blue" spaces (environments with running or still water) are especially beneficial for healthy aging. A study investigating the relationship of blue and green spaces, therapeutic landscapes, and well-being in later life revealed that features such as a koi pond or bench with a view of flowers promoted feelings of renewal, restoration, and spiritual connectedness as well as places for multigenerational social interactions and engagement (Global News Connect, 2015). "Green exercise" and walking in natural settings such as parks, as compared to walking in an urban environment, results in greater physiological stress recovery (see Fig. 5.6). Interaction with outdoor plants through horticulture therapy has also shown to have significant health benefits (Largo-Wight, 2011).

Two large-scale studies that link the health of seniors with exposure to green-space in the urban environment are noteworthy. In Tokyo, over 3000 people were surveyed during a five year period and the results showed that people lived longer if there was walkable greenspace near the person's residence, the streets were lined with trees, and if the person had chosen to live in that environment (Takano, Nakamura, & Watanabe, 2002). In another study conducted in the Netherlands, over 10,000 people's self-reported health data was combined with land-use data on proximate greenspace. Results indicated that people living in a green environment between 1 and 3km away were significantly healthier than those with less green-space. The effects were stronger for the elderly than for the sample population as a whole (de Vries, Verheij, Groenewegen, & Spreeuwenberg, 2003).

Building on this research is a concept called "forest bathing." In one project, "Forests and Human Health" launched by the European Co-operation in the Field of Scientific and Technical Research and the International Union of Forest Research Organizations, findings showed a positive impact of the forest environment for human health. Similarly, in many Asian countries, forest bathing, or spending extended time in a forest, is widely adopted by people. A study of young male forest bathers found that compared to those in an urban environment, they experienced stress reduction

Figure 5.6 Labyrinth at Mepkin Abbey, Monks Corner, SC.
Photo by Ellen Vincent.

mechanisms such as parasympathetic nervous system stimulation, reduction of cortisol, and reduction of pulse rate. Forest bathers also reported feelings of being soothed and refreshed, reported enhancement of positive mood states, and decreases in negative mood state compared with the urban environment subjects who experienced an increase in negative mood state (Lee et al., 2011).

Another pioneer in the field, Dr. Susan Rodiek has conducted multiple research studies and concluded that older adults who have outdoor nature contact enjoy better quality of life, improved recovery from illness, stimulated sensory perception, increased physical activity, increased social interactions, and an enhanced sense of self and well-being. She found that exposure to daylight had specific health benefits through increased levels of vitamin D, serotonin, and melatonin, improved hypertension management, hormone balance, sleep, mood, distraction from pain, as well as the reduction of reported pain and use of pain meds (Rodiek, 2009a). Daylight exposure has also been shown to be effective for regulating sleep-/wake-cycles, circadian cycle, and reducing incidence of Seasonal Affective Disorder. Dementia patients can have particular benefits from being outdoors as it helps elicit memories by stimulating senses, increasing brain plasticity, and reducing agitation (Rodiek, 2009b).

Indoor nature contact through interaction with plants, animals, or landscape views experienced inside of buildings also benefits the health of older adults. For example, animal-assisted therapy is a proven stress-reduction activity (Largo-Wight, 2011). Indirect nature contact, through viewing nature photography and art, or listening to recorded nature sounds has also been shown to benefit health (Frumkin, 2001; Largo-Wight, 2011). Finally, in a randomized study, Diette, Lechtzin, Haponik, Devrotes, and Rubin (2003) found that patients exposed to landscape photographs and recorded nature sounds reported a 43% increase in self-reported pain control compared to a randomized control group.

Technological supports connecting older adults to nature are showing promise as vehicles for health promotion

To conclude this chapter, this section argues that simulated natural environments using technological supports are advantageous for promoting health. Examples follow illustrating how various technological supports are showing promise for connecting older adults to nature through simulations, VEs, virtual reality (VR), and interactive screens.

Use of simulated natural environments to promote health

As technologies become more advanced, accessible and affordable, new applications are emerging in health promotion programs. Furthermore, technology is capable of reproducing high fidelity, realistic environments with multisensory enhancers. Thus, the question at hand is: Can technology make people feel like they are outdoors? Technology is proving to be effective for connecting people to natural environments through various applications such as simulations, VEs, and interactive screens. While immersion in real natural settings is known to be therapeutic as noted in the previous section, the question remains whether simulated natural environments are effective substitutes for the actual experience of being outdoors in nature (see Fig. 5.7).

While physical activity such as walking occurs naturally in well-designed green spaces, not everyone has access to safe walkable green areas. For example, people recovering from injuries, elders who are frail, and people who do not feel safe walking in their outdoor environments are ideal recipients of simulated therapeutic landscapes. In these cases, technology may be used to display therapeutic landscapes, which appear as art on the wall, images on a computer, phone, or exercise machine, and in video displays. Photographs have been found to be as effective as real immersive experiences in research studies and are often used to simulate nature indoors (Stamps, 1990).

However, how do people select images that promote health? Individual preference is always a good starting place, but for spaces that have shared clientele a more theory-based approach may be appropriate. In fact, not all images are equivalent and it is best to refer to research literature to identify the most appropriate images for a

Figure 5.7 Health benefits of nature through technological supports.
Photo by Dina Battisto.

specific population (Vincent, Battisto, Grimes, & McCubbin, 2010). Evolutionary theory provides an excellent starting point to understand how to select images. Evolutionary theory looks to history to understand humans' predisposition for specific landscapes (Appleton, 1996; Kaplan & Kaplan, 1989; Kellert & Wilson, 1993; Ulrich et al., 1991; Vincent et al., 2010). Appleton's prospect refuge theory of landscape preference is an evolutionary theory developed by studying historical landscape paintings that have been influential. Appleton's prospect refuge theory was used to select images for both a pilot project in a controlled setting as shown in Fig. 5.8 and a follow-up hospital study in upstate South Carolina. Appleton identified detailed categories of prospect, refuge, and hazard to describe landscape scenes. These categories, along with a mixed prospect and refuge category were used to guide the image selection process for a pilot study to understand which type of nature image was most therapeutic. Findings revealed that the mixed prospect and refuge scene significantly reduced sensory pain in participants who were subjected to a pain stressor (Vincent et al., 2010).

Prospect is an environmental condition, situation, object or arrangement that presents real or symbolic access to a view (Appleton, 1996). Elements that contribute to prospect include blue skies, low vegetative groundcover, and expansive viewing vantages, such as from high ground. Refuge in the landscape presents real or symbolic situations for hiding or sheltering. In comparison, refuge features in the landscape include dim light, and places to hide from inclement weather or threatening people. Low horizontal tree branches that are suitable for climbing are symbolic of

Figure 5.8 Nature images effect on pain research.
Photo by Ellen Vincent.

refuge. When equal amounts of prospect and refuge are visible in the landscape or image it is called mixed prospect refuge (Appleton, 1996; Vincent et al., 2010). Finally, hazard in the landscape present symbolic threats to life and well-being. Thunderstorms, thick thorns on vines or shrubs that prohibit movement, and forest fires are all examples of hazardous landscapes. Examples of these views are illustrated in Fig. 5.9.

Interestingly, the virtual environments (VEs) concept of *presence*, the ability to imagine oneself in the pictured landscape, of really being there in the image, surfaced in a hospital research study as being crucial to the selection of images for restorative health benefits (Ijsselsteijn & Giuseppe, 2003; de Kort, Meijnders, Sponselee, & IJsselsteijn, 2006). In a research experiment conducted in a hospital setting, images were clipped to surgery outpatient beds as well as mounted to post-surgery inpatients' walls. Post-surgery participant surveys revealed that images that exhibited high levels of presence were most effective for reducing pain (Vincent, 2015).

Virtual environments (VEs) are still in the developmental stage and will perhaps become a strong tool for restoration and health in the years to come. Medical virtual reality (VR) research is ongoing at University of Southern California-Institute for Creative Technologies to explore and discern how it can be used in the fields of psychology, medicine, neuroscience, physical and occupational therapy (USC Institute for Creative Technologies, 2017). In addition, VE are being used in the medical classroom to help students see human anatomy clearly (CBS News, 2017).

Figure 5.9 Natural landscapes capturing Appleton's Prospect Refuge Theory; (A) prospect (California); (B) refuge (Ireland); (C) prospect, refuge, mixed (England); (D) hazard (rock quarry in South Carolina).
Photos by Ellen Vincent.

Technological supports for increasing nature contact

Technological supports such as screens to display virtual landscape images, VR googles, and integrated technologies into the environment to simulate natural environments are helping older adults stay connected to nature. For example, videos of nature scenes and animals as well as virtual hikes can be viewed on YouTube, and wildlife can be observed in real time with wireless trail cameras. Watching videos of nature scenes and sounds has been shown to lower blood pressure and pulse rate compared to those who view daytime TV or videos of urban scenes and sounds (de Kort et al., 2006; Ulrich et al., 1991).

In one study, computers were used with 18 elderly research participants in a VE study in Spain (Banos, Quero, Etchemendy, & Botella, 2012). Two VE nature walks were designed to promote positive moods in the elderly. One walk symbolized joy while the other promoted relaxation. Elements of both environments involved walking on a path through a meadow under a blue sky, viewing a stone bridge, and listening to flowing water. The VE scenes created for the study were presented on a 21″ computer screen with integrated audio speakers, and large keyboard keys arranged in ABC order. This early study shows how adaptive technologies can be used to accommodate older people.

In another study, exercise bicycles with an attached interactive screen were used to display VEs at a retirement home in Denmark (Bruun-Pedersen, Pedersen, Serafin, & Kofoed, 2014). The VE was a summer-time countryside walk on a gravel path surrounding a lake. The visual scenes were displayed on a 46″ LED monitor and sounds were played through headphones. Fifteen participants pedaled while immersing themselves in the scene. Results indicated that the majority of the participants preferred bicycle exercising with the VEs, rather than the conventional way. Some reported exercising longer and with more excitement due to the access to nature scenes. This preliminary study indicates that adaptive technology coupled with virtual nature environments can stimulate physical activity and a positive mood for the elderly (see Fig. 5.10).

Taking simulated environments to a heightened experience level is through virtual reality (VR). For example, it has been shown that virtual reality (VR) goggles have tremendous potential to improve quality of life for older adults and those with dementia. Dr. Sonya Kim, Founder and CEO of One Caring Team, has developed a virtual reality (VR) program for the elderly that features nature images and sounds. Her company translated results of over 100 clinical research papers that reveal positive clinical outcomes using virtual reality (VR) in managing chronic pain, anxiety, and depression. The report included work by the Chronic Pain Research Institute found a virtual meditative nature walk helped users manage pain and stress (Platoni, 2016). Another startup called Rendever, established by graduate students at MIT, provides travel experiences to seniors using Google Maps footage and 360-degree films (Kelly-Barton, n.d.). In addition, at Aalborg University Copenhagen, VR landscapes are being used to encourage nursing home residents to use stationary bicycles (Aalborg University, 2016).

Figure 5.10 Nature scenes used for exercise.
Photo by Dina Battisto.

VR has unlimited applications for older adults. Dr. Marc Agronin, a geriatric psychiatrist at Miami Jewish Health Systems and author of "How We Age" and "The Dementia Caregiver: A guide to Caring for Some with Alzheimer's Disease and Other Neurocognitive Disorders," sees several applications of VR for older adults including simulating nature experiences. He cautions, however, that headsets must account for age-related changes in visual acuity and hearing loss, and should be integrated with existing glasses or hearing aids (see Fig. 5.11). He recommends the exploration of nonheadset forms of interface such as wearables on arms or wrists, and that design features must be familiar to older users such as the haptic and auditory feedback of buttons, knobs, and switches (Agronin, 2016). Dr. Sonya Kim is a physician and founder of One Caring Team, a company devoted to improving quality of life of older adults. One Caring Team incorporates research supporting use of VR in managing chronic pain, anxiety, and depression and has found VR googles to be effective with elderly including those with dementia. Challenges remain regarding the weight of the headsets and the cost, but One Caring Team continues to build VEs and to pursue business partners for help in overcoming VR challenges for older adults (Platoni, 2016).

Moving forward, technological supports are being seamlessly integrated within the physical environment. One example that demonstrates this is the Lantern at Chagrin, an assisted living and dementia care unit aimed to use environmental cues as therapeutic aids for residents with memory impairments. Informed by the tenets of biophilic architecture (Wilson, 1984), the memory care facility is organized

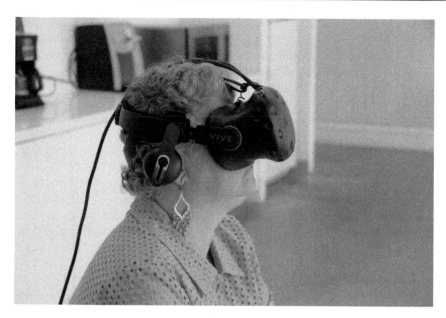

Figure 5.11 Virtual reality used to connect the elderly to nature.
Photo by Dina Battisto.

Figure 5.12 Lantern at Chagrin.
From Carter, M. (August 25, 2016). *This assisted living facility is designed to look like a small town from the 1940s*. Retrieved from CountryLiving <http://www.countryliving.com/life/a39630/nursing-home-tiny-houses/>.

around a large community courtyard that simulates an outdoor golf course lined by tiny houses representing the 1930s and 1940s era with front porches that overlook the golf course (see Fig. 5.12). To simulate grass for the golf course, there is green turf carpet and other parts of the floor are painted green. In the interior courtyard, a "sky ceiling" utilizes fiber optics that mimic daylight and nighttime skies corresponding to the time of the day. The simulated sky aims to regulate circadian system and regulate a person's biological clock to recognize day and night cycles. To reinforce the feeling of being outside, there are nature sounds with birds chirping to stimulate the feeling of being outdoors. Another environmental cue to reinforce the feeling of being outdoors are porch lights that come on at night (Carter, 2016).

In conclusion, opportunities to utilize technologies for connecting older adults to nature are increasing. The challenges will continue to be how to create high fidelity, realistic settings using technologies to substitute from actually going outside and immersing oneself in nature. Finally, developing technological interfaces, formats and controls that are affordable, age appropriate and easy to use, continues to be a challenge. Nevertheless, this appears to be a burgeoning field suitable for future research and new technological applications, and supports to seek ways to connect older adults to nature to promote health and encourage healthy lifestyles to ensure a high quality of life.

References

Aalborg University. (October 18, 2016). *Virtual experience gets the elderly to exercise.* Retrieved from ScienceDaily <https://www.sciencedaily.com/releases/2016/10/161018093824.htm>.

Administration on Aging, Administration for Community Living, US Department of Health and Human Services. (2016). *Profile of older Americans.* Retrieved from Administration for Community Living <https://aoa.acl.gov/aging_statistics/profile/index.aspx>.

Agronin, M. (March 21, 2016). *How virtual reality can enhance the life of older adults.* Retrieved from The Wall Street Journal <http://blogs.wsj.com/experts/2016/03/21/how-virtual-reality-can-enhance-the-life-of-older-adults/>.

Appleton, J. (1996). *The experience of landscape.* Chichester: John Wiley and Sons.

Baernholdt, M., Hinton, I., Yan, G., Rose, K., & Mattos, M. (April 2012). Factors associated with quality of life in older adults in the United States. *Quality of Life Research: An International Journal of Quality of Life Aspects of Treatment, Care, and Rehabilitation, 21*(3), 527–534. Available from http://dx.doi.org/10.1007/s11136-011-9954-z.

Banos, R. M., Quero, S., Etchemendy, E., & Botella, C. (2012). Positive mood induction procedures for virtual environments designed for elderly people. *Interacting with Computers, 24*(3), 131–138. Available from http://dx.doi.org/10.1016/j.intcom.2012.04.002.

Barton, H., & Grant, M. (2006). A health map for the local human habitat. *The Journal for the Royal Society for the Promotion of Health, 126*(6), 252–253. Available from http://dx.doi.org/10.1177/1466424006070466.

van den Berg, A. E. (2005). *Health impacts of healing environments: The architecture of hospitals.* Groningen: Foundation 200 Years University Hospital.

Bowling, A., Banister, D., Sutton, S., Evans, O., & Windsor, J. (2002). A multidimensional model of the quality of life in older age. *Aging & Mental Health, 6*(4), 355−371. Available from http://dx.doi.org/10.1080/1360786021000006983.

Bruun-Pedersen, J. R., Pedersen, K. S., Serafin, S., & Kofoed, L. (2014). Augmented exercise biking with virtual environments for elderly users: A preliminary study for retirement home physical therapy. *2014 2nd workshop on Virtual and Augmented Assistive Technology (VAAT)* (pp. 23−27). Minneapolis, MN: IEEE Press. Available from http://dx.doi.org/10.1109/VAAT.2014.6799464.

Carter, M. (August 25, 2016). *This assisted living facility is designed to look like a small town from the 1940s.* Retrieved from CountryLiving <http://www.countryliving.com/life/a39630/nursing-home-tiny-houses/>.

CBS News. (January 8, 2017). *Virtual reality check.* Retrieved from CBS News <http://www.cbsnews.com/news/virtual-reality-check/>.

Center for Technology and Aging. (2014). *Center for technology and aging.* Retrieved from Center for Technology and Aging <http://www.techandaging.org/>.

Center for Technology and Aging (CTA), Center for Information Technology Research in the Interest of Society (CITRIS), Public Health Institute (PHI) (2014). *The new era of connected aging: A framework for understanding technologies that support older adults in aging in place.* Berkeley, CA: CITRIS.

Cunliffe, B. (1971). *Roman bath discovered.* London: Routledge & Kegan Paul.

Diette, G. B., Lechtzin, N., Haponik, E., Devrotes, A., & Rubin, H. R. (March 2003). Distraction therapy with nature sights and sounds reduces pain during flexible bronchoscopy: A complementary approach to routine analgesia. *Chest, 123*(3), 941−948.

Farber, N., Shinkle, D., Lynott, J., Fox-Grage, W., & Harrell, R. (2011). *Aging in place: A state survey of livability policies and practices.* AARP Public Policy Institute, National Conference of State Legislatures. Washington, DC: AARP. Retrieved from <http://assets.aarp.org/rgcenter/ppi/liv-com/aging-in-place-2011-full.pdf>.

Fanshel, S., & Bush, J. W. (1970). A health-status index and its application to health-services outcomes. *Operations Research, 18*(6), 1021−1066. Available from http://dx.doi.org/10.1287/opre.18.6.1021.

Frumkin, H. (April 2001). Beyond toxicity: Human health and the natural environment. *American Journal of Preventive Medicine, 20*(3), 234−240.

Gesler, W. M. (2003). *Healing places..* Lanham, MD: Rowman & Littlefield.

Global News Connect. (July 4, 2015). *Global News Connect.* Retrieved from Everyday access to nature improves quality of life in older adults <http://globalnewsconnect.com/everyday-access-to-nature-improves-quality-of-life-in-older-adults/>.

Ijsselsteijn, W., & Giuseppe, R. (2003). Chapter 1: Being there: The experience of presence in mediated environments. In R. Giuseppe (Ed.), *Being there: Concepts, effects and measurements of user presence in synthetic environments* (pp. 1−14). Amsterdam: IOS Press.

Kaplan, R., & Kaplan, S. (1989). *The experience of nature.* Cambridge: Cambridge University Press.

Kellert, S. R., & Wilson, E. O. (1993). *The biophilia hypothesis.* Washington, DC: Island Press.

Kelly-Barton, C. (n.d.). *Scientists test virtual reality tools to help seniors.* Retrieved from SeniorAdvisor.com <https://www.senioradvisor.com/blog/2016/08/scientists-test-virtual-reality-tools-to-help-seniors/>.

de Kort, Y. A., Meijnders, A. L., Sponselee, A. A., & IJsselsteijn, W. A. (2006). What's wrong with virtual trees? Restoring from stress in a mediated environment. *Journal of Environmental Psychology, 26*(4), 309−320. Available from http://dx.doi.org/10.1016/j.jenvp.2006.09.001.

Largo-Wight, E. (January 2011). Cultivating healthy places and communities: Evidenced-based nature contact recommendations. *International Journal of Environmental Health Research*, *21*(1), 41−61. Available from http://dx.doi.org/10.1080/09603123.2010.499452.

Lawton, M. P. (August 1983a). *Environmental and other determinants of well-being on older people. Gerontologist*, *23*(4), 349−357.

Lawton, M. P. (1983b). The varieties of wellbeing. *Experimental Aging Research*, *9*(2), 65−72. Available from http://dx.doi.org/10.1080/03610738308258427.

Lawton, M. P., Windley, P. G., & Byerts, T. O. (1982). Competence, environmental press and adaptation of older people. In M. P. Lawton, P. G. Windley, & T. O. Byerts (Eds.), *Aging and the environment: Theoretical approaches* (pp. 33−59). New York: Springer.

Lee, J., Park, B. J., Tsunetsugu, Y., Ohira, T., Kagawa, T., & Miyazaki, Y. (2011). Effect of forest bathing on physiological and psychological responses in young Japanese male subjects. *Public Health*, *125*(2), 93−100. Available from http://dx.doi.org/10.1016/j.puhe.2010.09.005.

Levasseur, M., Desrosiers, J., & Tribble, D. S.-C. (2008). Do quality of life, participation and environment of older adults differ according to level of activity? *Health and Quality of Life Outcomes*, *6*(1), 30. Available from http://dx.doi.org/10.1186/1477-7525-6-30.

National Institute on Aging, National Institutes of Health, US Department of Health & Human Services. (July 2010). *Healthy aging: Lessons from the Baltimore Longitudinal Study of Aging. 08-6440.* Retrieved from National Institute on Aging <https://www.nia.nih.gov/health/publication/healthy-aging-lessons-baltimore-longitudinal-study-aging/introduction>.

Norris, T., & Pittman, M. (2000). The healthy communities movement and the coalition for healthier cities and communities. *Public Health Reports*, *115*(2−3), 118−124.

Perissinotto, C., Cenzer, I. S., & Covinsky, K. E. (2012). Loneliness in older persons: A predictor of functional decline and death. *Archives of Internal Medicine*, *172*(14), 1078−1083. Available from http://dx.doi.org/10.1001/archinternmed.2012.1993.

Platoni, K. (June 29, 2016). *Virtual reality aimed at the elderly finds new fans.* Retrieved from Shots - Health News from NPR <http://www.npr.org/sections/health-shots/2016/06/29/483790504/virtual-reality-aimed-at-the-elderly-finds-new-fans>.

Rodiek, S. (2009a). *Access to nature: Planning outdoor space for aging.* Retrieved from Access to Nature <http://www.accesstonature.org/index.asp>.

Rodiek, S. (2009b). *The value of nature for older adults* [Motion Picture].

Schroeder, S. A. (2017). We can do better − Improving the health of the American people. *The New England Journal of Medicine*, *357*, 1221−1228.

Stamps, A. E. (1990). Use of photographs to simulate environments: A meta-analysis. *Perceptual and Motor Skills*, *71*(7), 907−913. Available from http://dx.doi.org/10.2466/PMS.71.7.907-913.

Takano, T., Nakamura, K., & Watanabe, M. (2002). Urban residential environments and senior citizens' longevity in megacity areas: The importance of walkable green spaces. *Journal of Epidemiology and Community Health*, *56*(12), 913−918.

Tarlov, A. R. (1999). Public policy framework for improving population health. *Annals of the New York Academy of Sciences*, *896*, 281−293. Available from http://dx.doi.org/10.1111/j.1749-6632.1999.tb08123.x.

The Schmieding Center for Senior Health and Education, The International Longevity Center-USA. (n.d.). *Caregiving in America.* Retrieved from <http://www.caregiverslibrary.org/portals/0/CGM.Caregiving%20in%20America-Final.pdf>.

The WHOQOL Group (1995). The World Health Organization quality of life assessment (WHOQOL): Position paper from the World Health Organization. *Social Science and Medicine, 41*(10), 1403–1409.

Ulrich, R. (1984). *View through a window may influence recovery from surgery. 224*(4647), 420–421.

Ulrich, R. S., Simons, R. F., Losito, B. D., & Zelson, M. (September 1991). Stress recovery during exposure to natural and urban environments. *Journal of Environmental Psychology, 11* (3), 201–230. Available from http://dx.doi.org/10.1016/S0272-4944(05)80184-7.

USC Institute for Creative Technologies. (2017). *Medical virtual reality.* Retrieved from USC Institute for Creative Technologies <http://ict.usc.edu/groups/medical-vr/>.

Vincent, E. (2015). Health wellness and trees: Effects of nature images on pain research. In *International Society of Arboriculture conference.* Orlando, Florida.

Vincent, E., Battisto, D., Grimes, L., & McCubbin, J. (2010). The effects of nature images on pain in a simulated hospital patient room. *Health Environments Research & Design Journal, 3*(3), 42–55.

de Vries, S., Verheij, R. A., Groenewegen, P. P., & Spreeuwenberg, P. (2003). Natural environments – Healthy environments? An exploratory analysis of the relationship between greenspace and health. *Environment and Planning A, 35*(10), 1717–1731. Available from http://dx.doi.org/10.1068/a35111.

Webb, E., Blane, D., McMunn, A., & Netuveli, G. (2011). Proximal predictors of change in quality of life at older ages. *Journal of Epidemiology and Community Health, 65*(6), 542–547. Available from http://dx.doi.org/10.1136/jech.2009.101758.

Wilson, E. O. (1984). *Biophilia.* Cambridge, MA: Harvard University Press.

World Health Organization. (2017). *Constitution of WHO: Principles.* Retrieved from World Health Organization <http://www.who.int/about/mission/en/>.

Further reading

Kaplan, R., Kaplan, S., & Ryan, R. (1998). *With people in mind.* Washington, DC: Island Press.

Design and development of an automated fall risk assessment system for older adults

6

Ruopeng Sun[1], Vignesh R. Paramathayalan[2], Rama Ratnam[1,2], Sanjiv Jain[3], Daniel G. Morrow[1] and Jacob J. Sosnoff[1]

[1]University of Illinois at Urbana-Champaign, IL, United States, [2]Advanced Digital Sciences Center, Illinois at Singapore PTE Ltd, Singapore, Singapore, [3]Carle Foundation Hospital, Urbana, IL, United States

Aging, falls, and technology

Falls are the leading cause of accidental death and injury in older adults (Rubenstein, 2006). One in three older adults experience a fall yearly and a significant portion of those that fall will suffer an injury (Stevens, 2005). Moreover, fall-related injuries incur more than $30 billion direct medical cost annually and is expected to increase to $100 billion by 2030 (Stevens & Phelan, 2013). Given the adverse impact of falls, they have been the focus of significant research. To date over 80,000 older adults have participated in clinical trials focusing on fall prevention (Gillespie et al., 2012). This collective research has made it clear that falls are predictable and preventable with interventions targeting modifiable risk factors such as environmental hazards, muscle strength, balance, and mobility (Gillespie et al., 2012). However, despite the increase in the understanding of falls and their prevention, the age-adjusted fall death-rate among older adults nearly doubled in the last decade (Kramarow, Chen, Hedegaard, & Warner, 2015). This dramatic increase in death rate highlights the need for innovative approaches. The development and refinement of various technologies has the potential to improve fall risk assessment and ultimately prevention of falls (Patel, Park, Bonato, Chan, & Rodgers, 2012).

The obvious first step to implementing effective fall prevention and risk reduction involves identification of modifiable fall risk factors. This is necessary for both identifying individuals at risk for falls and providing appropriate targets for the design of therapeutic interventions aimed at reducing falls. Indeed the American Geriatric Society as well as the Centers for Disease Control and Prevention (CDC) recommends screening of fall risk for older adults at least annually by physicians (Ambrose, Cruz, & Paul, 2015). Specifically, it is recommended that fall history (number of falls in the past year), concerns about falling, and patient self-reported balance or walking impairment are assessed as part of a clinical fall risk screen.

Aging, Technology and Health. DOI: http://dx.doi.org/10.1016/B978-0-12-811272-4.00006-3

It is also recommended that functional measures of cognition, static/dynamic balance and muscle strength are conducted.

There are several limitations with current fall risk screenings. Self-report measures and subjective clinical judgement are frequently used for clinical fall risk assessment. Although these approaches are clinically feasible, they lack psychometric robustness (Howcroft, Kofman, & Lemaire, 2013) (e.g., validity and reliability), which should be central in the allocation of healthcare resources. Functional balance and gait assessments such as the Romberg test, 5-time sit to stand, and timed up-and-go have been promoted as fall risk assessment tools (Buatois et al., 2008; Maki, Holliday, & Topper, 1994; Podsiadlo & Richardson, 1991). Although these measures have several advantages, they still have a subjective component and require staff time and some clinical expertise. Laboratory based measurement tools, such as motion capture (Hahn & Chou, 2003) and force platform (Maki et al., 1994) provide objective, quantitative measures of fall risk. However, the equipment is relatively expensive and requires expertise to be conducted. These limitations prevent this approach from being integrated into typical clinical scenarios. Additionally, although falls are multifactorial in nature (Rubenstein, 2006), the majority of the current fall risk assessments are unidimensional. At best, this results in an incomplete assessment of fall risk, and at worse, it results in an inaccurate fall risk profile.

Due in part to these limitations fall risk screenings are rarely performed. Data suggests that less than 20% of physicians screen older adults for fall risk and make appropriate treatment plans (Smith et al., 2015). Even when physicians are systematically encouraged to objectively measure fall risk (with external funding and best practices in place) over 75% report that time constraints and competing medical priorities are significant barriers to implementing fall screening in a clinical setting (Casey et al., 2016).

The recent development and refinement of imaging and sensor technology, coinciding with the limitations of fall screening practices has led to development of numerous fall-related technologies. Technologies, such as inertial sensors, low-cost video/depth camera and ambient sensing, offer an alternative approach to current practice in fall risk assessment. These technologies provide a platform to effectively capture and analyze movement data that may provide an easy-to-implement fall risk screening. More specifically: (1) inertial sensors contain miniaturized accelerometers and gyroscopes that can track triaxial linear acceleration and angular rotation velocity and capable of quantify movement patterns. These sensors have been used for continuous tracking of mobility, both in the clinic (Greene et al., 2012) and in the real world environment (van Schooten et al., 2015). (2) Low-cost video/depth camera provides marker-less 3D motion tracking of body joints by using its built-in and external validated human skeleton modeling algorithms. It enables fast and patient-friendly motion tracking that can be used for in-home habitual tracking (Rantz et al., 2015), as well as objective clinical measures of balance/mobility (Kargar et al., 2014). (3) Radar/laser sensing technology have also been used in unobtrusive tracking of human movement (Rantz et al., 2015). This technology can estimate the movement velocity of individual's body parts, and identify the movement abnormality in impaired individuals. Research has demonstrated its effectiveness for long-term habitual movement tracking (Rantz et al., 2015), as well as clinical movement assessment (Nishiguchi et al., 2013).

Although these approaches are promising, they are not without limitations. For instance, continuous monitoring of movement is computationally demanding, requires numerous sensors and has inherent privacy concerns (Hawley-Hague, Boulton, Hall, Pfeiffer, & Todd, 2014). In addition, inertial sensors usually only serve as a stand-alone recording device that does not interact with the user to provide guidance or feedback to facilitate the assessment procedure. Further, inertial sensors are body-worn and often prove cumbersome for older adults. It is also worth noting that most, if not all, systems are designed to be utilized/interpreted by clinicians or caregivers and not by older adults themselves (Hawley-Hague et al., 2014). Furthermore, all current technologies used for fall screening still require additional personnel to utilize and implement the system, thus potentially limiting the systems' cost benefit.

Based on these gaps, our research group is developing a comprehensive automated fall risk assessment system to be used by older adults. We envisioned a system that is automated, affordable, intuitive, touch free, unobtrusive, and safe. These criteria lead us to develop a system with a relatively inexpensive commercially available imaging device (the Microsoft Kinect). More specifically, we developed a system that incorporates assessments that can resemble clinical tests of balance and mobility (i.e., static/dynamic balance, rapid stepping, and sitting to standing transition, etc.) as well as collecting other pertinent information associated with risk of falling—i.e., health history, balance confidence, history of falling, etc. The following sections detail the design and refinement process, as well as some preliminary data highlighting the potential of the system.

Automated fall risk assessment system

The hardware components of the system include a Microsoft Kinect V2 camera, a PC-based computer and a display screen (Fig. 6.1). The software component includes three main features: (1) A Fall Risk Assessment Avatar (FRAAn); (2) assessment of movement during prescribed motor tasks; and (3) a cloud-based algorithm to determine individuals fall risk.

FRAAn is displayed on the screen and leads the participant through a comprehensive fall risk assessment. FRAAn was chosen as a gender- and ethnically neutral avatar to enhance user acceptance (Nass, Moon, & Green, 1997). FRAAn will ask participants their age, gender, if they have experienced a fall in the past 12 months, if they are concerned about falling and whether they feel unsteady during daily ambulatory activity. Voice recognition technology will be utilized to record the participant's verbal responses. These questions are based on CDC fall risk assessment recommendations (Stevens & Phelan, 2013). Following the collection of demographics, participants complete a series of balance and mobility tests. Prior to each

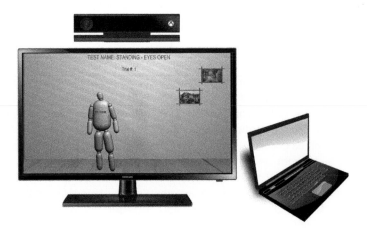

Figure 6.1 Schematic of the system.

test, FRAAn provides standardized verbal instructions and visual demonstration of the required movements.

It is important to note that the design of FRAAn (or computer agent) builds on progress in developing agents for human−computer systems. Agents with realistic facial expressions, gestures and other relational cues have been found to improve learning in automated tutoring systems compared to text-based systems (Mayer & DaPra, 2012; Moreno, 2005; Schroeder, Adesope, & Gilbert, 2013), in part by engendering social responses (Reeves & Nass, 1996). Agents are often used and evaluated in education settings, but much less so in healthcare. However, Bickmore and colleagues have developed agents that support a variety of patient goals and have helped diverse patients to follow self-care recommendations compared to text-based or lower fidelity interfaces (Bickmore, Gruber, & Picard, 2005; Bickmore et al., 2010; Bickmore, Pfeifer, & Paasche-Orlow, 2009). They may especially help older adults by emulating best practices for face-to-face communication. We are not aware of any agents besides FRAAn being implemented in a fall risk assessment scenario.

Fall risk assessment

Given the Kinect camera's capture range (1.5−4.5 m skeletal tracking range) and best practice recommendations for quantifying falls risk in older adults (Stevens & Phelan, 2013), a set of assessments were selected and integrated in the system. Briefly, the assessment consists of valid and reliable clinical test focusing on static and dynamic balance. Static balance assessments include a series of 30 s sway assessments varying visual input with eyes open (EO) and closed (EC), and/or modifications of base of support—semi-tandem stance (ST), tandem stance (T), and single-leg stance (SL), see Fig 6.2. Dynamic balance was assessed with the four

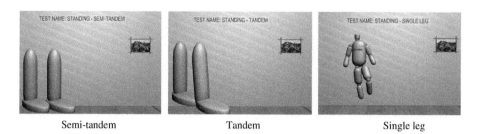

| Semi-tandem | Tandem | Single leg |

Figure 6.2 Sample FRAAn demonstration for semitandem, tandem, and single-leg standing tasks.

square step test (4SQT) (Dite & Temple, 2002). The 4SQT is a clinical test that requires participants to rapidly change direction while stepping forward, backward and sideways over a low obstacle. Lastly, muscle strength and coordination were assessed with the five-time sit-to-stand test (5STS) (Buatois et al., 2008) which is a clinical test that asks participants to stand up and sit down from a chair five times as quickly as possible.

In addition to utilizing validated balance assessments, we also took participant safety into account when designing the system. This is key given the ultimate goal of an automated unsupervised fall risk screening. In order to ensure safety of users, the designed tests were carried out in progressive difficulty (i.e., static balance eyes open precedes eyes closed test and semitandem precedes tandem test, and if an individual cannot complete a task after two attempts, the test will end and proceed to the next test, see Fig. 6.3). Additionally, participants will be able to verbally inform FRAAn when they need additional instructions, a rest, or if they want to skip a given task, or stop the assessment entirely. The total time for the assessment is less than 20 minutes.

Preliminary results

To test the system's validity and feasibility, the automated fall risk assessment system is currently being tested in a hospital setting with older adults at high risk of fall-related injuries. To date, 12 participants (mean age 76.5 years old, age range 65−88, 1 male/11 female) have participated in the automated fall risk assessment as well as clinical fall risk assessment. Following the automated fall risk assessment, user feedback was collected using the System Usability Scale (SUS) (Brooke, 1996). This feedback was used to enhance the iterative design of the system. Participants were included if they were at least 65 years of age, able to walk for 10 m (with or without walking aid), normal or corrected to normal vision, and ability to speak and comprehend written and spoken English. Upon arrival at the hospital, participants were verbally informed of the experimental procedures and provided an opportunity to ask questions. After all queries were satisfied,

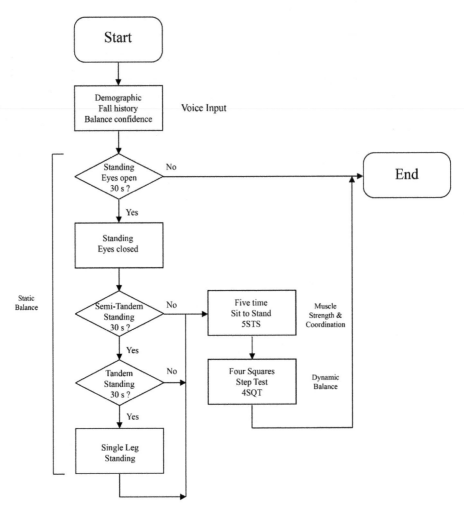

Figure 6.3 Flowchart of the Automated Fall Risk Assessment procedure. Yes, indicates participant successfully complete the task.

participants signed an informed consent document, which had been approved by the local Institutional Review Board.

To determine the validity of the automated fall risk assessment system, the measurement of postural sway during the various movements was compared to validated fall risk assessment tools—Berg Balance Scale—BBS (Muir, Berg, Chesworth, & Speechley, 2008), Timed-Up and Go test -TUG (Shumway-Cook, Brauer, & Woollacott, 2000). Briefly, each participant underwent an automated fall risk assessment session led by FRAAn, and completed the BBS and Timed Up-and-Go that was administered by a trained researcher. The BBS is comprised of 14 balance tasks (i.e., standing, sitting, turning, reaching forward, etc.) and the participants are scored (0−4) on the ability to complete the tasks. The TUG requires participant to rise from a chair, walk at a comfortable pace for 3 m, and walk back to the chair and sit down. The time to complete the TUG was recorded. The FRAAn session always preceded the research-led session. The association between measurement of fall risk by system (center of mass postural sway area, completion time of 4SQT and 5STS, as well as center of mass acceleration parameters during movement transition) and the BBS/TUG scores were used to determine the validity of FRAAn.

Sample measurements of center of mass sway in various balance tests are shown in Fig. 6.4. As expected, the postural sway amplitude increased when visual was occluded and when the base of support was reduced. Additionally, the BBS score (range 28−56), TUG completion time (range 7.76−36.91 seconds), sway measurement and completion time of 5STS were strongly correlated (Table 6.1). These results indicate that the systems measurement of balance and movement is valid. The demographic and fall history information collected through FRAAn were also verified with participants' written responses.

Regarding the completion of each automated test condition, all of the participants were able to complete the 30 seconds standing with- and without-vision and

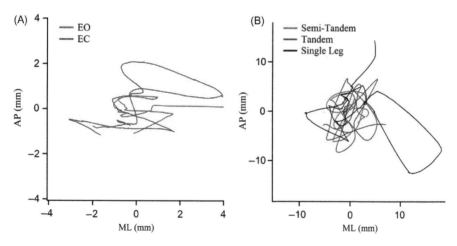

Figure 6.4 Sample postural sway trace from a representative participant (69 years old, female). (A) In eyes open (EO) and eyes closed (EC) condition; (B) in semitandem, tandem and single-leg condition.

Table 6.1 Correlation between measurement scores

Spearman Rho	TUG	BBS	FRAAn sway area
5STS	0.90, P < .01	−0.82, P < .01	0.68, P = .03
TUG	−	−0.96, P < .01	0.61, P = .04
BBS	−	−	−0.76, P < .01

Semi-Tandem condition. Four participants were unable to complete the tandem condition, seven participants did not complete the single-leg standing condition (four participants opted not to attempt the exercise, and three unable to complete it), one participant was unable to complete the 5STS test, and two participants were unable to complete the 4SQT test. No adverse events were reported.

User feedback and system refinement

After individuals underwent the automated fall risk assessment, user experience feedback was collected using the SUS (Brooke, 1996). Participants provided feedback on the interface, instruction, demonstration, task complexity, system integration, as well as potential barriers to implementing the technology.

Overall, participants provided positive feedback on the ease of use of the system, the clearness of visual demonstration and verbal instruction. For instance, one 65-year-old female reported that *Instructions were easy to follow and tests were not difficult.* Eleven of the twelve participants reported interest in using the FRAAn system on a regular basis, were able to follow the instructions provided by FRAAn, and confident to initiate fall screening assessment themselves after a brief tutorial. For instance, a 73-year-old female participant reported that *I needed someone to explain how to use it, then I was comfortable using it.*

Several modifications were implemented during the design process and initial testing. Specifically, the initial system utilized a synthetic voice for verbal instructions and was replaced with human voice with a natural pace to maximize comprehension. During initially testing, participants reported confusion with understanding the 4SQT task demonstration—there was confusion on whether they should step forward or backward, and whether they should mirror the figure or step to their own left or right. Consequently, the visual demonstration of the 4SQT was altered from a 3D mirror-view to a 2D bird-eye's view (Fig. 6.5).

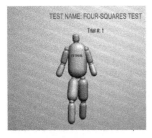 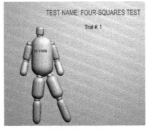 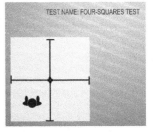

Forward stepping   Side stepping   Bird-eye demo

Figure 6.5 Refinement of FRAAn demonstration display for the 4SQT test.

Discussion

Technology-based fall screening and prevention tools have the potential to increase effectiveness of current healthcare practice without increasing the delivery costs. A novel self-initiated, affordable, automated fall risk assessment system was developed by our research team. It facilitates identification of fall risk factors that could allow for individualized fall prevention intervention. Furthermore, this affordable and portable system allows objective assessment to be conducted more regularly compared to clinic/laboratory based assessment.

Unlike most of the other existing technology for fall screening, this system is designed to be used by community-dwelling older adults. The FRAAn system enables objective assessment of static and dynamic balance, stepping, and Sit-to-Stand transition in a fully autonomous manner. In order to ensure safety and maximize the effectiveness of assessment, the system offers tests that are progressively designed and tailored to the ability of individual senior.

Preliminary results confirm the increase of postural sway in sensory removal and reduced base of support conditions. The sway measurement by FRAAn was also strongly correlated to validated clinical tests (TUG/BBS). These findings help validate FRAAn as a tool for balance/mobility screening. Initial user feedback confirms that seniors were comfortable using the system and confident in their ability to initiate the fall screening assessment themselves after a brief tutorial. It is worth noting that in the ongoing investigation, research personnel were present to offer fall protection during the "automated" assessment, and several participants with limited mobility required supervision to complete the assessments. Therefore, further research to determine proper safety measures for an unsupervised assessment is warranted.

Future directions

Given that numerous outcomes have been identified as fall risk factors, including a history of falls, muscle weakness, poor balance and gait, visual impairment, hearing loss, environmental risk factors, impaired cognition, psychoactive and multiple drug use, a comprehensive multifactorial approach is needed for fall risk screening. Thus, the next step of the current system is to integrate functions/tests that evaluate cognition (i.e., attention/executive control), functional mobility (i.e., TUG, Figure-8 walking), vision, hearing, and cognitive-motor interference. Additionally, questionnaires about drug use, comprehensive health history, fear of falling, and other psychometrics could be added as part of the fall screening. A composite fall risk index, detailed breakdown of each assessment, and recommendations for maintaining or improving their performance will be provided. The voice recognition function could be improved to enhance user comprehension and acceptance of the system, thus enabling FRAAn to interact more fully with older adults.

It is important to note that this system is designed to serve as a triage tool to better implement fall risk screening among older adults on a regular basis. Therefore, not all risk factors of falls (i.e., blood pressure, glucose test, vestibular function, etc.) need to be evaluated in this system, and should be further evaluated by physicians. And given the typical time allocation in a primary care office visit ($\sim$15 minutes) (Tai-Seale, McGuire, & Zhang, 2007), we envision to further optimize screening tasks and procedure so that the assessment can be completed within the time limit.

The finalized automated fall risk assessment system can be implemented in a primary care facility as an assistance device for clinicians, or in a community setting (i.e., senior residence center, public health screening events, etc.). If performed outside a healthcare setting, additional guidelines for interpreting results, intervention planning, and physician referral should be added. HIPPA compliance and proper procedure for patient's information sharing should also be investigated.

Acknowledgment

The research was funded in part by Carle Illinois Collaborative Seed Grant Program. The funding agency had no input on the experimental design or interpretation of the data.

References

Ambrose, A. F., Cruz, L., & Paul, G. (2015). Falls and fractures: A systematic approach to screening and prevention. *Maturitas*, *82*(1), 85−93.

Bickmore, T., Gruber, A., & Picard, R. (2005). Establishing the computer−patient working alliance in automated health behavior change interventions. *Patient Education and Counseling*, *59*(1), 21−30.

Bickmore, T. W., Pfeifer, L. M., Byron, D., Forsythe, S., Henault, L. E., Jack, B. W., ... Paasche-Orlow, M. K. (2010). Usability of conversational agents by patients with inadequate health literacy: Evidence from two clinical trials. *Journal of Health Communication*, *15*(S2), 197−210.

Bickmore, T. W., Pfeifer, L. M., & Paasche-Orlow, M. K. (2009). Using computer agents to explain medical documents to patients with low health literacy. *Patient Education and Counseling*, *75*(3), 315−320.

Brooke, J. (1996). SUS-A quick and dirty usability scale. *Usability Evaluation in Industry*, *189*(194), 4−7.

Buatois, S., Miljkovic, D., Manckoundia, P., Gueguen, R., Miget, P., Vançon, G., ... Benetos, A. (2008). Five times sit to stand test is a predictor of recurrent falls in healthy community-living subjects aged 65 and older. *Journal of the American Geriatrics Society*, *56*(8), 1575−1577.

Casey, C. M., Parker, E. M., Winkler, G., Liu, X., Lambert, G. H., & Eckstrom, E. (2016). Lessons learned from implementing CDC's STEADI falls prevention algorithm in primary care. *The Gerontologist*, gnw074.

Dite, W., & Temple, V. A. (2002). A clinical test of stepping and change of direction to identify multiple falling older adults. *Archives of Physical Medicine and Rehabilitation*, *83*(11), 1566–1571.

Gillespie, L. D., Robertson, M. C., Gillespie, W. J., Sherrington, C., Gates, S., Clemson, L. M., & Lamb, S. E. (2012). Interventions for preventing falls in older people living in the community. *Cochrane Database of Systemic Reviews*, *9*, 11.

Greene, B. R., Doheny, E. P., Walsh, C., Cunningham, C., Crosby, L., & Kenny, R. A. (2012). Evaluation of falls risk in community-dwelling older adults using body-worn sensors. *Gerontology*, *58*(5), 472–480. Available from http://dx.doi.org/10.1159/000337259.

Hahn, M. E., & Chou, L.-S. (2003). Can motion of individual body segments identify dynamic instability in the elderly? *Clinical Biomechanics*, *18*(8), 737–744.

Hawley-Hague, H., Boulton, E., Hall, A., Pfeiffer, K., & Todd, C. (2014). Older adults' perceptions of technologies aimed at falls prevention, detection or monitoring: A systematic review. *International Journal of Medical Informatics*, *83*(6), 416–426.

Howcroft, J., Kofman, J., & Lemaire, E. D. (2013). Review of fall risk assessment in geriatric populations using inertial sensors. *Journal of Neuroengineering and Rehabilitation*, *10*(1), 91.

Kargar, B. A., Mollahosseini, A., Struemph, T., Pace, W., Nielsen, R. D., & Mahoor, M. H. (2014). Automatic measurement of physical mobility in Get-Up-and-Go Test using Kinect sensor. *Conference Proceedings: IEEE Engineering in Medicine and Biology Society*, *2014*, 3492–3495. Available from http://dx.doi.org/10.1109/embc.2014.6944375.

Kramarow, E., Chen, L.-H., Hedegaard, H., & Warner, M. (2015). Deaths from unintentional injury among adults aged 65 and over: United States, 2000–2013. *NCHS Data Brief*, 199.

Maki, B. E., Holliday, P. J., & Topper, A. K. (1994). A prospective study of postural balance and risk of falling in an ambulatory and independent elderly population. *Journal of Gerontology*, *49*(2), M72–M84.

Mayer, R. E., & DaPra, C. S. (2012). An embodiment effect in computer-based learning with animated pedagogical agents. *Journal of Experimental Psychology: Applied*, *18*(3), 239.

Moreno, R. (2005). Multimedia learning with animated pedagogical agents. In R. E. Mayer (Ed.), *The Cambridge handbook of multimedia learning* (pp. 507–523). New York: University of Cambridge.

Muir, S. W., Berg, K., Chesworth, B., & Speechley, M. (2008). Use of the Berg Balance Scale for predicting multiple falls in community-dwelling elderly people: A prospective study. *Physical Therapy*, *88*(4), 449.

Nass, C., Moon, Y., & Green, N. (1997). Are machines gender neutral? Gender-stereotypic responses to computers with voices. *Journal of Applied Social Psychology*, *27*(10), 864–876.

Nishiguchi, S., Yamada, M., Uemura, K., Matsumura, T., Takahashi, M., Moriguchi, T., & Aoyama, T. (2013). A novel infrared laser device that measures multilateral parameters of stepping performance for assessment of all risk in elderly individuals. *Aging Clinical and Experimental Research*, *25*(3), 311–316.

Patel, S., Park, H., Bonato, P., Chan, L., & Rodgers, M. (2012). A review of wearable sensors and systems with application in rehabilitation. *Journal of Neuroengineering and Rehabilitation*, *9*(1), 21.

Podsiadlo, D., & Richardson, S. (1991). The timed "Up & Go": A test of basic functional mobility for frail elderly persons. *Journal of the American Geriatrics Society*, *39*(2), 142−148.

Rantz, M., Skubic, M., Abbott, C., Galambos, C., Popescu, M., Keller, J., ... Petroski, G. F. (2015). Automated in-home fall risk assessment and detection sensor system for elders. *Gerontologist*, *55*, S78−87. Available from http://dx.doi.org/10.1093/geront/gnv044.

Reeves, B., & Nass, C. (1996). *How people treat computers, television, and new media like real people and places*. Cambridge, UK: CSLI Publications and Cambridge University Press.

Rubenstein, L. Z. (2006). Falls in older people: Epidemiology, risk factors and strategies for prevention. *Age and Ageing*, *35*(Suppl. 2), ii37−ii41.

van Schooten, K. S., Pijnappels, M., Rispens, S. M., Elders, P. J., Lips, P., & van Dieën, J. H. (2015). Ambulatory fall-risk assessment: amount and quality of daily-life gait predict falls in older adults. *The Journals of Gerontology Series A: Biological Sciences and Medical Sciences*, *70*(5), 608−615.

Schroeder, N. L., Adesope, O. O., & Gilbert, R. B. (2013). How effective are pedagogical agents for learning? A meta-analytic review. *Journal of Educational Computing Research*, *49*(1), 1−39.

Shumway-Cook, A., Brauer, S., & Woollacott, M. (2000). Predicting the probability for falls in community-dwelling older adults using the Timed Up & Go Test. *Physical Therapy*, *80*(9), 896.

Smith, M. L., Stevens, J. A., Ehrenreich, H., Wilson, A. D., Schuster, R. J., Cherry, C. O. B., & Ory, M. G. (2015). Healthcare providers' perceptions and self-reported fall prevention practices: Findings from a large New York health system. *Frontiers in Public Health*, *3*, 17.

Stevens, J. A. (2005). Falls among older adults—Risk factors and prevention strategies. *Journal of Safety Research*, *36*(4), 409−411.

Stevens, J. A., & Phelan, E. A. (2013). Development of STEADI: A fall prevention resource for health care providers. *Health Promotion Practice*, *14*(5), 706−714.

Tai-Seale, M., McGuire, T. G., & Zhang, W. (2007). Time allocation in primary care office visits. *Health Services Research*, *42*(5), 1871−1894.

Checking-in with my friends: Results from an in-situ deployment of peer-to-peer aging in place technologies

7

Yifang Li[1], Subina Saini[1], Kelly Caine[1] and Kay Connelly[2]
[1]Clemson University, Clemson, SC, United States, [2]Indiana University, Bloomington, IN, United States

Introduction

As the population and proportion of older adults continues to increase worldwide, with a projected estimate of approximately 2 billion people living until age 60 or over in 2050 (Doyle, Bailey, Scanaill, & van den Berg, 2014), the need to address the shortage of healthcare personnel (Hanson, Takahashi, & Pecina, 2013), the problem of caregiver burden (Pinquart & Sörensen, 2003a), and rising healthcare costs (Hanson et al., 2013) is becoming more and more pressing.

While 3.2% of older adults in the United States live in institutional settings such as nursing homes, many older adults (29%) live alone (Administration on Aging, 2015). Living alone is often challenging for older adults, however in-home technologies aimed at improving the well-being of older adults may help. In-home technologies typically collect and share older adults' information with family members, as well as care providers (Courtney, Demeris, Rantz, & Skubic, 2008). They address common healthcare issues facing older adults, such as the shortage of healthcare personnel (Hanson et al., 2013), caregiver burden (Pinquart & Sörensen, 2003a), and rising healthcare costs (Hanson et al., 2013). Researchers have studied older adults and other relevant users such as home care workers' and relatives of older adults' experiences with a variety of in-home healthcare technologies and found that these technologies could support cooperative home care, and had a positive impact on both older adults and their care network members (Bossen, Christensen, Grönvall, & Vestergaard, 2013; Consolvo, Roessler, & Shelton, 2004; Cornejo, Tentori, & Favela, 2013; Leonardi, Albertini, Pianesi, & Zancanaro, 2010).

However, much of this research has been conducted with high-socioeconomic older adults who have more resources in terms of care (Adler & Newman, 2002). On the other hand, we know less about low-socioeconomic status (SES) older adults' in-home care needs and resources. SES is measured by several indicators, including income, occupation, personal wealth, and education level. Besides the obvious relationship between these factors and overall resources, income and education level are also related to physiological impairments (Coppin et al., 2006). Taken

Aging, Technology and Health. DOI: http://dx.doi.org/10.1016/B978-0-12-811272-4.00007-5

together, the lack of overall resources and the increased incidence of physiological impairments means that this group of older adults is more vulnerable. Moreover, low-SES older adults have fewer opportunities for formal and informal care. Low-SES older adults are less able to afford formal caregivers (Andrews & Boyle, 2008). Many low-SES older adults do not have ready access to informal family caregivers since their family members often move away in search of economic opportunities, or have limited time due to jobs and taking care of their own children (White, Singh, Caine, & Connelly, 2015). However, many low-SES older adults have a rich network of fellow older adults within their community (White et al., 2015). Therefore, one underexplored opportunity is the potential to engage this network of community-dwelling older adults in peer-care.

Inspired by this opportunity, we developed a suite of peer-to-peer healthcare technologies to enable older adults to provide care for each other (Arreola et al., 2014). These technologies include the Activity Clock, Community Window, Check-In Tree (Arreola et al., 2014), and Trip Coordinator. See "SOLACE in-home PeerCare technologies for urban low-SES older adults" section for a complete description of these technologies.

One concern with any technology solution that incorporates sensing and monitoring technology, such as the suite we designed, is privacy. Some researchers take the stance that privacy issues are a nonnegligible barrier to the long-term success of in-home healthcare systems (Hong & Landay, 2004). Some evidence supports this stance: Though these technologies offer many advantages, findings from one study indicate that privacy concerns outweigh the potential benefits brought by home-based technologies (Cook, Augusto, & Jakkula, 2009), while other research suggests that older adults see simultaneous benefits and concerns of such technologies (Caine, Fisk, & Rogers, 2006).

Early on, we identified privacy as a key design goal. To mitigate privacy concerns, we developed the "DigiSwitch" (Caine et al., 2010) which puts users in control of all data gathered about them in their home. DigiSwitch is designed to be used with home-based health technologies, although is relevant and applicable to any Internet of Things devices, and we modified it to be used with the four technologies in our study. Using DigiSwitch, users are able to manage their privacy by seeing what information is being collected about them, controlling who it is shared with, and ceasing data transmission at any time.

In the study, we let older adults use the suite of technologies in their home for 8 weeks, conducted weekly surveys that measured loneliness, quality of life, social support, perceived burden, privacy perception, usability, and satisfaction of the four in-home health technologies to gain insight in participants' perceptions while using these technologies. We also studied the impact of DigiSwitch on perceived privacy.

Specifically, we sought to answer the following research question:

- How does the peer-care suite impact low-SES older adults' experiences, including quality of life, loneliness, peer-care burden, interpersonal support, satisfaction and usability of technologies, and privacy perception?

  With regards to the research question, we have the following hypotheses:
- H1—The peer-care suite will reduce loneliness over time.

- H2—The peer-care suite will enhance older adults' sense of interpersonal support.
- H3—The peer-care suite will increase perceived peer-care burden.
- H4—The peer-care suite will increase older adults' perceived quality of life.
- H5—The older adults' overall satisfaction of using the peer-care suite will increase over time.
- H6—Older adults who use DigiSwitch will be more concerned with privacy than those who did not use DigiSwitch.

Related work

Previous in-home technologies for older adults

Home-based living assistance technologies, which are quickly gaining interest as attractive caregiving interventions (Lorenzen-Huber, Boutain, Camp, Shankar, & Connelly, 2011) are cost-effective (Hanson et al., 2013) and match older adults' preferences to receive care in either their homes or in assisted living communities (Hanson et al., 2013). There are six categories of in-home technologies: Physiological monitoring (collecting and analyzing physiological indicators such as pulse or blood pressure), functional monitoring and emergency detection (collecting and analyzing the activity level, motion, or diet etc.), safety monitoring and assistance (detecting gas leak or fire etc.), security monitoring and assistance (detecting intruders), social interaction monitoring and assistance (facilitating social interaction) and, cognitive and sensory assistance such as medication reminders etc. (Demiris & Hensel, 2008).

The primary focus of our work was on functional monitoring, emergency detection, social interaction monitoring, and assistance. The gator tech smart house developed by researchers from University of Florida is a good example that involves both categories. It aims to provide assistive environments for disabled and older adults by installing multiple sensors in the house. For example, smart bed, smart floor, and ultrasonic location track users' activity and location. Users can also use the social-distant dining module installed in the breakfast area to have immersive video and audio calls with distant family and friends (Helal et al., 2005).

The Georgia Tech Aware Home is another example that deploys multiple aging support technologies, including motion and activity detection, and social interaction assistance. The smart floor, RFID room location system, and optical sensors are used to detect users' location and activity. The Digital Family Portrait is used to support communications between family members, which shows the family member's photo and the sensing data from their home (Abowd, Bobick, Essa, Mynatt, & Rogers, 2002; Kidd et al., 1999; Kientz et al., 2008). Researchers at the Aware Home also focused on preserving the privacy of older adults (e.g., Caine et al., 2006; Caine, Fisk, & Rogers, 2007; Caine, Rogers, & Fisk, 2005).

Other technologies in functional monitoring and emergency detection category include Health Integrated Smart Home Information System that monitors users' activity through location sensors installed in each room of users' home (Demongeot et al., 2002), and the Tiger Place where proximity sensors and displacement sensors are deployed to detect users' motion (Demiris et al., 2006).

Within the social interaction monitoring and assistance category, the CareNet Display was an early work in providing support to informal caregivers of older adults living on their own. It used an interactive digital picture frame to help people in an older adult's care network to coordinate care-related activities through displaying photos of older adults with information about their daily lives. The amount of stress the caregivers felt about caregiving reduced, while the quality of older adults' lives and care for them was improved (Consolvo et al., 2004).

Tlatoque, a situated display, provides older adults' information being shared by their relatives in a social network site (Facebook). Older adults were able to exchange ideas and share thoughts about information relatives posted. The results showed older adults learning about their relatives' lives and which made them more independent. Similarly, relatives gained awareness of the older adults' lives (Cornejo et al., 2013).

A tabletop device named MobiTable was introduced to assist older adults to communicate with their social network. It is a gestural touch-based interface embedded in a movable device that shared multimedia user-generated contents within the community (Leonardi et al., 2010).

Low-SES urban-dwelling older adults and PeerCare

Technology to support low-SES older adults is under researched, despite the fact that residents of low-SES neighborhoods have higher incidence of multiple problems, e.g., physical function loss, than their high-SES counterparts (Balfour & Kaplan, 2002). Moreover, many low-SES older adults living in urban areas are not able to afford formal caregivers or assisted living facilities (Andrews & Boyle, 2008). Adjusting to this limitation, many low-SES older adults rely heavily on their peer-group for their needs (Arreola et al., 2014). Therefore, a peer-to-peer model where older adults provide care for each other, instead of the caregiver-to-older adult model, may better serve this user group (Arreola et al., 2014). Reciprocal peer-to-peer support relationship, where older adults within a community develop small social networks that include social and care exchanges, has been termed "PeerCare," (Riche & Mackay, 2010). In the SOLACE model for low-SES older adults, we further incorporate four different peer-care technologies into a suite, to facilitate their lives from different perspectives, e.g., remote check-in, social interaction, or trip resource pooling.

SOLACE in-home PeerCare technologies for urban low-SES older adults

Based on the SOLACE model, we developed four technologies to address the individual needs for independent living in low-SES communities (Arreola et al., 2014).

Activity Clock

Challenges associated with independent living include healthcare problems/risks, caregiver burden, and small social networks (Demiris et al., 2004; Doyle, Skrba, McDonnell, & Arent, 2010). Older adults are afflicted by a range of health conditions, including falls, visual/hearing impairments, immobility and isolation (Demiris et al., 2004). Problems such as immobility are addressed with the Activity Clock (Fig. 7.1), which detects the older adult's motion and measures their level of activity. There are 48 lights on the face of the clock. Each one represents a 15-minute block of time. Brightly lit LED lights represent high levels of physical activity, including cleaning or doing exercise, while dim or dark LED lights represent low levels, e.g., watching television, or inactivity. Caregivers, who are older adults in the same community, can access activity logs on a tablet using the "Activity Monitor" application, and are given the option of representing the data in graphical form. The activity monitor interface in Fig. 7.2 shows the data from older adults'

Figure 7.1 Activity clock. A technology that detects the older adult's motion and measures their level of activity.

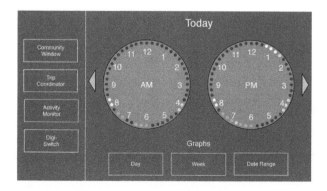

Figure 7.2 Activity monitor that shows the older adult's activity data from activity clock.

clocks for the morning and evening. Activity data is transmitted from the clock to the app every 15 minutes. Older adults can compare their activity levels to the rest of the group.

Check-In Tree

About a third of older adults experience some form of limited mobility, and thirty percent are at risk for experiencing social isolation (Demiris et al., 2004). The Check-In Tree is another technology that addresses the problem of falls or getting ill. For example, if someone does not check-in, his or her peer group can make sure this person is okay by phoning him or her. Moreover, it reduces social isolation by encouraging peers to check-in on each other. The tree in Fig. 7.3 connects older adults and seven peers. It has two basic parts: Picture frames with LEDs, and a button on the base of the tree. Every older adult in the network has an identical tree with a photo of each person in the network (including themselves). In the middle of the night, the LED shining on each picture starts to slowly pulse. When an older adult wakes up, they check-in with their peers by pressing the button on their tree, which makes the light shining on their picture on all of the tress go from pulsing to constantly on. Whenever an older adult looks at their tree, they can quickly assess who has checked-in for the day based on whose light is still pulsing. Depending on their knowledge of each of their friends, they can call someone who has not checked-in by their normal time to make sure they are ok. In this way, older adults

Figure 7.3 Check-in tree. A technology that older adults can check-in on their peers.

care for each other and make sure nothing has happened to them in the middle of the night, such as falling or becoming ill.

Community Window

Social connectedness plays an important role in older adults' well-being (Ashida & Heaney, 2008; Gardner, 2011; Haslam et al., 2008), and has a positive effect on physical and mental health (Cornwell, Laumann, & Schumm, 2008). Social connectedness can be enhanced with two easy-to-use technologies: The Community Window and the Trip Coordinator.

By using Community Window (Fig. 7.4), older adults are able to video call other members of their peer group. After opening the Community Window application on their tablet, besides their own window, they will see three more windows that show recent pictures from the cameras of three of their peers. The camera takes a picture every minute and sends it to the community window neighbors. Users have the option to protect their privacy by pressing the close button and putting a curtain over their own window. They can make a video call by tapping the "Call" button next to the picture of the person they wish to contact. A box that gives the option of accepting or declining a call appears to participants who are contacted by a peer requesting a video call (Fig. 7.5).

Trip Coordinator

Rural older adults often have difficulty making trips (either local trips, such as to the grocery store, or more remote trips, such as to a medical facility in the nearest metropolitan area) (Black, Dobbs, & Young, 2015; Heinz et al., 2013). Barriers can include no longer being allowed to drive due to a mental or physical impairment, not having the physical strength to drive for long periods, and not having the

Figure 7.4 Community window. A technology enables older adults to make video calling with other members of their peer group.

Figure 7.5 Community window call, that gives the option of accepting or declining a call from the peer.

financial resources to maintain a car. The trip coordinator assists older adults in pooling their resources (i.e., vehicles, driving time, and money for fuel) to make trips. A magnet board detailing a calendar for the current and following weeks is used to indicate trips older adults would like to make and resources they can provide (Fig. 7.6). A user moves a magnet that illustrates an activity to a date on the calendar in order to plan a trip. The 12 magnets are divided into two types: Places and resources, including restaurants, cafés, museums, senior centers, doctors, churches, shopping, parks, groceries, theaters, pharmacies, and gyms. After adding the activity magnet to the system, users will see the trip appear on the app (Fig. 7.7). Other users in the peer group are then informed of the trip and can choose to accompany their peer on the trip. Once the trip is confirmed, a printout detailing the location and date of the trip, all trip-goers, and the contact information of the trip planner is provided. In addition, users can place a special organizer magnet next to the trip and the app assistant will contact them to help them plan the trip.

Both of these technologies encourage social interaction to address the problem of declining social relationships—an issue that affects isolated older adults and is associated with notable health risks (Doyle et al., 2010).

Further research is needed to investigate low-SES older adults' experience on using these technologies through in-home evaluation.

Privacy concerns and "DigiSwitch"

The technologies described earlier provide benefits to older adults, but may also introduce privacy concerns (Caine et al., 2006). Since the home is a place which has a relatively high privacy level, privacy becomes a significant consideration when older adults use in-home technologies. After data is collected from in-home sensors, it is transmitted via the Internet, which may cause a potential threat to the

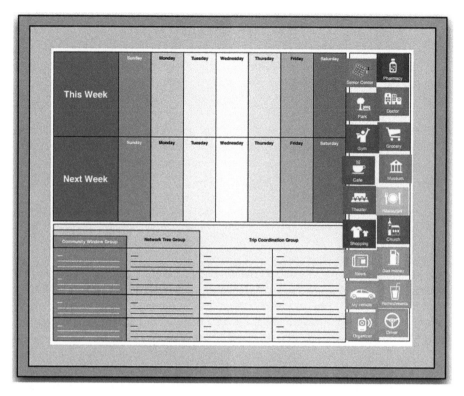

Figure 7.6 Trip coordinator. A magnet board detailing a calendar for the current and following weeks is used to indicate trips older adults would like to make and resources they can provide.

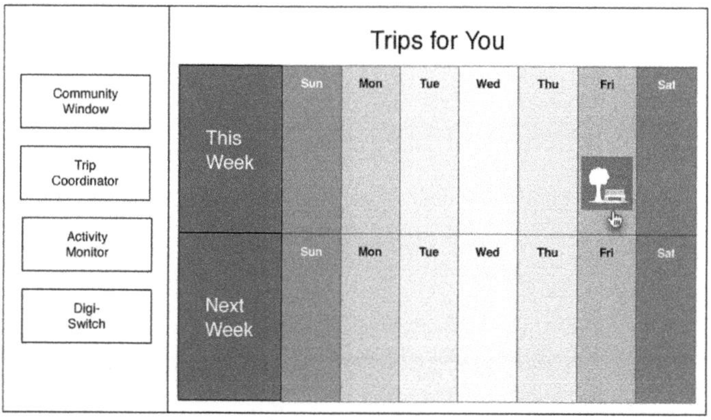

Figure 7.7 Plan a trip on trip coordinator.

security and privacy of users (Meingast, Roosta, & Sastry, 2006). Moreover, some in-home technologies, like small sensors installed in the corner of a user's home, are hardly visible to users. Users may find it difficult to access and control the computational processing and environmental sensing functions of these kinds of technologies (Edwards & Grinter, 2001; Langheinrich, 2002). Therefore, it is very important to understand the impacts on perceived privacy when deploying in-home technologies for older adults.

A health informatics technology, DigiSwitch, was originally designed for higher-SES older adults to manage their privacy with home-based technologies (Caine et al., 2010). It allows users to see what information the technology is collecting, control whether the information is being shared with others, and cease data transmission at any time.

Users are able to check the status of each home health monitoring device in their home and turn them on and off (Fig. 7.8). Fig. 7.9 is the caregiver's view, which allows the user to see exactly what their caregiver is seeing, to provide data awareness (Caine et al., 2011).

In this project, we adapted DigiSwitch to the four SOLACE technologies as a privacy control apparatus to allow participants to control which peers in their peer network could view their information (Fig. 7.10). Participants could select a technology, such as the Community Window for example, by clicking on the respective icon. Next, a screen displaying a "Play All" button in column 1, a "Stop All" button in column 2, and a "Pause All" button in column 3, would appear alongside pictures of peers located in the far-right column. The participant could then drag each peer to the desired column. Column 1 represents peers who can view the participant's activity. Column 2 represents peers who cannot view the participant's activity. Column 3 represents peers who view fake data and no real activity. This way, participants can control which peers can view (or not view) their activity for each technology. The Activity Monitor, the Check-in Tree, and the Community Window are all equipped with this functionality. For the Trip Coordinator, participants choose which peers they would or would not like to go on a trip with by dragging peers to respective columns.

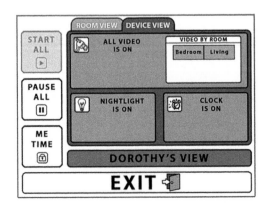

Figure 7.8 Original main screen of DigiSwitch.

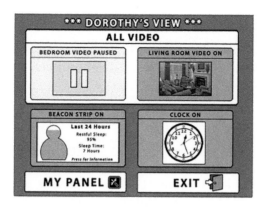

Figure 7.9 Original caregiver's view screen of DigiSwitch.

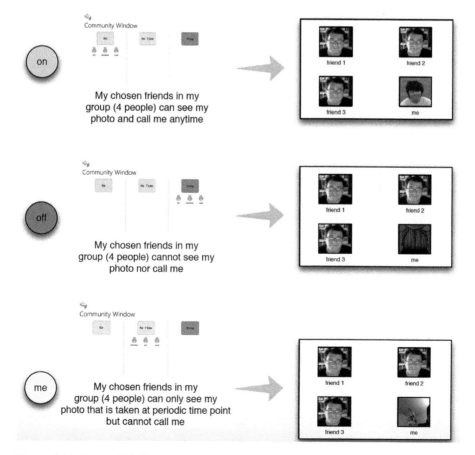

Figure 7.10 Adapted DigiSwitch.

Methods

We conducted an in-situ experiment with 16 participants over a period of 8 weeks to determine the effects of using the adapted DigiSwitch with peer-to-peer, in-home technologies.

Participants

We recruited 16 low-SES older adults aged 65 and older from an urban community in Indiana. Three participants were male and 13 were female. Most participants were female (81.2%) for two reasons: (1) It is representative of the population (i.e., the majority of older adults are women) (U.S. Census Bureau, 2017) and (2) the percentage of older women living alone is almost twice the percentage of men living alone (32% and 18% respectively Stepler, 2016). We recruited participants through advertisements at a local community center. Participants were compensated $200 for participating in the study. Of the sixteen older adults that participated in this study, we eliminated one participant from data analysis due to frequent incidences of nonresponse.

SOLACE technology prototypes and DigiSwitch apparatus

The four technologies described earlier form a suite designed to address the needs of the urban, low-income population of older adults. In addition to the suite of four technologies, eight participants were randomly assigned to receive the DigiSwitch, while the remaining eight participants did not. The presence or absence of the DigiSwitch functioned as an independent variable that manipulated privacy control. Participants were divided into peer groups throughout the study. All sixteen participants shared the Trip Coordinator. Eight participants with DigiSwitch shared a Check-in Tree, and eight without DigiSwitch shared another tree, then these two groups were further divided into groups of four for the Community Window. The Activity Clock is a self-reflection technology that only has one user.

Questionnaires

We administered both prestudy, weekly, and poststudy questionnaires. However, due to low-response rates, we did not include posttest data in our analysis. The Suite Questionnaire and Custom Privacy Index With(out) DigiSwitch were administered only at the conclusion of the deployment of the technologies because these questionnaires were designed to collect data once participants had experience with the technology suite and DigiSwitch. Weekly questionnaires were designed to measure usability of, and satisfaction with, the technology, privacy perception for DigiSwitch versus non-DigiSwitch users, feelings of social connectedness (interpersonal support), mental health and wellness (i.e., loneliness, quality of life), and peer-care burden.

Suite Questionnaire

We designed the Suite Questionnaire specifically for this study to examine participants' overall satisfaction with, and usability of, the technologies. Questions
included: "Using the suite would give me more peace of mind," "Using the suite
would be something I could rely on," and "Using the suite would be hard to learn
how to use." Participants rated their responses on a scale from 1 (Strongly disagree)
to 5 (Strongly agree), where the higher score means more usable and satisfying.
Negatively-framed items were reverse coded, e.g., *"Using the suite would be hard
to learn how to use."*

Custom Privacy Index With and Without DigiSwitch

We also created a privacy questionnaire specifically for this study. It focused on the
privacy concerns of the participants with respect to each SOLACE technology. We
used two different surveys based on whether or not the participant had DigiSwitch
or not. A few of the questions varied slightly to accommodate this difference. For
instance, a participant who had DigiSwitch would be asked: "I am more likely to
use the trip coordinator because I can pick which user I want to go on a trip with,"
while a participant who does not have DigiSwitch would be asked "I would be
more likely to use the trip coordinator if I could pick which user I want to go on a
trip with." Participants rated their response on a scale from 1 (Strongly disagree) to
5 (Strongly agree), where a higher score indicates a higher privacy concern.

The World Health Organization (WHO) Quality of Life—BREF

We measured quality of life using a 12-question scale (World Health Organization,
2012). For example, "I have the freedom to make my own decisions," and "I am
able to do things I like to do." Participants responded with their agreement to each
item on a scale from 1 (Not at all true for me) to 5 (Very true for me), where a
higher score indicates better life quality.

Interpersonal Support Evaluation List (ISEL)—Short Form

We measured interpersonal support using a modified 15 item version of the original
40 item scale (Cohen, Mermelstein, Kamarck, & Hoberman, 1985). Participants
gave their responses on a range of 1 (Completely false) to 4 (Completely true),
where a higher score indicates higher levels of social support. This scale was scored
by splitting the items into three different groups. Items 1−5 were used as a composite score to measure *Tangible Support*. These items contained questions like: "If
I needed help moving, I would be able to find someone to help me." Items 6−10
were used to measure *Appraisal Support* with statements such as: "There is at least
one person I know whose advice I really trust." Items 11−15 were used to measure
Belonging Support with statements like: "When I feel lonely, there are several
people I could talk to."

UCLA-R subscale

We measured loneliness this three-question subscale derived from the original UCLA-R scale (Hughes, Waite, Hawkley, & Cacioppo, 2004). Participants rated how often they felt they lacked companionship, felt left out, and felt isolated from others on a scale from 1 (Hardly ever) to 3 (Often), where a higher score indicates higher loneliness.

Zarit Burden Short Form

Participants functioned as caregivers for their peers in a peer-to-peer network through the SOLACE technologies. For example, if a participant noticed that a peer had not checked-in (as indicated by a pulsing green light above the peer's photograph), the participant could call to confirm the peer's safety. Because of this, we measured caregiver burden using the 12-question scale (Bédard et al., 2001). It included questions such as: "Because of the time I spend providing care for older adults in my community, I don't have enough time for myself." Participants rated their responses on a scale from 1 (Never) to 5 (Nearly always), where a higher score indicates a higher level of burden.

Procedure

After receiving IRB approval and participant consent, we conducted an in-situ study where researchers installed all SOLACE prototypes in participants' homes. After the technology was installed, participants received training on each technology, and were given an instructional manual that explained how to use each technology. Participants passed a competency test before training was considered complete. Training lasted around an hour.

Upon successfully passing the technology competency test, participants were interviewed and completed prestudy questionnaires. Beginning the following week, participants were given six questionnaires that were administered weekly over the phone for 8 weeks. Calls were conducted according to a phone script that was identical for all the participants. Researchers inquired about participants' difficulties with the technologies at the end of each call. Participants were given copies of the scales that detailed the response choices on each questionnaire so they could see the possible responses while they answered over the phone.

Results

We created a linear mixed-effect model that included the between-subject variable "(with/without) DigiSwitch" and the within-subject variable "Time (weeks)." To analyze loneliness, interpersonal support, burden, and quality of life more accurately, we recoded the "time (weeks)" variable to two time variables "Suite intervention" and "Time." For "Suite intervention," the preweek was coded as 0, and week 1−8 were 1, so that we could see the difference before and after technologies were introduced. For "Time," we were able to see how these technologies affect users' experience over time by coding the preweek and week 1 as 0, and week 2−8 as 1.

In Tables 7.1−7.4, the variable "DigiSwitch" shows the differences between Non-DigiSwitch and DigiSwitch before the suite's intervention. The variable "Suite intervention" shows the effect after using the technologies for users who did not use DigiSwitch. Combining this with "DigiSwitch*Suite intervention," we could measure the difference between Non-DigiSwitch and DigiSwitch with the intervention. Similarly, combining the variables "Time" and "DigiSwitch*Time," we could measure the differences between Non-DigiSwitch and DigiSwitch as the weeks progress.

In Tables 7.5 and 7.6, the variable "DigiSwitch" shows the difference between Non-DigiSwitch and DigiSwitch. The variable "Time" shows the difference between users' satisfaction about the technologies and the privacy perception over the 8 weeks. The interaction "DigiSwitch*Time" is not significant.

We will explain the results individually in the following paragraphs.

Table 7.1 **Loneliness result summary: coefficient estimates, standard errors SE, *t*-score, and significance level *P* for all parameters in the analysis**

Parameters	Coef.	SE	df	t	P
Intercept	1.24	0.16	85	7.89	<.001
DigiSwitch	−0.03	0.21	13	−0.14	>.05
Suite Intervention	0.30	0.13	85	2.26	<.05
Time	−0.06	0.02	85	−2.83	<.01
DigiSwitch*Suite Intervention	−0.37	0.18	85	−2.04	<.05
DigiSwitch*Time	0.04	0.03	85	1.42	>.05

Table 7.2 **Interpersonal support result summary: coefficient estimates, standard errors SE, *t*-score, and significance level *P* for all parameters in the analysis**

Parameters	Coef.	SE	df	t	P
Intercept	3.68	0.12	85	31.96	<.001
DigiSwitch	0.05	0.16	13	0.30	>.05
Suite Intervention	−0.12	0.11	85	−1.09	>.05
Time	0.00	0.02	85	0.02	>.05
DigiSwitch*Suite Intervention	0.19	0.15	85	1.33	>.05
DigiSwitch*Time	0.00	0.02	85	0.03	>.05

Table 7.3 Peer-care burden result summary: coefficient estimates, standard errors SE, *t*-score, and significance level *P* for all parameters in the analysis

Parameters	Coef.	SE	df	t	P
Intercept	1.35	0.17	85	7.94	<.001
DigiSwitch	0.33	0.23	13	1.44	>.05
Suite Intervention	0.13	0.15	85	0.87	>.05
Time	−0.03	0.02	85	−1.50	>.05
DigiSwitch*Suite Intervention	−0.34	0.20	85	−1.68	>.05
DigiSwitch*Time	0.01	0.03	85	0.17	>.05

Table 7.4 Quality of life result summary: coefficient estimates, standard errors SE, *t*-score, and significance level *P* for all parameters in the analysis

Parameters	Coef.	SE	df	t	P
Intercept	4.51	0.20	85	22.41	<.001
DigiSwitch	0.27	0.28	13	0.97	>.05
Suite Intervention	−0.16	0.13	85	−1.25	>.05
Time	0.06	0.02	85	3.27	<.01
DigiSwitch*Suite Intervention	0.04	0.17	85	0.23	>.05
DigiSwitch*Time	−0.04	0.03	85	−1.68	>.05

Table 7.5 Suite satisfaction and usability result summary: coefficient estimates, standard errors SE, *t*-score, and significance level *P* for all parameters in the analysis

Parameters	Coef.	SE	df	t	P
Intercept	3.11	0.20	72	15.73	<.001
DigiSwitch	0.07	0.27	13	0.26	>.05
Time	0.02	0.03	72	0.51	>.05
DigiSwitch*Time	−0.02	0.05	72	−0.43	>.05

Table 7.6 Privacy perception result summary: coefficient estimates, standard errors SE, *t*-score, and significance level *P* for all parameters in the analysis

Parameters	Coef.	SE	df	t	P
Intercept	3.38	0.23	72	14.59	<.001
DigiSwitch	−0.13	0.32	13	−0.40	>.05
Time	0.02	0.04	72	0.34	>.05
DigiSwitch*Time	−0.03	0.06	72	−0.53	>.05

Loneliness

The model shows that the peer-care suite intervention, time, and the interaction between DigiSwitch and technologies intervention have a significant effect on older adults' perceived loneliness. From Table 7.1 and Fig. 7.11, we see that when the technologies are introduced, the group without DigiSwitch shows a peak in loneliness, and the perceived loneliness of people using DigiSwitch is significantly lower than those not using DigiSwitch, $b = -0.37$, $t(85) = -2.04$, $P < .05$. Specifically, the effect for people who do not use DigiSwitch is an increase of 0.30 after using the technologies, while the effect for people who do use DigiSwitch is a decrease of 0.07.

As weeks progress, the perceived loneliness for people who do not use DigiSwitch decreases 0.057 per week, $b = -0.06$, $t(85) = -2.83$, $P < .01$. Though the perceived loneliness for people who use DigiSwitch decreases slightly, it did not change significantly.

Interpersonal support

From Fig. 7.12, we see that the mean scores for interpersonal support of the DigiSwitch group and non-DigiSwitch group are similar at the beginning of the study. Then, the mean scores for non-DigiSwitch users go down slightly while the mean scores for DigiSwitch users stay approximately the same. However, the model shows that neither the DigiSwitch, the technologies intervention, nor time have a significant effect on interpersonal support (Table 7.2). Note however that interpersonal support begins and remains at ceiling, limiting our ability to discover changes.

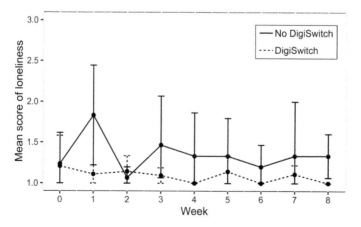

Figure 7.11 Mean scores of loneliness from preweek to week 8.

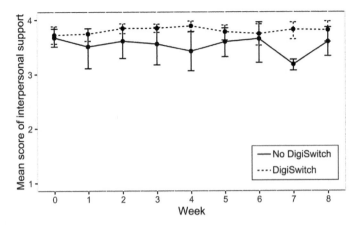

Figure 7.12 Mean scores of interpersonal support from preweek to week 8.

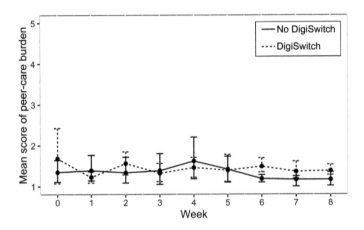

Figure 7.13 Mean scores of peer-care burden from preweek to week 8.

Peer-care burden

From Fig. 7.13, we see that the two lines for with and without DigiSwitch inter-
twine, and are nearly horizontal. There is no major difference between with and
without DigiSwitch users, which means the DigiSwitch does not increase peer-caregiver's burden. On the other hand, technologies intervention and weeks progress do
not have significant effects on perceived burden, which means there is no additional
burden when older adults provide peer-care (Table 7.3). The results are reconfirmed
in Table 7.1, that none of the variables had a significant effect. Similar to interpersonal support, the remaining floor effect of perceived burden also places restrictions
to find changes.

Quality of life

The time has a significant effect on life quality for older adults who do not use DigiSwitch, $b = 0.06$, t (85) $= 3.27$, $P < .01$. This means that the life quality of participants who did not use DigiSwitch increases significantly over time. In contrast, from both Table 7.4 and Fig. 7.14, the life quality of older adults using DigiSwitch does not change much, seeing as the *dotted line* is almost horizontal. In addition, there is no significant difference before and after the peer-care suite gets introduced. Again, a ceiling effect appears here.

Overall satisfaction and the usability of the peer-care suite

The Suite Questionnaire was administered only after the suite was installed, and is therefore analyzed from week 1 to week 8. From Table 7.5 and Fig. 7.15, participants' overall satisfaction with the technologies and their perceptions of the usability of the technology suite does not increase or decrease from week 1 to 8 and is similar for users with and without DigiSwitch, which means adding DigiSwitch does not worsen the user experience, and long-term usage of the technologies does not make users feel more unsatisfied.

Privacy perception

We also conducted the privacy perception questionnaire (Custom Privacy Index With and Without DigiSwitch) from week 1 to 8. As the model shows (Table 7.6), DigiSwitch and time do not significantly influence older adults' privacy perception, but non-DigiSwitch users have higher privacy concern than DigiSwitch users from Fig. 7.16.

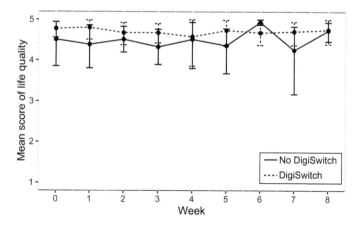

Figure 7.14 Mean scores of quality of life from preweek to week 8.

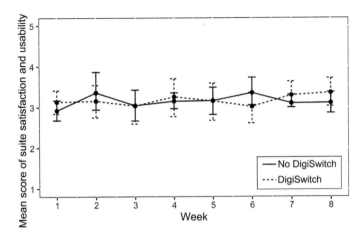

Figure 7.15 Mean scores of suite satisfaction and usability from week 1 to 8.

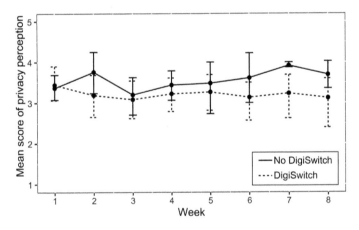

Figure 7.16 Mean scores of privacy perception from week 1 to 8.

Discussion

Participants' levels of loneliness, interpersonal support, peer-care burden, quality of life, satisfaction with the technology suite, and privacy were measured over an 8-week period. We aimed to see how participants' perceptions of the technologies changed over time and if significant differences were found between DigiSwitch users versus non-DigiSwitch users.

Reviewing the hypotheses, we find that:

- **H1—Mixed Support.** *Overall, the peer-care suite reduces loneliness over time.* For older adults who did not use DigiSwitch, their perceived loneliness decreases significantly, while it does not decrease much for those who used DigiSwitch. Therefore, we find mixed evidence for H1.

- **H2—Reject.** *The peer-care suite enhances older adults' interpersonal support over time.* For both DigiSwitch users and non-DigiSwitch users, perceived interpersonal support is not enhanced over time. Therefore, we reject H2, but note a ceiling effect.
- **H3—Reject.** *Overall, the peer-care suite increases the perceived peer-care burden over time.* Neither of the DigiSwitch and time has an effect on peer-care burden. Therefore, we reject H3, but note a floor effect.
- **H4—Mixed Support.** *Overall, the peer-care suite increases older adults' perceived quality of life over time.* For older adults who did not use DigiSwitch, their quality of life increases significantly over time, but it is not true for those who used DigiSwitch. Note that their quality of life does not decrease over time. Therefore, we find mixed evidence for H4, and note a ceiling effect.
- **H5—Reject.** *The users' overall satisfaction of using the peer-care suite increases over time.* From week 1 to 8, there is no significant difference of older adults' feelings about the technologies suite between using DigiSwitch or not. Therefore, we reject H5.
- **H6—Reject.** *Older adults who used DigiSwitch are more concerned with privacy than those who did not use DigiSwitch.* From week 1 to 8, there is no significant difference of older adults' privacy concern between participant who used DigiSwitch or not. Therefore, we reject H6.

Loneliness

Participants in this study reported they hardly ever felt lonely. This is different from many studies of older adults where participants report feeling lonely sometimes or often (Holmén, Ericsson, & Winblad, 1999; Weeks, 1994). Because the participants in this study were hardly ever lonely, we were limited in our ability to investigate the impact of the suite on loneliness.

When we investigated this effect, we found that older adults who did not use DigiSwitch had a small spike in loneliness immediately after the suite was installed, but then it leveled off in week 2. Those with the DigiSwitch reported a fairly stable level of (lack of) loneliness throughout the study.

Overall, our result indicates the peer-care suite decreases loneliness over time for older adults who did not use DigiSwitch, which casts doubt on previous research suggesting that in-home technologies may replace older adults' human contact with their caregivers (Lorenzen-Huber et al., 2011; Rogers & Fisk, 2010), and confirms the interview result from Huber et al.'s work that with using these technologies, the communication level stays the same or increases (Huber et al., 2013). For older adults who used DigiSwitch, their loneliness also slightly decreases over time, though there is no significant improvement.

Non-DigiSwitch users were lonelier when the suite was first introduced, but their loneliness went back to baseline very quickly. One possible reason for the short spike in loneliness in week 1 is that some members of peer groups were assigned to use DigiSwitch when using the Trip Coordinator. Hence, these people had the option to conceal themselves and not offer help. It is possible that this could make the participants who did not have a DigiSwitch feel a lack of companionship or a sense of isolation. After the first week, however, they felt the support from their peers went back to normal and their loneliness returned to baseline as the weeks progressed. One possible reason could be in week 1, participants who had a DigiSwitch used it more frequently when first introduced, then they reduced the usage frequency over time.

Unlike the spike in loneliness of older adults without DigiSwitch, participants with DigiSwitch, on the other hand, did not feel lonelier when the peer-care suite was introduced. Their loneliness did not decline over time as it did for non-DigiSwitch users. The floor effect probably led to this result. Participants' responses for loneliness were mostly 1 (Hardly ever) and a few were 2 (Some of the time) from week 1, which limits the change of their perceived loneliness throughout the 8-week period.

Interpersonal support

Overall, neither the presence of the DigiSwitch, nor time affected perceived interpersonal support. However, as shown in Fig. 7.12, ratings of interpersonal support were at ceiling for the duration of the study. The ceiling effect may possibly explain our findings. Participants were generally very satisfied with their level of interpersonal support, reporting responses of 4 (Completely True) or 3 (Somewhat True) to questions about their level of appraisal support, tangible support, and belonging support during week 1 of the study. We did not see any improvement in the level of interpersonal support throughout the 8-week period because participants were already very satisfied at the beginning of the study, and 4 (Completely True) was the highest response category (i.e., the highest level of satisfaction) that participants could report. In addition, participants took the survey via mobile phone every week with our researchers. Although telephone survey is better than face-to-face survey when involving some sensitive personal issues, it cannot provide as accurate a reflection as other anonymous surveys (Opdenakker, 2006). They might feel uncomfortable if they admitted they were lacking help when answering some questions, e.g., "There is no one I know who will tell me honestly how I am handling my problems."

Peer-care burden

Despite introducing peer-care into the lives of participants, we found that all participants reported very low levels of burden. This finding is notable because it indicates that we may be able to facilitate communities of peers providing support to one another without an increase in the burden they experience.

Care-giving for older adults is considered a stressful task and may harm caregivers' physical and psychological health (Aneshensel, Pearlin, Mullan, Zarit, & Whitlatch, 1995; Pinquart & Sörensen, 2003a, 2003b; Vitaliano, Zhang, & Scanlan, 2003). However, we find that the level of perceived peer-care burden did not change significantly over time. It is possible that peer-care burden never arose as a problem, seeing as participants consistently reported 1 (Never) or 2 (Rarely) to questions throughout the study about their perceived level of caregiver burden on the Zarit Burden Short Form. In fact, from our qualitative data, one participant commented on how her fellow participants actively helped her use the technologies (e.g., "We get together and we talk about this stuff (the technologies) all the time. I don't talk to them about the whole system. They explain to me what to do ... I would ask them if their tablets were working, or their tree."). For this user, the technology suite stimulated conversation, which facilitated peers to help each other use the technologies. Another participant commented on how the technologies and the peer-to-peer network created a feeling of togetherness more so than a feeling of responsibility for others, indicating that the act of caregiving was likely not perceived as a burden by that participant. For this user, the joint experience of using the technologies and being a part of a peer-based caregiving network promoted a sense of unity, or "togetherness." This finding is interesting because it suggests that the technology suite may help older adults feel more connected to their peers in the community because of the shared element of their caregiving experience. For some participants, this feeling of togetherness may overshadow the feeling of burden that can accompany the responsibility of caring for others.

In general, participants did not report that the caregiver element of the technology suite was a burden. We also found that the DigiSwitch did not increase perceived burden. This finding is important because two studies on the privacy management burden in Facebook's privacy setting, and location privacy setting indicate that privacy management generally poses additional user burden (Benisch, Kelley, Sadeh, & Cranor, 2011; Liu, Gummadi, Krishnamurthy, & Mislove, 2011), while our result suggests that participants in the DigiSwitch group were not additionally burdened by the need to manage their privacy. We also found that participants were not burdened by the responsibility of peer care, which is promising for the future of peer-based caregiving technologies for communities of low-SES older adults. This suggests that the peer-based, community-level design of the SOLACE technologies has potential as an effective caregiving intervention. Perhaps, the technologies work well at the level of the community to facilitate communication, peer-to-peer help, and a sense of togetherness—without making low-SES older adults feel like the responsibility of caring for each other is burdensome.

Quality of life

For both groups with and without DigiSwitch, participants' quality of life stayed the same as it was before introducing the peer-care suite and the first time introducing it, though we added peer-care tasks to the older adults' life. This could indicate that the benefits of the suite outweighed any inconvenience. On the other hand, we could argue that the suite should have increased their quality of life. However, we did not see an increase in quality of life after introducing the suite. One reason for this could be because participants were not familiar with these technologies and did not realize the potential benefits. The motivation for older adults to learn new technologies is very low, especially in our case where four technologies were employed together (Tacken, Marcellini, Mollenkopf, Ruoppila, & Széman, 2005). Some factors that influence older adults' willingness to adopt, and accept, new technologies include the fear of the new, a lack of motivation, difficulties related to usability, and insufficient training (Mollenkopf, 2003). Our participants were low-SES people with a relatively low education level. The use of technology is dependent on education level and income (Tacken et al., 2005). For example, older adults with higher education and better cognitive abilities, may find it easier to use the technologies which could contribute to seeing the technologies as improving their quality of life. Another reason may be that the participants were asked to use these technologies, so they felt they must accomplish the tasks as the researchers requested. In the WHO Quality of Life questionnaire, some questions such as "I have the freedom to make my own decisions," and "I am able to do things I like to do," may have been in conflict with the role of research participant which asks participants to perform certain activities.

However, we did see differences in the life quality of participants based on whether or not they had the DigiSwitch over time. The quality of life ratings for those users without DigiSwitch increased significantly over time, while the life quality ratings of those who used DigiSwitch was not enhanced as the weeks progressed. One reason may be the usability of DigiSwitch. Since DigiSwitch controls the privacy settings of all four technologies, it may not be as straight-forward to use as the other peer-care technologies. Users may get confused when operating it. However, participants were not asked about the usability of DigiSwitch specifically, only the technology suite as a whole. Future work may involve asking users about the usability of each individual technology so that data about the usability of DigiSwitch can be collected and comparisons can be drawn between the usability of DigiSwitch and the other four technologies. However, in Fig. 7.14 we see that the ceiling effect also occurred. The participants were generally satisfied with their life, so there was not much room for improvement over time.

From the qualitative data, participants had mixed reactions about whether or not the technologies helped them live more independently, but most agreed that the technologies were useful and, at least, helped them somewhat When one participant was asked if the technologies enhanced his independence, he answered "Moderately." When the same participant was asked if it would be more difficult for him to plan his activities if he did not have the technology suite, he answered "Yes. Pretty much."

Overall satisfaction and the usability of the peer-care suite

Users' satisfaction with, and perceived usability of, the technologies did not change over time. On the one hand, it is positive that we find satisfaction and perceived usability of these technologies did not decrease, because it means the participants did not become frustrated with the technologies over time. On the other hand, ideally, we would have expected satisfaction and usability to increase over time as participants became more familiar with the technologies. One reason for the similar ratings across time could be that we provided training initially, but did not provide additional training throughout the study. Many participants expressed that they did not fully understand how the technologies worked. For example, two participants mentioned that they did not know how the Presence Clock tracked their movements (e.g., "I don't get the clock. I just walk past it all the time when I go to my door") and another participant detailed her confusion about the community window, commenting that she could not find the "Close Out" button, thought that she could not call anybody at all, tried calling people when they were not on, and was not aware of the people who were on her calling list.

Moreover, one participant reported that she did not know instruction manuals were provided for each technology, and believed that she was not given enough training on how to use the technologies (e.g., "I thought we all were going to do a class on how to work it. I wish we had it because it could've been more useful and then we could've done something with it.") More training could have increased the older adults' knowledge of the technologies and how they function. One older adult, e.g., expressed heightened interest in using his tablet after finding out that it had Internet access. It is possible that participants' limited knowledge of the technologies and their functions could have influenced their perception of the technologies (e.g., "I may even pick the tablet if I learn how to work it."). This claim is supported by the statement of one participant who expressed an overall positive attitude towards the technologies, but asserted that she did not know how to use them (e.g., "I would like to learn a little more about the technologies to get going. I think it (i.e., learning about the technologies) is worthwhile. It's like a toy—you play with it and once you learn it, you get all excited."). Many participants also relied on family members to teach them how to use the technologies, e.g., "(My god-daughter) taught me a lot of things. When she was over here, my goodness, she had the whole Internet on (the tablet), and I haven't been able to get it. If I learn how to use this more, it'll be better." In general, participants suggested a more interactive, hands-on method of instruction that incorporated weekly assessments designed to gauge each participants' understanding of the technologies would have helped. For example, on participant said, "If you show us and tell us, then we will know more about the system. . . It would be better for somebody to come once a week or every week to touch base with that person and see how much they have learned." Overall, most participants reported a positive impression of the technologies and claimed that they would continue using the technologies after the study was over if that was an option (e.g., "I would keep those. It feels like I'm connected with the people. I'm connected with them and I am not bothered." "Overall, I've enjoyed it. I want to buy one.").

Furthermore, many participants reported that they liked the Presence Clock because it looked "cool" and displayed the time. Other participants reported that they liked the Check-in Tree because it looked "pretty," displayed pictures, and incorporated a light-up functionality to indicate their check-in status (e.g., "I like it how it is. It lights up at night." "I love this tree . . . you have a favorite and you hit that button. I mean, it's something different.") Several participants preferred Skype to the Community Window because it allowed them to communicate with family members rather than just their peer group. In addition, several participants expressed confusion about the Trip Coordinator (e.g., "I go in and all it says is my trip, so what do I put in there?") even though most liked the concept underlying it.

Privacy perception

Older adults who did not use DigiSwitch had slightly higher privacy concerns than DigiSwitch users, though generally DigiSwitch and time do not significantly affect older adults' privacy perception.

Users' privacy concerns decrease after users read and use the information in the website privacy policies if the policies are comprehensible (Wu, Huang, Yen, & Popova, 2012). The line chart in Fig. 7.16 shows a similar result. Though DigiSwitch users and non-DigiSwitch users did not report significant differences in their attitudes about privacy throughout the 8-week period, the mean scores of non-DigiSwitch users were slightly higher than DigiSwitch users, which may be because with using DigiSwitch, older adults feel more in control of their privacy rather than just worrying about their privacy or not disclosing their information.

The qualitative data from the interviews may explain why we do not see a significant difference between the privacy perception of DigiSwitch users versus non-DigiSwitch users. Most participants (including both DigiSwitch users and non-DigiSwitch users) reported that the technologies did not invade their privacy. Previous research suggests in-home monitoring technology may cause privacy concerns, especially those that capture images (Caine et al., 2006). Nonetheless, in our peer-care suite, only one technology (Community Window) involved video chat or image capturing. Users are not monitored all the time, and they have the option to reject a video call from others, which does not pose a huge privacy threat. Some participants specifically reported that they did not care if their data from either the Check-In Tree, the Presence Clock, or the Trip Coordinator (or a combination of the three) could be seen by others. One participant reported never having used the DigiSwitch device, so the amount of DigiSwitch use may help explain our finding. Moreover, several participants expressed that they liked the DigiSwitch functionality because it could be used to communicate with others. They did not comment on DigiSwitch's privacy-enhancing capabilities, suggesting that they lacked complete knowledge of the purpose and functions of DigiSwitch. Two participants commented that they would not care if others saw their activity data as it could be used as a conversation piece, and another participant commented that she did not wish to have a privacy-controlling technology because "I will never do anything that I will be ashamed of." One other participant commented that she did not mind if others could see her data, as long as she was not the only person whose data could be seen, e.g., "[The Presence Clock data] would move for me and a couple of other people, so it wouldn't be all me. No, I don't mind (if they saw it). They can see it." Furthermore, one participant mentioned that she did not care if others saw her schedule, but if more personal information about her trips or her health was accessible, then she would not like it if that data was shown. The same participant also said, "if [my data] were coded, then I'd like it better." Moreover, another participant commented that the amount and type of data shown by the technologies was not enough to concern her about privacy, e.g., "So, are you monitoring just me or the activities in my house? That's [my son] smoking 'til 3 a.m. in the morning, but it looks like I'm a very active person at 2 a.m. and I'm not. That's him." One participant also mentioned he felt he had control over the technologies. In general, participants did not care whether their data was visible to others in their peer network.

Ceiling effect and floor effect

A notable limitation that affects many of our results is ceiling and floor effects. The results for some of the questionnaires produced either a ceiling effect, where most data points fall in the very high range of possible values, or a floor effect, where most data points fall in the very low range. For example, as can be seen in the per-ceived interpersonal support line chart (Fig. 7.12), most participants reported scores of four, which was the highest point available, and indicated the highest levels of perceived interpersonal support. All participants in our study felt they had very high interpersonal support at the beginning of the study, so this ceiling effect lim-ited our ability to see any improvement. We expect older adults who started with lower perceived interpersonal support might experience an increase. Similarly, the ceiling effect also occurs for quality of life (Fig. 7.14). Moreover, the peer-care bur-den scale produced a floor effect (Fig. 7.10). Participants' answers all fell into the lowest value available, which was one (Never). All participants felt they had very little burden from before introducing the technology suite to the end of the study, so again, the floor effect limits the change of peer-care burden throughout the 8-week period. If the response categories could be lengthened to seven instead of four in future studies, the result may be different because this change might allow for more variability in response scores, specifically for the scores patterned by a ceiling effect and a floor effect. The ceiling and floor effect for the responses to the inter-personal support scale, quality of life scale and the peer-care burden scale may also be explained by the nature of the interview, which was conducted over the phone. Perhaps, participants did not want to reveal that they lacked others' support, had low life quality, or felt burdened by the responsibility to care for others in their con-versations with researchers to protect their self-esteem and/or appear socially desirable.

Conclusion and future work

This paper presented results from an 8-week in-situ study of older adults' percep-tions while using a suite of four peer-care technologies, Activity Clock, Community Window, Check-In Tree, and Trip Coordinator, with the privacy-enhancing tool DigiSwitch. We were interested in investigating how DigiSwitch and time influence the low-SES older adults' experience (quality of life, loneliness, peer-care burden, interpersonal support, satisfaction and usability of technologies, and privacy percep-tion) when using the peer-care suite over 8 weeks.

Our results show that we can engage older adults in peer-care without increasing the burden they feel. This is important because as a stressful task for caregivers, care-giving for older adults has a negative effect on their physical and psychological health (Aneshensel et al., 1995; Pinquart & Sörensen, 2003a, 2003b; Vitaliano et al., 2003).

The loneliness of older adults decreased over time more or less, which addresses the concern that these kind of technologies may replace older adults' human contact with their caregiver (Lorenzen-Huber et al., 2011; Rogers & Fisk, 2010). Especially for participants who did not use DigiSwitch, loneliness decreased significantly throughout the 8-week period. We also found that the life quality of older adults without DigiSwitch increased significantly over time. In addition, the participants' satisfaction levels and ratings of the usability of these technologies did not decrease, which means the participants did not become more frustrated with the technologies over time.

The result of the suite usability also suggests that when designing for older adults, especially low-SES older adults, designers should put more effort into the usability of the system, along with making the technologies easy to learn and simple to use, since some participants reported some confusion and problems with the suite usage. Designers should also effectively train low-SES older adults, so that they fully understand the purpose and functionalities of each technology.

Our main finding shows that DigiSwitch use does not increase peer-caregiver burden, and there is no additional peer-caregiver burden when low-SES older adults provide peer care. In future work, we plan to investigate how the technology suite impacts low-SES older adults who are not already experiencing low burden.

In future work, we also plan to modify the design of the response scales of the questionnaires, and exclude the participants who are at ceiling- or floor-, to avoid ceiling effects and floor effects. Additionally, we plan to shorten the length of our surveys to increase response rates and administer the surveys to a larger sample to better represent target users.

Acknowledgments

This material is based on work supported by the National Science Foundation under Grant Number 1117860. We thank Dr. Bart Knijnenburg for help with data analysis, Matthew Francisco, Shenshen Han, and Ingrid Arreola for assistance with suite design and technology development, Ginger White, Megan Holder, Zachary Robinson, Justin Stephens and Natalie Smoot, David Byrd and Tanya Singh for assistance with data collection, Brian Justice and Duyen Nguyen for voice files transcription.

References

Abowd, G.D., Bobick, A.F., Essa, I.A., Mynatt, E.D., & Rogers, W.A. (July 2002). The aware home: A living laboratory for technologies for successful aging. In *Proceedings of the AAAI-02 Workshop "Automation as Caregiver"* (pp. 1−7).

Adler, N. E., & Newman, K. (2002). Socioeconomic disparities in health: Pathways and policies. *Health Affairs*, *21*(2), 60–76.

Administraton on Aging. (2015). *A profile of older Americans: 2015*. Retrieved March 2, 2017,
from <http://www.aoa.acl.gov/aging_statistics/profile/2015/docs/2015-Profile.pdf>.

Andrews, M. M., & Boyle, J. S. (Eds.), (2008). *Transcultural concepts in nursing care*.
Philidelphia, PA: Lippincott Williams & Wilkins.

Aneshensel, C. S., Pearlin, L. I., Mullan, J. T., Zarit, S. H., & Whitlatch, C. J. (1995).
Profiles in caregiving: The unexpected career. San Diego, CA: Academic Press.

Arreola, I., Morris, Z., Francisco, M., Connelly, K., Caine, K.E., & White, G.E. (April 2014).
From checking on to checking in: Designing for low socio-economic status older adults.
In *CHI* (Vol. 14).

Ashida, S., & Heaney, C. A. (2008). Differential associations of social support and social
connectedness with structural features of social networks and the health status of older
adults. *Journal of Aging and Health*, *20*(7), 872–893.

Balfour, J. L., & Kaplan, G. A. (2002). Neighborhood environment and loss of physical function in older adults: Evidence from the Alameda County Study. *American Journal of
Epidemiology*, *155*(6), 507–515.

Bédard, M., Molloy, D. W., Squire, L., Dubois, S., Lever, J. A., & O'Donnell, M. (2001).
The Zarit Burden interview a new short version and screening version. *The
Gerontologist*, *41*(5), 652–657.

Benisch, M., Kelley, P. G., Sadeh, N., & Cranor, L. F. (2011). Capturing location-privacy
preferences: Quantifying accuracy and user-burden tradeoffs. *Personal and Ubiquitous
Computing*, *15*(7), 679–694.

Black, K., Dobbs, D., & Young, T. L. (2015). Aging in community mobilizing a new para-
digm of older adults as a core social resource. *Journal of Applied Gerontology*, *34*(2),
219–243.

Bossen, C., Christensen, L. R., Grönvall, E., & Vestergaard, L. S. (2013). CareCoor:
Augmenting the coordination of cooperative home care work. *International Journal of
Medical Informatics*, *82*(5), e189–e199.

Caine, K. E., Fisk, A. D., & Rogers, W. A. (October 2006). Benefits and privacy concerns of
a home equipped with a visual sensing system: A perspective from older adults.
In *Proceedings of the human factors and ergonomics society annual meeting* (Vol. 50,
pp. 180–184). Los Angeles, CA: Sage Publications.

Caine, K.E., Fisk, A.D., & Rogers, W.A. (October 2007). Designing privacy conscious aware
homes for older adults. In *Proceedings of the human factors and ergonomics society
annual meeting* (pp. 1–5).

Caine, K. E., Rogers, W. A., & Fisk, A. D. (September 2005). Privacy perceptions of an
aware home with visual sensing devices. In *Proceedings of the human factors and ergonomics society annual meeting* (Vol. 49, pp. 1856–1858). Los Angeles, CA: SAGE
Publications.

Caine, K. E., Zimmerman, C. Y., Schall-Zimmerman, Z., Hazlewood, W. R., Camp, L. J.,
Connelly, K. H., ... Shankar, K. (2011). DigiSwitch: A device to allow older adults to
monitor and direct the collection and transmission of health information collected at
home. *Journal of Medical Systems*, *35*(5), 1181–1195.

Caine, K. E., Zimmerman, C. Y., Schall-Zimmerman, Z., Hazlewood, W. R., Sulgrove,
A. C., Camp, L. J., ... Shankar, K. (November 2010). DigiSwitch: Design and evaluation of a device for older adults to preserve privacy while monitoring health at home.
In *Proceedings of the 1st ACM international health informatics symposium*
(pp. 153–162). ACM.

Cohen, S., Mermelstein, R., Kamarck, T., & Hoberman, H. M. (1985). Measuring the functional components of social support. In *Social support: Theory, research and applications* (pp. 73−94). Springer Netherlands.

Consolvo, S., Roessler, P., & Shelton, B. E. (September 2004). The CareNet display: Lessons learned from an in home evaluation of an ambient display. In *International conference on ubiquitous computing* (pp. 1−17). Springer Berlin Heidelberg.

Cook, D. J., Augusto, J. C., & Jakkula, V. R. (2009). Ambient intelligence: Technologies, applications, and opportunities. *Pervasive and Mobile Computing, 5*(4), 277−298.

Coppin, A. K., Ferrucci, L., Lauretani, F., Phillips, C., Chang, M., Bandinelli, S., & Guralnik, J. M. (2006). Low socioeconomic status and disability in old age: Evidence from the InChianti study for the mediating role of physiological impairments. *The Journals of Gerontology Series A: Biological Sciences and Medical Sciences, 61*(1), 86−91.

Cornejo, R., Tentori, M., & Favela, J. (2013). Ambient awareness to strengthen the family social network of older adults. *Computer Supported Cooperative Work (CSCW), 22*(2−3), 309−344.

Cornwell, B., Laumann, E. O., & Schumm, L. P. (2008). The social connectedness of older adults: A national profile. *American Sociological Review, 73*(2), 185−203.

Courtney, K. L., Demeris, G., Rantz, M., & Skubic, M. (2008). Needing smart home technologies: The perspectives of older adults in continuing care retirement communities. *Informatics in Primary Care, 16*(3), 195−201.

Demiris, G., & Hensel, B. K. (2008). Technologies for an aging society: A systematic review of "smart home" applications. *Yearbook of Medical Informatics, 3*, 33−40.

Demiris, G., Rantz, M. J., Aud, M. A., Marek, K. D., Tyrer, H. W., Skubic, M., & Hussam, A. A. (2004). Older adults' attitudes towards and perceptions of 'smart home' technologies: A pilot study. *Medical Informatics and the Internet in Medicine, 29*(2), 87−94.

Demiris, G., Skubic, M., Keller, J., Rantz, M.J., Oliver, D.P., Aud, M.A., ... Green, N. (June 2006). Nurse participation in the design of user interfaces for a smart home system. In *Proceedings of the international conference on smart homes and health telematics, NI Belfast, Editor* (pp. 66−73).

Demongeot, J., Virone, G., Duchêne, F., Benchetrit, G., Hervé, T., Noury, N., & Rialle, V. (2002). Multi-sensors acquisition, data fusion, knowledge mining and alarm triggering in health smart homes for elderly people. *Comptes Rendus Biologies, 325*(6), 673−682.

Doyle, J., Bailey, C., Scanaill, C. N., & van den Berg, F. (2014). Lessons learned in deploying independent living technologies to older adults' homes. *Universal Access in the Information Society, 13*(2), 191−204.

Doyle, J., Skrba, Z., McDonnell, R., & Arent, B. (September 2010). Designing a touch screen communication device to support social interaction amongst older adults. In *Proceedings of the 24th BCS interaction specialist group conference* (pp. 177−185). British Computer Society.

Edwards, W., & Grinter, R. (2001). *At home with ubiquitous computing: Seven challenges. Ubicomp 2001: Ubiquitous computing* (pp. 256−272). Berlin/Heidelberg: Springer.

Gardner, P. J. (2011). Natural neighborhood networks—Important social networks in the lives of older adults aging in place. *Journal of Aging Studies, 25*(3), 263−271.

Hanson, G. J., Takahashi, P. Y., & Pecina, J. L. (2013). Emerging technologies to support independent living of older adults at risk. *Care Management Journals, 14*(1), 58−64.

Haslam, C., Holme, A., Haslam, S. A., Iyer, A., Jetten, J., & Williams, W. H. (2008). Maintaining group memberships: Social identity continuity predicts well-being after stroke. *Neuropsychological Rehabilitation, 18*(5-6), 671−691.

Heinz, M., Martin, P., Margrett, J. A., Yearns, M., Franke, W., Yang, H. I., ... Chang, C. K. (2013). Perceptions of technology among older adults. *Journal of Gerontological Nursing, 39*, 42–51.

Helal, S., Mann, W., El-Zabadani, H., King, J., Kaddoura, Y., & Jansen, E. (2005). The gator tech smart house: A programmable pervasive space. *Computer, 38*(3), 50–60.

Holmén, K., Ericsson, K., & Winblad, B. (1999). Quality of life among the elderly. *Scandinavian Journal of Caring Sciences, 13*(2), 91–95.

Hong, J. I., & Landay, J. A. (June 2004). An architecture for privacy-sensitive ubiquitous computing. In *Proceedings of the 2nd international conference on Mobile systems, applications, and services* (pp. 177–189). ACM.

Huber, L. L., Shankar, K., Caine, K., Connelly, K., Camp, L. J., Walker, B. A., & Borrero, L. (2013). How in-home technologies mediate caregiving relationships in later life. *International Journal of Human-Computer Interaction, 29*(7), 441–455.

Hughes, M. E., Waite, L. J., Hawkley, L. C., & Cacioppo, J. T. (2004). A short scale for measuring loneliness in large surveys results from two population-based studies. *Research on Aging, 26*(6), 655–672.

Kidd, C. D., Orr, R., Abowd, G. D., Atkeson, C. G., Essa, I. A., MacIntyre, B., ... Newstetter, W. (October 1999). The aware home: A living laboratory for ubiquitous computing research. In *International workshop on cooperative buildings* (pp. 191–198). Springer Berlin Heidelberg.

Kientz, J. A., Patel, S. N., Jones, B., Price, E. D., Mynatt, E. D., & Abowd, G. D. (April 2008). *The Georgia tech aware home. CHI'08 extended abstracts on Human factors in computing systems* (pp. 3675–3680). ACM.

Langheinrich, M. (2002). *A privacy awareness system for ubiquitous computing environ-ments. International conference on Ubiquitous computing* (pp. 237–245). Berlin/ Heidelberg: Springer.

Leonardi, C., Albertini, A., Pianesi, F., & Zancanaro, M. (October 2010). An exploratory study of a touch-based gestural interface for elderly. In *Proceedings of the 6th Nordic conference on human-computer interaction: Extending boundaries* (pp. 845–850). ACM.

Liu, Y., Gummadi, K. P., Krishnamurthy, B., & Mislove, A. (November 2011). Analyzing facebook privacy settings: User expectations vs. reality. In *Proceedings of the 2011 ACM SIGCOMM conference on Internet measurement conference* (pp. 61–70). ACM.

Lorenzen-Huber, L., Boutain, M., Camp, L. J., Shankar, K., & Connelly, K. H. (2011). Privacy, technology, and aging: A proposed framework. *Ageing International, 36*(2), 232–252.

Meingast, M., Roosta, T., & Sastry, S. (2006). *Security and privacy issues with health care information technology. Engineering in Medicine and Biology Society, 2006. EMBS'06. 28th Annual International Conference of the IEEE* (pp. 5453–5458). Piscataway, NJ: IEEE.

Mollenkopf, H. (2003). Assistive technology: Potential and preconditions of useful applica-tions. *Impact of Technology on Successful Aging*, 203–214.

Opdenakker, R. (September 2006). Advantages and disadvantages of four interview techni-ques in qualitative research. In *Forum qualitative sozialforschung/forum: Qualitative social research* (Vol. 7, No. 4).

Pinquart, M., & Sörensen, S. (2003a). Associations of stressors and uplifts of caregiving with caregiver burden and depressive mood: A meta-analysis. *The Journals of Gerontology Series B: Psychological Sciences and Social Sciences, 58*(2), P112–P128.

Pinquart, M., & Sörensen, S. (2003b). Differences between caregivers and noncaregivers in psychological health and physical health: A meta-analysis. *Psychology and Aging, 18*(2), 250.

Riche, Y., & Mackay, W. (2010). PeerCare: Supporting awareness of rhythms and routines for better aging in place. *Computer Supported Cooperative Work (CSCW), 19*(1), 73−104.

Rogers, W. A., & Fisk, A. D. (2010). Toward a psychological science of advanced technology design for older adults. *The Journals of Gerontology Series B: Psychological Sciences and Social Sciences, 65*, 645−653.

Stepler, R. (2016). *Smaller share of women ages 65 and older are living alone*. Retrieved March 2, 2017, from <http://www.pewsocialtrends.org/2016/02/18/smaller-share-of-women-ages-65-and-older-are-living-alone/>.

Tacken, M., Marcellini, F., Mollenkopf, H., Ruoppila, I., & Széman, Z. (2005). Use and acceptance of new technology by older people. Findings of the international MOBILATE survey: 'Enhancing mobility in later life'. *Gerontechnology, 3*(3), 126−137.

U.S. Census Bureau (2017). Estimates of U.S. Population by Age and Sex: April 1, 2010, to July 1, 2016. Retrieved September 6, 2017, from < https://www.census.gov/newsroom/press-releases/2017/cb17-tps38-population-estimates-single-year-age.html >.

Vitaliano, P. P., Zhang, J., & Scanlan, J. M. (2003). Is caregiving hazardous to one's physical health? A meta-analysis. *Psychological Bulletin, 129*(6), 946.

Weeks, D. J. (1994). A review of loneliness concepts, with particular reference to old age. *International Journal of Geriatric Psychiatry, 9*(5), 345−355.

White, G., Singh, T., Caine, K., & Connelly, K. (May 2015). *Limited but satisfied: Low SES older adults experiences of aging in place. Pervasive computing technologies for healthcare (PervasiveHealth), 2015 9th international conference on* (pp. 121−128). IEEE.

World Health Organization. (2012). *WHO Quality of Life-BREF (WHOQOL-BREF)*. Retrieved March 2, 2017, from <http://www.who.int/substance_abuse/research_tools/whoqolbref/en/>.

Wu, K. W., Huang, S. Y., Yen, D. C., & Popova, I. (2012). The effect of online privacy policy on consumer privacy concern and trust. *Computers in Human Behavior, 28*(3), 889−897.

Enhancing social engagement of older adults through technology

Michael T. Bixter[1], Kenneth A. Blocker[2] and Wendy A. Rogers[2]
[1]Arizona State University, Tempe, AZ, United States, [2]University of Illinois at Urbana-Champaign, Champaign, IL, United States

Introduction

Humans are social animals. Whether it is spending time with family members during meals, talking with friends about personal or societal events of the day, or interacting with coworkers and clients during work, interactions with others is a common, everyday activity. However, individuals vary in their levels of social engagement, and these differences may have consequential effects on quality of life. For instance, high levels of social engagement have been found to be associated with a variety of beneficial health outcomes such as mental well-being (Cohen, 2004; Thoits, 2011). Conversely, social isolation and loneliness have been shown to exert a strong negative effect on life and well-being outcomes, such as physiological health (Holt-Lunstad, Smith, Baker, Harris, & Stephenson, 2015; Kearns, Whitley, Tannahill, & Ellaway, 2015; Nicholson, 2012).

For older adults, social engagement may be particularly important due to the life-changing events that can accompany older adulthood, including retirement and the development of disease or immobility. In longitudinal studies, increased social engagement predicted reduced mortality rates (Bennett, 2002; Ceria et al., 2001; Dalgard & Håheim, 1998; Eng, Rimm, Fitzmaurice, & Kawachi, 2002; Kiely & Flacker, 2003; Kim et al., 2016; Sampson, Bulpitt, & Fletcher, 2009). Though the exact mechanism that accounts for this relationship with mortality remains debated, social engagement has been associated with a variety of consequential health outcomes for older adults. Examples include hypertension (Yang et al., 2016); the development of dementia (Crooks, Lubben, Petitti, Little, & Chiu, 2008; Fratiglioni, Wang, Ericsson, Maytan, Winblad, 2000; Kotwal, Kim, Waite, & Dale, 2016; Sörman, Sundström, Rönnlund, Adolfsson, & Nilsson, 2014); and mental health and psychological well-being (Fiori, Antonucci, & Cortina, 2006; Forsman, Nyqvist, Schierenbeck, Gustafson, & Wahlbeck, 2012; Litwin & Shiovitz-Ezra, 2011). In all of these instances, higher levels of social engagement were associated with more positive health and quality of life outcomes.

With the rapid development of information and communication technologies over the past few decades, particularly with the internet, the way that people interact socially has dramatically changed. A specific example is the advent of social

Aging, Technology and Health. DOI: http://dx.doi.org/10.1016/B978-0-12-811272-4.00008-7

engagement technologies, including email and social networking sites such as Facebook and Instagram. Though these technologies have impacted how individuals of all ages interact socially, we focus here on the current and potential opportunities these technologies have to bolster social engagement in older adults. Social engagement technologies allow older adults to keep in contact with friends and family members who may no longer reside in the same geographical area. This has the potential to strengthen existing social ties by allowing new forms of communication and the sharing of information between older adults and their social connections. Furthermore, these technologies also afford older adults the opportunity to forge new social ties by connecting with others who share similar interests or experiences (e.g., online health groups or book clubs).

Our goal in this chapter is to assess the relationship between social engagement and health outcomes for older adults, specifically with respect to the role technology can play in supporting and facilitating social engagement. Social engagement technologies include established forms of electronic communication such as email and social networking sites (e.g., Facebook), as well as emerging technologies such as telepresence, social robots, virtual reality (VR), and augmented reality (AR). Our analysis of the literature revealed that there are barriers for older adults in the adoption and use of technologies that foster social engagement. We make recommendations about how designers can overcome these barriers to better suit the needs and interests of older adults.

Social engagement

Defining social engagement

Social engagement has been defined and operationalized in different, and sometimes inconsistent, ways in the literature. We propose the following definition: *Social engagement refers to the degree of participation in interpersonal activities and the maintenance of meaningful connections with other people.* This definition relates to a number of terms that have been used in the researched literature, such as social integration, social support, and social connectedness. Though differences exist between the exact characteristics of these related terms, all deal with the extent that an individual is living an interpersonally engaged and active lifestyle while maintaining meaningful relationships with others.

Social engagement may be influenced by *social networks* (Stopczynski et al., 2014; Watts, Dodds, & Newman, 2002) and *social capital* (Adler & Kwon, 2002; Kawachi, Kennedy, & Glass, 1999; Putnam, 1995). These terms primarily refer to social interaction at a group or community level. Social networks deal with the interconnections of a group, whereas social capital deals with the level of social participation or social resources available for a particular community or geographical area. The structure of a social network and the degree of social capital present in a given community will likely influence the level of social engagement experienced by individual group members.

Measuring social engagement

Social engagement can be measured in a number of ways. One method is to simply count the number of social contacts of an individual. For instance, researchers can have participants self-report on the number of people they interact with socially during a specified length of time (e.g., daily, weekly, monthly). This numerical frequency-based measure of social engagement can provide information about the level of social connectedness for a particular individual.

However, even though a numerical count of social contacts can give an impression of the scope and size of the social network an individual resides in, it does not provide any information about the *quality* of the particular social relationships. For example, an individual may have to interact with another person on a frequent basis (e.g., due to work), but may not enjoy these interactions. Social interactions of these sorts could exert a negative influence on an individual's quality of life. As a result, other measures of social engagement have individuals rate the quality of their social relationships on a variety of functional dimensions. For instance, Zunzunegui, Alvarado, Del Ser, and Otero (2003) had participants qualify their relationships with social connections (e.g., relatives, friends) through the following questions: "How often do you feel you help your [social connection]?"; "How often do you feel useful to your [social connection]?"; "How often do you feel that you play an important role in your [social connection's] lives?" Responses to these questions help quantify the meaningfulness and usefulness individuals attach to their various social relationships.

Of course, measures of social engagement can contain items that quantify both the numerical count of an individual's social connections as well as the perceived quality of the specific social relationships. One frequently used example is the Lubben Social Network Scale (Lubben et al., 2006), wherein participants not only self-report on the number of active family and friend social ties, but also the perceived support of these respective social connections. By including indices of the scope and size of an individual's network, the quality of the individual's social support can be assessed from the single scale.

Other measures of social engagement do not focus on particular social connections themselves, but instead on the degree of social activity or participation experienced by the individual (e.g., Gerstorf et al., 2016). In these measures, participants self-report on whether they attend a variety of social events (e.g., community centers, civic engagements, religious services). Higher attendance and participation in social activities is taken as evidence of a more socially engaged lifestyle.

For any intervention or technology designed to enhance social engagement to be successful, it is critical that the values and social preferences of individuals are taken into account. Individuals vary in their social relationship preferences, as evidenced by individual differences in typologies of social networks (Fiori et al., 2006; Litwin, 2001). Whereas some social networks consist of individuals with a few strong ties, other networks consist of individuals with many ties that are weaker in strength. Moreover, whereas some social networks consist mainly of ties with family members or close friends, other networks consist of a greater variety of social relationships. Insofar as different social network typologies stem from the values and preferences of individuals who make up the network, any intervention or technology designed to target social engagement must accommodate these differences. Technologies that aim to facilitate social engagement in a large and diverse user base should be flexible and customizable to enable individuals with different social preferences the ability to tailor the technology to suit their needs.

The value of social engagement for health outcomes

High levels of social engagement for older adults have documented benefits for health and quality of life, as measured through mortality rates and longevity. Though the precise mechanisms that account for the positive effects of social engagement on longevity remain inconclusive, a high level of social engagement has been shown to have a beneficial impact on a variety of consequential health outcomes (see Table 8.1).

Table 8.1 Higher levels of social engagement are associated with a variety of health outcomes

	Example health outcomes	References
Physiological markers of health	• Stress responsiveness • Cardiovascular disease • Hypertension • Immune functioning	Cacioppo et al. (2002), Cohen, Doyle, Skoner, Rabin, and Gwaltney (1997), Hermes et al. (2009), Ramsay et al. (2008), Yang et al. (2016)
Cognitive-related issues	• Reduced occurrence and onset of dementia • Increased cognitive functioning, including episodic memory, semantic memory, working memory, perceptual speed, and visuospatial ability • Reduced declines in memory over time	Ertel et al. (2008), Holtzman et al. (2004), Krueger et al. (2009), Marioni et al. (2015), Saczynski et al. (2006)
Mental health	• Happiness and life satisfaction • Positive affect • Reduced levels of depression, anxiety, and suicide ideation	Barg et al. (2006), Cacioppo, Hughes, Waite, Hawkley, and Thisted (2006), Forsman, Herberts, Nyqvist, Wahlbeck, and Schierenbeck (2013), Golden et al. (2009), Huxhold et al. (2013), Nyqvist, Forsman, Giuntoli, and Cattan (2013)

Social engagement and mortality

One clear example of health benefits for older adults is longevity. The link between levels of social engagement and mortality rates (e.g., Ceria et al., 2001; Giles, Glonek, Luszcz, & Andrews, 2005; Kiely & Flacker, 2003; Thomas, 2012) has been explored through longitudinal studies assessing social engagement and subsequent mortality rates over a specified number of years.

In one such longitudinal study, Kiely, Simon, Jones, and Morris (2000) analyzed data from 927 long-term care residents over a 4.5-year period. Overall, individuals with the lowest score on their 6-point social engagement scale were 2.3 times more likely to die compared with individuals with the highest score. Even after controlling for a number of well-known risk factors, individuals with low social engagement were still 1.4 times more likely to die compared with high social engagement individuals. In a more recent study, Kim et al. (2016) analyzed data from 8234 participants enrolled in the Korean Longitudinal Study of Aging over a 6-year period. After adjusting for a number of covariates, they found that the all-cause mortality rate for individuals with the lowest level of social engagement was 1.84 times the rate for individuals with the highest level of social engagement.

The general pattern of these relationships was assessed in a meta-analysis of 148 studies (308,849 participants) of social relationship patterns and mortality (Holt-Lunstad, Smith, & Layton, 2010). The weighted average effect size was an odds ratio of 1.50, which represents a 50% increased likelihood of survival for individuals with higher levels of social engagement and other patterns of stronger social relationships. Holt-Lunstad et al. (2010) compared this effect size to the effect of smoking status on mortality in late life, with the effect size of social engagement even exceeding other well-known risk factors such as obesity and physical inactivity. In a follow-up meta-analysis, Holt-Lunstad et al. (2015) assessed three measures of low social engagement (loneliness, social isolation, or living alone) and their effects on mortality. The weighted average effect sizes for the three measures, after controlling for a number of covariates, represented an increase likelihood of mortality of 29%, 26%, and 32%, respectively.

Reduced mortality rates remained significant even after controlling for potential confounding variables, such as age, sex, socioeconomic status, physical health status, depression, and geographic region of study (Bennett, 2002; Dalgard & Håheim, 1998; Gerstorf et al., 2016; Giles et al., 2005; Sampson et al., 2009). Thus, the impact of social engagement on reducing mortality rates and increasing longevity is a general one, not solely affected by a specific culture or confined to a particular sub-population.

Social engagement and physical markers of health

Social engagement influences a number of consequential markers of physical health, including:

- *stress responsiveness* (Cohen & Wills, 1985; Heinrichs, Baumgartner, Kirschbaum, & Ehlert, 2003)

- *cardiovascular disease and risk factors* (Kamiya, Whelan, Timonen, & Kenny, 2010)
- *immune functioning* (Lutgendorf et al., 2005)
- *sleep quality* (Kurina et al., 2011)

These physical markers of health have their own impact on longevity and quality of life. Thus, a better understanding of the exact mechanisms that account for the influences of social engagement on physical health is a critical component in clarifying the link between high levels of social engagement and increased longevity. Regardless of the mechanism, there is apparent value in enhancing individuals' social engagement.

The degree of strength in the relationship between levels of social engagement and physical markers of health was recently demonstrated by Yang et al. (2016). They analyzed nationally representative samples to determine the impact of functional dimensions of social relationships on biomarkers of physical health (e.g., C-reactive protein, systolic and diastolic blood pressure, waist circumference, body mass index). The representative samples allowed the researchers to investigate the impact of social engagement on physical health across the human life span. For older adults, in a longitudinal change model applied to data from the National Social Life, Health, and Aging Project (NSHAP), a higher mean social integration level had a 54% reduction in the odds of developing hypertension over a 6-year period. In fact, the effect of social integration even exceeded well-known risk factors for hypertension in late adulthood, such as diabetes. This pattern of results demonstrates the high impact varying levels of social engagement have on physical health, and the potential benefits that exist in designing interventions and technologies geared toward enhancing social engagement.

Yang et al. (2016) proposed a conceptual model where physiological regulation mediates the link between social relationship patterns and diseases and longevity. As an example, they posited that low levels of social engagement create continuous stress exposures for individuals, which subsequently leads to the development of stress-related diseases as people age. Furthermore, Yang et al. (2016) found that social relationship patterns affected certain physical markers of health especially during adolescence and older adulthood. Social integration and social support may be more powerful in influencing health and related outcomes for individuals during the formative years of adolescence and during the life-changing events often associated with older adulthood. For older adults, issues of retirement and disease can have tremendous effects on daily routines and ways of life. Having an active and supportive social system may be especially important in providing the purpose and meaning that is critical in maintaining a healthy and high quality of life.

Social engagement and cognitive decline

Preserved cognitive functioning is an integral component of maintaining a healthy, active, and independent lifestyle for older adults. Whether it is managing multiple medications, learning new skills and hobbies, or managing finances and paying bills, many everyday activities require complex cognitive processes. As a result, a better understanding of the protective effect that social engagement has on cognitive functioning is vital for designing solutions or interventions targeting declines in cognitive ability in older adulthood.

The most severe and debilitating form of cognitive decline is the development of dementia, with Alzheimer's disease being the most common cause (Burns & Iliffe, 2009). Due to the high personal and societal costs associated with the condition, numerous studies have investigated the effect of social engagement on the occurrence and onset of dementia (e.g., Sörman, Rönnlund, Sundström, Adolfsson, & Nilsson, 2015; Wang, Karp, Winblad, & Fratiglioni, 2002).

Fratiglioni et al. (2000) conducted a study of 1,203 community-dwelling older adults (aged 75 and above). Social engagement was assessed by a measure that included both structural and qualitative aspects of individuals' social lives. This included items about marital status, living arrangement, having children, as well as contact frequency and relationship satisfaction with various social ties (e.g., children, relatives, close friends). During a 3-year follow up after the baseline interview, it was found that poor or limited social engagement increased the risk of dementia by 60%.

A recent meta-analysis was carried out on the effect of social relationship factors on dementia risk in longitudinal cohort studies (Kuiper et al., 2015). The results of the meta-analysis were that individuals with lower levels of social participation, individuals with lower frequency of social contacts, and individuals with higher levels of loneliness were, respectively, 1.41, 1.57, and 1.58 times more likely to have a higher risk to develop dementia than their more socially engaged counterparts.

Even though dementia has been a main research focus, the benefits of social engagement for cognitive functioning in older adults are not solely confined to the onset of dementia. Social engagement has been found to associate with cognitive functions more broadly (Barnes, de Leon, Wilson, Bienias, & Evans, 2004; Seeman, Lusignolo, Albert, & Berkman, 2001). For instance, in a sample of 838 older adults without dementia, measures of social activity and social support related to higher cognitive functioning (Krueger et al., 2009). In this particular study, cognitive functioning was assessed using multiple measures of a variety of cognitive processes, including episodic memory, semantic memory, working memory, perceptual speed, and visuospatial ability. These results demonstrate that a high degree of participation in social activities and the maintenance of social connections serve to preserve an array of cognitive functions in late adulthood.

The relationship between social engagement and cognitive functioning in older adulthood could be bidirectional. That is, cognitive decline may cause a reduction in social engagement, because successfully maintaining interpersonal social relationships requires cognitive processing. Moreover, older adults experiencing cognitive decline could face barriers in participating in social activities, which would result in lower reported levels of social engagement. However, evidence suggests that enhanced social engagement exerts a protective effect on cognitive functioning for older adults. In one longitudinal study that used data from the Health and Retirement Study (Ertel, Glymour, & Berkman, 2008), linear growth curve models were used to determine if social engagement predicted subsequent memory decline. In fact, higher levels of social engagement did predict a reduced rate of memory decline over a 6-year period. However, no reverse causality was found (i.e., earlier memory scores did not predict subsequent social engagement), suggesting a causal path from degrees of social engagement to levels of cognitive functioning in older adulthood.

Social engagement and mental health

Mental health issues can have deleterious effects on health and quality-of-life outcomes for older adults. As an example, depression has been found to be related to higher mortality rates (Cuijpers & Smit, 2002; Geerlings, Beekman, Deeg, & Twisk, 2002; Mallon, Broman, & Hetta, 2000; Schulz et al., 2000). Conversely, happiness and other measures of psychological well-being are positively associated with health benefits in older adults (Angner, Ray, Saag, & Allison, 2009; Diener & Chan, 2011; Ostir, Markides, Peek, & Goodwin, 2001). Participating in rewarding social activities, having a robust social support system, and maintaining a diverse array of social connections can all be sources of self-worth and meaning that consequently affect well-being in older adults.

Numerous studies have investigated the extent that the type and quality of social relationships relate to happiness and subjective well-being in older adults (Bowling, Farquhar, & Browne, 1991; Cheng, Lee, Chan, Leung, & Lee, 2009; McAuley et al., 2000; Park, 2009). In one study that included 1,334 community-dwelling older adults, even after adjusting for age, sex, depression, cognitive impairment, and disability, higher social engagement was associated with higher self-rated happiness and ratings of life as worth living (Golden, Conroy, & Lawlor, 2009). In a longitudinal study consisting of a sample of 2,034 older adults (Huxhold, Fiori, & Windsor, 2013), changes in social engagement over a 6-year timespan were associated with changes in life satisfaction and positive affect. Moreover, survey data from samples of older adults living in Beijing and Hong Kong indicated that individuals' social network size and perceived social support were even stronger predictors of happiness than variables such as income and education (Chan & Lee, 2006).

Low levels of social engagement (e.g., social isolation, loneliness) are related to the occurrence of mental health issues such as depression or anxiety in late adulthood (Adams, Sanders, & Auth, 2004; Alpass & Neville, 2003; Forsman et al., 2012). For instance, in a community sample of older adults, fewer social support resources were related to higher levels of depression as well as suicidal ideation (Vanderhorst & McLaren, 2005). Cornwell and Waite (2009) used population-based data from the NSHAP, and found that a measure of social isolation, which included items relating to loneliness and perceived social support, predicted the prevalence of depressive symptomatology. The New Haven Established Populations for the Epidemiologic Study of the Elderly showed that lower social engagement was associated with higher levels of depression, even after controlling for variables such as age, sex, education, marital status, health and functional status, and fitness activities (Glass, de Leon, Bassuk, & Berkman, 2006).

Proposed mechanisms

Though the research summarized earlier demonstrates the large body of empirical work on the relationships between social engagement and health outcomes, less attention has been given to providing theoretical accounts of the causal mechanisms that underlie these relationships. However, Berkman, Glass, Brissette, and Seeman (2000) did propose an overarching model of how social relationships affect physical and mental health. According to the model, macrosocial factors such as cultural norms and economic factors exert an impact on social network structure, which then influences the lower behavioral level of individuals through the following pathways: provision of social support, social influence, social engagement and attachment, and access to resources and material goods. Thoits (2011) went on to propose seven possible mechanisms that might account for the effect of social engagement on health: social influence/social comparison, social control, role-based purpose and meaning (mattering), self-esteem, sense of control, belonging and companionship, and perceived support availability. Of course, different forms of social engagement and health variables may be linked through different underlying mechanisms, so the above list is not mutually exclusive. However, future research is needed to elucidate the precise causal mechanisms for these various social engagement and health linkages. Results from this line of research will also contribute to the future success of social engagement technologies, by allowing designers to target and support the particular elements of social engagement that are associated with quality-of-life outcomes.

Barriers to social engagement for older adults

The older adult population is heterogeneous and consists of individuals with varying needs and facing different challenges in their everyday lives. Challenges at both the personal and societal levels can impair their ability to perform activities relevant to living independently, such as activities of daily living and instrumental activities of daily living (Katz, 1983). These activities, which can include bathing, feeding oneself, self-grooming, among others, are important for maintaining functional independence. Furthermore, impairments that hinder one's ability to complete these activities can severely impact levels of social engagement and quality of life as a result (Andersen, Wittrup-Jensen, Lolk, Andersen, & Kragh-Sørensen, 2004; Ballard et al., 2001).

   If technology is to be a tool that can bolster social engagement for older adults, it is necessary to identify the particular challenges faced by older adults that can inhibit an active and socially engaged lifestyle. Below we summarize some of the challenges that are disproportionally likely to affect older adults, including barriers that are physical, cognitive, financial, or cultural/societal in nature (see Table 8.2). Older adults are more likely to adopt a social engagement technology if they find the technology or the content communicated through the technology to be "personally relevant" (Xie, Watkins, Golbeck, & Huang, 2012). As a result, successful

Table 8.2 Barriers faced by some older adults that can prevent high levels of social engagement

Type of barrier	Examples	References
Physical	• Reduced mobility • Increased frailty • Declines in sensory-perceptual abilities	Blagojevic et al. (2010), Crews and Campbell (2004), Dalton et al. (2003), Fulop et al. (2010), Lin et al. (2011)
Cognitive	• Development of dementia • Declines in cognitive abilities such as attention, processing speed, and working memory • Self-perception of memory decline	Hasher and Zacks (1988), Lovelace and Twohig (1990), Raz (2000), Ryan (1992), Salthouse (1996), Schaie and Zanjani (2006)
Financial	• Retirement from a working salary • Living on a limited, fixed income (e.g., Social Security, pensions, investments) • Wealth tied up in non-liquid assets (e.g., home ownership)	Dunn and Olsen (2014), Gruber and Wise (1999), Lusardi and Mitchell (2007a, 2007b)
Cultural/ societal	• Social norms about living arrangements during older adulthood • Development of a nation's healthcare system • "Walkability" of a geographical area	de Jong Gierveld and van Tilburg (1999), Rogers, Halstead, Gardner, and Carlson (2011), Shrestha (2000), Wood et al. (2008)

technologies will be ones that have the ability to directly combat and overcome the barriers that prevent desired levels of social engagement.

Physical barriers

As some individuals age, they encounter physical limitations such as increased frailty, slower gait, as well as limitations due to the effects of chronic diseases such as osteoarthritis (e.g., Blagojevic, Jinks, Jeffery, & Jordan, 2010; Bohannon, 1997; Fulop et al., 2010). These limitations can inhibit their ability to perform important mobility-related actions such as navigating their home, shopping for groceries, or traveling to visit family and friends. For perspective on the impact of such difficulties, Rogers, Meyer, Walker, and Fisk (1998) performed a focus group study investigating the difficulties older adults were facing and found that motor limitations represented 38% of the reported problems, primarily concerning issues related to walking, climbing steps, and other common physical activities. These challenges not only inhibit self-management, but such difficulties can impact health and overall quality of life. For example, declines in mobility have been found to contribute to heightened rates of social isolation and loneliness, and both characteristics have been associated with increased rates of mortality (Steptoe, Shankar, Demakakos, & Wardle, 2013).

In addition, declines in sensory-perceptual abilities commonly accompany aging (e.g., hearing or vision loss) and can increase the difficulty older adults experience when conversing with others, navigating their environment, and participating in social events. It is estimated that over 60% of older adults in the United States aged 70 and older meet the World Health Organization's definition for hearing loss (Lin, Thorpe, Gordon-Salant, & Ferrucci, 2011), and about 12% of older adults aged 65 and older report having moderate or severe vision loss (Centers for Disease Control & Prevention, 2011). These abilities are relevant to maintaining social engagement in the community and with friends and family, as well as overall quality of life (Crews & Campbell, 2004; Dalton et al., 2003). Other than impacting the ability to socialize, associations between these losses and cognitive decline, as well as mortality, have been demonstrated (e.g., Arlinger, 2003; Baltes & Lindenberger, 1997; Genther et al., 2015; Lin et al., 2013; McCarty, Nanjan, & Taylor, 2001).

Cognitive barriers

Preserved cognitive functioning plays a vital role in ensuring that an individual can perform important activities and self-manage their life (Greiner, Snowdon, & Schmitt, 1996; Grigsby, Kaye, Baxter, Shetterly, & Hamman, 1998). The degree to which an individual experiences cognitive declines as they age varies from person to person, but evidence for general declines in attention, processing speed, and working memory, among other cognitive abilities, have been commonly found (e.g., Hasher & Zacks, 1988; Raz, 2000; Salthouse, 1996; Schaie & Zanjani, 2006). Moreover, declines in cognitive functioning have been found to be associated with level of social engagement and support, with those having more social lives experiencing less cognitive difficulties as they age (Béland, Zunzunegui, Alvarado, Otero, & del Ser, 2005; Crooks et al., 2008). Although not all older adults experience the same degree of general cognitive decline, the perception of the impact that aging has on cognitive performance may hinder their desire to engage socially and lead to the avoidance of situations that hold the potential to test these perceived declines and difficulties. When adults have been asked to reflect upon how they perceive memory ability over the life span, a trend portraying more negativity with increasing age has been found (e.g., Lovelace & Twohig, 1990; Ryan, 1992). Thus, self-perception of cognitive ability may then influence decisions regarding personal and social lives.

Financial barriers

Another impediment to social engagement relates to financial challenges faced by older adults. Staying socially active is often expensive. Going out to dinner with friends, entertainment activities such as going to the movies or attending a concert, or traveling to distant locations can all be costly endeavors. Moreover, high levels of social engagement that require frequent social interaction can make matters more difficult by requiring continuous expenditures to sustain the social connection. As a result, for many older adults, there may exist a gap between their desired and actual degree of social engagement, due solely to not having the financial resources available to maintain high levels of social activity.

Just like any age group, older adults are heterogenous with respect to financial resources. This means that financial challenges toward social engagement will disproportionately affect some older adults more than others (e.g., low SES individuals). Older adults should not be stereotyped as all struggling financially. In fact, the average level of wealth is higher for older adults compared to younger and middle-aged adults (Dunn & Olsen, 2014). However, this wealth can often be tied up in non-liquid assets (e.g., home ownership), which do not have much of an effect on day-to-day income expenditures. Consequently, it is still the case that many older adults live on fixed incomes (e.g., Social Security, pensions, investments), which can force them to prioritize the things and people they choose to spend money on. Furthermore, due to the uncertainty of knowing how long retirement funds will have to last into the future, many older adults adopt a conservative attitude toward money usage. Taken together, any intervention or policy aimed to increase social engagement must take into account financial constraints faced by individual older adults.

Cultural/societal barriers

In addition to the personal challenges mentioned above, various cultural and societal factors can provide challenges for older adults' ability to maintain high levels of social engagement. A clear example of this is that countries and cultures have different social norms about living arrangements during older adulthood (Bongaarts & Zimmer, 2002; De Vos, 1990; Wilmoth, 2001; Zimmer & Dayton, 2005). These differences can have substantial effects on the type of daily social activities experienced by older adults. For instance, older adults living in a society that expects them to live with younger family members will likely have different social bonds and networks than older adults who reside in a country that stresses either independence or retirement communities.

Many other factors at a society or community level influence older adults' ability to engage in social activities outside the home. Geographical areas will differ in the availability and quality of public transportation, the prevalence of social gathering places such as community centers or parks, as well as the density of other destination locations (e.g., restaurants, shops). There is also an extensive body of research on the relationship between the "walkability" of a geographical area and levels of social engagement for residents of the area (Beard & Petitot, 2010; Leyden, 2003; Richard, Gauvin, Gosselin, & Laforest, 2008; Scharlach & Lehning, 2013). Here, walkability usually refers to neighborhood design, but walkability can also refer to other external factors that can affect older adults' desire to freely move around outside (e.g., crime rates and perceived safety; King, 2008).

Societal factors can influence social engagement in older adulthood through their impact on individual older adults' ability to maintain a healthy and socially active lifestyle. As an example, the development of a nation's educational and healthcare systems will greatly affect the health and quality of life experienced by older adults residing in that nation. Older adults in more industrialized societies can not only be predicted to experience higher life expectancies on average (Hertz, Hebert, & Landon, 1994; Shrestha, 2000), but they are also more likely to have the resources available that can support and strengthen an active lifestyle into late adulthood— whether these resources be financial, health/medical, or technological in nature.

These cultural/societal challenges should not be seen as distinct from the personal challenges described above. All of these cultural/societal challenges can be seen as exacerbators of the personal challenges mentioned previously—namely physical, cognitive, and financial challenges. Less developed infrastructures, modes of transportation, and physical aids will intensify the physical challenges faced by many older adults. Limited educational systems will affect the cognitive challenges faced by individuals residing in those nations, and less economically developed nations will mean that a greater percentage of older adults will most likely not have the financial resources available to fulfill their social desires or needs. However, what these cultural and societal challenges make clear is that any technology designed to enhance social engagement, particularly in older adults, cannot assume that the adoption and use of a technology in one culture or society will automatically transfer to another. Older adults in different societies, as well as individuals within societies, will face different challenges and may hold different social values. Any technical solution to the problem of low levels of social engagement must take these and related issues into account during the design process.

Using technology to foster social engagement

Changes in social engagement in American society

There have occurred large and consequential declines in social capital and civic engagement in American communities during the last couple decades of the 20th century (McPherson, Smith-Lovin, & Brashears, 2006; Putnam, 2000). As Putnam (2000) extensively detailed in his book *Bowling Alone*, there have been massive drops in engagement rates in a variety of formal social institutions, such as participation in political organizations, membership in local civic groups such as parent-teacher associations, religious attendance, as well as workplace organizations such as union membership. Negative trends have been observed in informal social connections as well. For instance, metrics such as the percentage of adults who had friends over for dinner during the previous month showed a consistent decline from 1975 to 1995, as did membership in other local neighborhood groups such as bowling leagues.

The rapid development of social engagement technologies over the past two decades may counteract declines in social capital and civic engagement. However, a popular concern has been the idea that these technologies (e.g., Facebook, or the internet more generally) could be making matters worse, or in some cases might actually be the cause of the decline. But, as Putnam (2000, p. 170) stated in retort to this idea: "Voting, giving, trusting, meeting, visiting, and so on had all begun to decline while Bill Gates was still in grade school. By the time that the Internet reached 10 percent of American adults in 1996, the nationwide decline in social connectedness and civic engagement had been under way for at least a quarter of a century."

Yet, there remains the concern that online and other modes of virtual interaction have the potential to exacerbate the negative trends in social connectedness described above. Imagine that an individual has a roughly fixed amount of time that he or she allocates to social interaction. More time spent on social networking sites such as Facebook would allow less time spent interacting with others in a face-to-face fashion. Or, relatedly, if online or virtual communication is enough to satisfy the social needs of an individual, that individual might have less desire or motivation to join local community organizations or interact with others in informal ways (e.g., having friends over for dinner).

Though research exploring this potential "crowding out" or "displacement" effect is limited, a few studies suggest that the relationship between virtual and face-to-face social interaction is actually in the positive direction. In a sample of college students, Facebook use was positively associated with various social capital variables, including the extent individual students felt engaged or part of the campus community (Ellison, Steinfield, & Lampe, 2007). Similarly, Valenzuela, Park, and Kee (2009) found that greater intensity of Facebook use was positively related to college students' social trust, civic engagement, and political participation. In a 1-year longitudinal study with college students (Steinfield, Ellison, & Lampe, 2008), intensity of Facebook use positively predicted subsequent social capital variables. Among older adults as well, active users of information/communication technologies reported higher percentages of frequently interacting with family and friends (Vroman, Arthanat, & Lysack, 2015). Moreover, in a sample of adults 50 years or older, Internet users were more likely to have contacts with family and friends compared to non-users, as well as were more likely to participate in organizations or clubs (Hogeboom, McDermott, Perrin, Osman, & Bell-Ellison, 2010).

The degree social capital exists in online communities still remains an open question. However, social engagement technologies have started influencing some of even the most dramatic declines reported by Putnam (2000), including participation in local or neighborhood organizations. Online neighborhood message boards have increasingly come into existence, where members of a neighborhood have the ability to share information about upcoming events in the community. At a minimum, the dramatic increase in adoption rates for particular social engagement technologies (e.g., over 1.8 billion monthly users of Facebook as of 2016) suggests that individuals have a strong desire to interact, communicate, and share information with others. As a result, though certain aspects of social engagement may be changing in American and other societies, such as the decline in membership in certain civic and community organizations, it does not necessarily mean that there has also been a decline in individuals' desire to be socially engaged with other people. The challenge for technological solutions of declining social engagement is to ensure that the use of a particular technology is strengthening other modes of social connection instead of either negatively affecting it, or fully replacing it.

The impact of current social engagement technologies

Technological innovation over the last century has led to an evolution among how individuals are able to communicate and interact with one another. Prior to these advancements, social engagements were heavily reliant on proximity as it was necessary to be in the same physical location to communicate in real-time. However, developments in social engagement technologies have allowed for a facilitation and decentralization of this communication and delivered the ability to connect to anyone at any time with relatively little effort. Prior to the introduction of the Internet, if an individual wanted to discuss a favorite past time with a friend or debate a pressing civil issue, meetings would have to be arranged by ensuring that not only was a location available, but that others were also able to join and were not burdened by conflicting commitments. Now, the Internet, mobile phones, and other related technologies allow for the discussion of such topics with the use of social networking sites (e.g., Facebook, Twitter) and other messaging platforms such as Internet-based forums or text messaging. Whether an individual is available at a specific time is no longer vital for social engagement as online discussions may be read and contributed to at one's leisure (i.e., asynchronously).

To better understand the potential of technology to foster and maintain social engagement, it is beneficial to discuss which social engagement technologies are currently used, as well as the emerging technologies that may further revolutionize communication (see Table 8.3). A clear example of the impact of a current social engagement technology is the rapid adoption of smartphones that allow one to call, email, instant message, or update social media from anywhere at any time. For perspective, nearly 70% of adults in the United States currently own a smartphone (Anderson, 2015). In addition, social networking sites such as Facebook and Twitter have exploded in popularity, as 65% of US adults report using at least one such site in 2015, up from under 10% since 2005 (Perrin, 2015). The widespread adoption of these technologies has fundamentally changed how people communicate and manage their social lives, and these changes are expected to continue as technology advances.

The potential of emerging technologies

Emerging technologies hold the potential to influence how individuals socialize in the near future. An emerging technology is "a radically novel and relatively fast growing technology characterized by a certain degree of coherence persisting over time and with the potential to exert a considerable impact on the socioeconomic

Table 8.3 Current and emerging social engagement technologies

Technology	Description
Augmented Reality (AR)	"Augmented reality is a live view of a real-world environment where the elements of the environment are augmented by software, such as video or audio." (Cabero & Barroso, 2016, p. 4)
Email	Emails are "messages in text form sent via computer networks from one person to another or to many others." (Tao & Reinking, 1996, p. 4)
Smartphone	A smartphone is "a cell phone with advanced capabilities, which executes an identifiable operating system allowing users to extend its functionality with third party applications that are available from an application repository." (Theoharidou, Mylonas, & Gritzalis, 2012, pp. 429–430)
Social Networking Sites	Social networking sites are "web-based services that allow individuals to (1) construct a public or semi-public profile within a bounded system, (2) articulate a list of other users with whom they share a connection, and (3) view and traverse their list of connections and those made by others within the system. The nature and nomenclature of these connections may vary from site to site." (Ellison, 2007, p. 211)
Televideo	Televideo involves the "the use of two-way audio and video to exchange information, whether it be through a computer (e.g., Skype or Facetime) or through the use of a telepresence system or robot that allows a person to navigate around a remote environment (e.g., Kubi, Beam)." (Matthews, 1999; Mitzner, Stuck, Hartley, Beer, & Rogers, 2017, p. 2)
Virtual Reality (VR)	Virtual reality technologies provide "the illusion of participation in a synthetic environment rather than external observation of such environment. VR relies on three-dimensional (3D), stereoscopic, head-tracked displays, hand/body tracking and binaural sound. VR is an immersive, multi-sensory experience." (Gigante, 1993, p. 3)

domain" (Rotolo, Hicks, & Martin, 2015, p. 4). Such developments may further benefit those living with certain impairments that inhibit their ability to engage with others. For instance, advancements regarding the availability, speed, and consistency of the Internet have allowed for the introduction of televideo applications and devices that allow users to see and hear the individual(s) with whom they are communicating. Moreover, the visual component of these technologies allows for their potential utilization in areas such as telemedicine and caregiving for older adults, permitting users to receive remote care from the comfort of their own home despite any mobility impairments (e.g., Wu, Stuck, Mitzner, Rogers, & Beer, 2016). In combination with televideo technologies, developments in robotics could allow individuals to not only communicate with others over long distances, but also remotely traverse and interact with the environment.

Social robots are emerging as a means to provide engagement themselves, or to facilitate social engagement between people. For example, the robot PARO was designed to simulate the movements and sounds of a baby harp seal. In skilled nursing environments, PARO increased social engagement between residents by encouraging people to congregate in common areas and providing a point of conversation (Shibata & Wada, 2011; Wada & Shibata, 2006). For healthy elders, engagement with PARO for even just a short time increased positive affect (McGlynn, Kemple, Mitzner, King, & Rogers, 2017). This is only one example of a social robot—there are many more in development that are specifically targeted toward older adults and this category of emerging technology holds promise for the future (Beer, Mitzner, Stuck, & Rogers, 2015).

Likewise, AR and VR may enhance interpersonal socialization. AR allows for the introduction of graphical interfaces, rendered objects, and other computer-generated information to be inserted into one's surroundings. Some smartphone applications already have integrated AR-related features using the device's camera and head-worn devices (e.g., Microsoft HoloLens). These applications allow for the integration of social media and other communication technologies to be holographically projected onto one's surrounding environment.

Rather than simply inserting objects into one's surrounding environment, VR allows individuals to communicate, interact, and play in wholly virtual environments. These devices use head-mounted displays to present stereoscopic images to the user, allowing for the perception of three-dimensional environments. In combination with an Internet connection, VR users can interact with others to play games, partake in a wide-range of experiences, or communicate with friends or other users in computer-generated environments as if they were in the same location. A number of VR consumer devices have been recently released, that range from utilizing one's own VR-capable smartphone when inserted into a compatible headset (e.g., Samsung Gear VR), to devices that connect to desktop computers and allow for one to traverse and interact in room-scale environments (e.g., HTC Vive, Oculus Rift). The potential of these technologies for social engagement and communication is only beginning to be understood, and will continue to mature over the coming years as innovation continues and adoption rates increase. As shown by the emergence and subsequent popularity of social networking applications such as Facebook, Twitter, and Instagram, future applications developed to take advantage of such novel technologies like AR or VR may impact social engagement in ways unimaginable at the current time.

The reduced necessity for physically being in a location to foster and maintain social engagement may bring added benefits to those who are unable to travel to social events. The impact of mobility challenges may be reduced, improving the range of activities of which older adults may perform and, hopefully, leading to a higher quality of life, both personally and socially. For current and future technologies to support social engagement, older adults have to be willing and able to use them.

Current dissemination of social engagement technologies

The digital divide

Although the adoption of technologies that promote socialization has been increasing among older adults in recent years, an intergenerational "digital divide" still exists (Anderson, 2015; Friemel, 2016). Younger generations consistently report using the Internet, smartphones, and other related technologies at higher rates than older adults (Smith, 2014). With regard to social networking sites (e.g., Facebook, Twitter), only 35% of older adults (65 +) self-report using these social communication tools, in comparison to nearly 90% of younger adults (Perrin, 2015). However, older adults' use of these social engagement technologies has risen in recent years. For example, only 2% of older adults used social networking sites just over a decade ago (see Fig. 8.1), and smartphones have been increasingly adopted by the older population as 30% owned such a device by 2015 (Anderson, 2015; Perrin, 2015). As it relates to Internet use more generally, older adults showed the greatest rate of change from 2000 to 2015 out of any age group, increasing their adoption rates from 14% to 58% (Perrin & Duggan, 2015) (see Fig. 8.2). So, although older adults tend to be late-adopters to technologies in comparison to younger generations, the digital divide appears to be closing at least as it relates to various social engagement technologies.

Age is not the only notable factor when it comes to the digital divide, as intragenerational differences exist that may play an important role for older adults' technology adoption. That is, even within older adult groups, those who use these

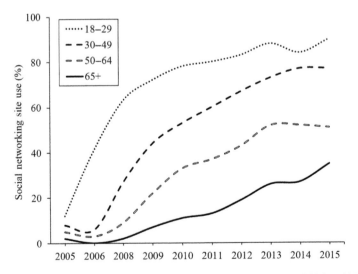

Figure 8.1 Social networking site use among different age groups from 2005 to 2015. *Source*: The figure is a recreation of data from the Pew Research Center (Perrin, 2015). Data from year 2007 were not collected.

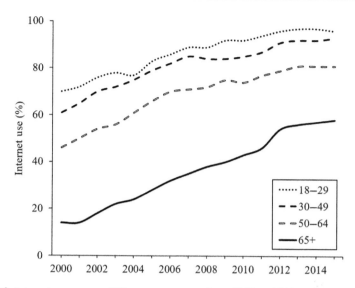

Figure 8.2 Internet use among different age groups from 2000 to 2015.
Source: The figure is a recreation of data from the Pew Research Center (Perrin & Duggan, 2015).

technologies tend to be more affluent, younger (i.e., less than 75), and more highly educated than their counterparts (Smith, 2014). For example, regarding Internet adoption, about 70% of older adults between the ages of 65−74 reported using the Internet or email, whereas 42% of older adults above the age of 75 report doing so (Smith, 2014). Thus, when understanding what may be hindering older adults from using these technologies, it is fruitful to also consider the characteristics of those who do choose to adopt them.

Benefits for older adults using social engagement technologies

As associations between social engagement and decreased cognitive, physical, and psychological impairments have been commonly observed (e.g., Nyqvist, Pape, Pellfolk, Forsman, & Wahlbeck, 2014; Yang et al., 2016), technologies that successfully increase levels of social engagement should yield positive benefits. Most of the research that has investigated the effects of the adoption and use of social engagement technologies has focused on younger adults (e.g., Ellison et al., 2007). Because different age groups may have divergent social needs and preferences, applying results found in one age group to another can be problematic. As a result, more research is needed to explore the direct benefits that use of various social engagement technologies have for older adults specifically.

Though more research is required to draw definitive conclusions on the consequences of social engagement technology use in older adults, the available research does suggest a variety of benefits. For instance, general Internet use among older adults has been found to positively relate to one's psychological well-being (Cotten, Ford, Ford, & Hale, 2012; Shapira, Barak, & Gal, 2007; White et al., 1999). Most current and emerging social engagement technologies rely on Internet use, making adoption of the Internet a prerequisite for technologies such as email or social networking sites. Any acquired benefits of general Internet use for older adults will therefore likely raise the probability that particular social engagement technologies will be tested and subsequently accepted by individual older adults.

Use of email and the Internet decreased loneliness for older adults who lived alone and were at risk for social isolations. Czaja et al. (2015) designed a computer system specifically for older adults called PRISM (Personal Reminder Information and Social Management) (see also Czaja, Boot, Charness, Rogers, and Sharit, 2017). In a randomized clinical trial, they found that after 6 months of system use, individuals who received the PRISM computer system had: significantly less loneliness; increased perceived social support and well-being; a trend toward a decline in social isolation; and an increase in computer self-efficacy, proficiency and comfort with computers when compared to those in the control group. The most frequently used function was email and the qualitative data showed that connecting with family and friends was viewed as a benefit of the system.

Benefits for older adults specifically using social engagement technologies have been demonstrated. For example, in a sample of adults, Facebook non-users reported higher levels of loneliness compared to users of the social networking site (Sheldon, 2012). However, the direction of causality in this study could not be established—it could be that happier individuals are more likely to become users of Facebook in the first place. In support of social networking site use providing mental health benefits to older adult users, a qualitative study that consisted of an Internet social networking intervention found that the use of a social networking site resulted in older adults reporting less loneliness (Ballantyne, Trenwith, Zubrinich, & Corlis, 2010). Furthermore, use of social networking sites have been shown to relieve stress and increase feelings of "empowerment" in older adults (for a review, see Leist, 2013), reduce the negative impact functional disability has on well-being (van Ingen, Rains, & Wright, 2017), and increase feelings of social well-being (Yu, Mccammon, Ellison, & Langa, 2016).

With the available research suggesting benefits of social engagement technology use to maintain and/or increase an older adult's social engagement and related health outcomes, it is then important to better understand why the aforementioned digital divide exists, and what might be influential regarding older adults' decisions to use these technologies.

Understanding technology use and acceptance predictors

To further design and improve the role technology can play in facilitating social engagement in older adulthood, understanding the factors that contribute to the adoption of information and communication technologies is necessary. Czaja et al. (2006) assessed the characteristics and opinions of a sample of over 1,200 adults between the ages of 18−91 to better understand the influence that many potential factors might have in contributing to whether an individual chooses to use technologies such as a computer or the Internet. They found evidence supporting the aforementioned age-related digital divide regarding technology use, with the older adults in the sample reporting less acceptance of such technologies, as well as the importance of cognitive ability relevant to learning to use novel technologies. Moreover, the findings also portrayed the impact that self-efficacy, which is the belief in one's ability to achieve certain goals with directed action (Bandura, 1977), has on technology use, and that this relationship was mediated by computer anxiety. Essentially, if an older adult does not perceive themselves to be able to learn to use technologies such as computers or the Internet, they may feel more anxious when attempting to do so, potentially hindering such technology use. Although this study further elucidated the contributions that many factors may have on older adults' use of various technologies, other factors may play important roles on these choices, and multiple models related to technology adoption have been proposed in an attempt to understand these variables.

Technology acceptance models

To understand the ability technology has to foster social engagement, a better understanding of the factors that predict whether a given person will use a particular technology is required. One general theory designed to address this issue is the Technology Acceptance Model (TAM; Davis, 1989). According to TAM, intention to use a particular technology can be predicted by the following two core constructs: perceived usefulness and perceived ease of use. Perceived usefulness refers to the degree an individual believes using a technology would enhance his or her performance. Perceived ease of use refers to the degree an individual believes using a technology would be relatively free of effort. In an updated version of the model (TAM 2; Venkatesh & Davis, 2000), three social influence processes were incorporated: (1) Whether an individual believes a *subjective norm* exists in using the technology, (2) Whether adopting the technology is being done on a *voluntary* or mandatory basis, and (3) Whether adopting the technology is believed to improve one's *image* with peers.

The Unified Theory of Acceptance and Use of Technology (UTAUT; Venkatesh, Morris, Davis, & Davis, 2003) was formulated to integrate elements from prior well-known models of technology acceptance. The UTAUT consists of the following four core constructs: (1) *Performance Expectancy*, which is defined as whether using a technology is believed to lead to gains in performance; (2) *Effort Expectancy*, which refers to the degree a technology is easy to use; (3) *Social Influence*, whether an individual believes important others think the individual should be using the technology; and (4) *Facilitating Conditions*, which is the extent an individual believes an organizational or technical infrastructure exists to aid in using the technology. In an updated version of the model (UTAUT2; Venkatesh, Thong, & Xu, 2012), the following three constructs were incorporated to help account for technology adoption in consumer contexts: hedonic motivation, price value, and habit.

Chen and Chan (2014) recently proposed a technology acceptance model specifically geared toward older adults, the Senior Technology Acceptance Model

(STAM). STAM extended prior technology acceptance models, such as the UTAUT, by incorporating health and ability issues often found to be associated with older adulthood. These additional factors included health conditions, cognitive ability, physical functioning, as well as factors such as gerontechnology self-efficacy and anxiety. Though future research is needed to further validate STAM, the incorporation of individual attributes and abilities will be beneficial in providing a theoretical account of technology acceptance in older adult samples in particular.

Factors contributing to the acceptance of social engagement technologies by older adults

The technology acceptance models described earlier have been used to explain older adults' adoption and use of various social engagement technologies. For example, perceived usefulness was the strongest unique predictor of intention to use social networking sites among a sample of older adults (Braun, 2013). However, perceived ease of use and social pressures to use social networking sites did not independently predict intention to use. Thus, whether an older adult adopts and uses a social engagement technology may be influenced by the extent that the person perceives the technology to be providing a particular benefit or utility to his or her life (for related findings, see Liu, 2015; Melenhorst, Rogers, & Bouwhuis, 2006).

Gaining a better understanding of the factors that contribute to the use or non-use of social engagement technologies was the focus of a recent study by Bixter, Prakash, Blocker, Mitzner, and Rogers (2016). In the study, older adult users and non-users of social networking sites participated in group interviews in which their perceptions of and attitudes toward these technologies were discussed. Using a modified version of the UTAUT model to capture the qualitative data produced by the group interviews, they found that performance expectancy was the category most frequently discussed. However, the users and non-users differed in whether they perceived these technologies as potentially providing benefits to their lives. For the users, the following three themes emerged from the data: information sharing, connection forming, and connection strengthening. The users focused on how social networking sites allow people to share information easily and effectively, as well as how these sites allow individuals to forge new social connections and strengthen existing bonds. In contrast, for the non-users, the following two themes emerged: time ineffectiveness and goal incongruity. Non-users focused on how these sites would not be good uses of their time and how using the sites would actually conflict with their social goals (e.g., maintaining face-to-face social interaction). These results helped elucidate the elements of social networking sites that older adult users find beneficial and enjoyable, as well as the elements that older adult non-users find disadvantageous. Further research along this line will help provide designers of social engagement technologies the ability to increase their user base and address the needs and preferences of older adults, an age group that is projected to sharply increase in numbers in the coming decades.

Other factors that were discussed frequently during the group interviews conducted by Bixter et al. (2016) were privacy and security concerns. These issues were discussed at comparable frequencies by both users and non-users, supporting prior work that has shown privacy and security issues exerting negative influences on older adults' perceptions of social engagement technologies (e.g., Lüders & Brandtzæg, 2017; Xie et al., 2012). These results are evidence that a perceived lack of control over content shared online, as well as the prevalence of malicious individuals and software, is either a barrier for some older adults adopting a social engagement technology in the first place, or a barrier for current users in enjoying the technology to its fullest extent. As a result, designers of current and future social engagement technologies will need to do more to not only combat security threats, but also ensure that the safety of the technologies is being communicated with users, particularly older adult users, clearly and effectively.

The role technology can play in combating barriers to social engagement

Social engagement technologies hold the potential to mitigate the barriers to social engagement that many older adults face—namely, physical, cognitive, and financial challenges. These challenges can impede older adults' ability to fulfill their social needs and, as a result, negatively affect quality of life. The unique role that technology can play in supporting and facilitating social engagement in older adulthood stems from its ability to provide individual older adults a powerful tool to overcome particular barriers they may experience as they age.

Physical challenges such as increased immobility can make traveling and participating in social events difficult for many older adults. Social engagement technologies allow individual older adults to remain socially active from the comforts of their own home through the use of the Internet and the various devices geared toward facilitating social interaction. Thus, no matter the distance between an older adult and the people with whom they want to communicate, they may be better able to retain the social connections that they highly value. Furthermore, with the development of televideo technologies such as Skype, the experience of face-to-face social interaction is increasingly being captured through technical means. Moreover, the variety in types of communication that technology allows provides benefits for individual older adults afflicted by a particular physical challenge. For instance, older adults who are experiencing sensory/perceptual impairments such as extreme hearing loss are able to communicate with others through text-based communication technologies without the difficulties that can accompany verbal interaction.

Cognitive-related challenges can negatively affect one's ability to remain socially engaged. For example, due to memory-related impairments that afflict certain older adults, successfully maintaining ongoing interpersonal communication with others can be difficult. In fact, in the group interviews carried out by Bixter et al. (2016), in which older adults discussed their perceptions of and attitudes toward particular social engagement technologies, the ability for communication and information to be documented and stored was a benefit that was often discussed. Using technology can provide direct cognitive benefits to users as well. For instance, Slegers, van Boxtel, and Jolles (2012) found that computer use had a protective effect in older adults for cognitive functions such as selective attention and memory. As a result, the adoption and use of social engagement technologies can serve a dual purpose by affording individual older adults the ability to maintain both a cognitively and socially stimulating lifestyle.

Maintaining a socially engaged lifestyle can often be costly. One of the benefits of technology for older adults relates to the ability for individuals to maintain high levels of social interaction at little-to-no additional financial cost. Many social networking sites and related applications are free to join, essentially eliminating the previously high cost of long-distance communication (e.g., long-distance telephone calls). Of course, some technologies can be financially expensive, particularly ones at an earlier stage of development or dissemination. However, as technological progress continues, devices and services that support social engagement and communication are rapidly dropping in price. Computers and smartphones that used to be exceedingly expensive and only within the financial reach of a privileged few are now more affordable. This high level of innovation and consequential reduction in costs have led certain technologies to be disseminated and adopted at high rates over the past few years, including by the older adult population.

For older adults to continue to benefit from the advancements made in social engagement technologies, their needs and capabilities must be considered during the design and innovation process. The result would not only be a reduction in the digital divide between younger and older adults, but the further accrual of material benefits in older adults' ability to stay socially active as well as experience associated increases in quality of life.

Recommendations for social engagement technologies

General design guidelines

Design of social engagement technologies should proceed similarly to design of any product or system with which people will interact. Follow the fundamental principles of design that have emerged from decades of research in the fields of human factors, human-automation interaction, human-robot interaction, and human-technology interaction (for reviews see Salvendy, 2012). When designing for older adult users, their specific considerations need to be incorporated (e.g., Fisk, Rogers, Charness, Czaja, & Sharit, 2009; Pak & McLaughlin, 2010; Rogers & Mitzner, 2017b).

Successful design (i.e., technologies integrated into the lives of people) will benefit from user-centered design (see Fisk et al., 2009; for more details). This process adheres to four principles of design:

1. Early focus on the user and the tasks the user will be performing, which often requires a task analysis.
2. Empirical measurement using questionnaires and surveys as well as usability testing studies that rely on observations and quantitative or qualitative performance data.

3. Iterative design and testing, which often requires the development of prototypes of products or system interfaces to support rapid development cycles and performing cost—benefit analyses to support tradeoff decisions.
4. Integrated design, wherein all aspects of the usability design process evolve in parallel, and are generally under the coordination of a single person.

A further extension of the idea of user-centered design is universal (or inclusive) design (Sanford, 2012), whereby products or environments are designed that are flexible enough to be usable by people with no limitations as well as by people with functional limitations related to disabilities or due to circumstances. In principle, good universal design benefits everyone and thus, would benefit many more people without disabilities than those with disabilities (e.g., those who are blind, cannot speak, cannot hear, or have learning disabilities) or those whose limitations are due to other reasons (e.g., those whose hands are temporarily occupied, cannot hear due to a noisy environment, or those who are very young or very old). Designing for older people can, similar to designs intended for accommodating people with functional limitations, also provide insights into designs that benefit all users.

Design guidelines specific to social engagement for older adults

In addition to following the standard human factors guidance for design, the specific context of social engagement will influence design considerations (e.g., Jaeger & Xie, 2009). As in many contexts, there are individual differences in preferences—herein instantiated in terms of types, frequency, and breadth of interactions; technology platform and other experience; tolerance for privacy and security risks; and so on.

Analysis of the barriers to use for older adults and current social engagement technologies can provide guidance as well. For example, Leist (2013) discussed some ways social engagement technologies can be improved to better suit the needs of older adults. Some sites can be overwhelming in the amount of applications, menus, etc., available to a new user, and preselecting functions or content to be available to different users could help with usability. However, at the same time, designers should not give in to ageist stereotypes and overly restrict the content available to older adult users. This could lead older adult users to assume a passive role in their engagement with the technology or prevent them from experiencing certain elements of the technology that they may enjoy. Leist (2013) concluded that design solutions will be strengthened through better understanding of the specific elements of social engagement technologies older adults are interested in.

Training and instruction

Older adults have more limited experience with social engagement technologies (such as social networking sites) compared to younger adults. As research summarized above demonstrated, older adults were more likely to adopt a communication technology the more personally relevant they found the technology or the perceived benefits associated with use of the technology. As a result, training might be more successful with older adults if it first focuses on older adults using either a site or part of a site that focuses on personally relevant topics. Nimrod (2010) provided some examples of online communities designed specifically for older adults (e.g., SeniorNet). Once individual older adults become more comfortable with personally relevant applications, they may become better equipped to explore sites or applications which are broader in scope and content (e.g., Facebook).

As a group, older adults prefer to receive guidance (i.e., instruction and training) to use new technologies, rather than to try it on their own (e.g., Mitzner et al., 2008). There are resources available for design of training specific to technology use by older adults (e.g., Rogers, Campbell, & Pak, 2001) or for broader age-related training considerations (e.g., Czaja & Sharit, 2012). However, the training/instruction need not be formal—older adults reported that they also liked receiving training from family members and friends (Mitzner et al., 2008).

Conclusion

Social engagement is a fundamental component of life quality. Of course, people differ in their preferred levels of engagement (with whom, for how long, engaging in what activities). Nonetheless, measures of social engagement are correlated with various measures of physical health, mental health, life quality, and even mortality—as we have reviewed in this chapter. Technology designers have an opportunity to design products, applications, robots, and other innovations that will enable social engagement—either by being engaging themselves, or by serving as a medium of engagement between people.

Older adults are willing and able to use technologies for social engagement, but, as a whole, they are slower to adopt and report some reticence related to usefulness, usability, privacy, and security. Moreover, older adults may not be targeted as potential users during the design process and thus their capabilities, limitations, and preferences may not be considered into the final implementation.

Our goal in this chapter was to provide an overview of: the importance of social engagement; the potential for technology to enable and enhance such engagement; the characteristics of older adults that should be considered during design; and an overview of current social-related technologies for older adults. Given the changing demographics (i.e., number of people over age 65 worldwide) and changing life-styles (i.e., people likely to live alone and/or geographically dispersed from family), the need for social engagement supports will only increase in the future (Rogers & Mitzner, 2017a). Designing technology with consideration of and involvement by older adults will yield more positive outcomes—and ultimately higher life quality.

References

Adams, K. B., Sanders, S., & Auth, E. A. (2004). Loneliness and depression in independent living retirement communities: Risk and resilience factors. *Aging & Mental Health*, 8(6), 475–485.

Adler, P. S., & Kwon, S.-W. (2002). Social capital: Prospects for a new concept. *The Academy of Management Review*, 27(1), 17–40.

Alpass, F. M., & Neville, S. (2003). Loneliness, health and depression in older males. *Aging & Mental Health, 7*(3), 212–216.

Andersen, C. K., Wittrup-Jensen, K. U., Lolk, A., Andersen, K., & Kragh-Sørensen, P. (2004). Ability to perform activities of daily living is the main factor affecting quality of life in patients with dementia. *Health and Quality of Life, 2,* 52.

Anderson, M. (2015). *Technology device ownership: 2015.* Pew Research Center.

Angner, E., Ray, M. N., Saag, K. G., & Allison, J. J. (2009). Health and happiness among older adults: A community-based study. *Journal of Health Psychology, 14*(4), 503–512.

Arlinger, S. (2003). Negative consequences of uncorrected hearing loss-a review. *International Journal of Audiology, 42,* 2S17–2S20.

Ballantyne, A., Trenwith, L., Zubrinich, S., & Corlis, M. (2010). 'I feel less lonely': What older people say about participating in a social networking website. *Quality in Ageing and Older Adults, 11*(3), 25–35.

Ballard, C., O'Brien, J., James, I., Mynt, P., Lana, M., Potkins, D., Reichelt, K., Lee, L., Swann, A., & Fossey, J. (2001). Quality of life for people with dementia living in residential and nursing home care: The impact of performance on activities of daily living, behavioral and psychological symptoms, language skills, and psychotropic drugs. *International Psychogeriatrics, 13*(1), 93–106.

Baltes, P. B., & Lindenberger, U. (1997). Emergence of a powerful connection between sensory and cognitive functions across the adult life span: A new window to the study of cognitive aging? *Psychology and Aging, 12*(1), 12.

Bandura, A. (1977). Self-efficacy: Toward a unifying theory of behavioral change. *Psychological Review, 84*(2), 191–215.

Barg, F. K., Huss-Ashmore, R., Wittink, M. N., Murray, G. F., Bogner, H. R., & Gallo, J. J. (2006). A mixed-methods approach to understanding loneliness and depression in older adults. *Journals of Gerontology: Series B: Psychological Sciences and Social Sciences, 61*(6), S329–S339.

Barnes, L. L., de Leon, M., Wilson, R. S., Bienias, J. L., & Evans, D. A. (2004). Social resources and cognitive decline in a population of older African Americans and whites. *Neurology, 63,* 2322–2326.

Beard, J. R., & Petitot, C. (2010). Ageing and urbanization: Can cities be designed to foster active ageing? *Public Health Reviews, 32*(2), 427–450.

Beer, J. M., Mitzner, T. L., Stuck, R. E., & Rogers, W. A. (2015). Design considerations for technology interventions to support social and physical wellness for older adults with disability. *International Journal of Automation and Smart Technology, 5,* 249–264.

Béland, F., Zunzunegui, M. V., Alvarado, B., Otero, A., & del Ser, T. (2005). Trajectories of cognitive decline and social relations. *The Journals of Gerontology Series B: Psychological Sciences and Social Sciences, 60*(6), P320–P330.

Bennett, K. M. (2002). Low level social engagement as a precursor of mortality among people in later life. *Age and Ageing, 31*(3), 165–168.

Berkman, L. F., Glass, T., Brissette, I., & Seeman, T. E. (2000). From social integration to health: Durkheim in the new millennium. *Social Science & Medicine, 51,* 843–857.

Bixter, M.T., Prakash, A., Blocker, K.A., Mitzner, T.L., & Rogers, W.A. (November 2016). A qualitative analysis of the adoption and use of social communication technologies by older adults. *Poster presented at the Gerontological Society of America's 69th annual scientific meeting: New Orleans, LA.*

Blagojevic, M., Jinks, C., Jeffery, A., & Jordan, K. P. (2010). Risk factors for onset of osteoarthritis of the knee in older adults: A systematic review and meta-analysis. *Osteoarthritis and Cartilage, 18*(1), 24–33.

Bohannon, R. W. (1997). Comfortable and maximum walking speed of adults aged 20−79 years: Reference values and determinants. *Age and Ageing*, *26*(1), 15−19.

Bongaarts, J., & Zimmer, Z. (2002). Living arrangements of older adults in the developing world: An analysis of demographic and health survey household surveys. *Journals of Gerontology: Series B: Psychological Sciences and Social Sciences*, *57*(3), S145−S157.

Bowling, A., Farquhar, M., & Browne, P. (1991). Life satisfaction and associations with social network and support variables in three samples of elderly people. *International Journal of Geriatric Psychiatry*, *6*(8), 549−566.

Braun, M. T. (2013). Obstacles to social networking website use among older adults. *Computers in Human Behavior*, *29*, 673−680.

Burns, A., & Iliffe, S. (2009). Alzheimer's disease. *BMJ*, *338*, 467−471.

Cabero, J., & Barroso, J. (2016). The educational possibilities of Augmented Reality. *Journal of New Approaches in Educational Research*, *5*(1), 44−50.

Cacioppo, J. T., Hawkley, L. C., Berntson, G. G., Ernst, J. M., Gibbs, A. C., Stickgold, R., & Hobson, J. A. (2002). Do lonely days invade the nights? Potential social modulation of sleep efficiency. *Psychological Science*, *13*(4), 384−387.

Cacioppo, J. T., Hughes, M. E., Waite, L. J., Hawkley, L. C., & Thisted, R. A. (2006). Loneliness as a specific risk factor for depressive symptoms: Cross-sectional and longitudinal analyses. *Psychology and Aging*, *21*(1), 140−151.

Centers for Disease Control and Prevention (2011). *The state of vision, aging, and public health in America*. Atlanta, GA: US Department of Health and Human Services. Retrieved from <http://www.cdc.gov/visionhealth/pdf/vision_brief.pdf>.

Ceria, C. D., Masaki, K. H., Rodriguez, B. L., Chen, R., Yano, K., & Curb, J. D. (2001). The relationship of psychosocial factors to total mortality among older Japanese-American men: The Honolulu Heart Program. *Journal of the American Geriatrics Society*, *49*, 725−731.

Chan, Y. K., & Lee, R. P. L. (2006). Network size, social support and happiness in later life: A comparative study of Beijing and Hong Kong. *Journal of Happiness Studies*, *7*, 87−112.

Chen, K., & Chan, A. H. S. (2014). Gerontechnology acceptance by elderly Hong Kong Chinese: A senior technology acceptance model (STAM). *Ergonomics*, *57*(5), 635−652.

Cheng, S.-T., Lee, C. K. L., Chang, A. C. M., Leung, E. M. F., & Lee, J.-J. (2009). Social network types and subjective well-being in Chinese older adults. *Journal of Gerontology: Psychological Sciences*, *64B*(6), 713−722.

Cohen, S. (2004). Social relationships and health. *American Psychologist*, *59*(8), 676−684.

Cohen, S., Doyle, W. J., Skoner, D. P., Rabin, B. S., & Gwaltney, J. M., Jr. (1997). Social ties and susceptibility to the common cold. *JAMA*, *277*, 1940−1944.

Cohen, S., & Wills, T. A. (1985). Stress, social support, and the buffering hypothesis. *Psychological Bulletin*, *98*(2), 310−357.

Cornwell, E. Y., & Waite, L. J. (2009). Social disconnectedness, perceived isolation, and health among older adults. *Journal of Health and Social Behavior*, *50*, 31−48.

Cotten, S. R., Ford, G., Ford, S., & Hale, T. M. (2012). Internet use and depression among older adults. *Computers in Human Behavior*, *28*(2), 496−499.

Crews, J. E., & Campbell, V. A. (2004). Vision impairment and hearing loss among community-dwelling older Americans: Implications for health and functioning. *American Journal of Public Health*, *94*(5), 823−829.

Crooks, V. C., Lubben, J., Petitti, D. B., Little, D., & Chiu, V. (2008). Social network, cognitive function, and dementia incidence among elderly women. *American Journal of Public Health*, *98*(7), 1221−1227.

Cuijpers, P., & Smit, F. (2002). Excess mortality in depression: A meta-analysis of community studies. *Journal of Affective Disorders, 72*(3), 227–236.

Czaja, S. J., Boot, W. R., Charness, N., Rogers, W. A., & Sharit, J. Improving social support for older adults through technology: Findings from the PRISM randomized controlled trial. *The Gerontologist*, 2017.

Czaja, S. J., Boot, W. R., Charness, N., Rogers, W. A., Sharit, J., Fisk, A. D., Lee, C. C., & Nair, S. (2015). The Personalized Reminder Information and Social Management System (PRISM) Trial: Rationale, methods and baseline characteristics. *Contemporary Clinical Trials, 40*, 35–46.

Czaja, S. J., Charness, N., Fisk, A. D., Hertzog, C., Nair, S. N., Rogers, W. A., & Sharit, J. (2006). Factors predicting the use of technology: Findings from the Center for Research and Education on Aging and Technology Enhancement (CREATE). *Psychology and Aging, 21*(2), 333.

Czaja, S. J., & Sharit, J. (2012). *Designing training and instructional programs for older adults*. Boca Raton, FL: CRC Press.

Dalgard, O. S., & Håheim, L. L. (1998). Psychosocial risk factors and mortality: A prospective study with special focus on social support, social participation, and locus of control in Norway. *Journal of Epidemiology and Community Health, 52*, 476–481.

Dalton, D. S., Cruickshanks, K. J., Klein, B. E., Klein, R., Wiley, T. L., & Nondahl, D. M. (2003). The impact of hearing loss on quality of life in older adults. *The Gerontologist, 43*(5), 661–668.

Davis, F. D. (1989). Perceived usefulness, perceived ease of use, and user acceptance of information technology. *MIS Quarterly, 13*(3), 319–339.

De Vos, S. (1990). Extended family living among older people in six Latin American countries. *Journal of Gerontology, 45*(3), S87–S94.

Diener, E., & Chan, M. Y. (2011). Happy people live longer: Subjective well-being contributes to health and longevity. *Applied Psychology: Health and Well-Being, 3*(1), 1–43.

Dunn, L., & Olsen, R. (2014). US household real net worth through the Great Recession and beyond: Have we recovered? *Economic Letters, 122*(2), 272–275.

Ellison, N. B. (2007). Social network sites: Definition, history, and scholarship. *Journal of Computer-Mediated Communication, 13*(1), 210–230.

Ellison, N. B., Steinfield, C., & Lampe, C. (2007). The benefits of Facebook "friends": Social capital and college students' use of online social network sites. *Journal of Computer-Mediated Communication, 12*, 1143–1168.

Eng, P. M., Rimm, E. B., Fitzmaurice, G., & Kawachi, I. (2002). Social ties and change in social ties in relation to subsequent total and cause-specific mortality and coronary heart disease incidence in men. *American Journal of Epidemiology, 155*(8), 700–709.

Ertel, K. A., Glymour, M. M., & Berkman, L. F. (2008). Effects of social integration on preserving memory function in a nationally representative US elderly population. *American Journal of Public Health, 98*(7), 1215–1220.

Fiori, K. L., Antonucci, T. C., & Cortina, K. S. (2006). Social network typologies and mental health among older adults. *Journal of Gerontology: Psychological Sciences, 61B*(1), P25–P32.

Fisk, A. D., Rogers, W. A., Charness, N., Czaja, S. J., & Sharit, J. (2009). *Designing for older adults: Principles and creative human factors approaches* (2nd ed.). Boca Raton, FL: CRC Press.

Forsman, A. K., Herberts, C., Nyqvist, F., Wahlbeck, K., & Schierenbeck, I. (2013). Understanding the role of social capital for mental wellbeing among older adults. *Ageing & Society, 33*, 804–825.

Forsman, A. K., Nyqvist, F., Schierenbeck, I., Gustafson, Y., & Wahlbeck, K. (2012). Structural and cognitive social capital and depression among older adults in two Nordic regions. *Aging & Mental Health, 16*(6), 771−779.

Fratiglioni, L., Wang, H.-X., Ericsson, K., Maytan, M., & Winblad, B. (2000). Influence of social network on occurrence of dementia: A community-based longitudinal study. *The Lancet, 355*, 1315−1319.

Friemel, T. N. (2016). The digital divide has grown old: Determinants of a digital divide among seniors. *New Media & Society, 18*(2), 313−331.

Fulop, T., Larbi, A., Witkowski, J. M., McElhaney, J., Loeb, M., Mitnitski, A., & Pawelec, G. (2010). Aging, frailty and age-related diseases. *Biogerontology, 11*(5), 547−563.

Geerlings, S. W., Beekman, A. T. F., Deeg, D. J. H., & Twisk, J. W. R. (2002). Duration and severity of depression predict mortality in older adults in the community. *Psychological Medicine, 32*(4), 609−618.

Genther, D. J., Betz, J., Pratt, S., Kritchevsky, S. B., Martin, K. R., Harris, T. B., Helzner, E., Satterfield, S., Xue, Q., Yaffe, K., Simonsick, E. M., & Lin, F. (2015). Association of hearing impairment and mortality in older adults. *The Journals of Gerontology Series A: Biological Sciences and Medical Sciences, 70*(1), 85−90.

Gerstorf, D., Hoppmann, C. A., Löckenhoff, C. E., Infurna, F. J., Schupp, J., Wagner, G. G., & Ram, N. (2016). Terminal decline in well-being: The role of social orientation. *Psychology and Aging, 31*(2), 149−165.

Gigante, M. A. (1993). Virtual Reality: Definitions, history, and applications. In R. A. Earnshaw, M. A. Gigante, & H. Jones (Eds.), *Virtual reality systems* (pp. 3−14). London: Academic Press.

Giles, L. C., Glonek, G. F. V., Luszcz, M. A., & Andrews, G. R. (2005). Effect of social networks on 10 year survival in very old Australians: The Australian longitudinal study of aging. *Journal of Epidemiology & Community Health, 59*, 574−579.

Glass, T. A., de Leon, C. F. M., Bassuk, S. S., & Berkman, L. F. (2006). Social engagement and depressive symptoms in late life: Longitudinal findings. *Journal of Aging and Health, 18*(4), 604−628.

Golden, J., Conroy, R. M., & Lawlor, B. A. (2009). Social support network structure in older people: Underlying dimensions and association with psychological and physical health. *Psychology, Health & Medicine, 14*(3), 280−290.

Greiner, P. A., Snowdon, D. A., & Schmitt, F. A. (1996). The loss of independence in activities of daily living: The role of low normal cognitive function in elderly nuns. *American Journal of Public Health, 86*(1), 62−66.

Grigsby, J., Kaye, K., Baxter, J., Shetterly, S. M., & Hamman, R. F. (1998). Executive cognitive abilities and functional status among community-dwelling older persons in the San Luis Valley Health and Aging Study. *Journal of the American Geriatrics Society, 46*(5), 590−596.

Gruber, J., & Wise, D. A. (1999). Social security programs and retirement around the world. *Research in Labor Economics, 18*, 1−40.

Hasher, L., & Zacks, R. T. (1988). Working memory, comprehension, and aging: A review and a new view. *Psychology of Learning and Motivation, 22*, 193−225.

Heinrichs, M., Baumgartner, T., Kirschbaum, C., & Ehlert, U. (2003). Social support and oxytocin interact to suppress cortisol and subjective responses to psychosocial stress. *Biological Psychiatry, 54*, 1389−1398.

Hermes, G. L., Delgado, B., Tretiakova, M., Cavigelli, S. A., Krausz, T., Conzen, S. D., & McClintock, M. K. (2009). Social isolation dysregulates endocrine and behavioral stress while increasing malignant burden of spontaneous mammary tumors. *PNAS, 106*(52), 22393−22398.

Hertz, E., Hebert, J. R., & Landon, J. (1994). Social and environmental factors and life expectancy, infant mortality, and maternal mortality rates: Results of a cross-national comparison. *Social Science & Medicine, 39*(1), 105–114.

Hogeboom, D. L., McDermott, R. J., Perrin, K. M., Osman, H., & Bell-Ellison, B. A. (2010). Internet use and social networking among middle aged and older adults. *Educational Gerontology, 36*, 93–111.

Holt-Lunstad, J., Smith, T. B., Baker, M., Harris, T., & Stephenson, D. (2015). Loneliness and social isolation as risk factors for mortality: A meta-analytic review. *Perspectives on Psychological Science, 10*(2), 227–237.

Holt-Lunstad, J., Smith, T. B., & Layton, J. B. (2010). Social relationships and mortality risk: A meta-analytic review. *PLoS Medicine, 7*(7), e1000316.

Holtzman, R. E., Rebok, G. W., Saczynski, J. S., Kouzis, A. C., Doyle, K. W., & Eaton, W. W. (2004). Social network characteristics and cognition in middle-aged and older adults. *Journal of Gerontology: Psychological Sciences, 59B*(6), P278–P284.

Huxhold, O., Fiori, K. L., & Windsor, T. D. (2013). The dynamic interplay of social network characteristics, subjective well-being, and health: The costs and benefits of socio-emotional selectivity. *Psychology and Aging, 28*(1), 3–16.

van Ingen, E., Rains, S. A., & Wright, K. B. (2017). Does social network site use buffer against well-being loss when older adults face reduced functional ability? *Computers in Human Behavior, 70*, 168–177.

Jaeger, P. T., & Xie, B. (2009). Developing online community accessibility guidelines for persons with disabilities and older adults. *Journal of Disability Policy Studies, 20*(1), 55–63.

de Jong Gierveld, J., & van Tilburg, T. (1999). Living arrangements of older adults in the Netherlands and Italy: Coresidence values and behavior and their consequences for loneliness. *Journal of Cross-Cultural Gerontology, 14*(1), 1–24.

Kamiya, Y., Whelan, B., Timonen, V., & Kenny, R. A. (2010). The differential impact of subjective and objective aspects of social engagement on cardiovascular risk factors. *BMC Geriatrics, 10*, 81.

Katz, S. (1983). Assessing self-maintenance: Activities of daily living, mobility, and instrumental activities of daily living. *Journal of the American Geriatrics Society, 31*(12), 721–727.

Kawachi, I., Kennedy, B. P., & Glass, R. (1999). Social capital and self-rated health: A contextual analysis. *American Journal of Public Health, 89*(8), 1187–1193.

Kearns, A., Whitley, E., Tannahill, C., & Ellaway, A. (2015). Loneliness, social relations and health and well-being in deprived communities. *Psychology, Health & Medicine, 20*(3), 332–344.

Kiely, D. K., & Flacker, J. M. (2003). The protective effect of social engagement on 1-year mortality in a long-stay nursing home population. *Journal of Clinical Epidemiology, 56*(5), 472–478.

Kiely, D. K., Simon, S. E., Jones, R. N., & Morris, J. N. (2000). The protective effect of social engagement on mortality in long-term care. *Journal of the American Geriatrics Society, 48*, 1367–1372.

Kim, J.-H., Lee, S. G., Kim, T.-H., Choi, Y., Lee, Y., & Park, E.-C. (2016). Influence of social engagement on mortality in Korea: Analysis of the Korean Longitudinal Study of Aging (2006–2012). *Journal of Korean Medical Science, 31*(7), 1020–1026.

King, D. (2008). Neighborhood and individual factors in activity in older adults: Results from the Neighborhood and Senior Health Study. *Journal of Aging and Physical Activity, 16*(2), 144–170.

Kotwal, A. A., Kim, J., Waite, L., & Dale, W. (2016). Social function and cognitive status: Results from a US nationally representative survey of older adults. *Journal of General Internal Medicine, 31*(8), 854–862.

Krueger, K. R., Wilson, R. S., Kamenetsky, J. M., Barnes, L. L., Bienias, J. L., & Bennett, D. A. (2009). Social engagement and cognitive function in old age. *Experimental Aging Research, 35*, 45–60.

Kuiper, J. S., Zuidersma, M., Oude Voshaar, R. C., Zuidema, S. U., van den Heuvel, E. R., Stolk, R. P., & Smidt, N. (2015). Social relationships and risk of dementia: A systematic review and meta-analysis of longitudinal cohort studies. *Ageing Research Reviews, 22*, 39–57.

Kurina, L. M., Knutson, K. L., Hawkley, L. C., Cacioppo, J. T., Lauderdale, D. S., & Ober, C. (2011). Loneliness is associated with sleep fragmentation in a communal society. *Sleep, 34*(11), 1519–1526.

Leist, A. K. (2013). Social media use of older adults: A mini-review. *Gerontology, 59*, 378–384.

Leyden, K. M. (2003). Social capital and the built environment: The importance of walkable neighborhoods. *American Journal of Public Health, 93*(9), 1546–1551.

Lin, F. R., Thorpe, R., Gordon-Salant, S., & Ferrucci, L. (2011). Hearing loss prevalence and risk factors among older adults in the United States. *The Journals of Gerontology Series A: Biological Sciences and Medical Sciences, 66*(5), 582–590.

Lin, F. R., Yaffe, K., Xia, J., Xue, Q. L., Harris, T. B., Purchase-Helzner, E., Satterfield, S., Ayonayon, H. N., Ferrucci, L., & Simonsick, S. (2013). Hearing loss and cognitive decline in older adults. *JAMA Internal Medicine, 173*(4), 293–299.

Litwin, H. (2001). Social network type and morale in old age. *The Gerontologist, 41*(4), 516–524.

Litwin, H., & Shiovitz-Ezra, S. (2011). Social network type and subjective well-being in a national sample of older-Americans. *The Gerontologist, 51*(3), 379–388.

Liu, W. (2015). A hybrid model for explaining older adults' continuance intention toward SNSs. *International Journal of Smart Home, 9*(1), 93–102.

Lovelace, E. A., & Twohig, P. T. (1990). Healthy older adults' perceptions of their memory functioning and use of mnemonics. *Bulletin of the Psychonomic Society, 28*(2), 115–118.

Lubben, J., Blozik, E., Gillmann, G., Iliffe, S., Kruse, W. V. R., Beck, J. C., & Stuck, A. E. (2006). Performance of an abbreviated version of the Lubben Social Network Scale among three European community-dwelling older adult populations. *The Gerontologist, 46*(4), 503–513.

Lusardi, A., & Mitchell, O. S. (2007a). Baby Boomer retirement security: The roles of planning, financial literacy, and housing wealth. *Journal of Monetary Economics, 54*(1), 205–224.

Lusardi, A., & Mitchell, O. S. (2007b). Financial literacy and retirement preparedness: Evidence and implications for financial education. *Business Economics, 42*(1), 35–44.

Lutgendorf, S. K., Sood, A. K., Anderson, B., McGinn, S., Maiseri, H., Dao, M., ... Lubaroff, D. M. (2005). Social support, psychosocial distress, and natural killer cell activity in ovarian cancer. *Journal of Clinical Oncology, 23*(28), 7105–7113.

Lüders, M., & Brandtzæg, P.B. (2017). 'My children tell me it's so simple': A mixed-methods approach to understand older non-users' perceptions of social networking sites. *New Media & Society, 19*(2), 181–198.

Mallon, L., Broman, J.-E., & Hetta, J. (2000). Relationship between insomnia, depression, and mortality: A 12-year follow-up of older adults in the community. *International Psychogeriatrics, 12*(3), 295–306.

Marioni, R. E., Proust-Lima, C., Amieva, H., Brayne, C., Matthews, F. E., Dartigues, J.-F., & Jacqmin-Gadda, H. (2015). Social activity, cognitive decline and dementia risk: A 20-year prospective cohort study. *BMC Public Health*, *15*, 1089.

Matthews, J.H., III. (1999). *U.S. Patent No. 5,874,985*. Washington, DC: U.S. Patent and Trademark Office.

McAuley, E., Blissmer, B., Marquez, D. X., Jerome, G. J., Kramer, A. F., & Katula, J. (2000). Social relations, physical activity, and well-being in older adults. *Preventative Medicine*, *31*(5), 608−617.

McCarty, C. A., Nanjan, M. B., & Taylor, H. R. (2001). Vision impairment predicts 5 year mortality. *British Journal of Ophthalmology*, *85*(3), 322−326.

McGlynn, S., Kemple, S., Mitzner, T. L., King, A., & Rogers, W. A. (2017). Understanding the potential of PARO for healthy older adults. *International Journal of Human-Computer Studies*, *100*, 33−47.

McPherson, M., Smith-Lovin, L., & Brashears, M. E. (2006). Social isolation in America: Changes in core discussion networks over two decades. *American Sociological Review*, *71*, 353−375.

Melenhorst, A. S., Rogers, W. A., & Bouwhuis, D. G. (2006). Older adults' motivated choice for technological innovation: Evidence for benefit-driven selectivity. *Psychology and Aging*, *21*(1), 190.

Mitzner, T. L., Fausset, C. B., Boron, J. B., Adams, A. E., Dijkstra, K., Lee, C. C., Rogers, W. A., & Fisk, A. D. (2008). *Older adults' training preferences for learning to use technology*. Proceedings of the Human Factors and Ergonomics Society 52nd annual meeting (pp. 2047−2051). Santa Monica, CA: Human Factors and Ergonomics Society.

Mitzner, T. L., Stuck, R., Hartley, J. Q., Beer, J. M., & Rogers, W. A. (2017). Acceptance of televideo technology by adults aging with a mobility impairment for health and wellness interventions. *Journal of Rehabilitation and Assistive Technologies Engineering*, *4*.

Nicholson, N. R. (2012). A review of social isolation: An important but underassessed condition in older adults. *Journal of Primary Prevention*, *33*, 137−152.

Nimrod, G. (2010). Seniors' online communities: A quantitative content analysis. *The Gerontologist*, *50*(3), 382−392.

Nyqvist, F., Forsman, A. K., Giuntoli, G., & Cattan, M. (2013). Social capital as a resource for mental well-being in older people: A systematic review. *Aging & Mental Health*, *17*(4), 394−410.

Nyqvist, F., Pape, B., Pellfolk, T., Forsman, A. K., & Wahlbeck, K. (2014). Structural and cognitive aspects of social capital and all-cause mortality: A meta-analysis of cohort studies. *Social Indicators Research*, *116*(2), 545−566.

Ostir, G. V., Markides, K. S., Peek, M. K., & Goodwin, J. S. (2001). The association between emotional well-being and the incidence of stroke in older adults. *Psychosomatic Medicine*, *63*, 210−215.

Pak, R., & McLaughlin, A. C. (2010). *Designing displays for older adults*. Boca Raton, FL: CRC Press.

Park, S. N. (2009). The relationship of social engagement to psychological well-being of older adults in assisted living facilities. *Journal of Applied Gerontology*, *28*(4), 461−481.

Perrin, A. (2015). *Social media usage*. Pew Research Center.

Perrin, A., & Duggan, M. (2015). *Americans' internet access: 2000−2015*. Pew Research Center.

Putnam, R. D. (1995). Bowling alone: America's declining social capital. *Journal of Democracy*, *6*(1), 65−78.

Putnam, R. D. (2000). *Bowling alone: The collapse and revival of American community*. New York, NY: Simon & Schuster, Inc.

Ramsay, S., Ebrahim, S., Whincup, P., Papacosta, O., Morris, R., Lennon, L., & Wannamethee, S. G. (2008). Social engagement and the risk of cardiovascular disease mortality: Results of a prospective population-based study of older men. *Annals of Epidemiology*, *18*(6), 476–483.

Raz, N. (2000). Aging of the brain and its impact on cognitive performance: Integration of structural and functional findings. In F. I. M. Craik, & T. A. Salthouse (Eds.), *Handbook of aging and cognition* (2nd ed., pp. 1–90). Mahwah, NJ: Erlbaum.

Richard, L., Gauvin, L., Gosselin, C., & Laforest, S. (2008). Staying connected: Neighborhood correlates of social participation among older adults living in an urban environment in Montréal, Québec. *Health Promotion International*, *24*(1), 46–57.

Rogers, S. H., Halstead, J. M., Gardner, K. H., & Carlson, C. H. (2011). Examining walkability and social capital as indicators of quality of life at the municipal and neighborhood scales. *Applied Research in Quality of Life*, *6*(2), 201–213.

Rogers, W. A., Campbell, R. H., & Pak, R. (2001). A systems approach for training older adults to use technology. In N. Charness, D. C. Park, & B. A. Sabel (Eds.), *Communication, technology, and aging: Opportunities and challenges for the future* (pp. 187–208). New York: Springer.

Rogers, W. A., Meyer, B., Walker, N., & Fisk, A. D. (1998). Functional limitations to daily living tasks in the aged: A focus group analysis. *Human Factors: The Journal of the Human Factors and Ergonomics Society*, *40*(1), 111–125.

Rogers, W. A., & Mitzner, T. L. (2017a). Envisioning the future for older adults: Autonomy, health, well-being, and social connectedness with technology support. *Futures Journal*, *87*, 133–139.

Rogers, W.A., & Mitzner, T.L. (2017b). Human-robot interaction for older adults. In *Encyclopedia of computer science and technology*, 1–11, Taylor and Francis, New York, NY.

Rotolo, D., Hicks, D., & Martin, B. R. (2015). What is an emerging technology? *Research Policy*, *44*(10), 1827–1843.

Ryan, E. B. (1992). Beliefs about memory changes across the adult life span. *Journal of Gerontology*, *47*(1), 41–46.

Saczynski, J. S., Pfeifer, L. A., Masaki, K., Korf, E. S. C., Laurin, D., White, L., & Launer, L. J. (2006). The effect of social engagement and incident dementia: The Honolulu-Asia Aging Study. *American Journal of Epidemiology*, *163*(5), 433–440.

Salthouse, T. A. (1996). The processing-speed theory of adult age differences in cognition. *Psychological Review*, *103*(3), 403.

Salvendy, G. (2012). *Handbook of human factors and ergonomics*. Hoboken, NJ: John Wiley & Sons.

Sampson, E. L., Bulpitt, C. J., & Fletcher, A. E. (2009). Survival of community-dwelling older people: The effect of cognitive impairment and social engagement. *Journal of the American Geriatrics Society*, *57*, 985–991.

Sanford, J. A. (2012). *Design for the ages: Universal design as a rehabilitation strategy*. New York: Springer.

Schaie, K. W., & Zanjani, F. A. (2006). *Intellectual development across adulthood*. *Handbook of adult development and learning* (pp. 99–122). New York, NY: Oxford University Press, Inc.

Scharlach, A. E., & Lehning, A. J. (2013). Ageing-friendly communities and social inclusion in the United States of America. *Ageing & Society*, *33*(1), 110–136.

Schulz, R., Beach, S. R., Ives, D. G., Martire, L. M., Ariyo, A. A., & Kop, W. J. (2000). Association between depression and mortality in older adults: The Cardiovascular Heart Study. *Archival of Internal Medicine*, *160*, 1761–1768.

Seeman, T. E., Lusignolo, T. M., Albert, M., & Berkman, L. (2001). Social relationships, social support, and patterns of cognitive aging in healthy, high-functioning older adults: MacArthur Studies of Successful Aging. *Health Psychology, 20*(4), 243–255.

Shapira, N., Barak, A., & Gal, I. (2007). Promoting older adults' well-being through Internet training and use. *Aging & Mental Health, 11*(5), 477–484.

Sheldon, P. (2012). Profiling the non-users: Examination of life-position indicators, sensation seeking, shyness, and loneliness among users and non-users of social network sites. *Computers in Human Behavior, 28*, 1960–1965.

Shibata, T., & Wada, K. (2011). Robot therapy: A new approach for mental healthcare of the elderly—A mini-review. *Gerontology, 57*, 378–386.

Shrestha, L. B. (2000). Population aging in developing countries. *Health Affairs, 19*(3), 204–212.

Slegers, K., van Boxtel, M. P. J., & Jolles, J. (2012). Computer use in older adults: Determinants and the relationship with cognitive change over a 6 year episode. *Computers in Human Behavior, 28*, 1–10.

Smith, A. (2014). *Older adults and technology use: Adoption is increasing, but many seniors remain isolated from digital life*. Pew Research Center.

Sörman, D. E., Rönnlund, M., Sundström, A., Adolfsson, R., & Nilsson, L.-G. (2015). Social relationships and risk of dementia: A population-based study. *International Psychogeriatrics, 27*(8), 1391–1399.

Sörman, D. E., Sundström, A., Rönnlund, M., Adolfsson, R., & Nilsson, L.-G. (2014). Leisure activity in old age and risk of dementia: A 15-year prospective study. *Journals of Gerontology, Series B: Psychological Sciences and Social Sciences, 69*(4), 493–501.

Steinfield, C., Ellison, N. B., & Lampe, C. (2008). Social capital, self-esteem, and use of online social network sites: A longitudinal analysis. *Journal of Applied Developmental Psychology, 29*, 434–445.

Steptoe, A., Shankar, A., Demakakos, P., & Wardle, J. (2013). Social isolation, loneliness, and all-cause mortality in older men and women. *Proceedings of the National Academy of Sciences, 110*(15), 5797–5801.

Stopczynski, A., Sekara, V., Sapiezynski, P., Cuttone, A., Madsen, M. M., Larsen, J. E., & Lehmann, S. (2014). Measuring large-scale social networks with high resolution. *PLoS One, 9*(4), e95978.

Tao, L., & Reinking, D. (1996) *What research reveals about email in education* (ERIC Document No. ED4085).

Theoharidou, M., Mylonas, A., & Gritzalis, D. (2012). *A risk assessment method for smart-phones. Proc. of the 27th IFIP international information security and privacy conference* (pp. 428–440). Springer.

Thoits, P. A. (2011). Mechanisms linking social ties and support to physical and mental health. *Journal of Health and Social Behavior, 52*(2), 145–161.

Thomas, P. A. (2012). Trajectories of social engagement and mortality in late life. *Journal of Aging and Health, 24*(4), 547–568.

Valenzuela, S., Park, N., & Kee, K. F. (2009). *Is there social capital in a social network site?: Facebook use and college students' life satisfaction, trust, and participation. Journal of Computer-Mediated Communication* (14, pp. 875–901).

Vanderhorst, R. K., & McLaren, S. (2005). Social relationships as predictors of depression and suicidal ideation in older adults. *Aging & Mental Health, 9*(6), 517–525.

Venkatesh, V., & Davis, F. D. (2000). A theoretical extension of the Technology Acceptance Model: Four longitudinal field studies. *Management Science, 46*(2), 186–204.

Venkatesh, V., Morris, M. G., Davis, G. B., & Davis, F. D. (2003). User acceptance of information technology: Toward a unified view. *MIS Quarterly, 27*(3), 425–478.

Venkatesh, V., Thong, J. Y. L., & Xu, X. (2012). Consumer acceptance and use of information technology: Extending the Unified Theory of Acceptance and Use of Technology. *MIS Quarterly*, *36*(1), 157−178.

Vroman, K. G., Arthanat, S., & Lysack, C. (2015). "Who over 65 is online?": Older adults' dispositions toward information communication technology. *Computers in Human Behavior*, *43*, 156−166.

Wada, K., & Shibata, T. (2006). Robot therapy in a care house: Its sociopsychological and physiological effects on the residents. In *Proceedings of the IEEE international conference on robotics and automation* (pp. 3966−3971).

Wang, H.-X., Karp, A., Winblad, B., & Fratiglioni, L. (2002). Late-life engagement in social and leisure activities is associated with a decreased risk of dementia: A longitudinal study from the Kungsholmen Project. *American Journal of Epidemiology*, *155*(12), 1081−1087.

Watts, D. J., Dodds, P. S., & Newman, M. E. J. (2002). Identity and search in social networks. *Science*, *296*(5571), 1302−1305.

White, H., McConnell, E., Clipp, E., Bynum, L., Teague, C., Navas, L., Craven, S., & Halbrecht, H. (1999). Surfing the net in later life: A review of the literature and pilot study of computer use and quality of life. *The Journal of Applied Gerontology*, *18*(3), 358−378.

Wilmoth, J. M. (2001). Living arrangements among older immigrants in the United States. *The Gerontologist*, *41*(2), 228−238.

Wood, L., Shannon, T., Bulsara, M., Pikora, T., McCormack, G., & Giles-Corti, B. (2008). The anatomy of the safe and social suburb: An exploratory study of the built environment, social capital and residents' perceptions of safety. *Health & Place*, *14*(1), 15−31.

Wu, X., Stuck, R.E., Mitzner, T.L., Rogers, W.A., & Beer, J.M. (2016). Televideo for older adults with mobility impairment: A needs assessment. *In Rehabilitation Engineering and Assistive Technology Society (RESNA) 2016 annual conference, Arlington, VA*.

Xie, B., Watkins, I., Golbeck, J., & Huang, M. (2012). Understanding and changing older adults' perceptions and learning of social media. *Educational Gerontology*, *38*, 282−296.

Yang, Y. C., Boen, C., Gerken, K., Li, T., Schorpp, K., & Harris, K. M. (2016). Social relationships and physiological determinants of longevity across the human life span. *PNAS*, *113*(3), 578−583.

Yu, R. P., Mccammon, R. J., Ellison, N. B., & Langa, K. M. (2016). The relationships that matter: Social network site use and social wellbeing among older adults in the United States of America. *Ageing & Society*, *36*, 1826−1852.

Zimmer, Z., & Dayton, J. (2005). Older adults in sub-Saharan Africa living with children and grandchildren. *Population Studies*, *59*(3), 295−312.

Zunzunegui, M.-V., Alvarado, B. E., Del Ser, T., & Otero, A. (2003). Social networks, social integration, and social engagement determine cognitive decline in community-dwelling Spanish older adults. *Journal of Gerontology: Social Sciences*, *58B*(2), S93−S100.

Further reading

Beer, J. M., & Takayama, L. (2011). Mobile remote presence systems for older adults: acceptance, benefits, and concerns. *Proceeding of Human-Robot Interaction* (pp. 19−26). ACM/IEEE.

Webber, S. C., Porter, M. M., & Menec, V. H. (2010). Mobility in older adults: a comprehensive framework. *The Gerontologist*, *50*(4), 443−450.

Virtual cognitive training in healthy aging and mild cognitive impairment

Chandramallika Basak and Shuo Qin
Center for Vital Longevity, University of Texas at Dallas, Richardson, TX, United States

The rapid change in technology over the past decade has not only made virtual tools handy, but is also causing a greater cohort gap between different age groups, particularly between children, their middle-aged parents and their older grandparents. The advent of iPhone in 2007 brought forth not merely accessibility, but also popularity to mobile virtual tools, particularly to app-based games and learning tools. These virtual tools have proven to be efficient learning tools for children and younger adults, when compared to traditional classroom-based learning (van Doorn & van Doorn, 2014; Finlay, Desmet, & Evans, 2004). But little is known about the efficacy of these virtual tools in enhancing learning experiences in adults over the age of 60. Although children and younger adults have eagerly latched onto these learning tools and games, older adults have been more reluctant to adapt to this shift in lifestyle. When learning to use virtual tools, such as smart phones and computers, older adults must utilize active learning process (Chan, Haber, Drew, & Park, 2014), which is an important component of most intervention studies aimed to slow down age-related cognitive declines. We hypothesize that these tools will not merely be effective in teaching novel skills to older adults, but may also be effective in strengthening cognitive abilities in older adults. But not all virtual tools are created equal. It is therefore possible that only a few specific types of virtual tools may be beneficial in strengthening cognition in elderly.

The average life expectancy in the United States is increasing (Beller, 2013). As a result, the number of older adults with age-related neurodegenerative illnesses requiring continuous patient care is rapidly growing (Alzheimer's Association, 2015; Hebert, Weuve, Scherr, & Evans, 2013). Moreover, although there is continual shift in the life expectancy, but there has been almost no shift in the average age of onset of age-related neurodegenerative illnesses, including Alzheimer's disease (AD; Sperling et al., 2011). The increase in the number of people with dementia or AD creates a burden not only on the affected individual and his/her immediate family, but also on the society. If we continue to stay on the current course of aging and age-related neurodegenerative illnesses, it is expected that the national cost of caring for individuals with AD will increase to a staggering $1 trillion by 2050 in the United States (http://www.alz.org). This can bankrupt our medical system. Therefore, one of our greatest contemporary challenges is to deploy effective cognitive interventions not only when we are aging successfully, but also

Aging, Technology and Health. DOI: http://dx.doi.org/10.1016/B978-0-12-811272-4.00009-9

at the earliest signs of age-related neuropathology. We will, in this chapter, review one such proposed intervention mode which uses virtual tool-based cognitive training.

Cognitive declines in healthy aging and MCI

The most common complaints heard from older adults are regarding their memory lapses (McGillivray & Castel, 2010), such as forgetting where personal things are kept or confusing names of people. Such memory lapses can lead to socially embarrassing situations, and affect the mental well-being of the individual. Older adults also complain about inability to multitask or inefficiently perform complex real-world tasks, such as driving. In fact, older drivers over the age of 80 have the same crash rate per mile as younger drivers in their early 20s (Teftt, 2012). Thus, the subjective complaints of older adults are pronounced for two cognitive domains—episodic memory (e.g., recalling events) and executive functions (e.g., multitasking). Episodic memory refers to memories for past events, people and episodes (Tulving, 1972)—e.g., recalling vignettes in a story in the correct order, where each episode is linked to the subsequent episode. Executive functions refer to set of cognitive processes that require cognitive control of behaviors to successfully attain a goal. Three fundamental aspects of executive functions are inhibitory control (e.g., self-control, selective attention and resisting distractors), cognitive flexibility (e.g., switching from one task to another during multitasking, thinking of novel creative solutions), and working memory (maintaining and coordinating multiple information units simultaneously in mind) (Basak & Verhaeghen, 2011a, 2011b; Diamond, 2013; Miyake et al., 2000; Verhaeghen, Cerella, Bopp, & Basak, 2005). Deficits in episodic memory or executive functions are detrimental to the lives of the affected individuals. Such cognitive deficits may be caused by a disease or an accident, but the most common cause of deficits in memory and executive functions is chronological aging. Although cross-sectional data show a steady, gradual difference among different age cohorts in both of these cognitive domains, the actual episodic memory declines, as evidenced in longitudinal data, are visible only after 60 years of age, even after adjusting for practice effects (Rönnlund, Nyberg, Bäckman, & Nilsson, 2005).

It is well documented that after 60 years of age, our episodic memory, executive functioning, and reasoning skills decline steadily. In contrast, general knowledge, vocabulary, and semantic memory remain relatively stable or even show some increments during middle age till 55 years (Park et al., 2002; Rönnlund et al., 2005; Salthouse, 2010). Importantly, episodic memory, but not executive functions or reasoning, declines rapidly 3—4 years prior to diagnosis of mild cognitive impairment (MCI), compared to normal aging (Howieson et al., 2008). Fig. 9.1 shows our hypothesized model of progression from healthy aging to AD, involving four stages. These stages are: healthy aging, preclinical phase, MCI and AD. The preclinical phase, 3—4 years prior to MCI diagnosis, is neither marked by any striking brain

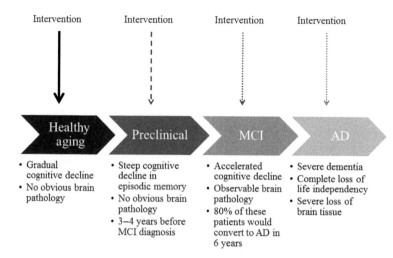

Figure 9.1 A model of progression to Alzheimer's Disease (AD) from healthy aging, which involves four stages.

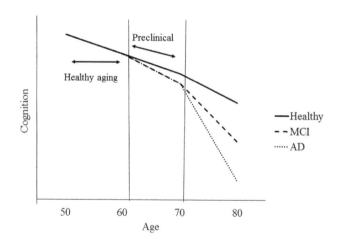

Figure 9.2 Hypothetical trajectory of age-related cognitive decline and progression to Alzheimer's Disease (AD) from in older adults.

pathology (Jack et al., 2013; Sperling et al., 2011) nor by accelerated declines in other age-sensitive cognitive abilities, such as executive functions or reasoning (Park et al., 2002). The detection, therefore, of this preclinical phase is extremely difficult, unless sensitive cognitive measures are used for evaluation. The MCI stage, in contrast, is marked by an accelerated decline not only in the episodic memory, but also in executive functions and reasoning. In other words, MCI and the preclinical phase differ with respect to the global cognitive declines, which are observable only in MCI stage. Fig. 9.2 displays a hypothetical trajectory of cognitive declines with the different stages of aging. These broader and detectable cognitive declines in MCI are accompanied with observable brain pathology, particularly in medial temporal lobes (MTLs) and frontoparietal brain regions. MTL serves episodic memory, whereas the frontoparietal regions serve executive functioning and reasoning (Nyberg, McIntosh, Houle, Nilsson, & Tulving, 1996; Naghavi & Nyberg, 2005). Importantly, about 20% of patients diagnosed with MCI convert to AD within 1 year and over 33% over 5 years (Ward, Tardiff, Dye, & Arrighi, 2013). AD is initially marked by severe memory loss, followed by loss of personality and mood leading to a complete loss of life independency. AD is also accompanied initially by a severe cortical atrophy, with severe tissue loss in memory-related areas, such as MTL and frontoparietal brain regions. Gradually, most of the cortex is severely affected causing loss of speech and communication. It is, therefore, extremely important to implement interventions that can maintain, and hopefully even improve, not only memory but also executive functions and everyday functioning through late adulthood.

Behavioral interventions to enhance cognition

In general, behavioral intervention studies fall into three categories: physical intervention, cognitive intervention, and social engagement. Of these three, the effects of physical and cognitive interventions on cognition have been studied most, with social engagement often used as a placebo. Metaanalytic studies on physical interventions, which have compared different types of physical exercises, such as aerobic (walking, bicycling, etc.), anaerobic (toning and stretching), and strength-training, have found aerobic interventions to be most beneficial in improving cognition in both healthy older adults and patients with dementia (Colcombe & Kramer, 2003; Heyn, Aberu, & Ottenbacher, 2004). In healthy older adults, the effect size of cognitive improvements for the physical fitness training group was moderate (Hedge's $g = 0.48$); this effect size was small for the control group (Hedge's $g = 0.16$) (Colcombe & Kramer, 2003). In patients with MCI and dementia, the effect size of cognitive improvements for the physical fitness training group was moderate (Hedge's $g = 0.57$), but the effects for control group were not reported (Heyn, Aberu, & Ottenbacher, 2004). Strength training has also been found to be beneficial in improving executive functions in healthy older adults (Liu-Ambrose et al., 2010), though more studies are required before drawing conclusions.

Although physical interventions are effective in improving cognition in older adults, physical exercise can be potentially dangerous to frail older adults. Moreover, adherence to physical exercise regimens is challenging even in younger adults, as evidenced from high gym attendance in January of any given year, driven plausibly by new year resolutions, to subsequent drop-outs in attendance and gym memberships within a few months (Watts, 2012). In contrast, development of smart devices and other virtual game-like tools has made cognitive interventions not only engaging, but also accessible to sedentary older adults, who can now participate in an intervention program from the comfort of their own homes.

Increasing popularity of cognitive interventions has resulted in commercial corporations creating "brain games" with claims of enhancing and training our brains, with little evidence of brain plasticity. Use of these commercial "brain training" products, some with exaggerated claims about the degree of transfer and brain changes, have led to recent criticism and scrutiny of cognitive training. One of the main goals of cognitive training is not only to establish improvements in skills similar to the trained task, i.e., *near transfer*, but also to evaluate the extent to which the training can engender *broad* improvements in untrained skills, i.e., *far transfer*. In 2014, two groups of scientists published open letters debating the effects of cognitive training, particularly the so-called brain games (www.cognitive-trainingdata. org). A comprehensive literature review on the effectiveness of brain games was recently published (Simons et al., 2016) where the authors concluded that most cognitive training studies showed small to moderate effects on improvements in the trained cognitive functions (near transfer), and that the corporation-developed brain games showed small effects of improvements to near transfer tasks, but there is little evidence of far transfer to tasks that are very different from the trained games. Moreover, many cognitive intervention studies did not follow strict clinical trial protocols, such as, having an active control group, or randomizing participants into the training group and the control group. Early cognitive interventions have focused on the improvement of cognition in the trained group only. Such experimental design was soon criticized due to the confounding test−retest, or practice, effects. Later studies then started to incorporate characteristics of rigid clinical trials by having one or more control groups that were either passive (a test−retest group) or active (a placebo group engaged in some activity), as well as by randomizing participants into the training or the control groups (e.g., Basak, Voss, Boot, & Kramer, 2008).

Today, most cognitive intervention studies are randomized controlled trials (RCTs), to the extent that a metaanalysis was conducted only on the RCTs that used computer-based cognitive training in healthy older adults (Lampit, Hallock, & Valenzuela, 2014). The result of this metaanalysis suggests a significant, but small, effect (Hedge's $g = 0.22$) of improvements in the training group on overall cognition. This result is not conclusive because improvements in the control group on overall cognition was not reported. Therefore, the cognitive changes in the training group cannot be compared to that of the control group. This issue is remedied in our recent metaanalyses (Basak, Qin, & O'Connell, submitted for publication), where the cognitive training using RCT protocols yielded significantly greater benefits to overall cognition than the control groups. Importantly, metaanalysis on cognitive interventions in MCI patients, though not limited to RCTs, has found a moderate effect (Hedge's $g = 0.41$) of cognitive training on improving cognition, compared to the negligible effects (Hedge's $g = -0.02$) on the age-matched controls (Li et al., 2011).

To summarize, systematic reviews on cognitive and physical interventions indicate that both types of interventions improve cognition in both healthy older adults (Lampit et al., 2014; Colcombe & Kramer, 2003) as well as MCI patients (Li et al., 2011; Heyn, Aberu, & Ottenbacher, 2004). Physical interventions seem to yield a larger effect on overall cognition than cognitive interventions in healthy older adults (0.48 vs 0.22), but this could be due to an artifact from the lack of rigor in the physical intervention metaanalysis (Colcombe & Kramer, 2003), where studies were not limited to RCTs. Moreover, physical interventions are usually most effective on cognition only after long training duration (greater than 6 months; Colcombe & Kramer, 2003). In contrast, cognitive training studies are of shorter durations, with most training lasting for 20 hours or less (Lampit et al., 2014). The two metaanalyses conducted on the MCI patients, one on physical interventions and another on cognitive interventions, lacked the rigor of limiting the studies to RCTs. In this case, both types of intervention yielded similar moderate benefits to cognition. Therefore, it is premature to conclude that physical interventions are more superior to cognitive intervention in elderly, unless a comprehensive metaanalysis is conducted that explicitly compares these effects in RCTs.

Most of these interventions reported in the metaanalyses have utilized traditional training tools. For example, cognitive intervention studies have used paper-pencil based or computer-based laboratory cognitive tasks, while physical intervention studies have used regular gym machines with supervision. With advancement of technology, especially with the development of smart devices, recent intervention studies have started to utilize virtual tools to improve cognition in older adults. We will therefore focus in the rest of this chapter on reviewing recent cognitive and physical RCTs that have used virtual tools to improve cognition in healthy older adults and MCI patients.

Cognitive interventions using virtual tools

The most common virtual cognitive intervention tool is video game. Early RCTs using first generation video games such as the Pacman and Tetris suggested that playing such games could improve processing speed in heathy older adults compared to controls (Belchior et al., 2013; Dustman, Emmerson, Steinhaus, Shearer, & Dustman, 1992). RCTs using more complex real-time strategy games (e.g., Rise of Nation, World of Warcraft) found that healthy older adults in the training group showed significant gains in attention (Whitlock, McLaughlin, & Allaire, 2012), working memory, executive functions and short-term memory (Basak et al., 2008), compared to those in the control group. Simple music game (Kim et al., 2015a, 2015b) has also been effective in improving executive function in healthy older adults, compared to controls. Results for action video games have been inconsistent: the Nintendo DS Mario Kart has resulted in no significant cognitive improvement in healthy older adults (Boot et al., 2013), while Medal of Honor has been found to improve selective attention in healthy older adults (Belchior et al., 2013), compared to the age-matched healthy controls.

While some researchers used off-the-shelf video games, some others have developed their own games to target cognitive declines in older adults. Space Fortress is one such example of an in-lab developed multicomponent video game that has been shown to improve executive functions in healthy older adults, compared to both passive and active controls (Stern et al., 2011). van Muijden and colleagues (2012) developed a series of short-play computer games, often referred to as "casual games," and found that healthy older adults trained on all of these games improved in executive functions more than the active controls, who were not playing any casual games. Another study found lab-developed multicomponent game to be more effective in improving attention and working memory in healthy older adults than single-component game (Anguera et al., 2013). In short, video games that employ multiple cognitive components, either simultaneously (Anguera et al., 2013; Basak et al., 2008; Stern et al., 2011) or sequentially (van Muijden et al., 2012), are more effective in improving executive functions in healthy older adults.

Aside from off-the shelf and laboratory video games, many commercially available "brain training" packages have been used in cognitive intervention studies. In healthy older adults, training with Posit Science programs showed improvements in both episodic memory and attention, compared to controls (Smith et al., 2009). An intervention study using Lumosity programs found that trained healthy older adults improved in executive functions compared to controls (Mayas, Parmentier, Andrés, & Ballesteros, 2014). Another intervention study using Lumosity programs in healthy older adults found improvements in selective attention, processing speed and episodic memory, but not in working memory and executive functions (Ballesteros et al., 2014). In MCI patients, training on such programs has shown improvements in episodic memory (Posit Science, Barnes et al., 2009; Rosen, Sugiura, Kramer, Whitfield-Gabrieli, & Gabrieli, 2011; Complete Brain Workout, Stavros, Fotini, & Magda, 2010), attention (Lumosity, Finn & McDonald, 2011; Complete Brain Workout, Stavros et al., 2010), and verbal fluency (Complete Brain Workout, Stavros et al., 2010). Both Posit Science's and Lumosity's websites provide detailed scientific background materials and citations to scientific literature, but both make claims about effectiveness of their products not only on cognition but also on "brain training." It is important to note that Lumosity program uses laboratory-based tasks of executive function, attention and working memory. Therefore, the findings from Lumosity can be considered evidence for near transfer at best. In contrast, improvements in episodic memory can be considered evidence for far transfer, because the training protocol (e.g., Posit Science) did not involve measures of episodic memory.

Most of the above mentioned cognitive interventions have used personal computers and internet as the training tools. Some researchers, with technology advancement, have adapted other devices as cognitive intervention tools for healthy older adults and MCI patients. compared a tablet-based cognitive training to robot-assisted cognitive training in healthy older adults, but they found that robot-assisted cognitive training was not superior to the tablet-based training. Two recent intervention studies with MCI patients have utilized the new virtual reality (VR) technology. One study had participants looking at moving objects (e.g., a moving swing or a flying seagull) in the VR world, and compared this group to an active control group which underwent musical therapy (Optale et al., 2010). Cognition was assessed at two time points: Before the training (baseline) and 6 months after the training. The main interest was to evaluate the difference between the two MCI groups (VR vs Music therapy) regarding their changes in cognition from baseline to 6 months after the training. Regarding general cognitive functioning, the VR group improved in mini-mental status examination (MMSE) but not in Mental Status in Neurology, compared to the controls. The VR group improved significantly more than the control group in measures of verbal short-term memory and verbal episodic memory, but no differential improvements were observed in tasks of executive functions, visuospatial processing, and daily living activities. In the other study, MCI patients underwent episodic memory training that was either VR immersed or was therapist led on paper-pencil tasks (Man, Chung, & Lee, 2012). Both groups showed equivalence in encoding objects in their memory, but the VR group outperformed in both immediate and delayed retrieval of the encoded objects. In summary, VR technology has been found to be more effective than other approaches in improving both short-term memory and long-term episodic memory in MCI patients, who suffer specifically from marked memory-impairments.

Based on the literature reviewed, we conclude that cognitive intervention studies using virtual tools have been effective in improving cognitive functions in both healthy older adults and MCI patients. However, retention of such improvements over long term (e.g., months after completion of the training) has not been thoroughly investigated. Also, most video game intervention studies targeted healthy older adults, while the VR intervention studies have targeted only the MCI patients. Future research should further explore the potential of video game training in MCI patients, as well as the potential of VR training in healthy older adults, given the positive evidence from MCI patients. For details of each study mentioned above, see Table 9.1.

Physical intervention using virtual tools

We discussed the issues with adherence to physical exercise regimen, not only in older but also in younger adults. Unlike video games, which can be addictive, physical exercise is usually seen as a "chore" by many of us. Motivating people to not only initiate but also to continue to exercise is therefore an important factor to a successful physical intervention. One way to motivate older adults to do physical exercise is to incorporate game play or other feedback-providing virtual tools. Such combination of physical exercise with game play has been coined "exergames." These exergame RCTs are gaining popularity as behavioral interventions, compared to traditional physical exercise interventions. We will hereby review these exergame intervention studies.

Two of the exergame intervention studies used VR stationary bicycles, and compared them to an aerobic-only group that exercised on the stationary bike, but without the VR experience. In one study, the training group enjoyed visual scenery in the VR, thus emulating outdoor bicycling experience (Anderson-Hanley et al., 2012). Cognition on variety of domains were assessed, including episodic memory and executive functions. In the other study, the training group had to collect

Table 9.1 **Cognitive training studies using virtual tools**

Author last name	Technology used	Mean age	Control group	Mental status	Transfer to cognition
Anguera et al., 2013	Neuro-racer	67	Active	Healthy	Attention and working memory
Barnes et al., 2009	Posit Science	74	Active	MCI	Episodic memory
Basak et al., 2008	Rise of Nation	69	Passive	Healthy	Working memory, executive functions and short-term memory
Ballesteros et al., 2014	Lumosity	69	Passive	Healthy	Processing speed, attention, and episodic memory
Belchoir et al., 2013	Medal of Honor, Tetris	69	Passive	Healthy	Selective attention
Boot et al., 2013	Nintendo DS Mario Kart and Brain Age	70	Passive	Healthy	No significant improvement compared to the control group
Dustman et al., 1992	Casual computer games (e.g., Pacman)	65	Active	Healthy	Processing speed
Finn (2011)	Lumosity	74	Passive	MCI	Attention
Kim, G., et al,., 2015	Robot	72	Passive	Healthy	Executive functions
Kim, K., et al., 2015	Music game	67	Passive	Healthy	Executive functions
Man Chung, & Li, 2012	Virtual Reality	80	Active	MCI	Memory
Mayas et al., 2014	Lumosity	68	Active	Healthy	Executive functions
McDougall & House, 2012	Nintendo Brain Age	75	Passive	Healthy	Working memory
van Muijden, Band, & Hommel, 2012	Brain training games	67	Active	Healthy	Executive function and reasoning

(Continued)

Table 9.1 **(Continued)**

Author last name	Technology used	Mean age	Control group	Mental status	Transfer to cognition
Nouchi et al., 2012	Nintendo Brain Age	68	Active	Healthy	Executive functions and processing speed
Optale et al., 2010	Virtual Reality	79	Active	MCI	Episodic memory
Rosen et al., 2011	Posit Science	75	Active	MCI	Episodic memory
Smith, 2009	Posit Science	75	Active	Healthy	Episodic memory and attention
Stavros, Fotini, & Magda, 2010	Complete Brain Workout	68	Passive	MCI	Attention, verbal fluency and episodic memory
Stern et al., 2011	Space Fortress	66	Active	Healthy	Executive functions
Whitlock et al., 2012	World of Warcraft	65	Passive	Healthy	Attention

color-appropriate coins and dragons (thus training their episodic memory) as they bicycled along a route (Barcelos et al., 2015). The targeted cognitive outcomes were three tasks of executive functions. In both studies, the exergame training groups significantly improved in measures of executive functions compared to the aerobic-only groups.

In another study using VR technology, 12 healthy older adults were taught to juggle three balls in a VR environment, and 12 were taught to juggle three balls with visual biofeedback (Bisson, Contant, Sveistrup, & Lajoie, 2007). Although both groups improved in reaction times during a dual task, VR group did not improve more than the standard biofeedback training group. These trained older adults improved in processing speed compared to controls. It is important to note that the study was underpowered for a behavioral intervention study, and juggling doesn't require the same degree of aerobic exercise as a bicycle ride.

An exergame intervention RCT study on 32 individuals used Dance Revolution (15 participants), an aerobic exercise which combines working memory and physical coordination, and compared this training group with a no-contact passive control group (17 participants; Schoene et al., 2013). This study assessed transfer on only one cognitive task of executive function (Trails B-A), although dual task ability was assessed in a timed-task, where verbal fluency task was imposed onto a standard physical mobility measurement (up and go test). The exergame group improved more than the controls in both tasks of executive functions, one cognitive (Trails B-A) and another a combination of cognitive-physical ability (dual task).

A cluster of exergame studies have utilized the Nintendo Wii system (Wii Fit) as an intervention tool. Results from these Wii exergame studies are mixed. Malliot and colleagues (Malliot, Perrot, & Hartley, 2012) found that healthy older adults trained on Wii Fit improved in executive functions and processing speed compared to a control group. Two other Wii Fit exergame intervention studies in healthy older adults found no significant cognitive improvements in the trained group compared to a control group (Franco, Jacobs, Inzerillo, & Kluzik, 2012; Wittelsberger, Krug, Tittlbach, & Bös, 2013). Another Wii Fit exergame intervention study on MCI patients found no significant cognitive improvements for the Wii Fit group compared to the control group (Padala et al., 2012). However, training on a Nintendo Wii-based exergame system (FitForAll), especially designed for older adults, improved episodic memory in the MCI patients (Franco et al., 2013).

The Microsoft Kinect, paired with Xbox 360, has also been used as an exergame intervention tool in older adults. Kayama and colleagues (2014) trained healthy older adults to practice TaiChi using the Microsoft Kinect system and found improvements in executive functions in the trained group. In contrast, another study using the Microsoft Kinect system with sports games found no significant cognitive improvements for the trained older adults (Ordnung, Hoff, Kaminski, Villringer, & Ragert, 2017).

Aside from exergames, some physical intervention studies have combined physical exercise with cognitive training packages. A 3-month long intervention study combined Posit Science programs and aerobic exercise in a 2 (Posit Science vs Educational DVD) × 2 (Dance-based Aerobic vs stretching) factorial design (Barnes, Santos-Modesitt, Poelke, & Kramer, 2013). Participants were assessed before and after the training on episodic memory, processing speed, visuospatial function and executive function. Results were reported on a composite score of all assessed cognitive abilities, and found that all four groups improved in this composite score of global cognitive functioning, but there were no significant differences between the four groups. When each cognitive task was analyzed individually, two tasks showed significant improvements for the two training groups that underwent Posit Science training, regardless of the type of physical intervention used. Both tasks assessed visuospatial attention, one for selective attention and another for divided attention. The active controls, who saw an education DVD, did not improve in any cognitive task. It is important to note that only two of the twelve tasks used showed any significant results, although these two tasks belonged to the same cognitive construct. Therefore, this study does not provide sufficient evidence for effectiveness of combining aerobic exercise training with virtual tools in healthy older adults. Another intervention study combined Lumosity programs, conducted in both individual and group settings, with aerobic exercise and daily heart rate tracker in the MCI patients (Dannhauser et al., 2014). Participants were wait-listed for the first 6−12 week run in period, and then underwent training for 12 weeks. Participants improved in working memory after 12-weeks of intervention, compared to their wait-list period, but lack of an independent control, group as warranted in an RCT, makes it difficult to disambiguate whether the cognitive gains are due to training or due to practice effects.

To summarize, physical interventions using virtual tools have yielded inconsistent cognitive benefits for both healthy older adults and MCI patients. However, interventions that combined traditional aerobic fitness regimens with VR tools have resulted in significant improvements in executive functions in older adults (Anderson-Hanley et al., 2012; Barcelos et al., 2015). Importantly, when compared to traditional aerobic fitness regimens, the VR-enhanced training has consistently shown greater gains in executive functions in healthy older adults, although more studies are needed before making any conclusive claims.

The effectiveness of the Nintendo Wii Fit and Microsoft Kinect systems in improving cognition in older adults is negligible, based on the current evidence. It is possible that with the wide range of available games in these two systems, researchers in some studies did not select games with high aerobic demands that could improve cognition in older adults. Also in some of the Wii Fit studies, cognitive outcomes were secondary to physical outcomes, such as balance and gait (Padala et al., 2012; Wittelsberger et al., 2013). The only cognitive outcome reported by these two studies (Padala et al., 2012; Wittelsberger et al., 2013) was the score for the MMSE, an assessment of general cognitive functioning. It is therefore possible that nuanced cognitive benefits to episodic memory or executive functions were simply overlooked. Therefore, more exergame intervention studies using the Wii Fit and Kinect systems in older adults with multiple cognitive outcomes are needed to evaluate any long-term benefit from using these exergames. For details of each above mentioned study, see Table 9.2.

Non-specific interventions using virtual tools

In addition to directly targeting cognitive or physical health of older adults, some researchers have implemented interventions that encourage social and mental stimulation of older adults in classroom settings. An intervention study taught healthy older adults to use an iPad in a classroom setting, and found that learning to use iPad, compared to active controls, improved processing speed and episodic memory in older adults (Chan et al., 2014). Two intervention studies that enrolled healthy older adults in computer classes found that learning to use a computer improved episodic memory (Klusmann et al., 2010; Nascimento et al., 2011), and language (Nascimento et al., 2011) in the trained older adults, compared to the controls. These studies provide limited evidence that nonspecific interventions using virtual tools produce broad transfer to cognition.

Discussion

The evidence from aerobic interventions and from exergames that have combined virtual tools with traditional aerobic exercises provide sufficient evidence for broad transfer to cognition from aerobic fitness training. In short, targeting our cardiovascular health proves not only beneficial for our heart, but also our brains. Further support for this statement comes from neuroimaging studies that have assessed brain structure and brain functions before and after aerobic fitness training.

Table 9.2 Physical exercise training studies using virtual tools with cognitive outcomes

Author last name	Technology used	Mean age	Control group	Mental status	Transfer to cognition
Anderson-Hanley, et al., 2012	Virtual reality stationary cycling	78	Active	Healthy	Executive function
Barcelos et al., 2015	Virtual reality stationary cycling	82	Active	Healthy	Executive function
Barnes et al., 2013	Posit Science plus aerobic exercise	73	Active	Healthy	Attention
Bisson et al., 2007	Virtual Reality ball juggling	74	Active	Healthy	Reaction time
Dannhauser et al., 2014	Heart rate tracker plus Lumosity	75	Passive	MCI	Working memory
Franco et al., 2012	Nintendo Wii Fit	78	Active	Healthy	No significant improvement compared to the control group
Franco et al., 2013	Nintendo Wii FitForAll	76	Passive	MCI	Episodic memory
Kayama et al., 2014	Microsoft Kinect	75	Active	Healthy	Executive function
Maillot Perrot, & Hartley, 2012	Nintendo Wii Fit	73	Passive	Healthy	Executive functions and processing speed
Ordnung et al., 2017	Microsoft Kinect	68	Passive	Healthy	No significant improvement compared to the control group
Padala et al., 2012	Nintendo Wii Fit	80	Active	MCI	No significant improvement compared to the control group
Schoene et al., 2013	Dance Revolution	78	Passive	Healthy	Executive functions
Wittelsberger et al., 2013	Nintendo Wii Fit	71	Passive	Healthy	No significant improvement compared to the control group

Sustained aerobic fitness training in healthy, but sedentary, older adults for 1 year (3 days per week, 45 minutes for each session) results not only improvements in spatial working memory, but also increases in both anterior and posterior hippocampus volume (Erickson et al., 2011). Hippocampus, an essential part of MTL, not only underlies episodic memory, but also spatial memory (Broadbent, Squire, & Clark, 2004; Clark, Zola, & Squire, 2000). In the same RCT (Erickson et al., 2011), training-related changes were also observed for resting-state functional connectivity in networks that underlie executive control and attention, and incorporate frontoparietal regions (Voss et al., 2013). Older adults who underwent aerobic fitness training showed increased connectivity between frontoparietal regions in cognitive networks, compared to the active controls. Interesting, healthy older adults undergoing the aerobic fitness training, compared to active controls who underwent toning and stretching, did not show any gains in brain volume after 6-month of intervention. This implies that gains in physical interventions are only effective at long training durations, usually lasting for 6 months or more (Colcombe & Kramer, 2003). Additionally, evidence from interventions using Nintendo Wii Fit and Microsoft Kinect systems suggest that cognitive gains from these interventions in older adults is negligible, plausibly because of the short training durations (<6 months) or not sufficiently engaging cardiovascular functions that are engaged in aerobic fitness training.

In contrast, cognitive interventions in older adults are usually of shorter durations and are found to be effective even at 20 hours or less (Lampit et al., 2014). Although cognitive training regimens targeting single cognitive components typically yield near transfer to the trained cognition in healthy older adults (e.g., Ball et al., 2002; Verhaeghen, Marcoens, & Gossens, 1992; for a review, see Stine-Morrow & Basak, 2011), those targeting multiple cognitive components through video games (except action games) show transfer to a wide range of age-sensitive cognitive skills, including executive functions. Evidence for the video game based training comes from both off-the-self games (Basak et al., 2008; Whitlock et al., 2012;) and laboratory designed games (Anguera et al., 2013; van Muijden et al., 2012; Stern et al., 2011). For brain training programs, results from Posit Science hold promise, given the consistent evidence for episodic memory improvements in both healthy older adults (Barnes et al., 2013; Smith et al., 2009) and MCI patients (Barnes et al., 2009; Rosen et al., 2011). Much of the evidence supporting video game based cognitive training comes from healthy older adults, whereas MCI patients seem to benefit in both episodic memory and short-term memory from VR-based training. We propose that future research should consider RCTs where video game and VR-based training are compared in both healthy older adults and MCI patients, allowing for us to understand what cognitive challenges warrant far transfer, and whether these challenges are modulated by stages of aging.

Interestingly, the only study that compared aerobic training to cognitive training found that cognitive training improved attention, whereas aerobic fitness did not (Barnes et al., 2013). Moreover, adding aerobic fitness to Posit Science-based virtual cognitive training did not enhance the transfer effects. On the other hand, adding virtual cognitive tools to aerobic fitness training has shown to be more effective at improving frontoparietal based executive functions (Anderson-Hanley et al., 2012; Barcelos et al., 2015). Such direct comparisons of different behavioral interventions, such as physical versus cognitive, is needed for future research. The evidence so far favors cognitive training over physical fitness training, once we account for duration and frequency of the training.

In is important to note that far transfer, if any, is usually limited to measures of episodic memory, short-term memory, processing speed, and executive functions. There were a handful of studies that investigated transfer to real-world skills or daily living activities, but no evidence was found to support far transfer to these everyday skills. In summary, we conclude that virtual cognitive training tools are more effective in improving executive functions than physical exercise, and that they can enhance executive functions and episodic memory in not only in healthy older adults, but also in MCI patients, but there is no present evidence supporting that such training effects last beyond its duration or that the training generalizes to everyday real-world skills.

References

Alzheimer's Association (2015). Alzheimer's Association Report 2015 Alzheimer's disease facts and figures. *Alzheimers & Dementia*, *11*(3), 332−384. Available from http://dx. doi.org/10.1016/j.jalz.2015.02.003.

Anderson-Hanley, C., Arciero, P. J., Brickman, A. M., Nimon, J. P., Okuma, N., Westen, S. C., & Zimmerman, E. A. (2012). Exergaming and older adult cognition: A cluster randomized clinical trial. *American Journal of Preventive Medicine*, *42*(2), 109−119. Available from http://dx.doi.org/10.1016/j.amepre.2011.10.016.

Anguera, J. A., Boccanfuso, J., Rintoul, J. L., Al-Hashimi, O., Faraji, F., Janowich, J., & Gazzaley, A. (2013). Video game training enhances cognitive control in older adults. *Nature*, *501*(7465), 97−101. Available from http://dx.doi.org/10.1038/nature12486.

Ball, K., Berch, D. B., Helmers, K. F., Jobe, J. B., Leveck, M. D., Marsiske, M., ... Willis, S. (2002). Effects of cognitive training interventions with older adults. *JAMA*, *288*(18), 2271. Available from http://dx.doi.org/10.1001/jama.288.18.2271.

Ballesteros, S., Prieto, A., Mayas, J., Toril, P., Pita, C., Ponce de LeÃn, L., & Waterworth, J. (2014). Brain training with non-action video games enhances aspects of cognition in older adults: A randomized controlled trial. *Frontiers in Aging Neuroscience*, *6*(October), 1−14. Available from http://dx.doi.org/10.3389/fnagi.2014.00277.

Barcelos, N., Shah, N., Cohen, K., Hogan, M. J., Mulkerrin, E., Arciero, P. J., & Anderson-Hanley, C. (2015). Aerobic and Cognitive Exercise (ACE) pilot study for older adults: Executive function improves with cognitive challenge while exergaming. *Journal of the International Neuropsychological Society*, *21*(10), 768−779. Available from http://dx. doi.org/10.1017/S1355617715001083.

Barnes, D. E., Santos-Modesitt, W., Poelke, G., & Kramer, A. F. (2013). The Mental Activity and eXercise (MAX) trial. *JAMA Internal Medicine*, *173*(9), 797−804. Available from http://dx.doi.org/10.1001/jamainternmed.2013.189.

Barnes, D. E., Yaffe, K., Belfor, N., Jagust, W. J., DeCarli, C., Reed, B. R., & Kramer, J. H. (2009). Computer-based cognitive training for mild cognitive impairment: Results from a pilot randomized, controlled trial. *Alzheimer Disease and Associated Disorders, 23*(3), 205–210. Available from http://dx.doi.org/10.1097/WAD.0b013e31819c6137.

Basak, C., Boot, W. R., Voss, M. W., & Kramer, A. F. (2008). Can training in a real-time strategy video game attenuate cognitive decline in older adults? *Psychology and Aging, 23*(4), 765–777. Available from http://dx.doi.org/10.1037/a0013494.

Basak, C., Qin, S., & O'Connell, M.A. Improving cognition through cognitive training in healthy aging and mild cognitive impairment: A meta-analysis of randomized controlled trials, submitted for publication.

Basak, C., & Verhaeghen, P. (2011a). Aging and switching the focus of attention in working memory: Age differences in item availability but not in item accessibility. *Journals of Gerontology Series B-Psychological Sciences and Social Sciences, 66*(5), 519–526. Available from http://dx.doi.org/10.1093/geronb/gbr028.

Basak, C., & Verhaeghen, P. (2011b). Aging and switching the focus of attention in working memory: Age differences in item availability but not in item accessibility. *The Journals of Gerontology: Series B: Psychological Sciences and Social Sciences, 66*(5), 519–526. Available from http://dx.doi.org/10.1093/geronb/gbr028.

Belchior, P., Marsiske, M., Sisco, S. M., Yam, A., Bavelier, D., Ball, K., & Mann, W. C. (2013). Video game training to improve selective visual attention in older adults. *Computers in Human Behavior, 29*(4), 1318–1324. Available from http://dx.doi.org/10.1016/j.chb.2013.01.034.

Beller, G. A. (2013). The United States has lower life expectancy than other developed nations, despite having highest health care costs. *Journal of Nuclear Cardiology, 20*(2), 177–178. Available from http://dx.doi.org/10.1007/s12350-013-9692-4.

Bisson, E., Contant, B., Sveistrup, H., & Lajoie, Y. (2007). Functional balance and dual-task reaction times in older adults are improved by virtual reality and biofeedback training. *CyberPsychology & Behavior, 10*(1), 16–23. Available from http://dx.doi.org/10.1089/cpb.2006.9997.

Boot, W. R., Champion, M., Blakely, D. P., Wright, T., Souders, D. J., & Charness, N. (2013). Video games as a means to reduce age-related cognitive decline: attitudes, compliance, and effectiveness. *Frontiers in Psychology, 4*(February), 31. Available from http://dx.doi.org/10.3389/fpsyg.2013.00031.

Broadbent, N. J., Squire, L. R., & Clark, R. E. (2004). Spatial memory, recognition memory, and the hippocampus. *Proceedings of the National Academy of Sciences of the United States of America, 101*(40), 14515–14520. Available from http://dx.doi.org/10.1073/pnas.0406344101.

Chan, M. Y., Haber, S., Drew, L. M., & Park, D. C. (2014). Training older adults to use tablet computers: Does it enhance cognitive function? *The Gerontologist, 0*(0), 1–11. Available from http://dx.doi.org/10.1093/geront/gnu057.

Clark, R. E., Zola, S. M., & Squire, L. R. (2000). Impaired recognition memory in rats after damage to the hippocampus. *Journal of Neuroscience, 20*(23), 8853–8860.

Colcombe, S., & Kramer, A. F. (2003). Fitness effects on the cognitive function of older adults: A Meta-Analytic Study. *Psychological Science*, 125–130.

Dannhauser, T. M., Cleverley, M., Whitfield, T. J., Fletcher, B. C., Stevens, T., & Walker, Z. (2014). A complex multimodal activity intervention to reduce the risk of dementia in mild cognitive impairment—Thinking Fit: Pilot and feasibility study for a randomized controlled trial. *BMC Psychiatry, 14*, 129. Available from http://dx.doi.org/10.1186/1471-244X-14-129.

Diamond, A. (2013). Executive functions. *Annual Review of Psychology, 64,* 135−168. http://dx.doi.org/10.1146/annurev-psych-113011-143750.

van Doorn, J. R., & van Doorn, J. D. (2014). The quest for knowledge transfer efficacy: Blended teaching, online and in-class, with consideration of learning typologies for non-traditional and traditional students. *Frontiers in Psychology, 5*(04), 1−14. Available from http://dx.doi.org/10.3389/fpsyg.2014.00324.

Dustman, R. E., Emmerson, R. Y., Steinhaus, L. A., Shearer, D. E., & Dustman, T. J. (1992). The effects of videogame playing on neuropsychological performance of elderly individuals. *Journal of Gerontology, 47*(3), 168−171.

Erickson, K. I., Voss, M. W., Prakash, R. S., Basak, C., Szabo, A., Chaddock, L., & Kramer, A. F. (2011). Exercise training increases size of hippocampus and improves memory. *Proceedings of the National Academy of Sciences of the United States of America, 108* (7), 3017−3022. Available from http://dx.doi.org/10.1073/pnas.1015950108.

Finlay, W., Desmet, C., & Evans, L. (2004). Is it the technology or the teacher? A comparison of online and traditional English composition classes. *Journal of Educational Computing Research, 31*(2), 163−180. Available from http://dx.doi.org/10.2190/URJJ-HXHA-JA08-5LVL.

Finn, M., & McDonald, S. (2011). Computerised cognitive training for older persons with mild cognitive impairment: A pilot study using a randomised controlled trial design. *Brain Impairment, 12*(3), 187−199. Available from http://dx.doi.org/10.1375/brim.12.3.187.

Franco, J. R., Jacobs, K., Inzerillo, C., & Kluzik, J. (2012). The effect of the Nintendo Wii Fit and exercise in improving balance and quality of life in community dwelling elders. *Technology and Health Care.* Available from http://dx.doi.org/10.3233/THC-2011-0661.

Franco, M., Jiménez, F., Parra, E., Toribio, J. M., Ruiz, Y., Solis, A., & Bueno, Y. (2013). *Converging Clinical and Engineering Research on Neurorehabilitation* (Vol. 1, pp. 917−921). Available from http://dx.doi.org/10.1007/978-3-642-34546-3.

Hebert, L. E., Weuve, J., Scherr, P. A., & Evans, D. A. (2013). Alzheimer disease in the United States (2010−2050) estimated using the 2010 census. *Neurology, 80*(19), 1778−1783. Available from http://dx.doi.org/10.1212/WNL.0b013e31828726f5.

Heyn, P., Abreu, B. C., & Ottenbacher, K. J. (2004). The effects of exercise training on elderly persons with cognitive impairment and dementia: A meta-analysis. *Archives of Physical Medicine and Rehabilitation, 85*(10), 1694−1704. Available from http://dx.doi.org/10.1016/j.apmr.2004.03.019.

Howieson, D. B., Carlson, N. E., Moore, M. M., Wasserman, D., Abendroth, C. D., ... Kaye, J. A. (2008). Trajectory of mild cognitive impairment onset. *Journal of the International Neuropsychological Society: JINS, 14*(2), 192−198. Available from http://dx.doi.org/10.1017/S1355617708080375.

Jack, C. R., Knopman, D. S., Jagust, W. J., Petersen, R. C., Weiner, M. W., Aisen, P. S., & Trojanowski, J. Q. (2013). Update on hypothetical model of Alzheimer's disease biomarkers. *Lancet Neurology, 12*(2), 207−216. Available from http://dx.doi.org/10.1016/S1474-4422(12)70291-0.

Kayama, H., Okamoto, K., Nishiguchi, S., Yamada, M., Kuroda, T., & Aoyama, T. (2014). Effect of a Kinect-based exercise game on improving executive cognitive performance in community-dwelling elderly: Case control study. *Journal of Medical Internet Research, 16*(2), e61. Available from http://dx.doi.org/10.2196/jmir.3108.

Kim, G. H., Jeon, S., Im, K., Kwon, H., Lee, B. H., Kim, G. Y., ... Na, D. L. (2015a). Structural brain changes after traditional and robot-assisted multi-domain cognitive training in community-dwelling healthy elderly. *PLoS One, 10*(4), 1−20. Available from http://dx.doi.org/10.1371/journal.pone.0123251.

Kim, K.-W., Choi, Y., Na, D. L., Yoh, M.-S., Park, J.-K., Seo, J.-H., & Ko, M.-H. (2015b). Effects of a serious game training on cognitive functions in older adults. *JAGS*, *63*(3), 603−605.

Klusmann, V., Evers, A., Schwarzer, R., Schlattmann, P., Reischies, F. M., Heuser, I., & Dimeo, F. C. (2010). Complex mental and physical activity in older women and cognitive performance: A 6-month randomized controlled trial. *The Journals of Gerontology. Series A, Biological Sciences and Medical Sciences*, *65*(6), 680−688. Available from http://dx.doi.org/10.1093/gerona/glq053.

Lampit, A., Hallock, H., & Valenzuela, M. (2014). Computerized cognitive training in cognitively healthy older adults: a systematic review and meta-analysis of effect modifiers. *PLoS Medicine*, *11*(11), e1001756. Available from http://dx.doi.org/10.1371/journal.pmed.1001756.

Li, H., Li, J., Li, N., Li, B., Wang, P., & Zhou, T. (2011). Cognitive intervention for persons with mild cognitive impairment: A meta-analysis. *Ageing Research Reviews*, *10*(2), 285−296. Available from http://dx.doi.org/10.1016/j.arr.2010.11.003.

Liu-Ambrose, T., Nagamatsu, L. S., Graf, P., Beattie, B. L., Ashe, M. C., & Handy, T. C. (2010). Resistance training and executive functions: A 12-month randomized controlled trial. *Archives of Internal Medicine*, *170*(2), 170−178. Available from http://dx.doi.org/10.1001/archinternmed.2009.494.

Maillot, P., Perrot, A., & Hartley, A. (2012). Effects of interactive physical-activity video-game training on physical and cognitive function in older adults. *Psychology and Aging*, *27*(3), 589−600. Available from http://dx.doi.org/10.1037/a0026268.

Man, D. W. K., Chung, J. C. C., & Lee, G. Y. Y. (2012). Evaluation of a virtual reality-based memory training programme for Hong Kong Chinese older adults with questionable dementia: A pilot study. *International Journal of Geriatric Psychiatry*, *27*(5), 513−520. Available from http://dx.doi.org/10.1002/gps.2746.

Mayas, J., Parmentier, F. B. R., Andrés, P., & Ballesteros, S. (2014). Plasticity of attentional functions in older adults after non-action video game training: A randomized controlled trial. *PLoS One*, *9*(3), e92269. Available from http://dx.doi.org/10.1371/journal.pone.0092269.

McDougall, S., & House, B. (2012). Brain training in older adults: Evidence of transfer to memory span performance and pseudo-Matthew effects. *Neuropsychology, Development, and Cognition. Section B, Aging, Neuropsychology and Cognition*, *19*(1−2), 195−221. Available from http://dx.doi.org/10.1080/13825585.2011.640656.

McGillivray, S., & Castel, A. D. (2010). Memory for age−face associations in younger and older adults: The role of generation and schematic support. *Psychology and Aging*, *25*(4), 822−832. Available from http://dx.doi.org/10.1037/a0021044.

Miyake, A., Friedman, N. P., Emerson, M. J., Witzki, A. H., Howerter, A., & Wager, T. D. (2000). The unity and diversity of executive functions and their contributions to complex "Frontal Lobe" tasks: A latent variable analysis. *Cognitive Psychology*, *41*(1), 49−100. Available from http://dx.doi.org/10.1006/cogp.1999.0734.

van Muijden, J., Band, G. P. H., & Hommel, B. (2012). Online games training aging brains: Limited transfer to cognitive control functions. *Frontiers in Human Neuroscience*, *6*(08), 221. Available from http://dx.doi.org/10.3389/fnhum.2012.00221.

Nascimento, T. O., Yassuda, M. S., & Cachioni, M. (2011). Elderly online: Effects of a digital inclusion program in cognitive performance. *Archives of Gerontology and Geriatrics*, *53*(2), 216−219. Available from http://dx.doi.org/10.1016/j.archger.2010.11.007.

Naghavi, H. R., & Nyberg, L. (2005). Common fronto-parietal activity in attention, memory, and consciousness: Shared demands on integration? *Consciousness and Cognition*. Available from http://dx.doi.org/10.1016/j.concog.2004.10.003.

Nouchi, R., Taki, Y., Takeuchi, H., Hashizume, H., Akitsuki, Y., Shigemune, Y., & Kawashima, R. (2012). Brain training game improves executive functions and processing speed in the elderly: A randomized controlled trial. *PLoS One*, *7*(1), e29676. Available from http://dx.doi.org/10.1371/journal.pone.0029676.

Nyberg, L., McIntosh, A. R., Houle, S., Nilsson, L.-G., & Tulving, E. (1996). Activation of medial temporal structures during episodic memory retrieval. *Nature*, *380*(6576), 715−717. Available from http://dx.doi.org/10.1038/380715a0.

Optale, G., Urgesi, C., Busato, V., Marin, S., Piron, L., Priftis, K., & Bordin, A. (2010). Controlling memory impairment in elderly adults using virtual reality memory training: A randomized controlled pilot study. *Neurorehabilitation and Neural Repair*, *24*(4), 348−357. Available from http://dx.doi.org/10.1177/1545968309353328.

Ordnung, M., Hoff, M., Kaminski, E., Villringer, A., & Ragert, P. (2017). No overt effects of a 6-week exergame training on sensorimotor and cognitive function in older adults. A preliminary investigation. *Frontiers in Human Neuroscience*, *11*(April), 1−17. Available from http://dx.doi.org/10.3389/fnhum.2017.00160.

Padala, K. P., Padala, P. R., Malloy, T. R., Geske, J. A., Dubbert, P. M., Dennis, R. A., & Sullivan, D. H. (2012). Wii-fit for improving gait and balance in an assisted living facility: A pilot study. *Journal of Aging Research*, 2012. Available from http://dx.doi.org/10.1155/2012/597573.

Park, D. C., Lautenschlager, G., Hedden, T., Davidson, N. S., Smith, A. D., & Smith, P. K. (2002). Models of visuospatial and verbal memory across the adult life span. *Psychology and Aging*, *17*(2), 299.

Rönnlund, M., Nyberg, L., Bäckman, L., & Nilsson, L. G. (2005). Stability, growth, and decline in adult life span development of declarative memory: Cross-sectional and longitudinal data from a population-based study. *Psychology and Aging*, *20*(1), 3.

Rosen, A. C., Sugiura, L., Kramer, J. H., Whitfield-Gabrieli, S., & Gabrieli, J. D. (2011). Cognitive training changes hippocampal function in mild cognitive impairment: A pilot study. *Journal of Alzheimer's Disease: JAD*, *26*(Suppl. 3), 349−357. Available from http://dx.doi.org/10.3233/JAD-2011-0009.

Salthouse, T. A. (2010). Selective review of cognitive aging. *Journal of the International Neuropsychological Society*, *16*(5), 754−760. Available from http://dx.doi.org/10.1017/S1355617710000706.

Schoene, D., Lord, S. S. R., Delbaere, K., Severino, C., Davies, T. A., & Smith, S. T. (2013). A randomized controlled pilot study of home-based step training in older people using videogame technology. *PLoS One*, *8*(3), e57734. Available from http://dx.doi.org/10.1371/journal.pone.0057734.

Simons, D. J., Boot, W. R., Charness, N., Gathercole, S. E., Chabris, C. F., Hambrick, D. Z., & Stine-Morrow, E. A. L. (2016). Do "Brain-Training" programs work? *Psychological Science in the Public Interest*, *17*(3), 103−186. Available from http://dx.doi.org/10.1177/1529100616661983.

Smith, G. E., Housen, Ã. P., Yaffe, K., Ruff, R., Kennison, R. F., Mahncke, H. W., & Zelinski, E. M. (2009). A cognitive training program based on principles of brain plasticity: Results from the Improvement in Memory with Plasticity-based Adaptive Cognitive Training (IMPACT) study. *Journal of the American Geriatrics Society*, 594−603. Available from http://dx.doi.org/10.1111/j.1532-5415.2008, 02167.x.

Sperling, R. A., Aisen, P. S., Beckett, L. A., Bennett, D. A., Craft, S., Fagan, A. M., & Phelps, C. H. (2011). Toward defining the preclinical stages of Alzheimer's disease: Recommendations from the National Institute on Aging-Alzheimer's Association workgroups on diagnostic guidelines for Alzheimer's disease. *Alzheimer's and Dementia.* Available from http://dx.doi.org/10.1016/j.jalz.2011.03.003.

Stavros, Z., Fotini, K., & Magda, T. (2010). Computer based cognitive training for patients with mild cognitive impairment (MCI). In *Proceedings of the 3rd International Conference on PErvasive Technologies Related to Assistive Environments — PETRA '10*, (Mci), 1. http://dx.doi.org/10.1145/1839294.1839319.

Stern, Y., Blumen, H. M., Rich, L. W., Richards, A., Herzberg, G., & Gopher, D. (2011). Space Fortress game training and executive control in older adults: a pilot intervention. *Neuropsychology, Development, and Cognition. Section B, Aging, Neuropsychology and Cognition, 18*(6), 653–677. Available from http://dx.doi.org/10.1080/13825585.2011.613450.

Stine-Morrow, E. A. L., & Basak, C. (2011). *Cognitive interventions. Handbook of the Psychology of Aging* (pp. 153–171). Elsevier Inc. Available from http://dx.doi.org/10.1016/B978-0-12-380882-0.00010-3.

Tefft, B.C. (2012). *Motor vehicle crashes, injuries, and deaths in relation to driver age: United States, 1995–2010, (November)* (pp. 1–13). Retrieved from <https://www.aaafoundation.org/sites/default/files/2012OlderDriverRisk.pdf>.

Tulving, E. (1972). Episodic and semantic memory. *Organization of Memory.* Available from http://dx.doi.org/10.1017/S0140525X00047257.

Verhaeghen, P., Cerella, J., Bopp, K. L., & Basak, C. (2005). Aging and varieties of cognitive control: A review of meta-analyses on resistance to interference, coordination, and task switching, and an experimental exploration of age-sensitivity in the newly identified process of focus switching. In R. W. Engle, G. Sedek, U. von Hecker, D. N. McIntosh, R. W. Engle, G. Sedek, U. von Hecker, & D. N. McIntosh (Eds.), *Cognitive limitations in aging and psychopathology* (pp. 160–189). New York: Cambridge University Press.

Verhaeghen, P., Marcoen, A., & Goossens, L. (1992). Improving memory performance in the aged through mnemonic training: A meta-analytic study. *Psychology and Aging, 7*(2), 242–251. Available from http://dx.doi.org/10.1037//0882-7974.7.2.242.

Voss, M. W., Heo, S., Prakash, R. S., Erickson, K. I., Alves, H., Chaddock, L., & Kramer, A. F. (2013). The influence of aerobic fitness on cerebral white matter integrity and cognitive function in older adults: Results of a one-year exercise intervention. *Human Brain Mapping, 34*(11), 2972–2985. Available from http://dx.doi.org/10.1002/hbm.22119.

Ward, A., Tardiff, S., Dye, C., & Arrighi, H. M. (2013). Rate of conversion from prodromal Alzheimer's disease to Alzheimer's dementia: A systematic review of the literature. *Dementia and Geriatric Cognitive Disorders EXTRA, 3*(1), 320–332. Available from http://dx.doi.org/10.1159/000354370.

Watts, H. (2012). A psychological approach to predicting membership retention in the fitness industry. *Dataquest, 22*(15), 19–98.

Wittelsberger, R., Krug, S., Tittlbach, S., & Bös, K. (2013). Auswirkungen von Nintendo-Wii® Bowling auf Altenheimbewohner. *Zeitschrift Fur Gerontologie Und Geriatrie, 46*(5), 425–430. Available from http://dx.doi.org/10.1007/s00391-012-0391-6.

Whitlock, L. A., McLaughlin, A. C., & Allaire, J. C. (2012). Individual differences in response to cognitive training: Using a multi-modal, attentionally demanding game-based intervention for older adults. *Computers in Human Behavior, 28*(4), 1091–1096. Available from http://dx.doi.org/10.1016/j.chb.2012.01.012.

Further reading

Bozoki, A., Radovanovic, M., Winn, B., Heeter, C., & Anthony, J. C. (2013). Effects of a computer-based cognitive exercise program on age-related cognitive decline. *Archives of Gerontology and Geriatrics*, *57*(1), 1–7. Available from http://dx.doi.org/10.1016/j.archger.2013.02.009.

Cadmus-Bertram, L. A., Marcus, B. H., Patterson, R. E., Parker, B. A., & Morey, B. L. (2015). Randomized trial of a fitbit-based physical activity intervention for women. *American Journal of Preventive Medicine*, *49*(3), 414–418. Available from http://dx.doi.org/10.1016/j.amepre.2015.01.020.

Edwards, J. D., Valdés, E. G., Peronto, C., Castora-binkley, M., Alwerdt, J., Andel, R., & Lister, J. J. (2013). The efficacy of insight cognitive training to improve useful field of view performance: A brief report. *The Journals of Gerontology: Series B: Psychological Sciences and Social Sciences*, *70*, 417–422. Available from http://dx.doi.org/10.1093/geronb/gbt113.

Miller, K. J., Dye, R. V., Kim, J., Jennings, J. L., O'Toole, E., Wong, J., & Siddarth, P. (2013). Effect of a computerized brain exercise program on cognitive performance in older adults. *The American Journal of Geriatric Psychiatry: Official Journal of the American Association for Geriatric Psychiatry*, *21*(7), 655–663. Available from http://dx.doi.org/10.1016/j.jagp.2013.01.077.

Social agents for aging-in-place: A focus on health education and communication

Jenay M. Beer and Otis L. Owens
University of South Carolina, Columbia, SC, United States

Introduction

Goals of chapter

Modern advances in technology development are making the application of interactive assistive technology in the home a very real possibility. Such technologies not only hold promise for assisting older adults to age-in-place, but also ease the burden on our healthcare system. Although there is no standard definition, persons over the age of 60 or 65 are typically classified as older adults (Fisk, Rogers, Charness, Czaja, & Sharit, 2009). Both in the United States and worldwide, the older adult population is expected to increase exponentially (AOA, 2010), and providing care for our aging society presents a societal challenge. Older adults wish to *age-in-place*, that is, grow old in their home environment (AARP, 2008). However, there are challenges that make managing health and living independently difficult for older adults. Technology holds much potential for mitigating these challenges. In this chapter, we provide a review on the application of socially interactive technologies, namely social agents, for health education and health communication for aging-in-place.

We will emphasize the following scope in this chapter. First, we will only report on interactions between the end user and the social agent (e.g., not interaction between multiple social agents) to emphasize products intended for our target population, older adults. Second, we will highlight applications in the home environment, to specifically focus the facilitators and challenges of applying such health-oriented technology to promote aging-in-place. Third, we will discuss applications related to *social agents*, specifically embodied conversational agents and robots, as we identify these forms of technology holding much future potential in the home. Fourth, we will cover specifically health education and communication. We focus on these two application areas because increasingly assistive technology can provide more than just physical assistance (Smarr, Fausset, & Rogers, 2011). We identify health education and health communication as two emerging research applications for social agents, with potential to help older adults in managing their health. In the following sections, we will provide a literature review on the

Aging, Technology and Health. DOI: http://dx.doi.org/10.1016/B978-0-12-811272-4.00010-5

application of social agents for health education and communication, then discuss challenges and future research directions.

Defining social agents

Because this chapter focuses on the application of social agents, it is important to define this term. We refer to social agents as an umbrella term, which encompasses two subcategories: embodied conversational agents and robotic agents. *Embodied conversational agents* are a virtual incarnation, embodiment, or manifestation of a person with a high level of behavior, flexible motion, realistic appearance, and the ability to react to its environment (Magnenat-Thalmann & Thalmann, 2005). One of the first embodied conversational agents resembling a human was William Fetter's Landing Signal Officer, which was developed for Boeing in 1959 to be used to study the instrument panel of a Boeing 747 (Magnenat-Thalmann & Ichalkaranje, 2008; Magnenat-Thalmann & Thalmann, 2005). Since then "virtual humans" have been used for a number of purposes including simulations for trainings (e.g., training for soldiers and surgery practice) characters for games, actors for movies, and presenters for TV, web programs, and virtual worlds such as SecondLife (Boulos, Hetherington, & Wheeler, 2007; Magnenat-Thalmann & Thalmann, 2005). It is important to note that some literature refers to embodied conversational agents as avatars (Lisetti et al., 2012). Although commonly described in a similar manner to embodied conversational agents, avatars are characters that are controlled externally by a human to engage in an activity and are a representation of the user, much similar to a video game character (Ducheneaut, Wen, Yee, & Wadley, 2009).

There is no agreed upon definition of *robotic agent*, though most people have ideas or definitions of what a robot should be like (Ezer, Fisk, & Rogers, 2009). The term "robot" derives from the Czech word "robota" which translates to forced labor. Within the research community, a robot has often been broadly described as a machine that can sense, think/plan, and act (e.g., Bekey, 2005). This definition may be criticized as being broad, as many types of technology could potentially be described as such. A synthesis of varying definitions of the term "robot" (i.e., Bekey, 2005; Murphy, 2000; Russell & Norvig, 2003) suggests that a robot is a physical computational agent. Robots are equipped with sensors for perceiving the environment, and typically contain effectors, or actuators, that manipulate and exert physical forces on the environment. For this chapter, a certain type of robot will be of focus: *socially assistive robots (SARs)*. SAR is defined as an intersection of assistive robotics and socially interactive robotics (Feil-Seifer & Mataric, 2005). SAR maintain the goal of social interactions with a human user for the purpose of providing assistance and achieving measurable progress in health and well-being.

In summary, this chapter will explore the countless benefits of social agents, which includes both embodied conversational agents and robotic agents. More specifically, we emphasize the promising future these technologies hold for providing assistance to the aging population and supporting health interventions through social interactivity. As the following sections will highlight, socially interactive technologies have a critical role in advancing health education and communication, as well as the potential to supplement other interdisciplinary and transdisciplinary approaches to promoting healthy aging and aging in place.

Benefits of using social agents within health interventions

Although there are many general advantages to using social agents in health interventions such as eliminating variability in intervention implementation, employing doctor—patient race concordance and addressing low literacy by including audio-visual components (Lisetti, 2012), there are also other benefits of using agents that build on the effectiveness of face-to-face communication. These benefits include the fact that social agents can make use of nonverbal communication (e.g., gestures, expressions) that can enhance the conveyance of messages and build rapport with patients. For instance, in a study about the acceptance of embodied conversational agents for motivational interviewing, Lisetti et al., (2012) found that 75% of participants felt either as comfortable or more comfortable interacting with an embodied conversational agent during a motivational interviewing session about reducing alcohol consumption than they would with a real counselor (Lisetti et al., 2012). Also, many participants who favored the agent-led interview felt positive about the experience because they felt the embodied conversational agent was unbiased and could not judge or them for their alcohol consumption behavior (Lisetti et al., 2012). These findings suggest that social agents may be especially efficacious in instances where conversations might be sensitive and behavior change is contingent on trust between the interventionist and the patient.

Another key benefit that is afforded by social agents is that the fact that the agent is available for as long as the user has access to a given system. According to a recent report on physician compensation, an average doctor/patient conversation during a doctor's visit is 15 minutes (Peckham, 2016). While there is limited evidence showing a positive correlation between the time spent with the patient and other constructs such as patient satisfaction and adherence (which can also be linked to patient trust of their doctor), time constraints may present limitations in circumstances where the disease and resulting regiment is more complex and/or the patient has lower health literacy. Therefore, Bickmore, Pfeiffer, and Paasche-Orlow (2009) tested the feasibility of a bed-side virtual nurse agent to teach hospital patients about their post-hospital discharge self-care regiment. Bickmore et al. (2009) found that participants' acceptability of the intervention was high because of the depth of information provided by the social agent and the fact that the agent was available for as much time as the participant needed (Bickmore et al., 2009).

Older adults may generally be reliant on a physician for guidance on their health, but physicians often have limited time. Social agents can supplement the education and communication provided by the doctor at a pace that is comfortable for the caregiver and the older adult. Furthermore, older adults may feel more comfortable discussing embarrassing topics with a social agent rather than a human, or prefer the agent so they do not feel they are wasting a doctor's time with questions (Mahani & Eklundh, 2009). Thus, social agents, such as embodied conversational agents and robots, can be active in promoting healthy behavior/ decision making, as well as promote health communication. In the following sections we will discuss these two application areas in more detail.

Social agents for health education and decision making

For almost eight decades, health education practitioners have developed programs to educate diverse populations on strategies for improving their personal health (Auld & Gambescia, 2011). Green and Kreuter (2005) define health education as "any combination of learning experiences designed to facilitate voluntary actions conducive to health". In more simple terms, health education is the provision of information to promote both general awareness and knowledge about disease prevention (World Health Organization, 2016). When coupled with access to the appropriate resource (not ignoring the many other contextual factors that contribute to human behavior) (Sallis & Carlson, 2015), health education can facilitate an individual's ability to change health-related behaviors (Zimmerman & Woolf, 2014) or make health decisions. The most successful health education programs have used a socioecological approach, which targets the individual and/or their physical/social environment (Auld & Gambescia, 2011).

While health education is critical to behavior change, it has been demonstrated through some studies that health education alone does not always directly affect behavior change. Rather, behavior change is more likely to occur when there is a collaborative relationship between patients and their healthcare providers with health education forming a critical arm in the larger decision making process. In the health decision literature, there are three main types of health decision making described: Paternalistic model, informed model, and shared model (Charles, Gafni, & Whelan, 1997).

In the paternalistic model the patient allows the healthcare provider make their health decision with little to no input from the patient. In an informed decision making model, the patient seeks or is provided with all of the necessary information to support their decision, but the onus of the final decision is placed on the patient (Charles et al., 1997).

In shared decision-making (which is most often recommended) the patient is "informed" about the available treatment options, but engage in a conversation about the options before making a joint decision with their healthcare provider about the best course of action (Charles, Gafni, & Whelan, 1999). The specific type of decision making preferred by an individual can vary based on factors such as their age, sex, socioeconomic status, education, and proximity of the decision, and type of disease (Hawley et al., 2007; Levinson, Kao, Kuby, & Thisted, 2005; Minton & Stone, 2008). For example, Levinson and colleagues (2005) found that individuals over 45 preferred less active roles in shared decision making as opposed to younger patients. Other factors that mediate the type of decision making elected by patients can range from patient-related constructs such as trust of healthcare provider or anxiety (Peek et al., 2013) to clinician-specific barriers (e.g., healthcare provider's perception of patients ability to engage in shared decision making) (Kane, Halpern, Squiers, Treiman, & McCormack, 2014). To facilitate quality health decisions, the Institute of Medicine and the Department of Health and Human Services support the use of informing individuals using plain language and culturally appropriate communication strategies (Health et al., 2010; Nielsen-Bohlman, Panzer, & Kindig, 2004).

For older adults, health information should be presented in a way that accommodates the physiological (e.g., vision, hearing, motor skills), psychological (e.g., information processing speed) and social (e.g., health literacy levels) challenges experienced by a population. For example, Speros (2009) recommends that when written health information is disseminated, it should not only support verbal instruction but be written at a fifth grade level or below, appear in print that is 14 to 16 point font, and should have high contrast between the print and paper color. Similarly, recommendations apply to multimedia/computer-based education interventions (Mayer, 2014).

Applying social agents to health education and health decision making

Health education programs and decision-making interventions have been delivered through several mediums over the years such as in-person administration or paper-based literature. However, with the expansion of computer and mobile-based technologies across the United States, there has been an increasing number of health education programs (Bull, 2010; Webb, Joseph, Yardley, & Michie, 2010) and decision aids (O'Connor et al., 2009; Stacey et al., 2011) that have been disseminated though computer and mobile applications.

It is, however, recognized that there are some disparities in general access to these technologies among poor, less educated and older populations. Compared to 86% of all adults, only 56% of older adults use the Internet or email. In addition, older adults who go online are more likely to have higher annual incomes (i.e., incomes above that received by seniors with Medicare) and education levels beyond a high school level (Cresci, Yarandi, & Morrell, 2010; Smith, 2014). Despite these disparities, social/health scientists and engineers have successfully developed and evaluated multiple technology-based interventions to support the health education and decision making of older adults. These interventions have ranged from mobile/web-based technologies (Joe & Demiris, 2013; Kueider, Parisi, Gross, & Rebok, 2012; Muellmann, Forberger, Möllers, Zeeb, & Pischke, 2016; Thomson et al., 2007) to advanced interactive communication technologies that are inclusive of embodied conversational agents and social robots (Bickmore, Caruso, Clough-Gorr, & Heeren, 2005; Bickmore et al., 2009; Fasola & Mataric, 2012; Robinson, MacDonald, & Broadbent, 2014).

Embodied conversational agents are also beginning to appear in health-related interventions for diverse populations. While many studies have focused primarily on the acceptability and satisfaction of agents for health promotion among younger and older adults (Lisetti et al., 2012; Schulman, Bickmore, & Sidner, 2011), there are also some (but few) studies that discuss the effectiveness of agents for providing health education or decision support specifically for older adults.

Most academic efforts on the acceptance and use of embodied conversational agents have been led by Timothy W. Bickmore and his team at the Boston University School of Medicine. One of Bickmore's first embodied conversational-led trainings specifically tailored for older adults was based on the MIT FitTrack program (Bickmore, Caruso, et al., 2005; Bickmore, Gruber, & Picard, 2005). FitTrack was originally designed to study the relationship between agents and users and whether these relationships could be used to enhance the effectiveness of health promotion programs (Bickmore, Gruber, and Picard, 2005). In the initial study, Bickmore, Gruber, and Picard (2005) discovered that individuals in agent-led groups had significant increases in their number of days per week of moderate-or-greater physical activity as compared to individuals receiving general web pages of educational content on the topic of walking for exercise.

In a follow-up study, FitTrack was redesigned and tested among an older population (Bickmore, Caruso, Clough-Gorr, & Heeren, 2005). The findings demonstrated that the intervention increased older adults steps per day significantly more than the control group. A similar study, demonstrated that individuals with higher literacy levels performed significantly more steps during the intervention than the control group (Bickmore et al., 2013). These results demonstrate that increasing short-term physical activity among older adults by using agent-based education programs is plausible, but effectiveness may depend on the literacy level of the user. Bickmore et al. (2005; 2013) findings also support the need for further exploration of the use of embodied conversational agents to support health behavior change and health decision making.

In summary, technology has become more ubiquitous. Therefore, technology has become more popular vehicles for disseminating health education and facilitating health decision making. More recently, exploration has taken place to test the efficacy of more advanced technologies (such as social agents) for supporting older adults. While, there may be some current disparities in technology access, research is demonstrating that older adults are accepting of technology when it is designed for their demographic and these technologies are leading to positive behavior change. Similar trends exist in terms of implementing social agents in health communication applications.

Social agents for health communication applications

Social agents hold promise far beyond health education. This technology has ample potential to be successful in health communication applications. Health communication is the study and practice of disseminating health information between healthcare professionals and patients. In this section, we will discuss how social agents have potential to refine and enhance communication strategies connecting older adults with remotely located doctors.

There are many products, both commercially available and in development, that are designed for health communication. Often, these technologies fall under the umbrella term "telepresence" which may be defined as having the sense of being present in another environment. The sense of presence is a complex construct. Briefly defined, presence can be described as feeling present either/both spatially (i.e., feeling of being in a remote location) and socially (natural communication with others) (Kristoffersson, Coradeschi, & Loutfi, 2013). Telepresence technology may range from televideo conferencing (e.g., skype), to mobile robotic telepresence (e.g., a screen with two-way audio and video, with the added value of a mobile base; Kristoffersson et al., 2013) to humanoid robots that elicit tele-interaction between end users via two-way audio and/or a screen mounted on the robot itself (e.g., Care-O-bot (Graf, Hans, & Schraft, 2004); Hector (Kite-Powell, 2012), Pearl (Pollack et al., 2002)). The primary function of social agents that promote communication is to foster connection *between* users. Within the context of health communication, this connection is typically between the doctor−patient or caregiver−patient.

Applying social agents to health communication

Social agents hold the promise of enhancing communication between patients, doctors, and other healthcare providers. However, for technological advances to be successful, we must first understand their specific needs and challenges, particularly related to health communication for the older population. Many individuals already use or have access to health communication technology; currently there are over 165,000 million Health apps available on the Apple and Android app stores, many of which advertise to offer health communication services (e.g., connecting with caregivers) (Terry, 2015). However, many of these services are underutilized; adoption may be hindered either because the technology does not meet patient needs, is too costly, or it is difficult to use, possibly due to age-related limitations.

To date, the majority of studies have investigated the use of robotic communication systems in office settings (for review see Kristoffersson et al., 2013). Recently however, the application of social agents for assisting older adults to maintain their health has become a primary goal of the research community (Broadbent, Jayawardena, Kerse, Stafford, & MacDonald, 2011; Bugmann & Copleston, 2011; Robinson et al., 2014; Smarr et al., 2014). Findings support the potential of healthcare robotics in keeping older adults socially engaged with family, friends, and healthcare providers (Beer & Takayama, 2011; Bevilacqua et al., 2014; Cesta, Cortellessa, Orlandini, & Tiberio, 2012), with the potential for providing telehealth and monitoring (Liles, Stuck, Kacmar, & Beer, 2015a, 2015b). In addition to promoting communication, the video and mobility features of the robot allow a caregiver to actually observe the older adults' emotional affect and well-being (Beer & Takayama, 2011; Liles et al., 2015a, 2015b), as well as to observe the status of their home environment.

In particular, mobile telehealth robots have been investigated within the application of hospital environments. In these studies, the robot is typically used to assist health practitioners perform rounds in a hospital (i.e., telerounds). Findings from a number of case studies suggest that hospital patients thought telerounds could and should be a part of regular hospital care (Daruwalla, Collins, & Moore, 2010; Ellison et al., 2007). Furthermore, patients reported that they felt comfortable communicating with their doctor via the technology. In fact, patients expressed a preference for telerounds with their own remotely located doctor, rather than to be seen by another doctor (Daruwalla et al., 2010; Ellison et al., 2007). The use of telerounds in hospitals has also shown a reduction in doctor response time (Petelin, Nelson, & Goodman, 2007; Vespa, 2005; Vespa et al., 2007), a reduction in the length of a patient's hospital stay compared to patients who received only bed-side rounds (Gandsas, Parekh, Bleech, & Tong, 2007; Vespa et al., 2007), and reduced costs of care (Vespa et al., 2007). While these hospital studies included patients of a wide age-range, the potential benefit of telepresence in hospital-based care is evident, and similar benefits may expand to home-use (Beer & Takayama, 2011).

Additional studies have investigated the use of social agents in senior living environments. In fact, the use of telecommunication technology in nursing homes has been found to promote social contact with family members (Mickus & Luz, 2002). Senior care staff of continuous care retirement facilities (i.e., facilities that offer a range of independent to nursing care living environments) have expressed that mobile robotic telepresence may offer a similar benefit for older adults in both independent and assisted living (Liles et al., 2015a, 2015b). These professional healthcare providers (primarily CNAs, RNs, and administrators) discussed, at length, the importance of keeping family connected, and they envisioned a primary benefit of a robotic telecommunication system was to connect remote family caregivers. Remote family caregivers, often located in other states, have to make difficult decisions about their elderly relative's healthcare. Social agents have potential to keep remote family caregivers in touch and informed. Importantly, the professional healthcare providers advocated that such technology might be used as a form of "checking in on" and monitoring older adults (Liles et al., 2015a, 2015b).

Using social agents, whether they are virtual or robotic, for the purposes of health communication allows a patient to remain in the comfort of their home while caregivers perform routine check-ups. Thus, social agents provide a link for health professionals as well as family to connect and collect at-home data on the older adults, while also promoting communication.

As smart homes emerge, healthcare will increasingly move from institutionalized care to the home. Many researchers envision a range of use cases for social agents in health communication. In particular, much development is ongoing connecting social agents with other medical devices (e.g., to read vitals), connect to medical health records, and connect with other devices in the home (e.g., a smart TV) to facilitate not only health communication, but also provide health information and data on-demand (for review, see Kristoffersson et al., 2013).

Challenges in implementation

As discussed earlier, social agents have potential to transform the way in which patients and doctors interface in both health education and health communication. However, this technology will never meet its full potential unless a number of challenges are better understood and addressed. Specifically, we identify three primary challenges that may impede the diffusion of such innovation: (1) security and privacy; (2) technology acceptance and adoption; and (3) adapting the technology for use in the home. In the following subsections we will discuss each of these challenges.

Security and privacy

While privacy has been recognized as an important psychological variable in previous research on smart homes (Caine et al., 2011), it has been largely uninvestigated with regard to deployment of social agents. As discussed earlier, social agents can provide a means for health education and communication—allowing caregivers and healthcare providers to gain critical and timely information related to an older adult's health and well-being. However, despite these potential benefits, the use of social agents in the home poses a number of privacy challenges and concerns. Some privacy and security challenges include potential hacks or scams that could risk older adults' health information (e.g., information about a patients' chronic illness via health education software) and/or confidential patient-doctor discourse (e.g., hacking of telecommunication devices used for telehealth).

Designing to promote privacy (aka "privacy-enhanced design") in social agent technology is no easy task. For example, it is important to consider that there are many individual differences among older adults—the capabilities, limitations, and privacy preferences for a 65-year-old versus an 85-year-old are likely very different. Furthermore, many older adults initially underestimate privacy risks (Grimes, Hough, Mazur, & Signorella, 2010; Lorenzen-Huber, Boutain, Camp, Shankar, & Connelly, 2011). There is a challenge in balancing users' perceptions of privacy, with the actual privacy of a system—this challenge becomes the designer's responsibility (Beckwith, 2003). Effective approaches to overcoming privacy barriers include obfuscating or "clouding" the data (i.e., filtering video), providing feedback to enhance awareness (i.e., transparency), and providing control over when/where data is collected (Caine et al., 2011). Nonetheless, concerns about healthcare technology privacy still exist (Beach et al., 2009; Caine et al., 2011); thus advanced forms of technology, such as social agents, need to be carefully designed to provide caregivers with monitoring and communication features to remain informed about the older adults' well-being, while maintaining the older adults' sense of privacy and control.

Acceptance and adoption of technology

Social agent adoption is more complex than providing grandma with the technology, and telling her "use this agent to support your independence." There is a progression of acceptance that begins with an attitude (this social agent seems like a good idea), which leads to an intention (I will buy this technology), which then leads to behavioral integration (I love my social agent and use it daily). This progression is based on the theory of reasoned action described by Fishbein and Ajzen (1975). The fundamental idea is that user attitudes influence intentions, which in turn influence behavior.

One of the most prominent models of technology adoption is the Technology Acceptance Model (TAM; Davis, 1989; Davis, Bagozzi, & Warshaw, 1989). Research on TAM has identified Perceived Usefulness (PU) and Perceived Ease of Use (PEU) as the most prominent predictive variables of technology acceptance (Davis, 1989). PU is defined as the extent to which a technology is expected to improve a potential user's performance (Davis, 1989). In the case of health education and communication, an older adult may ask how the social will improve his/her daily health? PEU refers to the amount of effort required to effectively use a technology (Davis, 1989). Do potential users believe that the social agent will be easy and intuitive to interact with? Is the social agent easy for the doctor or caregiver to use?

There are many factors that influence whether an older user holds certain attitudes toward technology. For instance, aspects of technology that encouraged use among older adults include: enhanced communication, reduction in the time to complete a task, and accessibility of technology features (Mitzner et al., 2010). Factors that may reduce the likelihood of an older adult accepting technology in the home include: Inconvenience, cost, having too many or too few programming features, and lack of reliability (Mitzner et al., 2010), lack of PU (Fisk et al., 2009; Heart & Kalderon, 2013; Mitzner et al., 2010; Morris, Goodman, & Brading, 2007) computer anxiety (Cesario, 2009; Chu, Huber, Mastel-Smith, & Cesario, 2009; Czaja et al., 2006), lack of self-efficacy (Chu et al., 2009), and disability or poor health (Cresci et al., 2010; Czaja et al., 2006). These barriers may be overcome via training older adults on how to use a specific technology (Cesario, 2009) and using community-based methods to develop technology in collaboration with communities of older adults (Owens, 2015; Owens, Friedman, Brandt, Bernhardt, & Hébert, 2015a, 2015b). Training and user-centric technology development is especially critical given that social agents are a novel technology for many older users, and such rapid innovation cannot be attractive to aging adults if they must consistently have to replace or upgrade technology. While these technologies may become less expensive in the future through increased market competition, older adults in the United States are either on fixed or low incomes which may hinder their ability to afford agent or robot technologies in the near future. Most older adults may not be able to afford some of the technologies and accompanying services, therefore it is critical that the cost of these technologies are subsidized.

Home environment

Older adults hold varying preferences for housing environments. Today, there are many different kinds of housing options for older adults. Older adults may choose to age in traditional housing (e.g., remaining in original home, or moving in with family) or move to more formal care, such retirement communities, assisted living facilities, or a continuing-care retirement communities. Most older adults prefer to remain in their own homes and age-in-place (AARP, 2008), while some may voluntarily relocate to formal care facilities, anticipating the potential need for future assistance. Regardless of their living arrangements, older adults wish to preserve their independence, autonomy, and well-being. Social agents have potential to aid older adults in health management in the home (Mitzner, Chen, Kemp, & Rogers, 2014). However, the home operational environment poses unique challenges to the implementation of social agents. While the physical space itself may not be an issue for embodied on-screen agents, it certainly poses problems for mobile telecommunication robots.

Application of telepresence robots in a hospital revealed challenges with security, network stability, inability to open doors and move between hospital floors (Daruwalla et al., 2010). These limitations will also be present, if not more common, in the home. The home environment poses a large set of unknown or unpredictable factors that may influence the robot's performance. The robot's ability to refine and modify its actions in response to unpredictable environmental stimuli (e.g., path planning, obstacle avoidance) will be critical for efficient operation in the home. For instance, it has been suggested (e.g., Thrun, 2004) that service robots require a high level of autonomy due to the unpredictable and changing environment of a home or healthcare setting.

A number of technical challenges would need to be overcome before deploying a social agent in a person's private home. For instance, the social agent will need to navigate the home environment and accommodate for obstacles, stairs, low lighting conditions, uneven floors/thresholds, and pets (Wu, Stuck, Mitner, Rogers, & Beer, 2016). This means the social agent will be required to simultaneously monitor the environment for navigation obstacles while also interacting with the older adult. There are environmental differences between traditional homes and senior center residences, which would impact the design of social agents (Mitzner et al., 2014). For example, senior care residences are likely to meet ADA requirements, with wider doorways and hallways compared to a traditional home, making robot navigation much easier. Additionally, senior care residences are more likely to have a static floor plan (i.e., less dynamic obstacles). Furthermore, for both on screen agents and robots implemented in living environments, the technology is intended to be used over extended periods of time, with little to no technical support (compared to a hospital or workplace for instance). Considerations for ease of use, accessibility, and ease of troubleshooting will be critical in making long-term adoption by older adults possible.

To create the ideal connected home where agents and robots will assist an older adult with their health, each connected device will likely need to be compatible with a larger system (i.e., a smart home). While there are companies that are working toward this goal (e.g., Apple, Google, Amazon), we are still years away from having this shared infrastructure.

Social agents for health education and communication: Future opportunities

While there are several barriers to ubiquitous implementation of social agents into the lives of every older adult, there are many opportunities to utilize this innovative technology to promote healthy aging/aging-in-place. To age in place, social agents could have a tremendous impact on assisting older adults with the prevention and/ or management of chronic disease. These innovations may also be critical to the completion or coordination of activities of daily living and instrumental activities of daily living, which can have a reciprocal relationship to an individual's health. More specifically, an individual's health may hinder them from completing an activity such as bathing, but not being able to bathe can also affect an individual's health. While there are multiple ways that these agents and robots can assist an older adult, we will continue our focus on the opportunities and the challenges of using agents and robots for health education, decision making, and for enhancing social connections.

Connected health

As previously discussed, having access to culturally appropriate, timely, and plain-language information about health is critical for enabling older adults (with varying levels of health literacy) to make informed health decisions (Nielsen-Bohlman et al., 2004). Furthermore, by making positive health decisions, older adults can enhance their capacity for aging in place (National Institute on Aging & World Health Organization, 2011). Currently, health information is being sought or transmitted to older adults through both interpersonal (e.g., healthcare provider/relative) sources and paper-based/digital media (e.g., television, magazines) (Chaudhuri, Le, White, Thompson, & Demiris, 2013). They are also being monitored through both medical devices and out-of-the-box sensor technologies. In a connected health model, healthcare providers, patients, and the aforementioned technologies are connected through a common platform where health information can be presented to all stakeholders in real time (Caulfield & Donnelly, 2013). Having this information available can permit proactive patient care. For example, there are multiple wireless technologies that have been developed to collect biological and anthropometric measures such as blood pressure, heart rate, weight, and BMI (Patel, Park, Bonato, Chan, & Rodgers, 2012). These measures are then transmitted to either a caregiver, healthcare provider, or health educator that can act quickly in a circumstance when the older adult's measures are abnormal (Patel et al., 2012). Similarly, there are also several wearable or home-based technologies (some of which are commercially available) that can detect falls and transmit an occurrence to emergency personnel and the caregiver (Chaudhuri, Thompson, & Demiris, 2014; De Bruin, Hartmann, Uebelhart, Murer, & Zijlstra, 2008; El-Bendary, Tan, Pivot, & Lam, 2013).

In the future, we will become an even more connected society. With advancements in the technologies and progression in cyber infrastructure development, the older adults of tomorrow will have the opportunity to build the ideal healthcare/ caregiver team supported by a number of new sophisticated technologies that will enable the older adult to age in place (Kvedar, Coye, & Everett, 2014). These technologies include everything from using ingestible sensors to determine adherence to a prescribed medication (Eisenberger et al., 2013) to detecting an impending emergency (such as a heart attack) minutes to hours in advance (Kappiarukudil & Ramesh, 2010). In addition, these technologies will be capable of transmitting information in common languages (i.e., interoperable) so that the older adults and their healthcare team can make decisions based on multiple factors as opposed to considering data from each device separately (Gay & Leijdekkers, 2015). For example, one device could detect that an individual has not taken their medication (which could be interpreted as nonadherence), but it could be possible that the older adult is out of a desired breakfast food they routinely eat prior to taking this medication or that they are being affected by another health issue such as depression. Connected health devices will also be interoperable with other products/devices beyond the home (e.g., cars) (Adair et al., 2013; Swan, 2015). This interoperability may translate into cars that will have the ability to respond to nonadherence to available medication (e.g., car reminds older adult to take medication and will not start if that medication can hinder driving performance) or a medical emergency (e.g., car can call paramedics and automatically transport older adult to a safe space on the roadway).

In the future, all device data will be accessible in a common portal and displayed or communicated in a way that is most beneficial for the interventionist (i.e., older adult, care giver, or healthcare professional). For the older adults, we envision that all health information will be provided through an omnipresent social agent, which will assist adults with digesting information collected through external devices (including electronic medical records) and the preferences of their healthcare/ caregiver team. These agents may be embodied and accessible through the home and other computer-based or mobile devices or appear in a robotic form. Using our prior example with an older adult who did not take the medication due to lack of recommended foods in the home, an agent would receive communication from a refrigerator or pantry that this particular food is no longer available and ask the older adult if he/she would like to place an order for delivery (or automatically place an order). The agent will also be sophisticated enough to make other suggestions for breakfast based on options available within and or near the home. In instances where robotic agents are present, these new options can be automatically prepared based on a catalogue of recipes available online. Also, because all systems will be connected, the robotic agent will be aware of dietary needs of the older adults (based on electronic medical records) and be able to consider these needs in the preparation of the older adult's breakfast. In addition, embodied and robotic agents might also be able to provide temporary intervention in situations where the older adult is displaying signs of depression. These responses include actions such as contacting a loved one or friend, recommending a favorite movie or song, or finding accessible community activities. Therefore, the agent of the future will not only be an informational device or appliance, but also an intelligent companion capable of facilitating interventions based on available data and the input of a connected team.

Comprehensive health decision making

While making decisions about whether or not to receive a health screening might not be fraught with complexity, health decisions about certain treatments (e.g., cancer) can be dreadfully difficult, but especially for older adults. As we enter our golden years, our capacities to digest and analyze large amounts of information (which can include the opinions of friends and family members, doctor's recommendations, literature, experiences of other survivors), becomes limited (Carpenter & Yoon, 2011). While shared decision making has become the desired healthcare decision model by organizations such as the American Medical Association (2010), shared decision making requires that the older adult have adequate knowledge about the disease and desire/ efficacy to engage in a conversation with their healthcare provider (Dy & Purnell, 2012). Therefore, many older adults prefer to rely on their physician to make the right health/treatment decision for them in hopes that the physician and others involved in the decision (i.e., caregivers) have considered their personal values and their desired quality of life post treatment (Levinson et al., 2005). However, treatment outcomes for some diseases such as cancer can vary considerably based on factors such as stage of the disease, family history, age, and type of treatment (Ward et al., 2004).

Over the past 5 years, organizations such as Memorial Sloan Kettering Cancer Center and others have explored supercomputing and deep learning for assisting clinicians with pinpointing the most effective treatments for cancer patients (Savvy, 2015). According to Savvy (2015), their super computer was able to quickly review the 1.2 million patient medical records in tandem with published research, treatment guidelines and genetic data to identify the best evidence-based treatment strategy.

In the future, these supercomputers will be widely accessible by healthcare providers and the resulting data from various analyses will be available through an older adult's electronic medical record. Social agents will also have access to this data and act as intelligent decision aids. Not only will the agents be able to educate the older adult on the treatment types, but they will also be capable of (1) answering general health or treatment questions which include those about potential treatment outcomes, (2) assisting the older adult and caregiver(s) with narrowing down options for intervention based on their desired outcomes, personal values, and the affect of the older adult, and (3) offering an opportunity to practice their doctor—patient communication through role plays with the social agent. Furthermore, these social agents will be intelligent enough to assist with the translation of information between doctor and patient during a discussion to improve the conversation. The older adult will also be automatically sent pertinent information about their conversation with a healthcare provider following their visit that can be reviewed by the older adult and their caregiver, supported by the social agent. By improving the health decision making capacity of older adults, their physical and mental health may be preserved which also enhances their overall capacity to age in place.

Connected communities and globalization

Beyond being connected to their healthcare providers, healthcare data, and their caregivers, the older adults of tomorrow will also leverage technology to become more socially engaged. According to Pew Internet, one in four (26%) Internet users 65+ use social media to stay connected with family friends and relatives (Greenwood, Perrin, & Duggan, 2016). In the future, algorithms will be developed to connect to other individuals with similar interests in their community and globally. These invitations will be facilitated by social agents. Virtually, older adults will have opportunities to be involved in group chats, support groups, and joint game play with older and younger adults from across the globe. With the advancement of voice recognition and translation technologies in the future, conversations will be translated instantly, eliminating barriers that now stand between intercontinental connectedness. These new engagements may lend themselves to an overall growth in cultural-competency, preservation of cultural traditions, cross-cultural and intergenerational exchanges, and opportunities for virtual tourism. Furthermore, there will be exceedingly more opportunities for informal and formal education for older adults that may not only lead to new skills, but also equate to certifications and degrees for from academic institutions from around the world.

In addition to virtual engagement, social agents will be capable of arranging opportunities for older adults to attend events in-person. For example, if a social agent scans the Internet and finds a "senior friendly" event or excursion that is being advertised, the agent will inform the older adult about this opportunity. In addition, if the older adult has an interest in attending the event or excursion, the agent will act as virtual assistant which could include: Checking the older adult's calendar for conflicting appointments, assessing potential barriers/risks and recommended solutions to attendance (e.g., inclement weather, accessibility of venue, proximity of restrooms to the seating area, food availability, costs), and arranging transportation and/or companionship to the event or excursion. Similar to current social media, older adults will also be able to report their intention to attend the event or excursion to select system users (who may also want to join them), but the social agent will further be capable of informing caregivers and other stakeholders about the older adults' intentions.

Summary

In summary, social agents, such as embodied conversational agents and robotic agents, hold much promise for aiding older adults to live independently. In particular, we focus on two application areas: Health education and health communication. By applying social agents in this context, older adults may receive more timely health information, as well as remain better connected with doctors, caregivers, and the global community. However, for social agents to be effectively implemented in health education and communication, a number of challenges must be addressed, such as issues surrounding privacy, technology acceptance, home environment designs, and ethical use. If these challenges can be met, applying social agents to health education and communication provide many exciting future opportunities for smart and connected aging-in-place.

References

AARP. (2008). *Healthy at home*. Available at <http://assets.aarp.org/rgcenter/il/healthy_-home.pdf>.

Adair, B., Miller, K., Ozanne, E., Hansen, R., Pearce, A. J., Santamaria, N., ... Said, C. M. (2013). Smart-home technologies to assist older people to live well at home. *Journal of Aging Science, 1*(1), 1−9. Available from http://dx.doi.org/10.4172/jasc.1000101.

Admission on Aging. (2010). Available at <http://www.aoa.gov>.

American Medical Association. (2010). *Getting the most for our health care dollars: Shared decision-making*. Washington, DC. Available at <http://www.ama-assn.org/resources/doc/health-care-costs/shared-decision-making.pdf>.

Auld, E., & Gambescia, S. (2011). Health education. *Oxford Bibliographies in Public Health. Available from http://dx.doi.org/10.1093/obo/9780199756797-0044.*

Beach, S., Schulz, R., Downs, J., Matthews, J., Barron, B., & Seelman, K. (2009). Disability, age, and informational privacy attitudes in quality of life technology applications: Results from a national web survey. *ACM Transactions on Accessible Computing (TACCESS), 2*(1), 5.

Beckwith, R. (2003). Designing for ubiquity: The perception of privacy. *Pervasive Computing, 2*(2), 40−46.

Beer, J. M., & Takayama, L. (2011). *Mobile remote presence systems for older adults: Acceptance, benefits, and concerns*. Proceedings of international conference on Human-Robot Interaction (HRI) (pp. 19−26). ACM/IEEE.

Bekey, G. A. (2005). *Autonomous robots: From biological inspiration to implementation and control*. Cambridge, MA: The MIT Press.

Bevilacqua, R., Cesta, A., Cortellessa, G., Macchione, A., Orlandini, A., & Tiberio, L. (2014). Telepresence robot at home: A long-term case study. *Ambient Assisted Living*, 73−85.

Bickmore, T. W., Gruber, A., & Picard, R. (2005). Establishing the computer−patient working alliance in automated health behavior change interventions. *Patient Education and Counseling, 59*(1), 21−30. Available from http://dx.doi.org/10.1016/j.pec.2004.09.008.

Bickmore, T. W., Caruso, L., Clough-Gorr, K., & Heeren, T. (2005). 'It's just like you talk to a friend' relational agents for older adults. *Interacting with Computers, 17*(6), 711−735. Available from http://dx.doi.org/10.1016/j.intcom.2005.09.002.

Bickmore, T. W., Pfeifer, L. M., & Paasche-Orlow, M. K. (2009). Using computer agents to explain medical documents to patients with low health literacy. *Patient Education and Counseling, 75*(3), 315−320. Available from http://dx.doi.org/10.1016/j.pec.2009.02.007.

Bickmore, T. W., Silliman, R. A., Nelson, K., Cheng, D. M., Winter, M., Henault, L., & Paasche-Orlow, M. K. (2013). A randomized controlled trial of an automated exercise coach for older adults. *Journal of the American Geriatrics Society, 61*(10), 1676−1683. Available from http://dx.doi.org/10.1111/jgs.12449.

Boulos, M. N. K., Hetherington, L., & Wheeler, S. (2007). Second life: An overview of the potential of 3-D virtual worlds in medical and health education. *Health Information & Libraries Journal, 24*(4), 233−245. Available from http://dx.doi.org/10.1111/j.1471-1842.2007.00733.x.

Broadbent, E., Jayawardena, C., Kerse, N., Stafford, R., & MacDonald, B. A. (2011). Human-robot interaction research to improve quality of life in elder care-an approach and issues. In *The conference on artificial intelligence (AAAI-11), Workshop on human-robot interaction in elder care* (pp. 13−19).

De Bruin, E. D., Hartmann, A., Uebelhart, D., Murer, K., & Zijlstra, W. (2008). Wearable systems for monitoring mobility-related activities in older people: A systematic review. *Clinical Rehabilitation, 22*(10-11), 878−895. Available from http://dx.doi.org/10.1177/0269215508090675.

Bugmann, G., & Copleston, S. N. (2011). *What can a personal robot do for you? Conference Towards Autonomous Robotic Systems* (pp. 360−371). Springer Berlin Heidelberg.

Bull, S. (2010). *Technology-based health promotion.* Los Angeles, CA: Sage Publications.

Caine, K. E., Zimmerman, C. Y., Schall-Zimmerman, Z., Hazlewood, W. R., Camp, L. J., Connelly, K. H., ... Shankar, K. (2011). DigiSwitch: A device to allow older adults to monitor and direct the collection and transmission of health information collected at home. *Journal of Medical Systems, 35*(5), 1181−1195.

Carpenter, S. M., & Yoon, C. (2011). Aging and consumer decision making. *Annals of the New York Academy of Sciences, 1235*(1), E1−E12. Available from http://dx.doi.org/10.1111/j.1749-6632.2011.06390.x.

Caulfield, B. M., & Donnelly, S. C. (2013). What is Connected Health and why will it change your practice? *QJM, 106*(8), 703−707. Available from http://dx.doi.org/10.1093/qjmed/hct114.

Cesario, S. (2009). "Partnering with Seniors for Better Health": Computer use and internet health information retrieval among older adults in a low socioeconomic community. *Journal of the Medical Library Association, 97*(1). Available from http://dx.doi.org/10.3163/1536-5050.97.1.003.

Cesta, A., Cortellessa, G., Orlandini, A., & Tiberio, L. (2012). *Evaluating telepresence robots in the field. International conference on agents and artificial intelligence* (pp. 433−448). Springer Berlin Heidelberg.

Charles, C., Gafni, A., & Whelan, T. (1997). Shared decision-making in the medical encounter: What does it mean? (or it takes at least two to tango). *Social Science and Medicine, 44*(5), 681−692. Available from https://dx.doi.org/10.1016/S0277-9536(96)00221-3.

Charles, C., Gafni, A., & Whelan, T. (1999). Decision-making in the physician−patient encounter: Revisiting the shared treatment decision-making model. *Social Science and Medicine, 49*(5), 651−661.

Chaudhuri, S., Le, T., White, C., Thompson, H., & Demiris, G. (2013). Examining health information−seeking behaviors of older adults. *Computers, Informatics, Nursing: CIN, 31*(11), 547−553. Available from http://dx.doi.org/10.1097/01.NCN.0000432131.92020.42.

Chaudhuri, S., Thompson, H., & Demiris, G. (2014). Fall detection devices and their use with older adults: A systematic review. *Journal of Geriatric Physical Therapy, 37*(4), 178. Available from http://dx.doi.org/10.1519/JPT.0b013e3182abe779.

Chu, A., Huber, J., Mastel-Smith, B., & Cesario, S. (2009). "Partnering with Seniors for Better Health": Computer use and internet health information retrieval among older adults in a low socioeconomic community. *Journal of the Medical Library Association: JMLA, 97*(1), 12−20. Available from http://dx.doi.org/10.3163/1536-5050.97.1.003.

Cresci, M. K., Yarandi, H. N., & Morrell, R. W. (2010). The digital divide and urban older adults. *Computers Informatics Nursing, 28*(2), 88−94. Available from http://dx.doi.org/10.1097/NCN.0b013e3181cd8184.

Czaja, S. J., Charness, N., Fisk, A. D., Hertzog, C., Nair, S. N., Rogers, W. A., & Sharit, J. (2006). Factors predicting the use of technology: Findings from the center for research and education on aging and technology enhancement (CREATE). *Psychology and Aging, 21*(2), 333−352. Available from http://dx.doi.org/10.1037/0882-7974.21.2.333.

Daruwalla, J. Z., Collins, D., & Moore, P. D. (2010). "Orthobot, to your station!" The application of the remote presence robotic system in orthopaedic surgery in Ireland: A pilot study on patient and nursing staff satisfaction. *Journal of Robotic Surgery*, *4*(3), 177−182.

Davis, F. D. (1989). Perceived usefulness, perceived ease of use, and user acceptance of information technology. *MIS Quarterly*, 319−340.

Davis, F. D., Bagozzi, R. P., & Warshaw, P. R. (1989). User acceptance of computer technology: A comparison of two theoretical models. *Management Science*, *35*(8), 982−1003.

Ducheneaut, N., Wen, M.-H., Yee, N., & Wadley, G. (2009). Body and mind: A study of avatar personalization in three virtual worlds. *Proceedings of the SIGCHI Conference on Human Factors in Computing Systems. Available from http://dx.doi.org/10.1145/ 1518701.1518877.*

Dy, S. M., & Purnell, T. S. (2012). Key concepts relevant to quality of complex and shared decision-making in health care: A literature review. *Social Science and Medicine*, *74*(4), 582−587. Available from http://dx.doi.org/10.1016/j.socscimed.2011.11.015.

Eisenberger, U., Wüthrich, R. P., Bock, A., Ambühl, P., Steiger, J., Intondi, A., & DiCarlo, L. (2013). Medication adherence assessment: High accuracy of the new Ingestible Sensor System in kidney transplants. *Transplantation*, *96*(3), 245−250. Available from http://dx. doi.org/10.1097/TP.0b013e31829b7571.

El-Bendary, N., Tan, Q., Pivot, F. C., & Lam, A. (2013). Fall detection and prevention for the elderly: A review of trends and challenges. *International Journal on Smart Sensing and Intelligent Systems*, *6*(3), 1230−1266.

Ellison, L. M., Nguyen, M., Fabrizio, M. D., Soh, A., Permpongkosol, S., & Kavoussi, L. R. (2007). Postoperative robotic telerounding: A multicenter randomized assessment of patient outcomes and satisfaction. *Archives of Surgery*, *142*(12), 1177−1181.

Ezer, N., Fisk, A. D., & Rogers, W. A. (2009). Attitudinal and intentional acceptance of domestic robots by younger and older adults. In *Universal access in human-computer interaction. Intelligent and Ubiquitous Interaction Environments* (pp. 39−48). Springer Berlin Heidelberg.

Fasola, J., & Mataric, M. J. (2012). Using socially assistive human−robot interaction to motivate physical exercise for older adults. *Proceedings of the IEEE*, *100*(8), 2512−2526. Available from http://dx.doi.org/10.1109/JPROC.2012.2200539.

Feil-Seifer, D., & Mataric, M. J. (June 2005). *Defining socially assistive robotics. The international conference on rehabilitation robotics (ICORR)* (pp. 465−468). IEEE.

Fishbein, M., & Ajzen, I. (1975). *Belief, attitude, intention and behavior: An introduction to theory and research.* Reading, MA: Addison-Wesley Publishing Co.

Fisk, A. D., Rogers, W. A., Charness, N., Czaja, S. J., & Sharit, J. (2009). *Designing for older adults: Principles and creative human factors approaches* (2nd ed.). Boca Raton, FL: CRC Press.

Gandsas, A., Parekh, M., Bleech, M. M., & Tong, D. A. (2007). Robotic telepresence: Profit analysis in reducing length of stay after laparoscopic gastric bypass. *Journal of the American College of Surgeons*, *205*(1), 72−77.

Gay, V., & Leijdekkers, P. (2015). Bringing health and fitness data together for connected health care: Mobile apps as enablers of interoperability. *Journal of Medical Internet Research*, *17*(11). Available from http://dx.doi.org/10.2196/jmir.5094.

Graf, B., Hans, M., & Schraft, R. D. (2004). Care-O-bot II—Development of a next generation robotic home assistant. *Autonomous Robots*, *16*(2), 193−205.

Green, L. W., & Kreuter, M. W. (2005). *Health program planning: An educational and ecological approach.* McGraw-Hill Companies.

Greenwood, S., Perrin, A., & Duggan, M. (November 11, 2016). *Social media update 2016.* Available at <http://www.pewinternet.org/2016/11/11/social-media-update-2016/>.

Grimes, G. A., Hough, M. G., Mazur, E., & Signorella, M. L. (2010). Older adults' knowledge of internet hazards. *Educational Gerontology*, *36*(3), 173–192.

Hawley, S. T., Lantz, P. M., Janz, N. K., Salem, B., Morrow, M., Schwartz, K., ... Katz, S. J. (2007). Factors associated with patient involvement in surgical treatment decision making for breast cancer. *Patient Education and Counseling*, *65*(3), 387–395.

Heart, T., & Kalderon, E. (2013). Older adults: Are they ready to adopt health-related ICT? *International Journal of Medical Informatics*, *82*(11), e209–e231. https://dx.doi.org/10.1017/CBO9781139547369 https://nam.edu/perspectives-2014-understanding-the-relationship-between-education-and-health/.

Healthy People (2020). Washington, DC: U.S. Department of Health and Human Services, Office of Disease Prevention and Health Promotion. Available at <https://www.healthypeople.gov/>.

Joe, J., & Demiris, G. (2013). Older adults and mobile phones for health: A review. *Journal of Biomedical Informatics*, *46*(5), 947–954. Available from http://dx.doi.org/10.1016/j.jbi.2013.06.008.

Kane, H. L., Halpern, M. T., Squiers, L. B., Treiman, K. A., & McCormack, L. A. (2014). Implementing and evaluating shared decision making in oncology practice. *CA: A Cancer Journal for Clinicians*, *64*(6), 377–388. Available from http://dx.doi.org/10.3322/caac.21245.

Kappiarukudil, K. J., & Ramesh, M. V. (2010). Real-time monitoring and detection of "heart attack" using wireless sensor networks. In *Sensor technologies and applications (SENSORCOMM), 2010 fourth international conference on* (pp. 632–636). IEEE.

Kite-Powell, J. (2012). *Hector: Robotic assistance for the elderly*. Available at <https://www.forbes.com/sites/jenniferhicks/2012/08/13/hector-robotic-assistance-for-the-elderly/#146632224437>.

Kristoffersson, A., Coradeschi, S., & Loutfi, A. (2013). A review of mobile robotic telepresence. *Advances in Human-Computer Interaction*, 1–17.

Kueider, A. M., Parisi, J. M., Gross, A. L., & Rebok, G. W. (2012). Computerized cognitive training with older adults: A systematic review. *PLoS One*, *7*(7), e40588. Available from http://dx.doi.org/10.1371/journal.pone.0040588.

Kvedar, J., Coye, M. J., & Everett, W. (2014). Connected health: A review of technologies and strategies to improve patient care with telemedicine and telehealth. *Health Affairs*, *33*(2), 194–199. Available from http://dx.doi.org/10.1377/hlthaff.2013.0992.

Levinson, W., Kao, A., Kuby, A., & Thisted, R. A. (2005). Not all patients want to participate in decision making. *Journal of General Internal Medicine*, *20*(6), 531–535. Available from http://dx.doi.org/10.1111/j.1525-1497.2005.04101.x.

Liles, K. R., Stuck, R. E., Kacmar, A. A., & Beer, J. M. (2015a). Understanding retirement community employees' perceived benefits and concerns of smart presence technology. In: *Proceedings of the Human Factors and Ergonomics Society Annual Meeting (HFES)* (pp. 75–79). Los Angeles, CA: SAGE Publications.

Liles, K. R., Stuck, R. E., Kacmar, A. A., & Beer, J. M. (2015b). Use cases of smart presence for retirement communities. In: *Proceedings of the HCI International (HCII); Human Aspects of IT for the Aged Population* (pp. 446–455). Springer.

Lisetti, C., Yasavur, U., de Leon, C., Amini, R., Rishe, N., & Visser, U. (2012). Building an on-demand avatar-based health intervention for behavior change. Paper presented at the proceedings of the 25th international FLAIRS conference, Marco Island, FL, USA.

Lisetti, C. L. (2012). 10 advantages of using avatars in patient-centered computer-based interventions for behavior change. *SIGHIT Record*, *2*(1), 28.

Lorenzen-Huber, L., Boutain, M., Camp, L. J., Shankar, K., & Connelly, K. H. (2011). Privacy, technology, and aging: A proposed framework. *Ageing International, 36*(2), 232−252.

Magnenat-Thalmann, N., & Ichalkaranje, N. (2008). *New advances in virtual humans: Artificial Intelligence Environment.* Berlin: Springer. Available from http://dx.doi.org/ 10.1007/978-3-540-79868-2.

Magnenat-Thalmann, N., & Thalmann, D. (2005). *Handbook of virtual humans.* John Wiley & Sons.

Mahani, M., & Eklundh, K. S. (2009). *A survey on relation of the task assistance of a robot to its social role.* Stockholm: Communication KCSa Royal Institute of Technology.

Mayer, R. E. (2014). Cognitive theory of multimedia learning. *The Cambridge handbook of multimedia learning* (Vol. 43) Cambridge University Press.

Mickus, M. A., & Luz, C. (2002). Televisits: Sustaining long distance family relationships among institutionalized elders through technology. *Aging & Mental Health, 6*(4), 387−396.

Minton, O., & Stone, P. (2008). How common is fatigue in disease-free breast cancer survivors? A systematic review of the literature. *Breast Cancer Research and Treatment, 112*(1), 5−13. Available from http://dx.doi.org/10.1007/s10549-007-9831-1.

Mitzner, T. L., Boron, J. B., Fausset, C. B., Adams, A. E., Charness, N., Czaja, S. J., ... Sharit, J. (2010). Older adults talk technology: Their usage and attitudes. *Computers in Human Behavior, 269,* 1710−1721.

Mitzner, T. L., Chen, T. L., Kemp, C. C., & Rogers, W. A. (2014). Identifying the potential for robotics to assist older adults in different living environments. *International Journal of Social Robotics, 6*(2), 213−227.

Morris, A., Goodman, J., & Brading, H. (2007). Internet use and non-use: Views of older users. *Universal Access in the Information Society, 6*(1), 43−57, doi10.1007/s10209-006-0057-5.

Muellmann, S., Forberger, S., Möllers, T., Zeeb, H., & Pischke, C. R. (2016). Effectiveness of eHealth interventions for the promotion of physical activity in older adults: A systematic review protocol. *Systematic Reviews, 5*(1), 47. Available from http://dx.doi.org/ 10.1186/s13643-016-0223-7.

Murphy, R. R. (2000). *Introduction to AI robotics.* Cambridge, MA: The MIT Press.

National Institute on Aging, & World Health Organization. (2011). *Global health and aging.* Available at <http://www.who.int/ageing/publications/global_health.pdf>.

Nielsen-Bohlman, L., Panzer, A. M., & Kindig, D. A. (2004). *Health literacy: A prescription to end confusion. Committee on Health Literacy, Board on Neuroscience and Behavioral Health, Institute of Medicine.* Washington, DC: National Academies Press. Available from http://dx.doi.org/10.17226/10883.

O'Connor, A. M., Bennett, C. L., Stacey, D., Barry, M., Col, N. F., Eden, K. B., ... Khangura, S. (2009). Decision aids for people facing health treatment or screening decisions. *The Cochrane Library. Available from http://dx.doi.org/10.1002/14651858. CD001431.*

Owens, O. L. (2015). Principles for developing digital health interventions for prostate cancer: A community-based design approach with African American men. In J. Zhou, & G. Salvendy (Eds.), *Human aspects of IT for the aged population. Design for Everyday Life: First International Conference, ITAP 2015, Held as Part of HCI International 2015, Los Angeles, CA, USA, August 2−7, 2015. Proceedings, Part II* (pp. 134−145). Cham: Springer International Publishing. Available from http://dx.doi.org/10.1007/978-3-319-20913-5_13.

Owens, O. L., Friedman, D. B., Brandt, H. M., Bernhardt, J. M., & Hébert, J. R. (2015a). Digital solutions for informed decision making: An academic—community partnership for the development of a prostate cancer decision aid for African American men. *American Journal of Men's Health.* Available from http://dx.doi.org/10.1177/1557988314564178.

Owens, O. L., Friedman, D. B., Brandt, H. M., Bernhardt, J. M., & Hébert, J. R. (2015b). An iterative process for developing and evaluating a computer-based prostate cancer decision aid for African American men. *Health Promotion Practice, 16*(5), 642—655. Available from http://dx.doi.org/10.1177/1524839915585737.

Patel, S., Park, H., Bonato, P., Chan, L., & Rodgers, M. (2012). A review of wearable sensors and systems with application in rehabilitation. *Journal of Neuroengineering and Rehabilitation, 9*(1), 1. Available from http://dx.doi.org/10.1186/1743-0003-9-21.

Peckham, C. (2016). *Medscape physician compensation report 2016.* Available at <http://www.medscape.com/features/slideshow/compensation/2016/public/overview?src = wnl_physrep_160401_mscpedit&uac = 232148CZ&impID = 1045700&faf = 1>.

Peek, M. E., Gorawara-Bhat, R., Quinn, M. T., Odoms-Young, A., Wilson, S. C., & Chin, M. H. (2013). Patient trust in physicians and shared decision-making among African-Americans with diabetes. *Health Communication, 28*(6), 616—623.

Petelin, J. B., Nelson, M. E., & Goodman, J. (2007). Deployment and early experience with remote-presence patient care in a community hospital. *Surgical Endoscopy, 21*(1), 53—56.

Pollack, M. E., Brown, L., Colbry, D., Orosz, C., Peintner, B., Ramakrishnan, S., ... Thrun, S. (2002). Pearl: A mobile robotic assistant for the elderly. In *AAAI workshop on automation as eldercare* (pp. 85—91).

Robinson, H., MacDonald, B., & Broadbent, E. (2014). The role of healthcare robots for older people at home: A review. *International Journal of Social Robotics, 6*(4), 575—591. Available from http://dx.doi.org/10.1007/s12369-014-0242-2.

Russell, S. J., & Norvig, P. (2003). *Artificial intelligence: A modern approach* (2nd ed.). Upper Saddle River, NJ: Pearson Education, Inc.

Sallis, J. F., & Carlson, J. A. (2015). Physical activity: Numerous benefits and effective interventions. In R. Kaplan, M. Spittel, & D. David (Eds.), *Population health: Behavioral and social science insights.* Rockville, MD: Agency for Healthcare Research and Quality.

Savvy, T. (2015). Watson will see you now: A supercomputer to help clinicians make informed treatment decisions. *Clinical Journal of Oncology Nursing, 1*(31—32). Available from http://dx.doi.org/10.1188/15.CJON.31-32.

Schulman, D., Bickmore, T. W., & Sidner, C. L. (2011). An intelligent conversational agent for promoting long-term health behavior change using motivational interviewing. In *Proceedings of the AAAI Spring Symposium: AI and Health Communication.*

Smarr, C.-A., Fausset, C. B., & Rogers, W. A. (2011). *Understanding the potential for robot assistance for older adults in the home environment (HFA-TR-1102).* Atlanta, GA: Georgia Institute of Technology, School of Psychology, Human Factors and Aging Laboratory.

Smarr, C. A., Mitzner, T. L., Beer, J. M., Prakash, A., Chen, T. L., Kemp, C. C., & Rogers, W. A. (2014). Domestic robots for older adults: Attitudes, preferences, and potential. *International Journal of Social Robotics, 6*(2), 229—247.

Smith, A. (2014). *Older adults and technology use.* Available at <http://www.pewinternet.org/2014/04/03/older-adults-and-technology-use/>.

Speros, C. I. (2009). More than words: Promoting health literacy in older adults. *OJIN: The Online Journal of Issues in Nursing, 14*(3). Available from http://dx.doi.org/10.3912/OJIN.Vol14No03Man05.

Stacey, D., Bennett, C. L., Barry, M. J., Col, N. F., Eden, K. B., Holmes-Rovner, M., ...
Thomson, R. (2011). Decision aids for people facing health treatment or screening decisions. *The Cochrane Database of Systematic Reviews*, *10*(10). Available from http://dx.
doi.org/10.1002/14651858.CD001431.pub3.

Swan, M. (2015). Connected car: Quantified self becomes quantified car. *Journal of Sensor
and Actuator Networks*, *4*(1), 2−29. Available from http://dx.doi.org/10.3390/
jsan4010002.

Terry, K. (2015). *Number of health apps sours, but use does not always follow*. Retrieved
from <http://www.medscape.com/viewarticle/851226>.

Thomson, R. G., Eccles, M. P., Steen, I. N., Greenaway, J., Stobbart, L., Murtagh, M. J., &
May, C. R. (2007). A patient decision aid to support shared decision-making on anti-
thrombotic treatment of patients with atrial fibrillation: Randomised controlled trial.
Quality and Safety Health Care, *16*(3), 216−223. Available from http://dx.doi.org/
10.1136/qshc.2006.018481.

Thrun, S. (2004). Toward a framework for human-robot interaction. Human−Computer.
Interaction, *19*(1−2), 9−24.

Vespa, P. (2005). Robotic telepresence in the intensive care unit. *Critical Care*, *9*(4),
319−320.

Vespa, P. M., Miller, C., Hu, X., Nenov, V., Buxey, F., & Martin, N. A. (2007). Intensive
care unit robotic telepresence facilitates rapid physician response to unstable patients
and decreased cost in neurointensive care. *Surgical Neurology*, *67*(4), 331−337.

Ward, E., Jemal, A., Cokkinides, V., Singh, G. K., Cardinez, C., Ghafoor, A., & Thun, M.
(2004). Cancer disparities by race/ethnicity and socioeconomic status. *CA: A Cancer
Journal for Clinicians*, *54*(2), 78−93. Available from http://dx.doi.org/10.3322/
canjclin.54.2.78.

Webb, T. L., Joseph, J., Yardley, L., & Michie, S. (2010). Using the internet to promote
health behavior change: A systematic review and meta-analysis of the impact of theoretical basis, use of behavior change techniques, and mode of delivery on efficacy. *Journal
of Medical Internet Research*, *12*(1). Available from http://dx.doi.org/10.2196/jmir.1376.

World Health Organization. (2016). *Health education*. Available at <http://www.who.int/
topics/health_education/en/>.

Wu, X., Stuck, R. E., Mitner, T. L., Rogers, W. A., & Beer, J. M. (2016). Televideo for older
adults with mobility impairment: A needs assessment. In *Proceedings of the international conference on rehabilitation engineering and assistive technology (RESNA/
NCART)*.

Zimmerman, E., & Woolf, S. H. (2014). Understanding the relationship between education
and health. *National Academy of Medicine*.

Further reading

Coradeschi, S., & Kristoffersson, A. (2011). Towards a methodology for longitudinal evaluation of social robotic telepresence for elderly. In *The 1st workshop on social robotic telepresence, Proceedings of the international conference on human-robot interaction
(HRI)* (pp. 1−7). ACM/IEEE.

Kristoffersson, A., Coradeschi, S., Loutfi, A., & Severinson-Eklundh, K. (2011). An
Exploratory Study of Health Professionals' attitudes about robotic telepresence technology. *Journal of Technology in Human Services*, *29*(4), 263−283.

Nakanishi, H., Kato, K., & Ishiguro, H. (2011). Zoom cameras and movable displays enhance social telepresence. In *Proceedings of the SIGCHI conference on human factors in computing systems* (pp. 63−72). ACM.

Nakanishi, H., Murakami, Y., Nogami, D., & Ishiguro, H. (2008). Minimum movement matters: Impact of robot-mounted cameras on social telepresence. In *Proceedings of the 2008 conference on computer supported cooperative work* (pp. 303−312). ACM.

Tsui, K. M., & Yanco, H. A. (2007). Assistive, rehabilitation, and surgical robots from the perspective of medical and healthcare professionals. *Proceedings of the AAAI Workshop on Human Implications of Human-Robot Interaction*, 34−39.

Design of human centered augmented reality for managing chronic health conditions

Anne Collins McLaughlin[1], Laura A. Matalenas[1] and Maribeth Gandy Coleman[2]
[1]North Carolina State University, Raleigh, NC, United States, [2]Georgia Institute of Technology, Atlanta, GA, United States

As we have seen in the previous chapters, older adults' health can be greatly enhanced by the judicious use of technology. Knowledge of age-related changes can inform the design of technological supports that keep older adults active, mobile, healthy, connected, and entertained. Earlier chapters presented how technology could be used now with technologies that are currently available or upcoming. But given the fast-changing pace of technology, how should technology be used to enhance older adults' health and well-being in the future? We close this book with one vision of how technology could help by presenting the challenges, knowns, and unknowns associated with the use of augmented reality (AR) by older adults (OAs).

The potential role of AR in managing chronic health conditions

Joan, age 68, was just diagnosed with prediabetes. She's overwhelmed with the prospect of managing her diet, so her doctor has given her a new technological aid designed to unobtrusively offer suggestions about what and how to eat. She starts preparing lunch and takes a look in the mirror. She looks closely at her arm and her view zooms in so she can see her individual blood cells and how they are acting to resist insulin. She can see internal functions related to diabetes, including some fatty cells coursing through her bloodstream. Text information is overlaid on the visualization that helps her develop a mental model of how the food she just ate is acting on her body. She experiments by turning to her lunch and sees the carb counts and glycemic indices of the foods on her plate. When she picks up a bread roll, she can see the difference in glycemic index between white and whole grain. The system surprises Joan by asking her to guess the calories in the slice she's holding. "80," Joan says. "Close," says the system, "it's 120." "Hmm, higher than I expected," thinks Joan. Joan can't wait to try new meals and to show her friends.

The scenario above presents a possible technological advancement using AR and good psychological principles from the learning and design domains to help an older

Aging, Technology and Health. DOI: http://dx.doi.org/10.1016/B978-0-12-811272-4.00011-7

person recently diagnosed with diabetes learn to manage her condition. However, embedded in this scenario are a multitude of questions regarding the design of AR. What inputs would function best for older users? Voice, touch, or movement? What should the display look like, so the user can easily perceive the elements and understand what is being presented? Regarding AR, the answers to these questions are not known. However, in this chapter we draw information from the past literature on displays and interfaces for older adults and from the literature on training to come up with initial design principles and an outline of research questions that need to be answered.

Definition and examples of augmented reality

AR is a type of immersive computing that adds virtual elements to the real environment (Azuma, 1997). Hardware can consist of computer-controlled "mirror" displays, projectors, AR/VR specific headsets, heads-up displays, auditory displays, haptic displays, and smartphones. On the mixed reality spectrum, AR falls somewhere in the middle—i.e., it is different from virtual reality, which contains virtual elements in an entirely synthetic environment, and reality, which contains no virtual elements at all. AR does not attempt to transport or distract the user from the real environment—it augments the real world by seamlessly combining virtual elements with the physical world. Examples of AR programs include the *SnapShop* showroom used by Ikea to simulate the look of furniture in a given room using a smartphone or tablet camera (SnapShop Inc., 2015), the *Augmented Car Finder* smartphone application which provides an on-screen pointer to help find a car in a parking lot (AugmentedWorks, 2017), and *Pokémon Go*, a popular smartphone game that displays digital characters in the real environment for players to "catch" (Fig. 11.1; Niantic, 2016). These programs use smartphones and other ubiquitous mobile devices, but other hardware can also be used.

One example is *Magic Mirror*, an AR make-up tool that uses a mirror display to allow shoppers to "try on" certain make up choices before buying (Javornick, Rogers, Moutinho, & Freeman, 2016). *Microsoft HoloLens* allows users to view virtual content ranging from browser windows to *Minecraft* video game scenes visually combined with their living environment (Microsoft, 2017). With *HoloLens*, users can "project" a TV show on a wall, have a virtual pet move about their room, play games on their table, or use the *Microsoft Office Suite* without the constraints of a monitor or physical input device (e.g., a computer mouse). Fig. 11.2 shows AR being used in a study of estimating food portions, where the goal portion, shown as a 3D pyramid on the left, can only be seen by looking through the tablet camera (Matalenas, 2017). Despite these many example applications, AR technology is in its infancy and much about the principles needed to create interesting, informative, and seamless user experiences is unknown.

The many (inter)faces of AR

Because AR is such a new technology it is worth surveying the types of interfaces that incorporate AR, noting their affordances, and their limitations. One unique

Figure 11.1 Screenshots from a mobile phone playing Pokémon Go, an AR game that necessitates moving around to collect the characters. The game uses information from GPS, maps, and crowd-sourced location data to place characters along roadways and otherwise integrate them into the real environments of any city. The left panel shows an action that can be taken on the 2D interface ("throwing" the ball) that will act on the augmented figure. In the right panel, it is possible to see the virtual shadow helping to ground the augmented figure into a real environment.

Figure 11.2 Augmented reality being used to show proper food portion sizes. The patterned paper on the left informs the AR system of what size cone to show when viewed through the camera on a tablet computer. The human tries to measure out a portion of quinoa similar to the goal amount shown by the cone (Matalenas, 2017). Thus, the contextual environment remains the same, save the addition of "augmented" information available via the computer. View of such AR can be done via tablets, smartphones, glasses, or any computer-mediated display.

aspect of AR is the difficulty in classifying displays versus interfaces. In traditional technologies, such as PCs, tablets, and smartphones, the display is a screen of information that can change based on input. The interface is usually the type of input device, (e.g., a computer mouse or touchscreen) combined with on-screen controls (e.g., menus, buttons), that act on the display. However, in AR the display and interface are often inseparable, with the interface *being* the display. For example, when health information is displayed on the body to show actions taking place within the body, one might turn over their arm to see the "inside" from a different angle. Thus, the arm displaying the augmented information is both a display of that information, and the input device to see different information.

Another unique affordance of AR is the variety of interface styles. These interface styles can range from traditional user interface elements like buttons and menus to tangible interfaces in AR where the user picks up or touches an object that controls the interface. This allows for more environment- and context-specific, situated interactions in which the user interacts with the system using elements present in the environment or the context of the interaction. For example, the *Microsoft HoloLens* scans the room of the user to track items in the environment and display augmented content appropriately on tables, walls, and around other objects. This helps the virtual elements from the HoloLens to be more convincing and natural to the users as it is embedded into the actual room with the user.

A situated interaction is one in which the user is present in the relevant environment or context of the interaction. Situated interactions can provide benefits for learning and for recall of learned information. Additionally, situated interactions can provide information to clarify or guide understanding of an environment. For example, information is available online or on packaging about the nutrition in oatmeal. This can be combined with information on what nutrition and portions are best for a breakfast that adheres to a diabetes diet. However, integrating across these sources of information is difficult *and* the two pieces of information are physically separate from the physical oatmeal. In AR, the information can be situated on or in the oatmeal itself, in the context of breakfast, or even in the context of other foods intended to accompany the oatmeal. This reduces the need for the user to translate and integrate information across sources.

"Opportunistic controls" within AR (Henderson & Feiner, 2008) are another example of providing environment- and context-specific interfaces with situated interaction. With opportunistic controls, virtual menus are visually overlaid on the relevant physical elements in the real world. The user can then touch (and potentially manipulate) the physical elements to browse and choose from items on a menu. For example, imagine an older user with type 2 diabetes is trying to choose healthy food from their fridge. With an AR device, the user can cycle through diabetes-related nutrition information and food choices using virtual menus. These menus can appear on the fridge or even on the food in "opportunistic" areas. If a user is curious how many grams of carbohydrates are in a slice of bread or what kind of recipes they can make with broccoli, they can look at the item for nutrition information, and once they've decided that's what they want to eat, they can pick up the item to display example meals with recipes. This way, the natural affordances of using a refrigerator and picking up items have become a part of the interface itself. For older adults self-managing their health, the benefits of these types of interactions include a reduction in the need for learning controls (i.e., opportunistic controls capitalize on affordances in the environment to create more natural interactions), increased context for learning and recall, and opportunities for perceptual and cognitive benefits (e.g., increased visual salience, lower working memory needs) due to the specificity of information.

AR information browser interfaces

Information browsers in AR are typically applications where the user looks around and sees augmentations registered with the physical world. Billinghurst, Clark, and Lee (2015) noted that the interfaces to such systems are often 2D controls on a touchscreen, allowing the user to filter layers of information or turn certain augmentations on and off. This class of applications encompasses the majority of AR systems since most are situated visualization viewers where all the user does is look around the environment for augmentations. An example relating to aging and health might be looking through a tablet at a meal choice at a restaurant. The AR display could show nutrition information and portion size on each food item. The user could turn off the nutrition information layer on the tablet, leaving only portion size remaining. A caveat is that more information is not necessarily better for information browser interfaces. It is easy to make the 2D interface unwieldy or difficult to operate while looking "through" the tablet or phone display.

Natural interfaces and 3D interfaces

Natural interfaces allow body movements to be used as input for the AR display. For example, a pinching motion on a tablet can allow a user to pick up a virtual item in AR or a spreading movement of the fingers can increase the size of a virtual item in AR. Natural interfaces allow for the body to be the input device and take away the need for other physical items or devices for interacting with the AR interface. The most widely known commercial example of this type of interface is the *Microsoft Kinect* gaming system. For some of the available games, player motion is mapped directly to the motion of an avatar on the screen for gesture-based control (e.g., the player raises their arm and the avatar raises their arm). Gesture-based controls may have cognitive benefits as well—being able to use gestures when explaining math problems has been shown to reduce the load on working memory (Cook, Yip, & Goldin-Meadow, 2012) and seems to aid memory in general (Cook, Nusbaum, & Goldin-Meadow, 2004). A similar literature on performing actions or imagining performing actions also indicates that gestures support learning and memory (Schmidt & Wrisberg, 2008). There are no studies yet of gesture-based natural interfaces supporting learning or memory or reducing load while learning, but the related literatures point toward a potential benefit. This is particularly interesting when brainstorming how to extend these results to AR for older adults. If gesture-based communication reduces working memory demands, gesture-based

AR interfaces may help to reduce the complexity of health management tasks. In the human factors literature, we often call these natural interfaces "direct input" devices.

Previous research suggested that direct interaction methods, such as using a touchscreen or stylus, are most suitable for older users (Charness, Holley, Feddon, & Jastrzembski, 2002; McLaughlin, Gandy, Allaire, & Whitlock, 2012; Rogers, Fisk, McLaughlin, & Pak, 2005). In the study by Charness et al., older adult performance was compared using a computer mouse or a light pen (essentially the same as a stylus.) Older users were faster and more accurate with the direct input device—the light pen. The benefit of direct devices made sense, as indirect devices involve mental and physical translation (i.e., moving a mouse forward moves it "up" on the screen and moving it a few inches on a mousepad moves it many inches across the display). There have been technological advances since then that also likely tip the scales in favor of direct input devices. In the 2002 study, participants were working with an upright screen. This is understandably more tiring with a direct device because the arm must be kept in the air. Current tablets and tablet-PCs such as the *Microsoft Surface* can be used comfortably on a table or lap.

McLaughlin, Rogers, and Fisk (2009) found that it was more important to match the type of input device (direct or indirect) to the type of task than it was to choose a particular input device for older adults. Older adults were faster to change settings on an interface when given an indirect device (a knob) when those settings required repetitive motion on a direct device (a touchscreen) (multiple taps). They were faster to operate an interface that just needed an activating tap or swipe if given a touchscreen instead of a knob.

Though the interface used in the study was not AR, similar indirect controls can be built into an AR interaction. For example, using input devices such as controllers (e.g., VR controllers such as the *Oculus Touch* controllers) to manipulate objects would be considered indirect. Even a device traditionally considered direct (the touchscreen on a tablet) can have indirect controls on it for AR where a movement on the tablet is translated to an action. For example, if AR is being viewed through a tablet and it is desirable to rotate an augmentation shown through the screen, this can be done by touching arrows on the 2D interface of the tablet. Because the arrows translate the tapping movement of the finger to a rotation of an object, it is an indirect input.

Another affordance of 3D interfaces is their tacit encouragement of physical exploration. Providing interfaces and devices that a user can interact with in 3D space encourages manipulation of objects (Piekarski, 2006). Further, when 3D AR visualizations allow 3D interaction (e.g., picking up, rotating, perspective change), this heightens the situatedness of the user—their connection to the natural world (Avery, Thomas, & Piekarski, 2008). We can assume (with caution) that many tasks in virtual and mixed reality will have similar results in AR (e.g., Lee, Rincon, Meyer, Höllerer, & Bowman, 2013). For example, Bisson, Contant, Sveistrup, and Lajoie (2007) explored the use of augmented virtuality (a type of mixed reality that integrates real objects into a virtual world) to successfully train and improve balance in older adults using a game where older adults would lean to one side or another to hit virtual items on a screen. The intervention would be considered mixed instead of augmented or virtual reality because the person was able to see their real body in the virtual game environment—compare this to AR where a person would see an augmented body or object in a real environment. These older users saw improvements in balance after 10 weeks of training. AR could allow similar interactions by projecting virtual items into the real environment. For example, projecting a virtual ball to the right side of the body to allow for the same leaning as in the prior example. Thus, if we examine these results and results from similar studies, we can integrate their design suggestions into AR for safer and more useful base designs for experiments with AR in older adults. Some researchers are currently exploring the use of virtual reality simulation environments to run AR studies. For example, one group of researchers explored the effects of AR visualizations for older adults in a driving environment (Schall et al., 2013). Because this environment is potentially dangerous to test in, the researchers used a driving simulator (VR) to provide a safe environment to test the AR visualizations. A potential drawback to 3D interfaces is that they often have unintentionally hidden information due to their dimensions. If a user does not investigate, or does not know to investigate, the other sides of a 3D interface, they may not receive the intended information or experience from the AR.

Tangible interfaces

Tangible interfaces take 3D interaction further through physical interaction with real objects. These types of interfaces involve the mapping of virtual elements by AR onto physical objects and the manipulation of these physical items in the real world to change the display of the virtual elements (Billinghurst, Grasset, & Looser, 2005). For example, if a medical device is accompanied by an AR manual, the user can see instructional projections of images above the page and they can interact with the manual to change, inspect, and rotate the image, or flip the page to remove the image or display a new one on another page. One of the first types of tangible interfaces was marker-based and consisted of a series of physical cards that users would move and place to interact with the display (Kato, Billinghurst, Poupyrev, Imamoto, & Tachibana, 2000). These marked cards allowed for 3D exploration through physical handling. Some manipulation methods suggested by the investigators included (1) inclining, (2) pushing down, (3) picking and pulling, (4) and shaking. These interactions with the virtual elements should lead to expected outcomes for users. For example, when inclining a card, any augmented object registered on the card should slide down the side of the card. When shaking the card, it may clear the card or change to a new object. Drawbacks are similar to those of 3D interfaces: when not all information is shown the user may not know it's possible to investigate further by handling the tangible interface.

Multimodal interfaces

Multimodal interfaces (MMIs) combine different input modalities (e.g., gesture, speech, eye gaze) to allow for more than one type of interaction using the same display. Irawati, Green, Billinghurst, Duenser, and Ko (2006) conducted a study using MMIs and found that participants were able to complete tasks with both gesture and voice inputs 35% faster than with gesture alone. This is beneficial to users who may need to perform multiple tasks or who may not know how to complete a task using a single input modality. MMIs are also useful to those who have issues with one or more senses: Those with impaired vision can utilize more of the auditory aspects of an interface, for example. One study incorporated audio in AR clothing for a role-playing patient that taught doctors to recognize the sound of a heart murmur (See, Billinghurst, Rengganaten, & Soo, 2016). Another, *Geo-Docent,* tags AR multimodal content to the environment (Chapman, Riddle, & Merlo, 2009). Users can access recordings of video and audio about the environment while they explore and other users can access that audio and video when they near the same locations.

Another study examined the usability of gesture and/or voice input for an AR display (Lee, Billinghurst, Baek, Green, & Woo, 2013). The researchers compared interaction with an AR display used to select and change the color and size of augmented objects. They compared the use of interfaces with only gestures, only voice, and an interface with both gesture and voice. From this work, they found that using that MMI, the users were faster at task completion than a gesture only interface, but no different than speech only. They also found that there were no differences in the number of errors committed by users, but that the users felt that the MMI was more natural, easy to use, and subjectively more effective than either of the other interfaces. The investigators also noted that speech commands were more helpful for descriptive commands, but that the gesture-based commands were better for spatial tasks. Thus, it is important to consider the task modality when integrating input modalities.

Issues with MMIs tend to be practical. To involve vision, hearing, and touch, these interfaces often need more sensors, speakers, and displays than other AR interfaces.

Social/collaborative interfaces

Social interfaces are those in which information from others is visible to the user, impacts the user's display, and/or influences the user to engage in certain behaviors. *Geo-Docent,* mentioned in the previous section, is a social/collaborative AR program. Collaborative AR interfaces can be socially co-located (all users are present in the same space) or socially remote (users are present in different spaces) and the interaction can be synchronous, where all users interact at the same time, or asynchronous. One example of a social application in AR is *WearCom,* a program that allows remote users to work together in synchronous time by projecting three-dimensional avatars of remote participants into the conference room (Billinghurst & Kato, 1999). Another AR system was created by Lukosch, Lukosch, Datcu, and Cidota (2015) to test how an individual and a remote viewer would work together on a highly detailed, spatial task (investigating a crime scene). Generally successful, those using the AR system were able to work together and reported high situational awareness via AR (though the system did increase subjective workload for the remote and present users.) It is not a difficult extension to imagine a similar system aiding the caretaker of an older adult family member in working together to solve a complex home or health task. A benefit of using AR rather than VR or teleconferencing is that AR produces higher feelings of social immersion (Billinghurst & Thomas, 2011). The roles of social support and social pressure are well-studied in the health psychology literature (e.g., Antonucci, 2001; Hayslip, Blumenthal, & Garner, 2015), making a socially present AR program likely desirable to bring people together.

Mirror interfaces

An AR "mirror" interface is a display (usually a computer screen) that mirrors the world in front of it through use of a camera. Looking into a mirror AR interface one can see oneself and the environment around and behind. The AR augmentation is to "mark up" what is viewable in the mirror-camera. For example, AR mirror displays allow users to virtually preview makeup (Rahman, Tran, Hossain, & El Saddik, 2010), jewelry (Chu, Dalal, Walendowski, & Begole, 2010), clothes (Begole et al., 2009; Eisert, Rurainsky, & Fechteler, 2007; Zhang, Begole, Chu, Liu, & Yee, 2008), and glasses (Yuan, Khan, Farbiz, Niswar, & Huang, 2011). AR mirrors can age a user's face (Kitanovski & Izquierdo, 2011), instruct in martial arts (Hämäläinen, Ilmonen, Höysniemi, Lindholm, & Nykänen, 2005) or assist in playing an instrument (Ng et al., 2007). One drawback to AR mirror systems is that they require larger displays or as well as precisely calibrated cameras and lighting, meaning they are less portable than other types of AR.

Information visualization across interfaces

Evaluation of AR visualization techniques has often focused on perception (e.g., depth and spatial perception; Avery, Sandor, & Thomas, 2009; Sandor, Cunningham, Dey, & Mattila, 2010). Mendez and Schmalstieg (2009) developed a variety of techniques to create visualizations and warned against "naive" augmentations, designed to reveal hidden structures inside a physical object that inadvertently obscure context or lack depth cues. They concluded that an effective augmentation considers what parts of the physical world should be occluded by the virtual content and then controls the information added to the physical scene. Similarly, Kalkofen, Mendez, and Schmalstieg (2009) framed the relationship of real and virtual objects in AR visualization as one of focus + context; the goal is to either provide virtual context to a physical object or for the user to focus on a virtual object embedded in a physical context. For example, an empty plate could have overlaid virtual representations for the portion size of fruits, grains, vegetables, and proteins, as recommended by MyPlate (www.choosemyplate. gov; USDA, 2017), giving user a virtual context to guide their physical portioning. In almost the same task, a virtual food item could be shown alongside actual food already on a plate to encourage the right choices, using the physical context of other foods to add more meaning to the virtual content. And these augmentations approaches can adapt throughout the experience, changing as the user interacts with the physical and virtual content and explore it in different ways (e.g., adding more food to the plate, pointing at a virtual or physical item, moving the plate closer to the camera etc.). Others such as Zollmann et al. (2012) have used these "focus + context" interaction techniques to guide the design of 4-D AR elements that show changes over time.

AR visualization techniques have been explored in the medical domain, ranging from a full-body system to teach ultrasound techniques (Blum, Heining, Kutter, & Navab, 2009), to delicate needle biopsies (State et al., 1996), down to laparoscopy (Bichlmeier, Heining, Rustaee, & Navab, 2007). The results have shown that virtual augmentations situated *on the body* at a variety of scales are an effective presentation method for physiological information and that medical professionals and trainees can use AR systems efficiently. For example, Navab, Mitschke, and Schütz (1999) first demonstrated the use of AR for more accuracy using a C-arm, which is a device used to guide a needle to a specific area of the body. Traditionally, to do this, physicians watch an ultrasound screen to see where the needle is in relation to the body. Providing the context of the body with AR allowed for higher accuracy and lower time to perform the procedure. Additional iterations on the design later revealed that users experienced increased depth perception when the virtual content was reduced to a small virtual "window" that allowed the user to look through the person's body (Erat et al., 2013). This work highlighted the importance of not overwhelming the user with virtual augmentations, but rather striking a delicate balance with the visual design between the virtual imagery and critical physical context.

Caution must be taken in assuming these medical visualization studies will apply directly to older adults' understanding of medicine and health. The target user in those systems was typically a medical expert, such as a doctor, nurse, or technician. The systems were designed either to train these experts or for use during live procedures. As a result, the virtual representations needed to be realistic and absolutely precise in registration representation. For example, one such study examined the use of VR and AR for a specific medical imaging procedure in 52 live surgeries (Okur, Ahmadi, Bigdelou, Wendler, & Navab, 2011). This visualization was used to guide medical professionals to specific areas in which a radioactive material was present to allow for a more accurate SPECT scan. These researchers found that AR visualization was used more often than VR visualization; however, they also noted that AR was used for more "big-picture" visualizations of what was happening in the body and more precise tasks were associated with more VR use.

Such system requirements differ from those for older adults managing health conditions, where the goal is for the user to gain a general understanding of their condition and knowledge and skills that will help them manage the condition. However, the medical domain does provide examples of proven techniques for conveying complex visual data of bodily process via AR and which rendering techniques work well in that context. For example, the *Mirracle* system is an AR mirror for teaching anatomy. The user sees a volumetric rendering of a CT dataset overlaid on their body and gestures to browse through "slices" of the self, augmented with 3D models of organs, text information, and images (Blum, Kleeberger, Bichlmeier, & Navab, 2012). This system works with the camera from the *Kinect* but is still a proof of concept rather than a system tested to see if it helps anatomy students learn. However, users were successful in interacting with the system to browse their body, showing that the interaction techniques were sound.

AR affordances and age-related changes in abilities

All of these AR interfaces, information visualizations, and interaction designs are viable for use by older persons, however designers must map the affordances of the interface to the needs of the user and the type of task being performed. Virtually no work has been done to assess older adult use of AR. However, to inform these fields we can turn to the well-established literature on age-related changes in perception, cognition, and movement ability to present the older adult needs that AR must support.

Cognitive factors

Adult cognition may be divided into two categories: crystallized intelligence and fluid abilities (Horn & Cattell, 1967). Crystallized intelligence refers to the amassing of knowledge across the lifespan, from declarative knowledge such as historical facts and general knowledge about the world to social knowledge, such as how to deal with or interpret the actions of others (Carstensen, Fung, & Charles, 2003; Scheibe & Blanchard-Fields, 2009; Urry & Gross, 2010). Seeing a wooden block with a letter on it and knowing that it is highly likely the other sides of the block also contain letters would be an example of this kind of intelligence as is the knowledge that a waving avatar is giving a greeting. Thus, it is possible to see how crystallized knowledge could be leveraged in the design of AR for older adults. Objects, such as blocks, can retain their real-world properties in AR even when they are added as an electronic augmentation to an environment. Plates, utensils, and food are all familiar items with predictable properties, helping the AR user to understand what can be done with them, often without instruction. Of course, in poorly designed AR (where familiar objects take on unfamiliar uses or don't allow expected interactions), older users may be adversely impacted by their dependence on crystallized intelligence to inform the interaction. Many of the types of AR interfaces (information browsers, natural interfaces, tangible interfaces, mirror interfaces) can incorporate the crystallized knowledge of the user for what interactions are available and what real-world objects are prior to being augmented, so the information display and controls are grounded in an understanding of the world. For example, projecting an AR "scale" on the ground would make it likely instantly understandable that one should step on it.

Fluid abilities include attention, spatial abilities, response time, reasoning, perceptual speed, visual search, memory recall, and numerical ability (Christensen et al., 1994; Finkel, Reynolds, McArdle, Gatz, & Pedersen, 2003; Finkel, Reynolds, McArdle, & Pedersen, 2007; Fisk, Hertzog, Lee, Rogers, & Anderson-Garlach, 1994; Hertzog, Dixon, Hultsch, & MacDonald, 2003; Schaie, 2005; Wilson et al., 2002; Rogers, 1992; Rogers & Fisk, 1991). These abilities tend to show age-related decline. Within the overarching category of attention there are several subabilities that are separable in how much they may be called upon to interact with an AR system. The subabilities specific to use of AR are likely working memory capacity (Hasher & Zacks, 1988), attentional control (Kane, Bleckley, Conway, & Engle, 2001; Milham et al., 2002), inhibition of unnecessary information (Hasher & Zacks, 1988), and the unprompted recall of long-term memory (Craik, 1983; Lindenberger & Mayr, 2014). Appropriately designed AR can support tasks that require these abilities. For example, many medications have multiple rules (with high working memory demands) that need to be integrated into a regimen (e.g., do not take with food, take twice a day, do not eat grapefruit while taking this medication, take with a meal, take if X symptom appears, stop taking if X symptom appears, do not take this medication if you drink three or more alcoholic beverages per day). The AARP reports that persons over 45 are managing an average of four different medications each day (AARP, 2005), meaning that planning and executing a regimen is challenging and error prone (Morrow et al., 2012). Studies show at least half of older adults do not take their medications correctly (Cutler & Everett, 2010; Morrow & Wilson, 2010).

Looking back through the affordances of AR interfaces, we can speculate how each might be harnessed to support lower working memory capacity, issues with attentional control and inhibition, and recall in medication tasks. For example, information browser interfaces can be mapped to show information about each medication as it is being examined, including records of when it was last taken or needs to be taken in the future. This augmentation could provide more information than the label on the bottle, but only what is important to the individual user. Pills themselves can be TUIs: Imagine the information about each pill responds to being in proximity to another. Pills sorted together on a table could warn the user about possible interactions. With a social or collaborative interface, a caregiver or healthcare provider could place or sort medications in their own space that then are shown to the patient in his or her own space, with appropriate groupings and instructions. AR allows faster localization of objects than other displays (i.e., LCD, HUD; Henderson & Feiner, 2009), meaning that the older user can be oriented to what needs their attention and extra information can be suppressed. All of these interfaces should reduce the load on the working memory of the user, their need for long-term recall of instructions or past behavior, and helping them to ignore information in the instructions or environment that doesn't apply to the current task.

The augmentations in AR should still be chosen carefully to avoid overloading the user with information. As another example of applying the literature on cognitive aging to the potential design of AR, previous research suggests that older adults tend to compensate for slowed visual search by using a serial scanning mechanism instead of a parallel processing mechanism (Gottlob & Madden, 1999). Thus, clutter in AR could be especially detrimental to older user performance due to serial scanning of each item. However, the affordances of AR, such as highlighting or otherwise making a target more salient, can help older users avoid the need for serial scanning. For example, if a diabetes diet is desired, low carbohydrate foods could be highlighted inside a refrigerator while less-desirable foods are dimmed.

Changes in learning associated with age are linked to changes in fluid abilities. This affects the acquisition of both knowledge and skill. One way to reduce the demands on fluid abilities is to provide more structured or repetitive learning, typically in the form of worked examples (Paas & Van Merriënboer, 1993; Sweller, 1988). Use of such prescribed content tends to result in greater performance for older adults compared to conceptual instruction or discovery-based learning (Morrell, Park, Mayhorn, & Kelley, 2000; Rogers, Campbell, & Pak, 2001). Unfortunately, such specific instruction also tends to result in "route following" behavior and when attributes of the task change, even superficially, the route follower is more easily confused than one with a conceptual understanding. Thus, in managing a complex health condition, highly specific training may be sufficient for tasks that never change but insufficient when the person is faced with a new situation that requires problem solving. Klein and Lippa (2008) called for conceptual training methods to be developed for older persons and suggested simulation training, which allows for a safe exploration of choices and has benefited training programs in aviation and medicine. AR is perfectly matched to the idea of simulations as it allows display of results from simulations as though they had actually happened. For example, a traditional display might allow the input of a meal and predict blood sugar changes, but an AR simulation can show those changes directly on (or a view inside) the body. The concern with such a system is that the older adult population is not selected in the same way as pilots or doctors; diabetes training must serve a large range of ability levels and simulations may not be appropriate for older adults due to the cognitive resources needed for trial-and-error exploration of a simulation (Klein & Lippa, 2008).

Perceptual factors

Age-related changes in perception are numerous, including visual changes, hearing changes, proprioceptive changes, and changes in the sense of touch (Schaie & Willis, 2016). The solutions that compensate for these losses tend to be technological: bifocals are a common solution for increased farsightedness, though they can make reading displays more difficult. Hearing aids bring back lost frequencies, but can be difficult to pair with headphones or other technologies. Solutions for balance include ramps and hand bars. The main benefits of AR for perceptual factors are that (1) AR can be adjusted to suit the perceptual ability of the user and (2) perceptual modalities can be added that would not be present without AR. For example, words shown in an information browsing display can be of any size or contrast, rather than being limited to a print size. MMIs can add visual, auditory, and haptic information to a display so that if the user has difficulty with one, there is information available through the other modalities. For example, AR paths can be shown on the ground to aid wayfinding and reduce the user's dependance on signage. Auditory AR can be triggered by being in certain locations, giving verbal guidance toward a room in a building, a car or transit location, or any number of desired targets.

This is not to say that perceptual difficulties have been solved for AR. Much of the literature in AR is on engineering better perceptual experiences, from providing more accurate depth perception of augmentations (e.g., Choi, Cho, Masamune, Hashizume, & Hong, 2015) to avoiding the sense that augmentations are "floating" rather than part of the environment (Furmanski, Azuma, & Daily, 2002), and how to reliably generate readable text on a multitude of complex backgrounds (Gabbard, Swan, & Hix, 2005; Gabbard et al., 2006; Leykin & Tuceryan, 2004). Progress continues on these problems but we believe that they need to be examined specifically for older adults rather than with the most common AR testers (students or adults younger than 35).

Movement factors

Age-related changes in movement are generally thought of as slowing—slowed reaction time, slowed choice-reaction time, and slower movements altogether (Verhaeghen, 2016). However, other age-related changes in movement include increased noise in the system, making for less accurate and controlled fine movements, some to the point of a diagnosis of tremor. There have been advances in traditional display and control technologies, such as "sticky" icons that draw a mouse cursor closer to them when it is nearby (Ahlström, Hitz, & Leitner, 2006; Worden, Walker, Bharat, & Hudson, 1997), and changing the gain on a computer mouse so that it moves more slowly to allow broader movements by the user to be translated into small movements by the cursor. These concepts should translate well to the affordances of AR interfaces. For example, a gesture-based interface can capture the ballistic movements of a user and interpret their intent. These gestures can be larger than the fine movements required for gesturing on a tablet touchscreen but accomplish the same task.

3D AR interfaces also allow exploration of objects and information without an input device as an intermediary *or* can allow any object to be that intermediary, such as a pen for pointing. This flexibility can allow appropriately designed AR to be matched to the movement capabilities of the user. For example, if an older user with movement control issues wanted to explore WebMD for medical information, they would be limited by the size of the clickable areas on the screen. An AR interface could display similar information on a tabletop, activated by an entire hand touching the target the user wants more information on. This translation of a website from a traditional display to being on a large physical object could also be augmented by 3D information when necessary—e.g., instead of showing a photo or illustration of a symptom from WebMD, it could be seen situated on a 3D body.

Table 11.1 provides a summary of previous research relating aging and AR. However, it is important to note that many of the topics researched in AR are more general and are not specific to the aging population. It is particularly important to discuss the implications of AR for older adults and the limitations of current AR systems for cognition, perception, and movement of older adults to provide a framework for future design of AR displays. The table provides a list of potential research questions yet to be answered.

Table 11.1 Age-related considerations for the design of AR

	Age-related change	AR knowns relevant to aging	AR unknowns for older adults
Cognition			
Attention	• Slowed attention allocation and preference for serial visual scanning (Gottlob & Madden, 1999) • Distracting information more detrimental as selective attention declines (Tipper, 1991) • Many components of attention decline (Braver & West, 2011)	• AR cueing increases attention to expected objects, but not unexpected ones (e.g., Yeh & Wickens, 2001) • Cueing increases detection of pedestrians and warning signs but not other vehicles in a driving task (Rusch et al., 2013) • AR allows faster localization of objects than other displays (i.e., LCD, HUD; Henderson & Feiner, 2009) • AR improves hazard detection by older adults during driving simulation, but does not interfere with secondary object detection or ability to maintain a safe distance from other drivers (Schall et al., 2013)	• How might AR utilize masking or hiding of unnecessary information to reduce cognitive load? • How should AR alerts be designed for older adults (e.g., while driving)? • Does use of AR require additional attention resources?
Working memory	• Working memory capacity decreases (Salthouse, 1994) • Compensatory strategies include using support from the external environment (e.g., checklists, timers, social cues; Hasher & Zacks, 1988)	• Reduction in spatial navigation errors and distraction in older adults using a simulated AR windshield for driving (Kim & Dey, 2009) • Spatial abilities improved from using an AR training tool due to gesture-based controls, spatial use of AR, 3D nature of display. This context also reduces cognitive load due to decreased complexity (Lee, Chen, & Chang, 2016)	• Can integrating objects, information, and location reduce working memory demands for health-related tasks? • How can we design AR to reduce the need for working memory in health tasks?
Long-term memory	• Knowledge preserved while fluid abilities decline (Horn & Cattell, 1967) • Memory for contextual information and source information decreases and the storage of such information is more effortful (Burke & Light, 1981)	• No research found on the impact of presenting information or experiences via AR on long-term memory of older adults	• How can AR remove short and long-term memory demands via virtual elements? • How should AR reminders and cues be integrated into the environment?

(Continued)

Table 11.1 (Continued)

	Age-related change	AR knowns relevant to aging	AR unknowns for older adults
	• Retrieval deficits present, especially without environmental support (e.g., Wingfield & Kahana, 2002) • Encoding deficits (e.g., Friedman, Nessler, & Johnson, 2007)		• Which health behaviors depend on long-term memory recall and how can they be assisted by AR?
Inhibition	• Difficult to ignore salient stimuli (e.g., flashing or brightly colored) (Hasher, Stoltzfus, Zacks, & Rypma, 1991; Hasher & Zacks, 1988; McDowd, 1997)	• Making the road more salient reduced some issues with multitasking for older drivers (Kim & Dey, 2016) • "Diminished reality" in AR attracts attention to the target by dimming real-world distractors (Ienaga et al., 2016)	• How can highlighting be used to simplify a complex environment or health task? • What should "diminished reality" look like to reduce clutter in the environment or health task? • How is "diminished reality" perceived by those who have age-related changes in vision? • Can AR displays increase inhibition of incorrect heuristics or recall (e.g., via masking or blocking) for health behaviors?
Perception			
Vision	• Decreased visual acuity (Klein, Klein, & Lee, 1996) • Increased prevalence of binocular vision and eye movement disorders (Leat et al., 2013) • Color vision deficits increase, especially blue-yellow deficits (Schneck, Haegerstrom-Portnoy, Lott, & Brabyn, 2014) • Loss of peripheral vision (e.g., glaucoma; Quigley & Broman, 2006) • Presbyopia (Glasser & Campbell, 1998) • Perception of motion (Tran, Silverman, Zimmerman, & Feldon, 1998)	• Allows 3D visualization of traditionally 2D information (e.g., Maps; Savova, 2016) • Allows projection of information to allow for better planning (Abhari et al., 2015) • Successfully increases restricted FOV (Vargas-Martín & Peli, 2002) • AR can change the amount of food consumed by augmenting the visual perception of the portion size (Narumi et al., 2012) • Depth information can be lost in AR and VR environments (e.g., Jones, Swan, Singh, Kolstad, & Ellis, 2008) • The brightness of an augmentation can make it difficult to see other real objects (Duh, Ma, & Billinghurst, 2006)	• How do people with bifocals perform with AR overlays? • How can age-related changes in acuity be supported by AR? • What types of AR depth cues can provide benefits to visual performance? • How should colors and contrast levels be chosen to best suit older adult users?

Sense	Age-related changes	AR applications	Questions
Touch	• Wickremaratchi and Llewelyn (2006) review overall changes in touch due to age • Thickening of skin on fingers (Carmeli, Patish, & Coleman, 2003) • Light touch threshold increased • Increased thermal pain threshold • Some vibration sense thresholds increased—light touch and pain preserved • Less fine touch sensation • Spatial acuity decreased	• Surgical tools can provide realistic haptic feedback and increase immersion during AR simulations (e.g., Lemole, Banerjee, Luciano, Neckrysh, & Charbel, 2007) • Haptics and tactile feedback through AR is developing and moving away from heavy wired gloves to TUIs (Bai, Lee, Ramakrishnan, & Billinghurst, 2014; Hürst & Vriens, 2013)	• How can augmented haptic information support age-related changes in touch sensitivity? • When a TUI is mapped to an object shaped differently than the augmentation, are there age differences in being able to translate it for use as an interface?
Hearing	• Presbycusis (NIDCD, 2016)—leads to decreased ability to hear high frequency sounds and decreased ability to differentiate words • Hearing loss is also linked to problems with memory (Tun, McCoy, & Wingfield, 2009)	• Augmented audio interfaces have been successfully used in museums and gaming to help with navigation and augmenting visual displays (e.g., Hatala, Kalantari, Wakkary, & Newby, 2004; Moustakas, Floros, & Grigoriou, 2011) • Audio in AR can be the entire experience, as in Voices of Oakland, a tour of a cemetery in Atlanta, GA (Dow et al., 2005)	• How does augmented audio need to be designed to support age-related changes in hearing? • Are there age differences in ability to use spatial audio from AR interfaces? • How does AR audio interact with hearing aids?
Proprioception	• Declines in proprioception (Skinner, Barrack, & Cook, 1984) • Balance more difficult especially when multitasking (Granacher, Muehlbauer, & Gruber, 2012) • Posture more unstable and compensatory strategies used (Granacher et al., 2012)	• AR was more effective for training balance exercises than a traditional training program (Im et al., 2015; Yoo, Chung, & Lee, 2013) • Many studies supporting AR for balance training (Bianco, Pedell, & Renda, 2016)	• How can AR be used to provide proprioceptive cues and feedback to help age-related changes in proprioception? • Does including AR elements in the environment affect balance or navigation for older persons?
Smell	• Increases in olfactory impairment (Murphy et al., 2002) • Smell and taste impairment in people with diabetes (e.g., Hillson, 2014)	• MetaCookie successfully provided augmentation of smell to change taste perception of foods (Narumi, Nishizaka, Kajinami, Tanikawa, & Hirose, 2011)	• Unclear how AR can provide benefits to age-related or diabetes-related olfactory changes • Can AR provide visual information that substitutes for age-related olfaction decline?

(Continued)

Table 11.1 (Continued)

	Age-related change	AR knowns relevant to aging	AR unknowns for older adults
Movement			
Movement time	• Generally slowed movements, particularly when task difficulty increases (Goggin & Meeuwsen, 1992)	• Engineering advances not caught up with human movements (e.g., difficult to track fingers, Hürst & Vriens, 2013) • Gestures are preferred interactions, but slower than using touchscreens (Bai et al., 2014) • Research on AR movement time not conducted with older users	• How can AR provide assistance with age-related general movement slowing? • How should AR interfaces be designed to accommodate slower gestures and movements? • What are the effects of making gestures indirectly related to their function in AR (e.g., large slow gestures could be translated to faster motions needed for a game)?
Movement control	• Less adaptation of velocity of movements or distances needed to travel (Ketcham, Seidler, Van Gemmert, & Stelmach, 2002) • More affected by changes in movement amplitude than target size (Ketcham et al., 2002; Ketcham & Stelmach, 2004) • Higher variability of movement termination location (Ketcham & Stelmach, 2004)	• AR has been used to rehabilitate loss of movement from stroke (de Assis, Corrêa, Martins, Pedrozo, & Lopes, 2016) • The broad movements often needed for AR/VR can be tiring (Jang, Stuerzlinger, Ambike, & Ramani, 2017)	• Can AR adapt to the increased variability in older adult movements (e.g., smooth jerky movements)? • Is AR accessible to persons with movement disorders? • How should AR interfaces be designed to capitalize on the preserved capabilities of older adults? • Can AR simulations be used to train coordination?
Strength	• Strength decreases (Metter, Conwit, Tobin, & Fozard, 1997) • Grasp force increases to compensate for slipperiness and higher variability in grip (Cole, Cook, Hynes, & Darling, 2010)	• No AR research dedicated to strength	• How does the use of AR change how older adults might interact with physical objects? • Does AR provide benefits for tasks that, with physical objects, would require more strength? • Can AR training promote gains or minimize loses to strength through augmented feedback or guidance

Posture and gait	• Severe perturbations affect posture and balance (Alexander, 1994) • Postural sway increases, particularly in complex balance (e.g., closing eyes; Alexander, 1994) • Gait speed slows, stride length shortens (JudgeRoy, Davis, & Õunpuu, 1996)	• AR visual cues may aid posture and gait for those with Parkinson's Disease (Espay et al., 2010)	• How can information provided using AR give proprioceptive and postural support? • How can AR provide walking support? • Can AR provide navigational cues to reduce cognitive load while walking?
Experience			
Knowledge	• Acquisition of new skills and knowledge is more difficult and takes longer (e.g., Smith et al., 2005) • Knowledge preserved while fluid abilities often decline (Horn & Cattell, 1967)	• AR has the potential to provide interesting experiences to help with encoding of new information. For example, exploring a cemetery using mixed-reality audio storytelling (Dow et al., 2005) • AR supports and increases engagement and learning through experiences in the real world (i.e., field trips) and increases student-centered learning (Kamarainen et al., 2013) • Most studies of presenting information via AR are not experiments and do not focus on older adults	• Can the literature on industrial training via AR be extended to older adult health behavior training?
Skills	• Skilled performance of learned tasks is well-preserved (e.g., Smith et al., 2005) • Social knowledge preserved (e.g., Carstensen et al., 2003)	• Though AR has been used to train skills in industry, no research on older adult skill acquisition could be found	• What are effective forms of feedback and practice for training via AR? • What is the impact of situated learning for skills acquired using AR? • How can AR design allow for skill practice for varied tasks via simulations? • What health tasks are most amenable to AR simulation?

Each age-related change is paired with what is known in relation to design of AR and what is still unknown regarding the design of AR for older adults.

Type 2 diabetes: A case study for AR, aging, and health

The case study presented is an overview of the challenges older adults face when diagnosed with type 2 diabetes and the (speculative) specific ways in which AR can be used to ameliorate these challenges.

By 2050 the number of adults over 60 will outnumber those under age 15 for the first time in history (CDC, 2011). With advanced age often comes health challenges and the need to manage complex health conditions. These health conditions require the acquisition of new knowledge, skills, and the motivation to change long-standing behaviors. It is not surprising that individuals fail in many cases: older adults experience frequent hospital readmissions and adverse events related to poor medication adherence (e.g., Gurwitz et al., 2003). With new conditions, chronic and otherwise, comes the need for new skills and knowledge to manage health and the need to change behavior.

One of the most complex health conditions to manage, and one often diagnosed in older age, is type 2 diabetes. Nearly 27% of persons over 65 have diabetes and a further 40% have prediabetes (Chan, 2011; Cowie et al., 2009). The difficulties of self-management for older adults with diabetes are not surprising given the intense cognitive, physical, and motivational task demands of the disease (Polly, 1992). Diabetes self-management is an especially difficult task as the effects of diabetes are often asymptomatic in the short term, making it challenging for a patient to understand the impact of daily choices on health. Further, the practice needed to comply with self-management recommendations balanced with each person's life-style can be dangerous as deviation from optimal blood sugar has a lasting deleterious effect on the body.

The good news for persons with type 2 diabetes is that symptoms and complications are linked to behavior. Accurate self-management, including carbohydrate management and diet, can delay onset or even prevent diabetes for those at high risk (DPPRG, 2002; Lindström et al., 2003) and greatly reduce (or eliminate symptoms) in those diagnosed with the disease (Steven et al., 2016). Unfortunately, few people self-manage well due to difficulty understanding complex recommendations, difficulty acquiring diabetes-related skills (Cavanaugh et al., 2008; Shigaki et al., 2010), and barriers such as a lack of feedback on their choices and difficulty maintaining motivation (Glasgow, Toobert, & Gillette, 2001).

Cognitive demands of managing diabetes

Understanding the variables affecting diabetic symptoms requires knowledge of numerous rules as well as the skill to use a variety of technologies (e.g., glucose meters, insulin pens, carbohydrate charts). Simple rules can be applied (e.g., avoid high-sugar foods), but many rules are more complex (e.g., exercise improves insulin response but over-exercise harms insulin response; insulin response changes when under stress or ill). The disease itself increases the challenge, as poor self-management of blood sugar impacts decision-making and cognitive ability (Ryan,

Williams, Feingold, & Orchard, 1993; Stewart & Liolitsa, 1999). Thus, the patients most in need of good management likely have the most difficulty doing so. Technology designed to make self-management easier is often not designed well for older users, requiring many steps and providing ill-designed feedback for errors (e.g., Rogers, Mykityshyn, Campbell, & Fisk, 2001). The outcome from this mixture of complex tasks, impacted cognition, and poorly designed technology is not surprising: even health-literate older adults mismanage self-care, relying on incorrect heuristics rather than developing an understanding of how their behaviors directly affect blood sugar levels and long-term disease outcomes (Boren, 2009; Klein & Meininger, 2004; Shigaki et al., 2010).

Klein and Meininger (2004) interviewed older persons with type 2 diabetes for their strategies in management, finding a dangerous predilection toward relying on a single, simple, but often incorrect, heuristic. For example, one patient knew that a lower blood sugar level was desirable, but having no idea how to properly achieve that goal, went without eating at all. Another thought that eating a sweet snack was the answer to either high or low blood sugar. All of these patients had received prior training from their healthcare providers or a diabetes educator, but all lacked continuous support or access to retraining in their day to day lives.

Perceptual and physical demands

Many of the perceptual and physical demands for managing type 2 diabetes are present in the environment and many are present in the technology specific to self-management. For example, the largest and most impactful task regarding self-management is food choice and amount. Successfully adhering to dietary recommendations depends on prior experience and knowledge, reading labels, reading measurements, and physically measuring food and medicine. A 2014 study found that 20 out of every 1000 persons over 65 with diabetes had visited an emergency room due to misuse of insulin (Geller et al., 2014) and it can be assumed that many more misused insulin but did not visit the ER. Clearly, matching insulin dose with a doctor's instructions and the amount of carbohydrates eaten is challenging. On the technology side, properly using self-management technologies often means gathering a drop of blood for glucose analysis where too much or too little blood on a test strip can cause a misreading. The visual and movement demands of measuring blood sugar are high. Reading and interpreting the results is also visually intensive, as is the reading of food labels and serving sizes. All of these challenging perceptual tasks must be carried out by older adults who are often suffering diabetes-related visual problems on top of normal age-related vision change.

Feedback and motivation

Last, across all of the cognitive, perceptual, and physical demands of self-management are motivational demands. Most obviously, these include hunger, preferences for nonrecommended foods, and a lifetime of habits in food choices that the older person is being asked to change. Though immediate feedback is recommended to help change health behaviors (Eriksen, Green, & Fultz, 1988; Rabbi, Pfammatter, Zhang, Spring, & Choudhury, 2015), little feedback (or reward) is available for making daily food, exercise, and medication choices. For example, the gold standard of progress toward managing diabetes is the A1C measure, but this must be done by a healthcare provider and is only given to the patient at long intervals (often months apart). Blood sugar measurements are the closest a patient has to immediate feedback, but trial-and-error is not encouraged as high blood sugar has lasting harmful effects, even after being lowered. A single study on using AR feedback to train carbohydrate estimation found improvements after experience with the AR display (Domhardt et al., 2015). Though this likely supports the importance of feedback, the study contained only eight participants who all had type 1 diabetes.

Potential for AR to aid self-management for persons with diabetes

We close with a speculative example of designing AR to aid in self-management of type 2 diabetes, taking into account the cognitive, perceptual, and motivational challenges older adults likely face with the disease. A promising solution is the introduction of technologies that allow older learners to experience successes and failures of health management in a safe setting: an AR simulation. In addition, AR can allow learners to see otherwise hidden information in their own bodies, providing an available and accessible platform for noninvasive investigation of bodily processes. AR can also allow for feedback on choices via simulation, so that the user can practice choices and learn from them. Last, AR can be designed to be easily tailored to the user: highly readable text, multimodal displays and interfaces, and situated in the environment of the individual.

An AR interface offering information display, natural interactions, and simulations is an AR Mirror (Hill, Barba, MacIntyre, Gandy, & Davidson, 2011). Using the mirror, older adults may see themselves and their environment reflected with additional information (Fig. 11.3). The AR mirror is a familiar metaphor, leveraging their many years of experience with real mirrors. For example, they may choose a plate of food and put it in front of the AR mirror to see how well they adhered to the American Diabetes Association (ADA) guidelines for protein, fat, and carbohydrates (ADA, 2013). Feedback can be displayed in multiple ways: on the plate as a whole or for each of the individual foods. Food could even be chosen virtually for practice, then appearing as though it is on a plate in front of the user (but only in the mirror) with feedback on choice of food and amount. It is easy to conceptualize practice and training programs utilizing this affordance of AR. Pointing at objects seen in the mirror, whether they be food or other objects in the environment, can trigger information displays on those items. The effects of a plate of food can be displayed on the body, changing exterior appearance (e.g., aging, weight) or inside the body, showing the actions of fats and carbohydrates on the organs or insulin levels. This essentially turns the person into a 3D tangible user interface, able to turn and point at different organs or areas of interest in their own body.

Figure 11.3 Mockup of a hypothetical AR mirror for diabetes nutrition education. Internal physiology and nutrition information are *situated* (i.e., visually registered) in real-time with the body and food. An *embodied interaction* (e.g., pointing) near the liver provides information at a different *physical scale* (e.g., cellular) and supports visual comparison of stages of the disease. Heads up display interface elements such as the slider allow exploration of body changes at different *timescales*. A plate of food provides input for the *simulation*. Selecting, portioning the food, and pointing with the fork are a *tangible user interface*. Such a hypothetical interface demonstrates the flexibility of AR HCI but leaves many unknowns for matching the design to suit a user's needs.

In sum, three specific affordances of information and feedback via an AR mirror could be used to teach or support diabetes self-management at older ages: control over time scale, physical scale, and the level of detail/abstraction shown.

1. *Time scale.* Many chronic diseases are linked to choices that affect physiology from the short term (minutes) to the long term (decades), but it can be difficult to comprehend these timescales when making day-to-day decisions. Biological feedback on lifestyle choices, such as diet and exercise, can be extremely delayed. Using AR, this feedback can be shown at any time scale, e.g., the effects of sun on the skin over many years of exposure or what incremental damage dietary choices have on the circulatory system. Various timescales for diabetes can be shown using the AR mirror, e.g., a simulation of what one will look like across ten years of a current diet versus ten years of a recommended diet. A caveat is that although AR is often called upon to convey changes over time (Zollmann et al., 2012) it remains an open question regarding how best to show such changes and how to permit the user to change or move through different timescales.
2. *Physical scale.* Health information can be provided at vastly different scales, from the entire body, to an organ system, to the cellular level. One could imagine an AR "microscope," able to present the effects of exercise, medications, or diet on the body at all levels. Also, because AR is a combination of physical items, virtual items, and information it is possible to situate objects and information in closer proximity than would be possible using only physical items. For example, looking up nutrition information online or

in a booklet presents the information on a display, while the food in question is on the table. AR would allow that information to be situated *on* the food itself. Physical scale of the body can be altered as well, bringing an organ or joint inside the body "out" to show at a larger size. Support for the effectiveness of such situatedness comes from *AnatOnMe*, where AR supported doctor/patient communication was explored in an experiment comparing the visual presentation of medical concepts to patients by projection on the wall (onto an outline of a body), onto a physical model of a body, or onto the patient's body (Ni, Karlson, & Wigdor, 2011). The results showed the body and model conditions were more desirable to patients across several measures. The patient's knee joint was no longer an abstracted diagram on a wall, it was *their* knee, seen and discussed inside their own body.

AR medical visualization research includes examples of systems that work at large and small scales (or support browsing layered views such as MRI data; Blum et al., 2012), but most are intended to be used at a single scale (Ni et al., 2011). For AR, it is unknown how to present changing scale in ways easily understandable by OA users (e.g., a zoomed view connected to the body via a leader line), but it is clear that a variety of scales can be useful for presenting information.

3. *Level of detail and abstraction*: When showing any object in an altered way the AR can also change the level of detail or abstraction, matching it to the current goal. For example, a too-realistic pancreas may be hard to understand when shown, but an abstracted diagram of one can still be situated "in" the body of the user. Or perhaps the user has been told to reduce carbohydrate intake but not pay attention to protein or fat—the interface can be tuned to provide the amount of detail needed. AR allows for a wide range of detail level and abstraction but it is necessary to know how the various levels translate to knowledge/skill increases and other measures of health management, such as motivation or adherence. For example, if a visualization is of a biological process, should the augmentations present high level information such as observable symptoms (e.g., nausea), lower level information (e.g., fluctuations of insulin levels), or the chemical processes at a cellular level? All levels of detail can be shown via AR but research is lacking on the information or motivations they convey to a user. The level of abstraction is another important HCI consideration. For example, production of insulin in the pancreas could be shown realistically (e.g., medical illustration), moderately abstracted (e.g., simple shapes, not necessarily of proper scale), or very abstracted (e.g., an anthropomorphized cartoon acts out the process).

Because there is no AR-specific research on levels of abstraction and older adult learning we must turn to more established domains. Animations, for example, often do not result in more learning than static pictures (Tversky, Morrison, & Betrancourt, 2002). One way to improve educational animations is to provide the user with a mental representation of the system by having their movements control or interact with the representation (de Koning & Tabbers, 2011). This can be done through AR, such as holding a model and receiving virtual information, or through natural gestures, such as making movements that map to the information being learned. Further, based on embodied theories of cognition, experiences will be more effective if the movements in the visualization are embodied by the users' movements, with specific guidelines for embodiment strategies that improve animated visualizations (de Koning & Tabbers, 2011). The importance of gesture is echoed in the educational literature, as gestures during learning encourage mental models (Beilock & Goldin-Meadow, 2010; Hostetter & Alibali, 2008). However, theories of embodied interfaces and their educational benefits need testing with a variety of users, particularly OAs.

This hypothetical AR interface is founded in the literature on aging and interaction with technology, but it is important to stress that they need to be tested. As with many new technologies, engineering is quickly outpacing our knowledge of how to make systems usable. It will soon not be a question of whether we can make such a system, but should we and if so, how?

Conclusion

AR is a promising technology coming of age in the commercial world. Because it allows for embedding information and action in an already present environmental context, it has the potential to be particularly effective for older users managing their health. One especially promising avenue is the ability to provide seemingly "real-world" simulations of daily decisions and tasks, allowing older users to develop their health management skills in a safe environment.

This is not to say AR will be a panacea: there are a number of difficulties yet to overcome, from the engineering of less cumbersome devices to the HCI questions of display and interaction. AR may add no benefit for decisions or tasks that are well-suited to traditional screen displays, such as feedback on progress over time via graphs or searching for text information on a condition. But for tasks that are embedded in the physical world or where there are learning benefits from simulations, AR shows high promise. Because of the capabilities and limitations that tend to come with age, interventions and technologies made for younger adults cannot be directly transferred (Fisk, Rogers, Charness, Czaja, & Sharit, 2009). This is why the person capabilities such as *cognition, perception,* and *movement ability* must be considered in design of AR technology.

Principles for AR design for older users

In closing, we offer four important considerations for implementing AR for OA.

1. Target the tasks most likely to benefit from the introduction of AR: spatial tasks, wayfinding, tasks requiring information integration, simulations.
2. Consider age-related changes that may affect perception and understanding of displays via AR.
3. Consider age-related changes that may affect use of interfaces in AR.
4. Iteratively test designs with a range of older adults—keeping in mind that abilities become more heterogeneous with age.

It is our hope that this chapter will inspire future research on older adults' use of AR to manage their health, resulting in concrete guidelines for design. AR will become a normal part of life in the future, and research is needed to make sure it is useful and accessible to everyone.

References

AARP. (2005). *Prescription drug use among midlife and older Americans*. Retrieved from <https://assets.aarp.org/rgcenter/health/rx_midlife_plus.pdf>.

Abhari, K., Baxter, J. S., Chen, E. C., Khan, A. R., Peters, T. M., de Ribaupierre, S., & Eagleson, R. (2015). Training for planning tumour resection: Augmented reality and human factors. *IEEE Transactions on Biomedical Engineering, 62*(6), 1466–1477.

Ahlström, D., Hitz, M., & Leitner, G. (2006). *An evaluation of sticky and force enhanced targets in multi target situations*. In: *Proceedings of the 4th Nordic conference on Human-computer interaction: Changing roles* (pp. 58–67). ACM.

Alexander, N. B. (1994). Postural control in older adults. *Journal of the American Geriatrics Society, 42*(1), 93–108.

American Diabetes Association (ADA). (2013). *American Diabetes Association releases new nutritional guidelines. Statement notes: When it comes to nutrition, there is no "One Size Fits All"*. Retrieved from <http://www.diabetes.org/for-media/2013/american-diabetes-association-releases-nutritional-guidelines.html>.

Antonucci, T. (2001). Social relations: An examination of social networks, social support, and a sense of control. In J. E. Birren, & K. W. Schaie (Eds.), *Handbook of the psychology of aging* (pp. 427–453). San Diego, CA: Academic Press.

de Assis, G. A. D., Corrêa, A. G. D., Martins, M. B. R., Pedrozo, W. G., & Lopes, R. D. D. (2016). An augmented reality system for upper-limb post-stroke motor rehabilitation: A feasibility study. *Disability and Rehabilitation: Assistive Technology, 11*(6), 521–528.

AugmentedWorks. (2017). *Find your car with AR: Augmented car finder (Version 3.3.1)* [Mobile application software]. Retrieved from <https://itunes.apple.com/us/app/find-your-car-with-ar-augmented-car-finder/id370836023?mt = 8>.

Avery, B., Sandor, C., & Thomas, B. H. (March 2009). *Improving spatial perception for augmented reality X-ray vision*. In: *Proceedings of the IEEE 2009 virtual reality conference* (pp. 79–82). IEEE.

Avery, B., Thomas, B. H., & Piekarski, W. (2008). *User evaluation of see-through vision for mobile outdoor augmented reality*. In: *Proceedings of the 7th IEEE/ACM international symposium on mixed and augmented reality* (pp. 69–72). IEEE Computer Society.

Azuma, R. T. (1997). A survey of augmented reality. *Presence: Teleoperators and virtual environments, 6*(4), 355–385.

Bai, H., Lee, G. A., Ramakrishnan, M., & Billinghurst, M. (2014). *3D gesture interaction for handheld augmented reality*. SIGGRAPH Asia 2014 Mobile graphics and interactive applications (p. 7) New York: ACM.

Begole, B., Matsumoto, T., Zhang, W., Yee, N., Liu, J., & Chu, M. (2009). Designed to fit: Challenges of interaction design for clothes fitting room technologies. In: *Proceedings of the international conference on human-computer interaction* (pp. 448–457). Berlin, Heidelberg: Springer.

Beilock, S. L., & Goldin-Meadow, S. (2010). Gesture changes thought by grounding it in action. *Psychological Science, 21*(11), 1605–1610.

Bianco, M. L., Pedell, S., & Renda, G. (2016). Augmented reality and home modifications: A tool to empower older adults in fall prevention. In: *Proceedings of the 28th Australian conference on computer-human interaction* (pp. 499–507). ACM.

Bichlmeier, C., Heining, S. M., Rustaee, M., & Navab, N. (2007). Laparoscopic virtual mirror for understanding vessel structure evaluation study by twelve surgeons.

In: *Proceedings from the 6th IEEE and ACM international symposium on mixed and augmented reality* (pp. 125–128). IEEE.

Billinghurst, M., Clark, A., & Lee, G. (2015). A survey of augmented reality. *Foundations and Trends® Human–Computer Interaction, 8*(2–3), 73–272.

Billinghurst, M., Grasset, R., & Looser, J. (2005). Designing augmented reality interfaces. *ACM Siggraph Computer Graphics, 39*(1), 17–22.

Billinghurst, M., & Kato, H. (1999). Collaborative mixed reality. *Proceedings of the first International Symposium on Mixed Reality (ISMR '99)* (pp. 261–284). Berlin: Springer Verlag.

Billinghurst, M., & Thomas, B. H. (2011). Mobile collaborative augmented reality. *Recent trends of mobile collaborative augmented reality systems* (pp. 1–19). New York: Springer.

Bisson, E., Contant, B., Sveistrup, H., & Lajoie,, Y. (2007). Functional balance and dual-task reaction times in older adults are improved by virtual reality biofeedback training. *CyberPsychology and Behavior, 10*(1), 16–23.

Blum, T., Heining, S. M., Kutter, O., & Navab, N. (2009). Advanced training methods using an augmented reality ultrasound simulator. In *Paper presented at the 8th IEEE international symposium on mixed and augmented reality, Orlando, FL* (pp. 177–178).

Blum, T., Kleeberger, V., Bichlmeier, C., & Navab, N. (2012). mirracle: An augmented reality magic mirror system for anatomy education. In *Paper presented at the virtual reality short papers and posters, IEEE* (pp. 115–116).

Boren, S. A. (2009). A review of health literacy and diabetes: Opportunities for technology. *Journal of Diabetes Science and Technology, 3*(1), 202–209.

Braver, T. S., & West, R. (2011). Working memory, executive control, and aging. In F. I. Craik, & T. A. Salthouse (Eds.), *The handbook of aging and cognition*. New York: Psychology Press.

Burke, D. M., & Light, L. L. (1981). Memory and ageing: The role of retrieval processes. *Psychological Bulletin, 90*, 513–546.

Carmeli, E., Patish, H., & Coleman, R. (2003). The aging hand. *Journals of Gerontology (Series A) Biological Sciences and Medical Sciences, 58*(2), M146–M152.

Carstensen, L. L., Fung, H. H., & Charles, S. T. (2003). Socioemotional selectivity theory and the regulation of emotion in the second half of life. *Motivation and Emotion, 27*(2), 103–123.

Cavanaugh, K., Huizinga, M. M., Wallston, K. A., Gebretsadik, T., Shintani, A., Davis, D., ... Rothman, R. L. (2008). Association of numeracy and diabetes control. *Annals of Internal Medicine, 148*(10), 737–746.

Centers for Disease Control and Prevention. (2011). *National diabetes fact sheet: National estimates and general information on diabetes and prediabetes in the United States, 2011*. Retrieved May 17, 2013 from <http://www.who.int/ageing/publications/global_health.pdf>.

Chan, M. (2011). *The worldwide rise of chronic noncommunicable disease: A slow-motion catastrophe*. Retrieved May 17, 2013 from <http://www.who.int/dg/speeches/2011/ministerial_conf_ncd_20110428/>.

Chapman, R. J., Riddle, D. L., & Merlo, J. L. (2009). Techniques for supporting the author of outdoor mobile multimodal augmented reality. In *Proceedings of the Human Factors and Ergonomics Society 53rd annual meeting*, 2009–2013.

Charness, N., Holley, P., Feddon, J., & Jastrzembski, T. (2002). Input devices: Minimizing age differences in performance. *Gerontechnology, 2*(1), 88.

Choi, H., Cho, B., Masamune, K., Hashizume, M., & Hong, J. (2015). An effective visualization technique for depth perception in augmented reality-based surgical navigation. *The International Journal of Medical Robotics and Computer Assisted Surgery, 12*(1), 62–72.

Christensen, H., Mackinnon, A., Jorm, A. F., Henderson, A. S., Scott, L. R., & Korten, A. E. (1994). Age differences and interindividual variation in cognition in community-dwelling elderly. *Psychology and Aging, 9*(3), 381–390.

Chu, M., Dalal, B., Walendowski, A., & Begole, B. (2010). Countertop responsive mirror: Supporting physical retail shopping for sellers, buyers and companions. In *Proceedings of the 28th international conference on human factors in computing systems* (pp. 2533–2542).

Cole, K. J., Cook, K. M., Hynes, S. M., & Darling, W. G. (2010). Slowing of dexterous manipulation in old age: Force and kinematic findings from the 'nut-and-rod' task. *Experimental Brain Research, 201*(2), 239–247.

Cook, S. W., Nusbaum, H., & Goldin-Meadow, S. (2004). Probing the mental representation of gesture: Is handwaving spatial? *Journal of Memory and Language, 50*(4), 395–407.

Cook, S. W., Yip, T. K., & Goldin-Meadow, S. (2012). Gestures, but not meaningless movements, lighten working memory load when explaining math. *Language and Cognitive Processes, 27*(4), 594–610.

Cowie, C. C., Rust, K. F., Ford, E. S., Eberhardt, M. S., Byrd-Holt, D. D., Li, C., ... Geiss, L. S. (2009). Full accounting of diabetes and pre-diabetes in the U.S. population in 1988-1994 and 2005-2006. *Diabetes Care, 32*(2), 287–294.

Craik, F. I. M. (1983). On the transfer of information from temporary to permanent memory. *Philosophical Transactions of the Royal Society of London. Series B, Biological Sciences, B301*, 341–359. Available from http://dx.doi.org/10.1098/rstb.1983.0059.

Cutler, D. M., & Everett, W. (2010). Thinking outside the pillbox − Medication adherence as a priority for health care reform. *The New England Journal of Medicine, 362*, 1553–1555.

Diabetes Prevention Program Research Group (DPPRG). (2002). Reduction in the incidence of type 2 diabetes with lifestyle intervention or metformin. *The New England Journal of Medicine, 346*, 393–403.

Domhardt, M., Tiefengrabner, M., Dinic, R., Fötschl, U., Oostingh, G. J., Stütz, T., ... Ginzinger, S. W. (2015). Training of carbohydrate estimation for people with diabetes using mobile augmented reality. *Journal of Diabetes Science and Technology, 9*(3), 516–524.

Dow, S., Lee, J., Oezbek, C., Maclntyre, B., Bolter, J. D., & Gandy, M. (2005). Exploring spatial narratives and mixed reality experiences in Oakland cemetery. In *Proceedings of the 2005 ACM SIGCHI international conference on advances in computer entertainment technology* (pp. 51–60). Valencia, Spain, June 15-17, 2005.

Duh, H. B. L., Ma, J., & Billinghurst, M. (2006). Human factors issues in augmented reality. In W. Karwowski (Ed.), *International encyclopedia of ergonomics and human factors*. London: Taylor & Francis.

Eisert, P., Rurainsky, J., & Fechteler, P. (2007). Virtual mirror: Real-time tracking of shoes in augmented reality environments. In *Paper presented at the IEEE international conference on image processing, San Antonio, TX* (pp. 557–560).

Erat, O., Pauly, O., Weidert, S., Thaller, P., Euler, E., Mutschler, W., ... Fallavollita, P. (2013). How a surgeon becomes superman by visualization of intelligently fused multimodalities. In *Proceedings from the SPIE medical imaging conference 2013: Image-guided procedures, robotic interventions, and modeling* (p. 8671).

Eriksen, M. P., Green, L. W., & Fultz, F. G. (1988). Principles of changing health behavior. *Cancer*, *62*(8 Suppl), 1768–1775.

Espay, A. J., Baram, Y., Dwivedi, A. K., Shukla, R., Gartner, M., Gaines, L., ... Revilla, F. J. (2010). At-home training with closed-loop augmented-reality cueing device for improving gait in patients with Parkinson disease. *Journal of Rehabilitation Research and Development*, *47*(6), 573.

Finkel, D., Reynolds, C. A., McArdle, J. J., Gatz, M., & Pedersen, N. L. (2003). Latent growth curve analyses of accelerating decline in cognitive abilities in late adulthood. *Developmental Psychology*, *39*(3), 535–550.

Finkel, D., Reynolds, C. A., McArdle, J. J., & Pedersen, N. L. (2007). Age changes in processing speed as a leading indicator of cognitive aging. *Psychology and Aging*, *22*(3), 558–568.

Fisk, A. D., Hertzog, C., Lee, M. D., Rogers, W. A., & Anderson-Garlach, M. (1994). Long-term retention of skilled visual search: Do young adults retain more than old adults? *Psychology and Aging*, *9*(2), 206–215.

Fisk, A. D., Rogers, W. A., Charness, N., Czaja, S. J., & Sharit, J. (2009). *Designing for OAs: Principles and creative human factors approaches*. Boca Raton, FL: CRC Press.

Friedman, D., Nessler, D., & Johnson, R., Jr (2007). Memory encoding and retrieval in the aging brain. *Clinical EEG and Neuroscience*, *38*(1), 2–7.

Furmanski, C., Azuma, R., & Daily, M. (2002). Augmented-reality visualizations guided by cognition: Perceptual heuristics for combining visible and obscured information. In *Proceedings of the IEEE and ACM International Symposium on Mixed and Augmented Reality (ISMAR 2002)* (pp. 215–224).

Gabbard, J. L., Swan, J. E., & Hix, D. (2006). The effects of text drawing styles, background textures, and natural lighting on text legibility in outdoor augmented reality. *Presence: Teleoperators and Virtual Environments*, *15*(1), 16–32.

Gabbard, J. L., Swan, J. E., Hix, D., Schulman, R. S., Lucas, J., & Gupta, D. (2005). An empirical user-based study of text drawing styles and outdoor background textures for augmented reality. In *Proceedings of the IEEE virtual reality* (pp. 11–18).

Geller, A. I., Shehab, N., Lovegrove, M. C., Kegler, S. R., Weidenbach, K. N., Ryan, G. J., & Budnitz, D. S. (2014). National estimates of insulin-related hypoglycemia and errors leading to emergency department visits and hospitalizations. *Journal of the American Medical Association: Internal Medicine*, *174*(5), 678–686. Available from http://dx.doi.org/10.1001/jamainternmed.2014.136.

Glasgow, R. E., Toobert, D. J., & Gillette, C. D. (2001). Psychosocial barriers to diabetes self-management and quality of life. *Diabetes Spectrum*, *14*(1), 33–41.

Glasser, A., & Campbell, M. C. (1998). Presbyopia and the optical changes in the human crystalline lens with age. *Vision Research*, *38*(2), 209–229.

Goggin, N. L., & Meeuwsen, H. J. (1992). Age-related differences in the control of spatial aiming movements. *Research Quarterly for Exercise and Sport*, *63*(4), 356–372.

Gottlob, L. R., & Madden, D. J. (1999). Age differences in the strategic allocation of visual attention. *The Journals of Gerontology*, *54B*(3), 165–172.

Granacher, U., Muehlbauer, T., & Gruber, M. (2012). A qualitative review of balance and strength performance in healthy older adults: Impact for testing and training. *Journal of Aging Research*, *2012*, 708905.

Gurwitz, J. H., Field, T. S., Harrold, L. R., Rothschild, J., Debellis, K., Seger, A. C., ... Bates, D. W. (2003). Incidence and preventability of adverse drug events among older persons in the ambulatory setting. *JAMA: The Journal of the American Medical Association*, *289*(9), 1107–1116.

Hämäläinen, P., Ilmonen, T., Höysniemi, J., Lindholm, M., & Nykänen, A. (April 2005). *Martial arts in artificial reality*. In: *Proceedings of the SIGCHI conference on Human factors in computing systems* (pp. 781–790). ACM.

Hasher, L., Stoltzfus, E. R., Zacks, R. T., & Rypma, B. (1991). Age and inhibition. *Journal of Experimental Psychology: Learning, Memory, and Cognition, 17*, 163–169.

Hasher, L., & Zacks, R. T. (1988). Working memory, comprehension, and aging: A review and a new view. In G. H. Bower (Ed.), *The psychology of learning and motivation* (Vol. 22, pp. 193–225). San Diego, CA: Academic Press.

Hatala, M., Kalantari, L., Wakkary, R., & Newby, K. (March 2004). *Ontology and rule based retrieval of sound objects in augmented audio reality system for museum visitors*. *Proceedings of the 2004 ACM symposium on Applied computing* (pp. 1045–1050). ACM.

Hayslip, B., Jr., Blumenthal, H., & Garner, A. (2015). Social support and grandparent caregiver health: One-year longitudinal findings for grandparents raising their grandchildren. *Journals of Gerontology: Series B, 70*(5), 804–812.

Henderson, S. J., & Feiner, S. (2008). Opportunistic controls: Leveraging natural affordances as Tangible User Interfaces for augmented reality. In *Proceedings of ACM Virtual Reality Software and Technology (VRST '08)* (pp. 211–218).

Henderson, S.J., & Feiner, S. (2009). Evaluating the benefits of augmented reality for task localization in maintenance of an armored personnel carrier turret. In *Proceedings of the 8th IEEE International Symposium of Mixed and Augmented Reality (ISMAR)* (pp. 135–144).

Hertzog, C., Dixon, R. A., Hultsch, D. F., & MacDonald, S. W. S. (2003). Latent change models of adult cognition: Are changes in processing speed and working memory associated with changes in episodic memory? *Psychology and Aging, 18*(4), 755–769.

Hill, A., Barba, E., MacIntyre, B., Gandy, M., & Davidson, B. (2011). Mirror worlds: Experimenting with heterogeneous AR. In *Paper presented at the 2011 international symposium on ubiquitous virtual reality, Jeju-si, Korea* (pp. 9–12).

Hillson, R. (2014). Taste and smell in diabetes. *Practical Diabetes, 31*(7), 269–270a.

Horn, J. L., & Cattell, R. B. (1967). Age differences in fluid and crystallized intelligence. *Acta Psychologica, 26*(2), 107–129.

Hostetter, A. B., & Alibali, M. W. (2008). Visible embodiment: Gestures as simulated action. *Psychonomic Bulletin & Review, 15*(3), 495–514.

Hürst, W., & Vriens, K. (2013). Mobile augmented reality interaction via finger tracking in a board game setting. In *Paper presented at the Mobile HCI 2013 AR-workshop, Designing Mobile Augmented Reality*.

Ienaga, N., Bork, F., Meerits, S., Mori, S., Fallavollita, P., Navab, N., & Saito, H. (2016). First deployment of diminished reality for anatomy education. In *Proceedings from the IEEE international symposium on mixed and augmented reality* (pp. 294–296).

Im, D. J., Ku, J., Kim, Y. J., Cho, S., Cho, Y. K., Lim, T., ... Kang, Y. J. (2015). Utility of a three-dimensional interactive augmented reality program for balance and mobility rehabilitation in the elderly: A feasibility study. *Annals of Rehabilitation Medicine, 39* (3), 462–472.

Irawati, S., Green, S., Billinghurst, M., Duenser, A., & Ko, H. (2006). An evaluation of an augmented reality multimodal interface using speech and paddle gestures. *Advances in Artificial Reality and Tele-Existence*, 272–283.

Jang, S., Stuerzlinger, W., Ambike, S., & Ramani, K. (2017). Modeling cumulative arm fatigue in mid-air interaction based on perceived exertion and kinetics of arm motion.

In: *Proceedings of the 2017 CHI conference on human factors in computing systems* (pp. 3328–3339). ACM.

Javornick, A., Rogers, Y., Moutinho, A. M., & Freeman, R. (2016). Revealing the shopper experience of using a 'Magic Mirror' augmented reality make-up application. In *Proceedings of the 2016 ACM conference on designing interactive systems* (pp. 871–882).

Jones, J. A., Swan, J. E., II, Singh, G., Kolstad, E., & Ellis, S. R. (2008). The effects of virtual reality, augmented reality, and motion parallax on egocentric depth perception. In: *Proceedings of the 5th symposium on Applied perception in graphics and visualization* (pp. 9–14). ACM.

JudgeRoy, J. O., Davis, B., & Õunpuu, S. (1996). Step length reductions in advanced age: The role of ankle and hip kinetics. *The Journals of Gerontology. Series A, Biological Sciences and Medical Sciences, 51A*(6), M303–M312.

Kalkofen, D., Mendez, E., & Schmalstieg, D. (2009). Comprehensible visualization for augmented reality. *IEEE Transactions on Visualization and Computer Graphics, 15*(2), 193–204.

Kamarainen, A. M., Metcalf, S., Grotzer, T., Browne, A., Mazzuca, D., Tutwiler, M. S., & Dede, C. (2013). EcoMOBILE: Integrating augmented reality and probeware with environmental education field trips. *Computers & Education, 68*, 545–556.

Kane, M. J., Bleckley, M. K., Conway, A. R., & Engle, R. W. (2001). A controlled-attention view of working-memory capacity. *Journal of Experimental Psychology: General, 130* (2), 169–183.

Kato, H., Billinghurst, M., Poupyrev, I., Imamoto, K., Tachibana, K. (2000). Virtual object manipulation on a table-top AR environment. In *Proceedings of the international symposium on augmented reality* (pp. 111–119). Munich, Germany.

Ketcham, C. J., Seidler, R. D., Van Gemmert, A. W., & Stelmach, G. E. (2002). Age-related kinematic differences as influenced by task difficulty, target size, and movement amplitude. *The Journals of Gerontology Series B: Psychological Sciences and Social Sciences, 57*(1), P54–P64.

Ketcham, C. J., & Stelmach, G. E. (2004). Movement control in the older adult. In R. W. Pew, & S. B. Van Hemel (Eds.), *National Research Council (US) Steering Committee for the Workshop on technology for adaptive aging, technology for adaptive aging*. Washington, DC: National Academies Press. Retrieved from <https://www.ncbi.nlm. nih.gov/books/NBK97342/>.

Kim, S., & Dey, A. K. (2009). Simulated augmented reality windshield display as a cognitive mapping aid for elder driver navigation. In *Proceedings of the SIGCHI conference on human factors in computing systems* (pp. 133–142).

Kim, S., & Dey, A. K. (2016). Augmenting human senses to improve the user experience in cars: Applying augmented reality and haptics approaches to reduce cognitive distances. *Multimedia Tools and Applications, 75*(16), 9587–9607.

Kitanovski, V., & Izquierdo, E. (2011). 3D tracking of facial features for augmented reality applications. In *Paper presented at the International workshop on image analysis for multimedia interactive services, Delft, The Netherlands*.

Klein, H. A., & Lippa, K. D. (2008). Type 2 diabetes self-management: Controlling a dynamic system. *Journal of Cognitive Engineering and Decision Making, 2*(1), 48–62.

Klein, H. A., & Meininger, A. R. (2004). Self management of medication and diabetes: Cognitive control. *Part A: Systems and Humans, IEEE Transactions on Systems, Man and Cybernetics, 34*(6), 718–725.

Klein, R., Klein, B. E. K., & Lee, K. E. (1996). Changes in visual acuity in a population: The Beaver Dam eye study. *Ophthalmology, 103*(8), 1169−1178.

de Koning, B. B., & Tabbers, H. K. (2011). Facilitating understanding of movements in dynamic visualizations: An embodied perspective. *Educational Psychology Review, 23* (4), 501−521.

Leat, S. J., Chan, L. L., Maharaj, P. D., Hrynchak, P. K., Mittelstaedt, A., Machan, C. M., & Irving, E. L. (2013). Binocular vision and eye movement disorders in older adults. *Investigative Ophthalmology & Visual Science, 54*(5), 3798−3805.

Lee, C., Rincon, G., Meyer, G., Höllerer, T., & Bowman, D. A. (2013). The effects of visual realism on search tasks in mixed reality simulation. *IEEE Transactions on Visualization and Computer Graphics, 19*(4), 547−556.

Lee, I. J., Chen, C. H., & Chang, K. P. (2016). Augmented reality technology combined with three-dimensional holography to train the mental rotation ability of older adults. *Computers in Human Behavior, 65*, 488−500.

Lee, M., Billinghurst, M., Baek, W., Green, R., & Woo, W. (2013). A usability study of multimodal input in an augmented reality environment. *Virtual Reality, 17*(4), 293−305.

Lemole, G. M., Jr, Banerjee, P. P., Luciano, C., Neckrysh, S., & Charbel, F. T. (2007). Virtual reality in neurosurgical education: Part-task ventriculostomy simulation with dynamic visual and haptic feedback. *Neurosurgery, 61*(1), 142−149.

Leykin, A., & Tuceryan, M. (2004). Automatic determination of text readability over textured backgrounds for augmented reality systems. In *Proceedings of the third IEEE and ACM international symposium on mixed and augmented reality* (pp. 224−230).

Lindenberger, U., & Mayr, U. (2014). Cognitive aging: Is there a dark side to environmental support? *Trends in Cognitive Sciences, 18*(1), 7−15.

Lindström, J., Louheranta, A., Mannelin, M., Rastas, M., Salminen, V., Eriksson, J., … Tuomilehto, J. (2003). The Finnish Diabetes Prevention Study (DPS): Lifestyle intervention and 3-year results on diet and physical activity. *Diabetes Care, 26*(12), 3230−3236.

Lukosch, S., Lukosch, H., Datcu, D., & Cidota, M. (2015). Providing information on the spot: Using augmented reality for situational awareness in the security domain. *Computer Supported Cooperative Work, 24*(6), 613−664.

Matalenas, L. A. (2017). *Examining spatial visualization feedback timing during food estimation* (Unpublished master's thesis). Raleigh, NC: North Carolina State University.

McDowd, J. M. (1997). Inhibition in attention and aging. *Journals of Gerontology. Series B: Psychological Sciences and Social Sciences, 52*, P265−P273.

McLaughlin, A. C., Gandy, M., Allaire, J. C., & Whitlock, L. A. (2012). Putting fun into video games for OAs. *Ergonomics in Design: The Quarterly of Human Factors Applications, 20*(2), 13−22.

McLaughlin, A. C., Rogers, W. A., & Fisk, A. D. (2009). Using direct and indirect input devices: Attention demands and age-related differences. *ACM Transactions on Computer-Human Interaction (TOCHI), 16*(1), 2.

Mendez, E., & Schmalstieg, D. (2009). Importance masks for revealing occluded objects in augmented reality. In *Paper presented at the Proceedings of the 16th ACM symposium on virtual reality software and technology, Kyoto, Japan.*

Metter, E. J., Conwit, R., Tobin, J., & Fozard, J. L. (1997). Age-associated loss of power and strength in the upper extremities in women and men. *The Journals of Gerontology Series A: Biological Sciences and Medical Sciences, 52*(5), B267−B276.

Microsoft Corporation. (2017). *Microsoft HoloLens.* Retrieved from <https://www.microsoft.com/en-us/hololens>.

Milham, M. P., Erickson, K. I., Banich, M. T., Kramer, A. F., Webb, A., Wszalek, T., & Cohen, N. J. (2002). Attentional control in the aging brain: Insights from an fMRI study of the Stroop Task. *Brain and Cognition*, *49*(3), 277–296.

Morrell, R. W., Park, D. C., Mayhorn, C. B., & Kelley, C. L. (2000). Effects of age and instructions on teaching older adults to use ELDERCOMM, an electronic bulletin board system. *Educational Gerontology*, *26*(3), 221–235.

Morrow, D., McKeever, S., Chin, C., Madison, A., Davis, K., Wilson, E., . . . Graumlich, J. (2012). An EMR-based tool to support collaborative planning for medication use among adults with diabetes: A multi-site randomized control trial. *Contemporary Clinical Trials*, *33*(5), 1023–1032.

Morrow, D., & Wilson, E. (2010). Medication adherence among older adults: A systems perspective. *Aging in America Volume II: Physical and mental health*. Santa Barbara, CA: Praeger.

Moustakas, N., Floros, A., & Grigoriou, N. (2011). Interactive audio realities: An augmented/mixed reality audio game prototype. *130th Audio Engineering Society convention*. Audio Engineering Society.

Murphy, C., Schubert, C. R., Cruickshanks, K. J., Klein, B. E., Klein, R., & Nondahl, D. M. (2002). Prevalence of olfactory impairment in older adults. *JAMA*, *288*(18), 2307–2312.

Narumi, T., Ban, Y., Kajinami, T., Tanikawa, T., & Hirose, M. (2012). *Augmented perception of satiety: Controlling food consumption by changing apparent size of food with augmented reality*. Proceedings of the SIGCHI conference on human factors in computing systems (pp. 109–118). New York, NY: ACM.

Narumi, T., Nishizaka, S., Kajinami, T., Tanikawa, T., & Hirose, M. (2011). Augmented reality flavors: Gustatory display based on edible marker and cross-modal interaction. In: *Proceedings of the SIGCHI conference on human factors in computing systems* (pp. 93–102). ACM.

National Institute on Deafness and Other Communication Disorders [NIDCD]. (2016). *Age-related hearing loss*. Retrieved from <https://www.nidcd.nih.gov/health/age-related-hearing-loss>.

Navab, N., Mitschke, M., & Schütz, O. (1999). Camera-Augmented Mobile C-arm (CAMC) application: 3D reconstruction using a low-cost mobile C-arm. In C. Taylor, & A. Colchester (Eds.), *Medical Image Computing and Computer-Assisted Intervention – MICCAI'99. MICCAI 1999*. Lecture Notes in Computer Science (Vol. 1679). Berlin, Heidelberg: Springer.

Ng, K., Larkin, O., Koerselman, T., Ong, B., Schwarz, D., & Bevilacqua, F. (2007). The 3D augmented mirror: Motion analysis for string practice training. In *Paper presented at the international computer music conference, Copenhagen, Denmark* (pp. 247–248).

Ni, T., Karlson, A. K., & Wigdor, D. (2011). AnatOnMe: Facilitating doctor-patient communication using a projection-based handheld device. In *Paper presented at the SIGCHI conference on human factors in computing systems, Vancouver, Canada* (pp. 3333–3342).

Niantic. (2016). *Pokemon Go (Version 0.63.1)* [Mobile application software]. Retrieved from <http://pokemongo.nianticlabs.com/en>.

Okur, A., Ahmadi, S. A., Bigdelou, A., Wendler, T., & Navab, N. (2011). MR in OR: First analysis of AR/VR visualization in 100 intra-operative freehand SPECT acquisitions. In *Paper presented at the International symposium on mixed and augmented reality, Basel, Switzerland* (pp. 211–218).

Paas, F., & Van Merriënboer, J. (1993). The efficiency of instructional conditions: An approach to combine mental effort and performance measures. *Human Factors: The Journal of the Human Factors and Ergonomics Society, 35*(4), 737−743.

Piekarski, W. (2006). 3D modelling with the Tinmith mobile outdoor augmented reality system. *IEEE Computer Graphics and Applications, 26*(1), 14−17.

Polly, R. K. (1992). Diabetes health beliefs, self-care behaviors, and glycemic control among older adults with non-insulin-dependent diabetes mellitus. *The Diabetes Educator, 18* (4), 321−327.

Quigley, H. A., & Broman, A. T. (2006). The number of people with glaucoma worldwide in 2010 and 2020. *British Journal of Ophthalmology, 90*(3), 262−267.

Rabbi, M., Pfammatter, A., Zhang, M., Spring, B., & Choudhury, T. (2015). Automated personalized feedback for physical activity and dietary behavior change with mobile phones: A randomized controlled trial on adults. *JMIR mHealth and uHealth, 3*(2), e42.

Rahman, A. M., Tran, T. T., Hossain, S. A., & El Saddik, A. (2010). Augmented rendering of makeup features in a smart interactive mirror system for decision support in cosmetic products selection. In *Paper presented at the 14th International symposium on distributed simulation and real time applications, Fairfax, VA* (pp. 203−206).

Rogers, W. A. (1992). Age differences in visual search: Target and distractor learning. *Psychology and Aging, 7*(4), 526−535.

Rogers, W. A., Campbell, R., & Pak, R. (2001). A systems approach for training older adults to use technology. In N. Charness, D. C. Park, & B. A. Sabel (Eds.), *Communication, technology, and aging: Opportunities and challenges for the future* (pp. 187−208). New York: Springer.

Rogers, W. A., & Fisk, A. D. (1991). Are age differences in consistent-mapping visual search due to feature learning or attention training? *Psychology and Aging, 6*(4), 542−550.

Rogers, W. A., Fisk, A. D., McLaughlin, A. C., & Pak, R. (2005). Touch a screen or turn a knob: Choosing the best device for the job. *Human Factors: The Journal of the Human Factors and Ergonomics Society, 47*(2), 271−288.

Rogers, W. A., Mykityshyn, A. L., Campbell, R. H., & Fisk, A. D. (2001). Analysis of a "simple" medical device. *Ergonomics in Design, 9*(1), 6−14.

Rusch, M. L., Schall, M. C., Gavin, P., Lee, J. D., Dawson, J. D., Vecera, S., & Rizzo, M. (2013). Directing driver attention with augmented reality cues. *Transportation Research Part F: Traffic Psychology and Behaviour, 16*, 127−137.

Ryan, C. M., Williams, T. M., Finegold, D. N., & Orchard, T. J. (1993). Cognitive dysfunction in adults with Type 1 (insulin-dependent) diabetes mellitus of long duration: Effects of recurrent hypoglycaemia and other chronic complications. *Diabetologia, 36*(4), 329.

Salthouse, T. A. (1994). The aging of working memory. *Neuropsychology, 8*(4), 535.

Sandor, C., Cunningham, A., Dey, A., & Mattila, V. V. (2010). An augmented reality X-ray system based on visual saliency. In *Paper presented at the 9th IEEE international symposium on mixed and augmented reality, Seoul, Korea* (pp. 27−36).

Savova, D. (2016). AR sandbox in educational programs for disaster response. In *Proceedings from the 6th international conference on cartography and GIS* (pp. 847−858). Albena, Bulgaria.

Schaie, K. W. (2005). What can we learn from longitudinal studies of adult development? *Research in Human Development, 2*(3), 133−158.

Schaie, K. W., & Willis, S. L. (Eds.), (2016). *Handbook of the psychology of aging* (8th ed.). Cambridge, MA: Academic Press.

Schall, M. C., Rusch, M., Lee, J. D., Dawson, J. D., Thomas, G., Aksan, N., & Rizzo, M. (2013). Augmented reality cues and elderly driver hazard perception. *Human Factors*, *55*(3), 643−658.

Scheibe, S., & Blanchard-Fields, F. (2009). Effects of regulating emotions on cognitive performance: What is costly for young adults is not so costly for older adults. *Psychology and Aging*, *24*(1), 217−223.

Schmidt, R. A., & Wrisberg, C. A. (2008). *Motor learning and performance: A situation-based approach* (4th ed.). Champaign, IL: Human Kinetics.

Schneck, M., Haegerstrom-Portnoy, G., Lott, L. A., & Brabyn, J. A. (2014). Comparison of panel D-15 tests in large older population. *Optometry and Vision Science*, *91*(3), 284−290.

See, Z. S., Billinghurst, M., Rengganaten, V., & Soo, S. (2016). Mobile audible AR experience for medical learning murmurs simulation. In: *Proceedings of the SIGGRAPH ASIA mobile graphics and interactive applications conference, Article 19*. New York: ACM.

Shigaki, C., Kruse, R. L., Mehr, D., Sheldon, K. M., Ge, B., Moore, C., & Lemaster, J. (2010). Motivation and diabetes self-management. *Chronic Illness*, *6*(3), 202−214.

Skinner, H. B., Barrack, R. L., & Cook, S. D. (1984). Age-related decline in proprioception. *Clinical Orthopaedics and Related Research*, *184*, 208−211.

Smith, C. D., Walton, A., Loveland, A. D., Umberger, G. H., Kryscio, R. J., & Gash, D. M. (2005). Memories that last in old age: Motor skill learning and memory preservation. *Neurobiology of Aging*, *26*(6), 883−890.

SnapShop Inc. (2015). *SnapShop Showroom (Version 2.4.4)* [Mobile application software]. Retrieved from <https://itunes.apple.com/us/app/snapshop-showroom/id373144101?mt = 8>.

State, A., Livingston, M. A., Hirota, G., Garrett, W.F., Whitton, M.C., Fuchs, H., & Pisano, E. D. (1996). Technologies for augmented-reality systems: Realizing ultrasound-guided needle biopsies. In *Paper presented at the Special interest group on graphics and interactive techniques, New Orleans, LA* (pp. 439−446).

Steven, S., Hollingsworth, K. G., Al-Mrabeh, A., Avery, L., Aribisala, B., Caslake, M., & Taylor, R. (2016). Very low-calorie diet and 6 months of weight stability in type 2 diabetes: Pathophysiological changes in responders and nonresponders. *Diabetes Care*, *39* (5), 808−815.

Stewart, R., & Liolitsa, D. (1999). Type 2 diabetes mellitus, cognitive impairment and dementia. *Diabetic Medicine*, *16*(2), 93−112.

Sweller, J. (1988). Cognitive load during problem solving: Effects on learning. *Cognitive Science*, *12*(2), 257−285.

Tipper, S. P. (1991). Less attentional selectivity as a result of declining inhibition in older adults. *Bulletin of the Psychonomic Society*, *29*(1), 45−47.

Tran, D. B., Silverman, S. E., Zimmerman, K., & Feldon, S. E. (1998). Age-related deterioration of motion perception and detection. *Graefe's Archive for Clinical and Experimental Ophthalmology*, *236*(4), 269−273.

Tun, P. A., McCoy, S., & Wingfield, A. (2009). Aging, hearing acuity, and the attentional costs of effortful listening. *Psychology and Aging*, *24*(3), 761.

Tversky, B., Morrison, J., & Betrancourt, M. (2002). Animation: Can it facilitate? *International Journal of Human-Computer Studies*, *57*(4), 247−262.

Urry, H. L., & Gross, J. J. (2010). Emotion regulation in older age. *Current Directions in Psychological Science*, *19*(6), 352−357.

USDA. (2017). *MyPlate*. Retrieved from <https://www.choosemyplate.gov/>.

Vargas-Martín, F., & Peli, E. (2002). Augmented-view for restricted visual field: Multiple device implementations. *Optometry & Vision Science*, *79*(11), 715–723.

Verhaeghen, P. (2016). Age-related slowing in response times, causes and consequences. In *Encyclopedia of geropsychology* (pp. 1–9). Springer Singapore http://dx.doi.org/10.1007/978-981-287-080-3.

Wickremaratchi, M. M., & Llewelyn, J. G. (2006). Effects of ageing on touch. *Postgraduate Medical Journal*, *82*(967), 301–304.

Wilson, R. S., Beckett, L. A., Barnes, L. L., Schneider, J. A., Bach, J., Evans, D. A., & Bennett, D. (2002). Individual differences in rates of change in cognitive abilities of older persons. *Psychology and Aging*, *17*(2), 179–193.

Wingfield, A., & Kahana, M. J. (2002). The dynamics of memory retrieval in older adulthood. *Canadian Journal of Experimental Psychology/Revue canadienne de psychologie expérimentale*, *56*(3), 187.

Worden, A., Walker, N., Bharat, K., & Hudson, S. (1997). Making computers easier for older adults to use: Area cursors and sticky icons. In: *Proceedings of the ACM SIGCHI conference on Human factors in computing systems (CHI '97)* (pp. 266–271). New York: ACM.

Yeh, M., & Wickens, C. D. (2001). Display signaling in augmented reality: Effects of cue reliability and image realism on attention allocation and trust calibration. *Human Factors: The Journal of the Human Factors and Ergonomics Society*, *43*(3), 355–365.

Yoo, H. N., Chung, E., & Lee, B. H. (2013). The effects of augmented reality-based Otago exercise on balance, gait, and falls efficacy of elderly women. *Journal of Physical Therapy Science*, *25*(7), 797–801.

Yuan, M., Khan, I. R., Farbiz, F., Niswar, A., & Huang, Z. (2011). A mixed reality system for virtual glasses try-on. In *Paper presented at the 10th International conference on virtual reality continuum and its applications in industry, Hong Kong, China* (pp. 363–366).

Zhang, W., Begole, B., Chu, M., Liu, J., & Yee, N. (2008). Real-time clothes comparison based on multi-view vision. In *Paper presented at the Second ACM/IEEE international conference on distributed smart cameras, Palo Alto, CA* (pp. 1–10).

Zollmann, S., Kalkofen, D., Hoppe, C., Kluckner, S., Bischof, H., & Reitmayr, G. (2012). Interactive 4D overview and detail visualization in augmented reality. In *Paper presented at the IEEE international symposium on mixed and augmented reality, Atlanta, GA* (pp. 167–176).

Index

CPI Antony Rowe
Chippenham, UK
2018-03-20 22:18